THIS GUIDE IS PART OF
THE PHILIPS BRASILIS PROJECT
WHOSE AIM IS TO PROMOTE
BRAZILIAN CULTURE AND
ART, AS WELL AS ITS HISTORICAL
AND NATURAL HERITAGE

NORTHEAST BRAZIL

THE NORTHEAST BRAZIL

4

HORIZONTE
GEOGRÁFICO

General Director: Peter Milko

PHILIPS GUIDES

THE NORTHEAST BRAZIL

Editor-in-chief: Peter Milko
Managing Editor: Martha San Juan França
Art Director: Marco Cançado

Editors: Fabrício Brasiliense and Maíra Rocha
Senior Writers: Beatriz Santomauro, Fabrício Brasiliense, Flávia Pegorin, Guilherme Sierra, Júlia Leme, Maíra Rocha, Marcelo Delduque and Marilena Rocha
Copy Editor: Luiz Francisco Senne (Portuguese), Kátia P. Pereira (English)
Translation to English: Damaris Vigar and David Andrew Hewitt
Art Manager: Jorge Toth and Marco Cançado
Page Layout: Ana Cristina Silveira and Gilda Lima
Photography Editor: Adriano Gambarini
Associate Contributors: Agência Estado, Fototeca, Pulsar, Imagenlatina, TBI Imagens **(agencies)**; Adriano Gambarini, Agliberto Lima, Alvaro Vilela, André Pessoa, Augusto Pessoa, Beatriz Santomauro, Christian Knepper, Cristiano F. Burmester, David Santos Junior, Delfim Martins, Evaldo Parreira, Fabio Bonotti, Fabricio Brasiliense, Ivan Carneiro, Jesus Carlos, Juca Martins, Leonardo Papini, Marcio Cabral, Maria Dania Junges, Pedro Ribeiro, Peter Milko, Ricardo Azoury, Robert Ostrowski, Roberto Cosulich, Rogerio Reis, Salomon Cytrynowicz, Stefan Kolumban, Tibico Brasil, Vidal Cavalcante, Vitor Andrade, Zig Koch **(photography)**; Geraldo Moura Filho **(Index of Fauna)** and Levi Grau **(Index of Flora)** (illustrations); Vera Grandisky Lerner **(maps)**; Leonardo Bussadori **(cover design)**; Adriana Férrer and Malu Campos **(research)**; Sueli Furlan **(consultant)**
Administrative Manager: Mauro de Melo Jucá • **Distribution:** José Augusto Pires de Abreu
Customer Service: Marcos Fernandes

Philips Guide of Amazônia
Copyright©Horizonte Geográfico, october 2002

Horizonte Geográfico
Av. Arruda Botelho, 684 – 5° floor
ZIP 05466-000, São Paulo – SP – Brasil
Phone: 55 (11) 3022-5599 – Fax: 55 (11) 3022-3751
E-mail: horizonte@horizontegeografico.com.br
www.horizontegeografico.com.br

All information in this guide was obtained by August 2002. We recommend users to always check schedules, prices and other useful data. The Publisher cannot hold responsible for possible losses due to changes in information.

Horizonte Geográfico would like to thank you for sending data to help us update the information and services included in this publication. Please send us information by mail, fax or e-mail: redacao@horizontegeografico.com.br. To keep updated and get further information, visit our site: **www.horizontegeografico.com.br**

Philips Guides Series of Brazilian Ecological Tourism
Published in October 2002 by Horizonte Geográfico

Summary

DEAR READER

Travel in Northeastern Brazil is, for most, synonymous with beach going, sunshine and, of course, carnival. This guide will astonish you by revealing countless options in ecological tourism opportunities within this striking region, which was scrutinized by our editorial team in search of new pleasure grounds and differentiated attractions and enjoyments.

The famous beaches are still there, alongside a selection of suggestions for travellers who wish to venture a little farther than the seaside; lots of information about different ecological and cultural points of interest, and opportunities for safe adventures have been compiled in this guide to assist you in your choice. We have also selected the finest places of visitation in the interior of each State, to where increasing numbers of visitors are lured, in their search for new horizons.

Northeastern Brazil surprises visitors with the quantity of breathtaking and dramatic natural landscapes and with its friendly, hospitable and festive people who live in the cities of great historical value, for Brazil and the rest of the world. From the Pillory district in Salvador to Alcântara in Maranhão, the fascination of colonial historical centers is intrinsically bound with religious and pagan festivities that are so popular and attract thousands, even millions, on their special days.

The diversity in landscape, and also in cultural aspects, is particularly apparent in the Northeast. Both the Dutch and the French tried to seize Brazil by force from the Portuguese, and left their respective marks in the architecture of Pernambuco and Maranhão. While magnificent, untouched beaches are still being unveiled to travellers, the interior hinterlands display unexpected alternatives. In Ceará, the Ubajara cave has a cable car; in the interior of Maranhão, in dozens of refreshing waterfalls visitors can mitigate the effect of the warm weather; in Paraíba, you can follow in the footsteps of a dinossaur!

In the Chapada de Diamantina plateau, abandoned mining towns such as Xique-Xique tell parts of Brazilian history. Not far from Recife, the adorable, roly-poly manatees have found a place of refuge, also for visitors to enjoy, right next door to the spectacular Fortress of Orange, built by the Dutch at the end of the 16th century. To discover Northeastern Brazil means getting to know the deepest roots of the history of Brazil. There are many towns and cities that once experienced much prosperity and opulence, as their gilded churches and some palace-like mansions still bear witness to. Such wealth was always associated with extractive activities, related first to brazilwood all along the coast; then cotton in Maranhão, cocoa in Bahia, sugarcane in Pernambuco.

To reach beyond the beaches – in themselves so extraordinarily attractive; that is the essence and aim of this guide and our collaborators, who toured thousands of kilometers in search of each little detail in order that you may plan, learn and enjoy your travels.

Peter Milko
Editor-in-chief

How to use THIS GUIDE

This travel guide enables you to access all the Northeast's natural and cultural wonders. To help you plan the trip, the guide offers useful information about how to reach each place, its festivities, main highlights, and an identification of the Northeastern animals and plants at the end. The contents are divided in two parts: the first offers general aspects of the region and the second includes the main cities in the States of Bahia, Sergipe, Alagoas, Pernambuco, Paraíba, Rio Grande do Norte, Ceará, Piauí, and Maranhão.

Discovering the Northeast, Ecological Scenery and The Man in the Northeast

In these chapters, there is a lot of information referring to the region, tips on how to prepare your trip, information on the main cares you should take with your health, along with cultural, historical and geographical aspects of the Northeast

Tours

Here you will find information on the varying human and geographical aspects of each State.

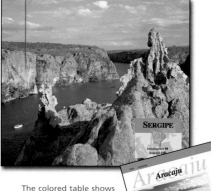

SERGIPE

List of the main highlights with their full addresses.

The colored table shows distances (in kilometers) to the main cities; number of inhabitants; area code and phone number of the main tourist information bureau in town.

Map of the town's central region, with location of the main attractions.

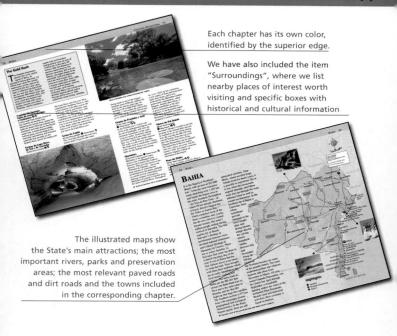

Each chapter has its own color, identified by the superior edge.

We have also included the item "Surroundings", where we list nearby places of interest worth visiting and specific boxes with historical and cultural information

The illustrated maps show the State's main attractions; the most important rivers, parks and preservation areas; the most relevant paved roads and dirt roads and the towns included in the corresponding chapter.

Services

Here there is a list of the main support services for tourists.
Detailed options on lodging, dining and useful phone numbers; airports, bus stations, car rental agencies, travel agencies, banks, hospitals, air companies, and places to shop. This chapter also provides a list of books, websites related to the Northeast and research institutions and their main projects.

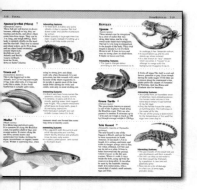

Animals and plants

To facilitate observation, we have included a list of the region's main species, with descriptions, habits and curiosities.

Index:

• To facilitate consultation, the guide has a table of contents including page numbers on the first page of each chapter. At the end there is an index of all the cities included in the book.

DISCOVERING THE NORTHEAST

DISCOVERING THE NORTHEAST

The contents of this guide cover the principal cities, the inland tourist resorts and the most famous beaches of all of the northeastern region. The ones who think that the Northeast is only a mixture of fascinating beaches and the backlands waiting to be conquered will be surprised by the diversity of climates, vegetation, soil and local colonization. In the northeastern vastness, there are steadfast rivers like the São Francisco and Parnaíba, by the side of hundreds of others that dry during part of the year. There are exuberant forests and inhospitable deserts; mountain ranges of more than 1,000 meters of altitude, where the temperature falls dramatically, and valleys in which the thermometer reaches higher than 40 ºC.

MANY LANDSCAPES

The forest zone, with a width that fluctuates between 100 and 200 kilometers, took its name because in the past, it was covered by the Atlantic Forest. After, the forest was largely substituted by sugarcane plantations and cocoa in the Southeast of Bahia. Nowadays, there are forests only in the extreme south of the region.

Bahia was the first region to be occupied by settlers, who demonstrated satisfaction with their new land. "For those who want to take advantage of it, the land gives everything," wrote the scribe Pero Vaz de Caminha in a letter to King D. Manuel of Portugal, referring to the discovery.

VARIED COLONIZING

Although it is rare today, it was from the Northeast that the red timber, which gave Brazil its name, originated. Settlement of the region happened along the coast during the 17th century and it was extended westwards in the following centuries. The brazilwood tree, in the first years after colonization, as well as sugarcane brought by the landowners, and cotton from the end of the 18th century, guaranteed the Northeast its position as the richest region of Portuguese America during three centuries. It is not without reason that the first capital of Brazil was Salvador, in the State of Bahia, and was only transferred to Rio de Janeiro in 1763. Salvador has, until today, one part of the rich colonial heritage, the greatest example of which can be found in the region today in the

Serra de Capivara: Semi-arid landscape in Piauí interior

◄ Praia do Forte: common vegetation of Bahia coast

Historic center of São Luís: colonial style

restored city of Pelourinho. West of the forest zone, is the sub-humid transitional zone called the *agreste*, where the elevations of the plateaus of Borborema in Rio Grande do Norte, Paraíba, Pernambuco and Diamantina in Bahia, which block the humid Atlantic winds. Erosion of the winds and the waters shaped the lands of the plateaus, bestowed with steep slopes, cliffs, canyons and valleys. With altitudes that vary from 400 meters above sea level in the valleys to peaks that reach 1,200 meters, the imposing plateaus separate the São Francisco River from the coastline of Bahia. Even farther westwards, the climate becomes semi-arid, giving start to the *sertão*. Although the term is often employed for the designation of regions far from the coast, in truth, the northeastern backlands almost reaches the coast in the States of Ceará and Rio Grande do Norte. The rainfalls are highly irregular, provoking periods of drought that can last for years. The typical vegetation is *caatinga*. Nowadays, national parks, such as those of Sete Cidades and Capivara, both in Piauí, can be visited. In the parks, evidence of the first inhabitants of the continent can also be found, natives who left, in their wake, designs and paintings on the rocks. In wetter areas (the 'swamps' at the foot of the mountain ranges), there are groves of palm-trees, chiefly of *carnaúba* trees. Due to the precarious conditions of subsistence, the area is sparsely populated. As a type of transition zone between the Amazon

rainforest and the semi-arid *sertão*, there's the Mid-north or Occidental Northeast consisting of the States of Maranhão and the west of Piauí. Here, the great natural riches are the babassu and carnauba trees. The climate is hot and humid in São Luís, but, the farther eastwards and inland you go, the lower the rainfall.

The Lençóis Maranhenses are located here, a region of dunes resulting from the action of the wind on the sands of the Preguiças and Parnaíba rivers.

WHAT TO EXPECT

Wars and occupations have left their marks in the architecture, the history and the northeastern cities, as can be seen in this guide. The society of the Northeast is, more than any other part of Brazil, a mixture of the White, Indian and Negro clans. The great cultural diversity of the population is probably due to this melting pot of races. This diversity is present in the rituals, folklore, the music and the local handicrafts. Nowadays, the beaches on the coastlines of Bahia, Pernambuco, Rio Grande do Norte and Ceará, have tourist-based economies. Hopefully, with this guide, it is possible to get to know and appreciate a little of the beauty of all this region even during the planning of the trip, and discover that it is impossible to fully relish the Northeast in merely one trip. It is necessary to visit with much spare time and you will be astonished with each one of its attributes.

HOW TO PREPARE

Northeast for everyone's taste: Trekking, ecological trails and beaches

The Brazilian Northeast is one of the most popular destinations in South America. For this it is one of the most developed from the point of view of tourism, and it is practically impossible to see all of it in just one visit. There is a Northeast for everyone's budget. Backpackers find the conditions ideal for an economical trip: simple accommodations, cheap meals and the possibility of meeting dozens of other travelers in the same conditions. The boarding houses have a preference for people who are looking for informality and good taste. Hotels are spread in the State capitals and are the most traditional option for package holidays. Families find comfort, and first-class service in the resorts.

Throughout this guide you will find diverse types of attractions, such as treks along the untouched beaches of south Bahia, trips through the archaeological sites in the *sertão* of Piauí, visits to fishing villages on the coast of Ceará, or city tours through the old center of Recife, getting to know the architecture of the 17th- century two-store buildings.

MUST-SEES

In all the places mentioned we have indicated with an asterisk (★) the places that must not be missed, besides recommending trips and indicating

festivals, handicraft markets, and tales. We emphasized what might help the visitor to better understand the essence of each place, always having in mind that the buyer of this guide is someone on holiday. For this, the following criteria were considered:

Rarity – Highlighting architectonic groups of buildings, archaeological findings and historical importance.

Accessibility – The degree of difficulty of access, road signs and demarcation.

Appeal – What each place offers in terms of entertainment and culture.

Infrastructure – What each city has to offer: shopping, restaurants and services.

Heritage – A little of the history contained in museums, theaters, buildings restored by cultural institutions, monuments and forts. We indicate the quality of the exhibits, the availability of on-site guides or of self-explanatory tours.

Ecological aspect – conservation of the ecosystem.

SERVICES

At the end of the guide, the services of each city mentioned on the itineraries are indicated. They are organized in geological order of States, starting from the south going north, that is, from Bahia to Maranhão. In the State capitals, we chose on average 10 hotels and 10 restaurants, from the cheapest to the most luxurious, distributed geographically. In the smaller towns, 5 hotels and restaurants were chosen, following the same criteria. It must be recognized that as this is the Northeast, a region of many contrasts, there are locations where the best place to stay is a boarding house without even electricity, but that has an astonishing landscape, an untouched scenery and the possibility of being with kind and simple people. Always when it is possible, we disclose characteristics of the restaurants, boarding houses and hotels that increase the attractiveness of the place – that might be located on the edge of a beach, inside a mansion from the colonial period or even a restaurant that can offer an unforgettable local dish.

The roads close to the coast are quieter

Airports and Highways

All the northeastern State capitals possess well-structured airports with regular flights, but the flights are more frequent in cities that operate with a high traffic of package holidays. These cities are also interlinked by the highway system, which is also connected to the smaller coastal and inland towns. Practically all of the itineraries mentioned in this guide are accessible both to whom is travelling by car or by bus. Some beaches have restricted access, generally where resorts and private condominiums are situated. For the ones traveling by car, the BR-101 highway, which starts in Rio Grande do Sul, crosses almost the entire Northeast, and ends in Touros in Rio Grande do Norte, is the best option.

Some States have State highways, such as the BA-001 in Bahia and the PE-060 in Pernambuco, near the coast. These highways were constructed so that the flow of cars would be freer, and are better when compared with the federal interstate highways that are almost always clogged and dangerous. Inland, the farther away from the State capital, the worse are the traffic conditions, as is the case of the BR-304 to Mossoró in Rio Grande do Norte, the final stretch of the AL-101, which goes to Penedo in Alagoas and the BR-242 which goes to Chapada Diamantina in Bahia. Watch out for warnings of animals on the roads, especially in the case of inland trips and ask about the safety of the roads, as there are frequent robberies. If you are traveling by car,

Espelho, in Bahia: visitors find different types of accommodations

always try to travel during the day. Buggy trips are also very popular mainly on the coast of Rio Grande do Norte and Ceará. It is important to always be with experienced buggy drivers, as on many stretches there are accidents, at river estuaries, and with stones and soft sand. Extra care should be taken on beaches where turtles lay eggs – in no way should vehicles drive around during the egg-laying season.

High and low seasons

Even though the sun shines practically all the year round in the Northeast, the months of Brazilian vacations – from December to March and July – and the bank holiday weekends are responsible for a phenomenon that can alter your decision to travel very much.

The high season is when the hotels and boarding houses are fully booked, all the bars and restaurants are open and all the attractions and trips are working at full capacity and the prices, including the plane tickets, are more expensive. In the cases of the New Year celebrations and carnival, bookings should be made as much as 6 months in advance.

The opposite, the low season, is when the cities return to their normal rhythm, many bars and restaurants close, daytrips are suspended (and when they are not the visitor may have to pay for the whole trip as in the case of boat trips). On the other hand, the daily rate in the hotels, the price in restaurants and attractions can fall by more than 50%. Exceptions can occur during times of festivities and local holidays (*read Man in the Northeast*).

Package-plan vacations

One of the greatest impetuses of tourism in the Northeast are the package-plan vacations. Tourist operators sign agreements with the hotel chains and airline companies and guarantee a constant flow of tourists, mainly to the most popular destinations, such as Porto Seguro, Natal, Salvador and Fortaleza.

The packages normally include the air ticket, accommodation and shuttle service. The advantage of this, above all is the price.

To buy a plane ticket and to book a good quality hotel on your own almost always turns out to be more expensive. You can buy the optional trips offered by the agency that sold the package, or set up your own itinerary.

THE BEST TIME OF THE YEAR

The average temperature in the Northeast is 26ºC, but it can easily reach 35ºC on many stretches of coastline, even though the thermal

Main highlights in Recife can be better appreciated in the low season

sensation is always lower due to the pleasant sea breeze. What might define the best time to visit is the rainy season. In the Northeast, generally, the rainy season is from April to June and in Bahia from May to August. But do not take this as a sworn fact, as the El Niño and La Niña phenomena provoked great meteorological variations.

Some attractions depend on climatic factors and only occur in determined periods of the year, such as the Lençóis Maranhenses.

Always, when possible, we indicated on the itineraries the occurrence of such phenomenon. For trips to the *sertão*, be prepared to face the hot ever-shining sun.

Spicy dishes: be careful

HEALTH CARE

All the state capitals in the Northeast have good hospitals, clinics and pharmacies, many of which are open 24-hours. In the chapter about services, we indicated the main emergency services in each city. But do not expect the same efficiency in the more remote areas that do not even have electricity. And take care with the hygiene of the food, avoid very typical dishes that you are not accustomed to eating. See below the more frequent health problems that can occur during a trip to the Northeast:

Jellyfish burns: do not rub the affected area so as not to spread the liquid that causes the burn. The fastest homemade solution is to wash with fresh water and pass vinegar to alleviate the burning sensation. The ideal is to use a cold compress of saline solution and apply a corticoid cream.

Dehydration: loss of liquids and mineral salts due to the heat. Replace the liquids. Particularly good is a home-made saline solution: a teaspoon of salt and a soupspoon of sugar dissolved in a litre of filtered or boiled water.

Mycosis: They are diseases caused by fungi. To avoid catching them, dry the body well after bathing, do not use tight underwear or clothes made of synthetic material. Try to use sandals or shoes that permit ventilation and never remove them on beaches that are used by many animals.

Foot Blisters: If the blister is large, puncture it with a sterilised needle – do not remove the skin – wash with antiseptic soap and after, use a dressing with scar-promoting cream. To prevent, avoid travelling with shoes that are not well worn in.

WATER AND FOOD

Throughout the guide we indicated diverse walks that pass through villages, river estuaries, deserted beaches and untouched landscapes. If you decide to choose one of these trips, remember that in certain places the possibility of finding a bar or market is remote. Take with you water, cereal bars, lotion, fruit, a cap and sunglasses.

MONEY AND EXCHANGE

In the State capital cities with the constant flow of visitors such as Porto Seguro, Arraial D'Ajuda, Pipa and Porto de Galinhas, the exchange bureaus are easy to find. But if you are far from a large center, plan how much you intend to spend in the period. In the chapter on Services, we indicated the appropriate places to exchange money in each place. Travelers checks are practically only exchanged in the State capitals. Credit cards are easily accepted in the State capitals but rarely in the smaller towns and villages. Try to always carry some lower value notes.

In nearly all the cities there are branches or cash machines of Banco do Brasil. International withdrawals are easier made in the bigger cities.

THE ECOLOGICAL SCENERY

INTRODUCTION TO THE NORTHEAST

The Northeast is composed of nine States: Maranhão, Piauí, Ceará, Rio Grande do Norte, Paraíba, Pernambuco, Alagoas, Sergipe and Bahia. In this area of 1,660,359 km², corresponding to 19.5% of the national territory, a total of 35,412,887 Brazilians currently live, which is 29.4% of the country's population. It is an immense area that presents a great diversity of relief, vegetation, soil and climate and, precisely because of this, it is divided into four large natural regions for study purposes: the Forest Zone, Agreste, Sertão and the Mid-North. This division is important in order to understand how colonization of the Northeast occurred, and with this, better enjoy the scenery, natural beauty spots and the history of each site.

In a general fashion, the region is formed of a vast level surface, from which some higher points protrude that rarely pass 1,000 meters of altitude. Consequently, the coast which runs from Rio Grande do Norte until the South of Bahia constitutes a one to two-hundred-kilometer wide plain of fertile soils, delimited to the west by two great plateaus, Borborema, which extends through the States of Rio Grande do Norte, Paraíba and Pernambuco; and Chapada Diamantina, in the State of Bahia. This is called the Forest Zone due to the humid tropical climate and because of the forest that prevailed here at the time of discovery.

FOREST ZONE

The most dynamic area of the Northeast, where almost all the northeastern State capitals are found, is the Forest Zone. This is where the majority of the population lives, and most of the tourist activities, industrial production and petroleum exploration take place. It is an area that is blessed with rains when compared with the remainder of the Northeast. The rains are regular and the average annual rainfall is greater than 1,000 mm. The climate is hot and humid, and it has only two well defined seasons: the rainy season, (March to August), and the dry season (September to February). Until today the vegetation of the Forest Zone is exuberant and it is still possible to see examples of how it must have been like in the past centuries when more forest survived, by the fragments which remain spread throughout the States. More than half the species of plants do

Nature is preserver in parks like Una, Bahia

◀ São Francisco River between Pernambuco and Bahia

The ecosystems ot the region

The region is divided
into 4 ecological
subsystems for study
purposes

- ■ Amazon Forest
- ▨ Tropical Forest
- ▨ Cerrado
- ▨ Caatinga
- ▨ Agreste
- ▨ Forest Zone - Mata Atlântica
- ■ Coastal Vegetation

not exist in other places, including the brazilwood tree which gave its name to the country. The forest is also the habitat for many species of animals, some of which are threatened, such as the mico-leão-dourado (*Leontopithecus rosalia*).

AGRESTE

Following the Forest Zone, there is a long, narrow stretch of semi-fertile lands, the Agreste, occasionally interrupted where the coastal plains come in direct contact with the *sertão*. This is a transitional zone and, therefore, badly defined. In the *agreste* of Pernambuco, for instance, it is possible to find the lush vegetation of the forest in some places and, in others, xerophil plants, which are plants that, to survive, adapt to conditions of little water, as has happened in the *caatinga*. The climate is tropical semi-arid, although with a higher rainfall than that of the *sertão*, of between 650 and 1,000 mm annually.

SERTÃO

The region named the Sertão includes large areas of the northeastern interior, found in the Chapadas or plateaus of Borborema and Diamantina. The *sertão* exists in every northeastern State with the exception of Maranhão. In this immense semi-arid region, the temperature is high during the entire year. It is also an area of few and

scattered rains, which are concentrated in three or four months of the year. In the *sertão*, the 400 to 800 mm of annual rainfall, depending on the region, is soon lost through evaporation and run off as the soil is little permeable and the relief is composed of steep slopes. The region suffers from periodical droughts, its rivers are temporary, and the thorny and aggressive vegetation is formed of plants of the cactaceae family. But there are also large islands of more dense vegetation here. These are found on the banks of certain enduring rivers, like the São Francisco, and others, which although they are temporary, preserve an underground water table.

MID-NORTH REGION

The Mid-north, represented by the states of Piauí and Maranhão, is composed of a low-altitude semi-humid plateau, whose appearance changes the farther you go westwards. The height and density of the vegetation changes from the typical *caatinga* of the sertão to the *cerrado* or savannah with sparse trees, and even to the terrain of the Babassu trees (*Orbignya speciosa*). The climatic conditions are reflected in the river system: the rivers situated in areas with more rains are permanent, whilst those of drier areas are intermittent. The Parnaíba River marks the limits of these two extremes.

COASTAL REGION

The 3,347 km of the northeastern coastline currently is considered one of the most attractive Brazilian regions for tourism. The beaches resemble images of tropical paradises with coconut trees, white sand and blue sea. As a matter of fact, these trees are considered to be a symbol of the Northeast, even though they are not originally from this region. Brought from Asia, they found on the northeastern coast an ideal habitat, exposed to the continuous actions of the sea winds. From Rio Grande do Norte to Bahia, the northeastern coast exhibits a great diversity of formations – *restingas*, dunes, lagoons, *tabuleiras* both of barricade and hill formation. Here, there is the estuary of the São Francisco River and Todos os Santos Bay, besides the volcanic islands, like Fernando de Noronha and Abrolhos, mixed (sedimentary and cragged) isles, such as Itamaracá and Itaparica, and islands formed from corals such as Atol das Rocas. A short distance from the coast, there are ribbons of

sand, which at high tide are submerged. These are the barrier reefs that exist in Traição and Mamanguape Bays in Paraíba, and in Cabo de Santo Agostinho in Pernambuco. By the side of the reefs facing the sea, there are steep crags or cliffs, as can be seen on the stretch between Ceará and Rio Grande do Norte, or in Porto Seguro in Bahia, set against the gently fashioned terrain on the land side whose limits are the cliffs or the beaches themselves. Also it presents *restingas,* or bands of sands deposited parallel to the coastline by the marine currents, at the entrances of the bays and coves, as in the case of Itacaré in Bahia. Lakes obstructed by the sediments of the rivers and the beaches, as in Maceió in Alagoas, are common too.

DUNES

The stretch that goes from Gurupi River in Maranhão to the Cabo de São Roque in Rio Grande do Norte corresponds to the continent's topmost side. There, the 'Rias Maranhenses' are located, sets of seawater channels where small rivers flow into the sea, as well as ribbons of sand, dunes and *tabuleiros*. Between Maranhão and Piauí, east of the great

Delta do Parnaíba: dunes reach as high as 30 meters

The mud and the vegetation constitute an important ecosystem for fishermen

The secrets of the seas

I t is important for those who want to move around in the Northeast to understand the periodic movement of rising and falling of the seawaters in relation to the coast. The tides are a result of the actions of the moon and the sun, and, to a lesser extent, of the planets. The name *preamar*, high tide, refers to the incoming phase of the seawaters. It lasts on average six hours. Long hikes, diving in natural swimming pools of the reefs, boat or buggy trips should be made during the low tide. At high tide, the sea advances and people can become stranded. For example, the visitor who is in Caraíva, Bahia, and who wants to walk to Espelho, 12 km to the north, should enquire about the receding tide. From the time that it starts and for the following five hours, a long band of sand is uncovered and the beach is more even, facilitation the crossing of Frades River bar and the cliffs. On the Internet site of the Navy there is a program that indicates the timetable of the tides (www.dhn.mar.mil.br/tabuas/TabuasMare.htm).

gulf formed by the São Marcos and São José Bays, as far as the Parnaíba River Delta, the dunes reach as high as 30 meters. In summer, when freshwater lakes appear, they are flooded by the rivers. Dunes are also present on the coasts of Ceará and Rio Grande do Norte, where the winds blow from the Northeast, displacing the sands inland. At river estuaries, the scenery is changed with the appearance of salt lakes. The dry climate, the high rate of evaporation, the tides and the low coastal terrain favors their formation in the Mossoró region in Rio Grande do Norte.

MANGROVES

Large expanses of the northeastern coast are comprised of mangroves, near to the banks of the river mouths, when they mix with seawater. The mud and the vegetation, adapted to the high salinity, are the habitat of crabs and shrimps and constitute an important ecosystem for fishermen, but are highly threatened by tourism and the commercial exploration of fish. In a general fashion, the northeast coast suffers from environmental degradation and the high population density at the tourist spots, as well as the disposal of industrial residues, which enter the sea without adequate treatment.

Mangroves cover large areas of the coast ▶

THE 'SERTÃO'

It stretches from the Northern coast to the Northern portion of Minas Gerais, the *sertão* encompasses an area of 962,300 km², nearly half of the Northeast of Brazil. It is the zone of the plateaus, large relief surfaces sometimes horizontal, which serve to block the passage of air masses inland. In this large extension where the temperature is elevated during the entire year causing a high level of evaporation, a small amount of rain falls that, to aggravate the situation, is concentrated in three or four months of the year. So, the 400 to 800 mm annual rainfall, depending on the region, is soon lost in evaporation or surface run off, as the terrain is little permeable and the relief slopes considerably. The scant amount of water is then carried by the São Francisco River to the sea.

'CAATINGA'

From here is the existence in the *sertão* of shallow soils, sometimes with big outcrops of rocks or flat areas of rock, of temporary rivers and a vegetation of *caatinga*, which loses its leaves during the long dry season. The loss of the leaves is an adaptation of the plants to climatic conditions and essential for their survival. But as soon as the rains start, all the dry vegetation of the *sertão* changes and in a few days the green sprouts as if by miracle from the dry stony soil. The variation of colors of the *caatinga* depending on the intensity of the rains is noticeable: from deep green it changes to red when the precipitation drops and the leaves become burnt, after yellow, grey and finally white. Because of this, the Indians call the *caatinga* 'white forests'. The cacti and bushes normally have large and eye-catching flowers, some of which only open at night. Some of the fruit of the *caatinga*, such as umbu, occasionally during prolonged droughts, make up the unique source of food for the *sertanejo*. One of the birds – a symbol of the Northeast and characteristic of the *sertão* is the *asa-branca* bird that marks the dry period. In contrast with the arid landscape, the *sertão* presents mountain ranges and plateaus, which rise to 900 or 1,000 meters above sea level and

The tragedy of the droughts

One of the biggest scourges of the Northeast is the drought, which is notorious since the colonial period. At that time, as the region was little populated, the drought did not represent the calamity that it does nowadays. From the 18th century, when more people moved to the *sertão*, due to the larger cattle herds and the cultivation of cotton, the drought started to have social repercussions. Technical commissions were entrusted to study the problem, while at the height of the disasters, thousands of *sertanejos* suffered from starvation, lost their crops and emigrated to other regions. Today, it is possible to determine some factors that influence the dryness, such as the difference of the surface water temperature of the North Atlantic and of the currents from the south, the appearance of El Niño, etc. But this does not stop the population from continuing to suffer. Emergency programs were set up but until now no solution has been found.

◄ Babassu, palm tree from Maranhão

The cacti and bushes have large and eye-catching flowers. They change the scenery

about 500 or 600 meters over the surrounding terrain. In these places, due to the altitude and consequently to greater exposure to the humid southern winds (the trade winds coming from the Atlantic Ocean), the scenery is more exuberant, because it benefits from a greater rainfall. It is the case of the Araripe forest, a region of fertile soils and diversified vegetation between the Amazon Rainforest and the Atlantic Forest, which has amenable temperatures during most of the year.

COCONUT GROVES

There is a transitional area between the *caatinga* and the Amazon Rainforest in Maranhão, parts of Piauí and Ceará and in short areas of other states. It is named Cocais forest, consisting, mainly, of babassu and carnauba palm trees, and to a lesser extent, by *buriti* (*Mauritia vinifera*). In the Cocais forests of Piauí, there are temporary rivers, but nearly all of the watercourses are permanent, some substantial like the Parnaíba between Piauí and Maranhão, together with the Itapecuru, Mearim and Pindaré. Apart from this, to the south of this region, characteristic vegetation of the central-western savannah predominates and to the Northwest, the Amazon Rainforest. In some points, these types of vegetation intermingle with the semi-arid.

The droughts have social repercussions in the semi-arid backlands

SÃO FRANCISCO RIVER

Old boats still cross the "Old Chico" as the river is called

The third biggest river in the country, only after the Amazon and Paraná rivers in size, was lovingly nicknamed "Velho Chico" (Old Francisco) by the Northeasterners because of the important role it represents in the lives of the population of the region. During a long time, it was the only means of communication between the Northeast and Minas Gerais, and for this, it was also grandiosely called the "River of National Integration". Discovered by the navigator Américo Vespúcio in 1501, the São Francisco River is born in the Serra da Canastra in Minas Gerais, and crosses four northeastern States: Bahia, Pernambuco, Alagoas and Sergipe. The length from its source to its estuary is 2,714 km. It traverses Minas Gerais and Bahia and from there it runs to the Northeast and, after a dog's leg in its course, it deviates to the southeast, flowing into the Atlantic Ocean between Alagoas and Sergipe. It is a plateau river, which has its course intersected by waterfalls and rapids in several points. Leaving Serra da Canastra, in its upper section, it forms the Casca d'Anta Waterfall, with a height of about 200 meters. From Salto de Pirapora, near to the city of the same name in Minas Gerais, is the start of what is called the middle segment, of between 370 and 480 meters in altitude, where it is navigable for 1,300 km to Juazeiro in Bahia, and Petrolina in Pernambuco, two cities linked by a river bridge. It is in this stretch that the river flows through the semi-arid *sertão*. Here, most of its tributaries are temporary rivers and the 'Velho Chico' assumes a fundamental role as a source of water and as a means of communication. In spite of the relative loss of importance of the river for transportation in more recent times, due to the expansion of the highway system, the river vessels called *gaiolas* (steamships) and *chatas* (barges), still navigate between Pirapora and Juazeiro, taking passengers and goods, always with figureheads on the bow. It also constitutes an important source of tourism and leisure in the region.

HYDROELECTRIC PLANTS AND DAMS

A long stretch with waterfalls downstream of Juazeiro marks the passage of the São Francisco River from the plateau to the plains and

Carrancas were figure heads used on the bow

Sobradinho Dam is used as a source of electricity too

eventually to its mouth in the Atlantic Ocean. The Paulo Afonso and Itaparica falls are located here. The São Francisco River has an important significance as a energy source: the Três Marias hydroelectric plant supplies energy to part of the southeast region in the upper section; the Paulo Afonso, Itaparica and Moxotó plants on the lower river supply energy to the Northeast. The need of regulating the middle river, an area subjected to the effects of the prolonged droughts, led to the construction of the Sobradinho Dam (used as a source of electricity too) and the formation of a lake, which in some places has a width of more than

Anjiquinho hydroeletric was build in 1913

30 km. Irrigation programs started the cultivation of fruits and vegetables over the last decades, mostly in the middle section, superimposing the traditional subsistence farming and extensive cattle ranching.

THREATS

Over the last years, a debate of a project to pump water of the São Francisco River re-started, which aims at transferring a volume of water to other river basins, an idea that exists since the times of the emperor Dom Pedro II, who was worried about the drought of 1850, one of the worst in the history of the region. The flow of the São Francisco River is in the order of 2,800 cubic meters per second. It was greater before. The construction of the dams increased the sediments removed at the barrages. The flow also reduced due to the indiscriminate use of the river waters in projects of irrigation. Other threats endanger the river. Its banks are obstructed by sediment, and there is no longer as much water or fish as in the past when the engineer Teodoro Sampaio, together with other explorers from the federal govern, made a trip along 'Velho Chico' in 1880. At that time, in a report to the hydraulic commission, Teodoro Sampaio summarized his impressions of the river in this way: "The São Francisco River is an enormous vivarium, which never lacks fish, as well as the *caatingas* and the riverside forests, an immense and inexhaustible treasure, easy to explore at moments, extremely rare moments, in which the universal laziness yields a little of its empire."

MAN IN THE NORTHEAST

THE EARLY TIMES

Pedra do Ingá inscriptions in Paraíba

A controversy splits palaeontologists who study the origin of man on the American continent: since when are there people on this side of the world? Whilst one group of researchers refuse to accept the existence of human remains dating more than 20,000 years old in South America, others sustain, mainly based on excavations performed in the Serra da Capivara region in Piauí, that the first human settlements in Brazil are from around 50,000 years ago. And so starts the history of man in the Northeast – a story, little understood and mysterious. Who were these first inhabitants who arrived here? And what about the tribes that followed, between 10,000 and 20,000 years ago, and who took advantage of the shelters carved from the rocks, such as in Boqueirão da Pedra Furada to draw colored designs? Anyway, during thousands of years, several tribes left their marks at sites in

Guajá Indians in Maranhão

◄ Fishermen in Parnaíba river, Piauí

the Northeast; for instance, in Pedra do Ingá in Paraíba and Lajedo de Soledade in Rio Grande do Norte. They could have been exterminated or moved on to other locations. It is known only that, when the Portuguese arrived here in the 16th century, the majority of the indigenous groups were of Tupi Indian stock. After having arrived in the region a few centuries previously, they were still forcing out the established occupants from other cultural backgrounds. They were hunter-gatherer populations who started to domesticate several plants. Despite having linguistic and tribal cultures in common, the Tupi Indian groups were never able to unite themselves into a political organization.

THE ARRIVAL OF THE PORTUGUESE

The first impression of the Europeans about these Brazilian Indians was of simple and sociable tribal groups. The explorer Américo Vespúcio wrote back to Portugal in 1502: "I imagined it is close to paradise on earth", he said referring to the life of these Natives. This impression lasted for a short time. After discovery, the northeastern territory was mainly visited by adventurers, above all the French, who, in exchange for trinkets, acquired from the Indians brazilwood and parrots. The red dye extracted from the brazilwood was

Indians try to preserve traditions ►

responsible for the carmine of the European clothes at a time when artificial dyes did not exist. To combat these adventurers and to guarantee possession of the land, the Portuguese Crown decided to send settlers to Brazil and introduced the system of hereditary captaincies. These captaincies were donated to land-less aristocrats who had earned a royal favor. They were ambitious people who were prepared to face the other side of the Atlantic. In exchange, they could enslave the natives and use them in the cultivation of the land.

THE CONFLICTS

The Indians, however, who had submitted themselves to the felling and transportation of the brazilwood trees in exchange for technological artifacts that they did not possess, refused to work in the plantations as they were not accustomed to this type of work and did not consider it profitable. The conflicts began. Although they were at a disadvantage (bows and arrows against muskets, swords and sometimes cannons) at first, the Indians devised strategies. Of the 17 captaincies that made up the territory of Brazil, almost all failed. In the Northeast, the captaincy of Pernambuco, which extended from the São Francisco River to Itamaracá Island, survived. It was given to Duarte Coelho, who disembarked here in 1535. The decision of the Portuguese Crown to send a governor-general to Brazil was aimed at retaking control of

Brazil by defending the captaincies weakened by the Indian attacks. The first Brazilian governor-general was Tomé de Souza, who settled in Bahia, a captaincy that, although it had started to prosper, had succumbed to the Indian attacks, exposing the city of Salvador to French invaders. In 1549, with the support of the Crown, Salvador was rebuilt. In a few decades the Indian populations that the discoverers of Brazil had found along the entire coastline, had disappeared. For this, the Portuguese, counted on, not only the weapons, but with diseases, that were introduced from Europe and thus unfamiliar to the Indians. And then at the end of the 16th century the sugar boom started. Each captaincy had at least one main village and some included several neighboring communities. It was at this time that cities such as Penedo, today in Alagoas, São Cristóvão and Laranjeiras in Sergipe, Fortaleza, Natal and João Pessoa (formerly called the Village of Filipéia), started being built around forts. The settlers who did not live permanently in the villages were found on the sugar plantations, small communities in themselves, where the 'Master' lived surrounded by his workers, both free men and slaves, Indians and Negroes. At the end of the 17th century, with the break up of the traditional indigenous culture and the crossbreeding of the population, the Negro slaves already constituted a majority in the plantations.

THE SUGARCANE CYCLE

Sugarcane was the main product of the Northeastern economy during centuries

The first governor-general, Tomé de Souza, arrived in Brazil in 1549, bringing with him civil and military workers, soldiers and craftsmen. New settlers also came with him as well as the first Jesuits. The new arrivals joined together with the Indians, taking as much land as possible. With this a generation of Brazilians originally 'mamelucos', a mixture of Europeans with Indians, appeared in the northeastern sugar regions, soon to by augmented by slaves brought from the African west coast. Brazil, in the words of the Jesuit and historian from this time, Antonil, was "the hell of the Negroes, the purgatory of the Whites and the paradise of the mulatto men and women." The Negroes played a fundamental role in the shaping of the local societies, centered on the Master's house and the slave quarters. They were the workforce which sustained the sugar plantations, immense sugar farms in the forest belt. In the plantations, the Master reigned, almost in an absolute form, the owner of the lands, the mansion, the plantations, the mill, the purgatory house, the slave quarters, the chapel, the rivers and brooks, the forests, the animals and the slaves themselves. And also, to a certain extent, the free people who

Articraft: villagers had commerce as function

rented lands to cultivate sugarcane and who were forced to sell it to their landlords.

THE COLONIAL SOCIETY

The towns and villages, which flowered during the colonial period, had, as their main function, commerce and services, besides the collection of taxes and religious assistance. Their principal buildings were the churches, convents and forts. The *casario* (a group of houses) of Pelourinho in Salvador, which nowadays is restored, was built by rich plantation owners as proof of their social improvement. During religious festivities, the rural aristocracy left their farms to live in the towns. At other times, the towns had a peaceful existence, only animated by the weekly market, the masses and novenas, and by the arrival of some sailing-vessel in the port. The tiered society of the plantations and the familiar character of the sugar companies permitted generations of Masters and slaves to preserve that world of domination even after abolition. In his classic, *Casa Grande e Senzala (Mansion and Slave Quarters)*, the author Gilberto Freire compares the social relationships in the plantation to those of a family, having the slave important to its prolongation in the same way as the lands. The continuity of this system in the following centuries forges one part of the north-eastern life, portrayed by other writers, such as José Lins do Rego and Graciliano Ramos. In the Ilhéus region of Southern Bahia, another author, a native of Bahia, Jorge Amado, showed a similar society forged into the cultivation of cocoa. In the mid 17th century, the wealth generated by the exportation of sugar allowed the establishment of cities like Recife, Olinda and Salvador, which constituted some of the biggest and richest urban centers of the American continent. The enormous, numerous and extremely rich churches and convents of these cities, their brilliant and ostentatious urban lifestyle were the expression of the Creole culture of the period. Not even the Dutch invasion (1580-1640) impaired this growth. On the contrary, the plantation owners just transferred

Sugarcane museum: colonial heritage

their businesses to these new controllers of the European sugar market. The problem is that when the Dutch left, they took their money to the plantations in the Antilles, which in the following century competed in the world market, eventually dominating it.

RESISTANCE

The plantation society only found active opposition on the part of the slaves who struggled for freedom. Daily they resisted the foreman's whipping and fled to distant places to found *quilombos* (escaped slave communities). The most famous of which, Palmares in Alagoas, resisted for nearly a century, being rebuilt after each of the landowners' attacks. Before being definitively destroyed in 1695, it brought together around 30,000 Negroes in diverse communities embedded between Pernambuco and Bahia. Another form of resistance was seen in the African religious services. Negroes, who by the end of the colonial period were integrated in the traditional Catholic religious organizations, were gradually abandoning it. In Salvador, Recife, and São Luis, 'candomblé' and the religious festivities, the Carnival, maracatu, and the dance of 'capoeira' developed in the absence of the official culture.

Berimbau: musical instrument ▶

THE 'SERTANEJO'

Since colonial times, cattle ranching constituted an activity of great relevance to the Northeastern economy. This happened, as sugarcane did not permit cattle for the subsistence of the population to evolve in the fertile plains of the forest belt. It was necessary to send the cattle inland, to the 'agreste' of Pernambuco and the edge of the Recôncavo in Bahia. There, the cattle proliferated and were dispersed in corrals along the permanent rivers, invading the backlands of São Francisco, proceeding southwards, and beyond in the lands of Piauí and Maranhão. At first, the plantation owners from the coast themselves took land on the edge of the backlands to breed cattle for their consumption. Afterwards the activity was passed to ranchers. As the corrals could only be located close to the rare permanent water supplies and as the inland pastures were very poor, the farms were immense. The corrals were distanced days away. The cowboys were paid in heads of cattle, some types of food and salt. Occasionally the cattle herders passed, rounded up the animals and led them to the coast. Caruaru in Pernambuco was one of the cities from this period that was founded as a stopping over point for travellers.

ISOLATION

The relationship between the landowner and the workers was rigidly organised, although not as brutal as in the

They settled where there was water

plantations. The proprietor had authority over the possessions of the workers, and sometimes, he aspired to have it over the daily life and over the women of the place. But there was not the same rigidity as in plantation work, which encouraged many half-castes to move inland, thus supplying a cheap workforce. These half-breeds entered into conflicts with the Indians who had found refuge in the interior of the country. Some interbred forming the typical characteristic of the flat-headed Northeasterner. These communities were slowly developing some forms of sociability. The necessity to recover and separate the cattle required cooperation, for example during

the roundups, which ended up being transformed in regional celebrations. The religious services for saints and the festivities of the religious calendar, centered in the chapels, forced regular interaction between families, which in turn resulted in parties, dances and weddings. They continue nowadays, for example the Junina (June) parties of Campina Grande and Caruaru. Outside of these times, the groups of cowboys remained isolated. These groups consisted of a few men recruited from among the Indians and half-breeds, as well as escapees from the coast, fleeing slaves and adventurers. They penetrated farther and farther until after three centuries they occupied almost the entire *sertão*. They settled where there was water and good pasture. Many of these settlements became villages and towns, famous as cattle and cotton markets.

RELIGIOUSNESS

Isolated, these *sertanejo* societies developed two forms of expression provoked by the poverty in which they lived: banditry and religious fanaticism. Until the middle of the 1930s, when the construction of highways in the region was accelerated, the backlands sheltered *jagunço* bands attired as well-armed cowboys. "Each gang member had his own moral justification for joining", Darcy Ribeiro said in *O Povo Brasileiro* (*The Brazilian People*). "All making banditry an expression of *sertanejo* revolt against the injustices of the world". The fact is that they constituted another motive of violence, even though frequently they were praised by the

population. The fanaticism was based on messianic beliefs experienced in the region that, one day, a savior would come to rescue the population from poverty. It was demonstrated many times by the presence of the people who led pilgrimages, attracted religious processions and those who said that they performed miracles. In the Juazeiro of Father Cícero, a prosperous religious commerce was created. In Bom Jesus da Lapa, in the 17th century, Francisco Soledade, after having a divine vision, chose a grotto on the banks of the São

Cowboys were the first to go to backlands

Francisco River as a chapel and created there one of the most traditional spots in Bahia for processions. Another form of popular expression among the Negroes coming as slaves, at that time, from the region known today as Benin. They kept their African gods appeased with the Christian religion in the territory of candomblé, and thus the religion fusion that influences the north-eastern cuture so much today.

The saga of Canudos

In about 1870, Antônio Mendes Maciel, the so-called Antônio Conselheiro, united a poor population who abandoned the farms to follow his preaching in the high *sertão* of São Francisco. Slowly they created the community of Canudos challenging the authorities and creating their own administrative rules. It was not long before they upset the big landowners who request the intervention of the state troops. The first attacks were repelled. An appeal was made to the army, who sent two large contingents, which were also beaten. It was then suggested that it should be interpreted as a monarchic rebellion against the republican regime. An army was sent against Canudos. The community did not resist. The event became renowned for the discordance of the two faces of the Brazilian society, portrayed in *Os Sertões* (*The Sertãos*), by Euclides da Cunha, and in the memory of the sertanejo that remembers this resistance.

◄ Procession in honor of orixá from candomblé, queen and protector of the waters

CONTRASTING LANDS

People in cities like Fortaleza lives in the past and in the future

It is possible to find in the Northeast, today, populations living in a state of extreme poverty and large cities with high-tech industries – without considering the luxurious resorts that share the space of the heavenly beaches with humble fishing villages. The inequality has been the motive of constant concern of the governments, although the measures adopted in the past to reduce the difference not always gave results. However, this picture of underdevelopment does not mean that the Northeast is insolvent from the economic point of view. Even the semi-arid regions can become areas producing wealth as long as a rational use of the land, the available water and the most neglected population is made. The best proof of the economic viability of the region is in Petrolina, where irrigation transformed the area in one of the biggest fruit producers in the world; and in some pockets on the banks of the São Francisco River and in the Chapada do Apodi. Besides this, tourism has increased on the beaches of Porto Seguro, Fortaleza, and on the coastlines of Natal and Pernambuco.

CHANGES

In recent years the isolation of the *sertão* has been slowly disappearing. With this the powerful farmers of the past are losing, little by little, their life and death authority over the population as the lands are being split by roads traversed by thousands of trucks which carry people, goods and new ideas. Even so, the development in some regions did not come together with corresponding urban planning. Remote and peaceful places were cut, from one day to the next, by highways without the necessary infrastructures such as sanitation. It is not rare to find places recently discovered by tourism, which do not have treated water and to see warnings of the presence of animals

on the paved highways. Pollution is also worrying, principally in threatened ecosystems such as the mangroves.

FESTIVITIES

Nowadays, in face of the vanishing isolation, the whole of Brazil knows the main cultural manifestations of the Northeast – and not only the Carnival. *Forró*, *baião*, *xote* and *xaxado* are some of the rhythms that were born in this region. Traditional styles such as that of the singers and 'repentistas' exist together with more commercial music such as axé-music and with styles more recent that incorporate the traditional to the new, like the mangue-beat. 'Literatura de cordel' was one of the most traditional printed poetry styles in the Northeast. It is still possible to find examples for sale in the inland markets. *Frevo*, currently a symbol of Carnival in Pernambuco, originates from the military bands from the end of the 19th

Music shows cultural vitality

century and the ballroom dances, such as *maxixe* (old popular dance). The *maracatu* tradition, which arrived with the slaves is really a type of Carnival group of music and dance. Due to its rich ethnic heritage, the Northeastern music is particularly valued and the folklore presentations such as the *pastoril* (theatrical play with music and dancing), the Holy Ghost festival and Bumba-Meu-Boi are extremely well appreciated.

The more traditional festivals of the Northeast

CELEBRATION	CITY	MONTH
Procession of Good Jesus of the Navigators	Salvador (BA)	1st January
Festival of the Master of Bonfim	Salvador (BA)	2º Thursday in January
Carnival	Salvador (BA)	*February or March
Festival of Iemanjá (Goddess of the Sea)	Salvador (BA)	2nd February
Festival of Our Mother of Conceição of the Beach	Salvador (BA)	8th December
Festival of Saint Sebastião	Trancoso (BA)	20th January
Festival of Saint Brás	Trancoso (BA)	3rd February
Holy Week Celebrations	Cachoeira (BA)	*March or April
Fair of Porto, Saint John and Independence	Cachoeira (BA)	From 22nd to 25th July
Our Mother of a Good Death	Cachoeira (BA)	Second half of August
Our Mother of Rosary	Cachoeira (BA)	Second half of October
Pilgrimage of Good Jesus	Bom Jesus da Lapa (BA)	July
Pilgrimage of Our Mother of Solitude	Bom Jesus da Lapa (BA)	15th September
Festival of Our Mother of Compassion	Porto Seguro (BA)	September
Procession of Saint Sebastião	Caraíva (BA)	January
Festival of Saint Benedict	Ponta do Corumbau (BA)	April
Festival of Our Mother of Conceição	Sta. Cruz de Cabrália (BA)	8th December
Pilgrimage in Praise of Father Cícero	Juazeiro do Norte (BA)	20th July
Roundup rodeo of Father Cícero	Juazeiro do Norte (BA)	July
Folklore week	Juazeiro do Norte (BA)	August
Pilgrim's Day	Juazeiro do Norte (BA)	1st November
Pilgrimage of Our Mother of Sorrows	Juazeiro do Norte (BA)	From 13th to 15th Sept.
Regatta of Rowing boats	Canoa Quebrada (CE)	July
Regatta of Jangadas (sailing rafts)	Majorlândia (CE)	October
Festival of the Patron Saint, Our Mother of Rosary	Aracati (CE)	7th October
Fortal – Carnival of Fortaleza	Fortaleza (CE)	June
MaceióFest	Maceió (AL)	November
Holy Ghost and Bumba-meu-boi	São Luis and Alcântara (MA)	May
Carnatal	Natal (RN)	December
Festival of Saint John	Petrolina (PE)	June
Junina (June) Party	Caruaru (PE)	June
Holy Week celebrations in Nova Jerusalém	Fazenda Nova (PE)	*March or April
Gathering of the merrymakers	Teresina (PI)	June

*DATE NOT SET

◀ Development did not come in some regions (BA)

GLOSSARY

Agogô – a percussion instrument made of iron and steel, brought to Brazil by Ioruba Africans. The sound is made by striking the instrument's two or sometimes three, bells with a stick. Alongside the drum and tambourine, it's used in samba and other types of Afro-Brazilian music making, such as in music for candomblé voodoo rituals, the very vigorous maculelê dance and capoeira kick-fighting.

Aperreado – peeved, annoyed

Arretado – can mean good-looking, smart and courageous, or upset

Arribar – leave, exit

Arroz de cuchá – a typical rice dish of Maranhão, prepared with dried shrimp, fish and sesame.

Avexar – vex, embarrass, humiliate

Berimbau – of African origin, this instrument marks the rhythm in capoeira kick dancing. It is basically a wooden bow curved by a metal string, with a resonating half-gourd attached toward one end. The cord vibrates when it is struck with a stick that the player holds in his right hand, while with the left, he changes this sound by touching the string with a metal ring or coin. It is played together with a small caxixi rattle which is attached to a right hand finger and shaken while striking the string.

Baião – a popular, lively type of song and dance that is accompanied by a small guitar and other instruments. Repentista improvisers who compose rhymes and music on the spur of the moment, often on subjects suggested by the audience, also call their musical interludes, a baião.

Baião-de-dois (also rubacão) – when rice and beans are cooked together, this is what the mixture is called.

Beiju – rather thick, manioc flour pancake that is either baked in the oven or griddled in a pan.

Buchada – casserole prepared with sheep or goat tripe

Bucho – belly, stomach.

Bumba-Meu-Boi – a wide-spread, very popular comic-dramatic street dance with human, animal and imaginary characters (Caipora, Babau, Jaraguá, etc.). It tells the story of the death and resurrection of an ox. In different regions it has other names (boi-bumbá, boi-de-mamão, boi de reis, boi-surubim) and is performed at different times (sometimes during the June/July festivities and sometimes around Christmas time).

Cangaço – the life style of nomadic bandit gangs (which the region's social injustices and abject poverty were also accountable for), that roamed the Northeastern hinterlands and terrified the population during the 19th and into the 20th century. Their weaponry and attire was also called cangaço.

Cordel Literature – booklets and leaflets with stories and verses based on the Northeastern culture and customs.

Cruzeiro – the section in a church between the main chapel (opposite the entrance door) and the central nave.

Desafio – a dual between repentista improvisers, in form of provocative but usually humorous dialogues and verses put to tunes.

Eira, beira e tribeira – the same as "sem eira nem beira": they say that in olden days, the rich houses had three layers of roofs, an eira, a beira and a tribeira, which was the top covering. The not so well-off were not able to have the three roofs, and therefore only covered their homes with the tribeira. Hence "sem eira nem beira" that used to designate underprivileged persons.

Forró – lively dance music bands that basically are accompanied by a zabumba bass drum, a triangle and an accordion. Couples dance together, holding each other tight. The origin of the word is unclear. According to one version, it derives from dances "for all" that foreigners, living in the Northeast during WWII, used to promote. Another possibility is "forró " being short for "forrobodó" which means a shindig dance, and also confusion.

Folguedo – fun time, merrymaking.

◀ Cowboys way of life remain the same (MA)

Frevo – an extremely rhythmic Carnival dance from Pernambuco in which the dancers carry out very frenetic choreographs holding a small, colorful umbrella in one hand which is swung sideways, and pushed up and down, in rhythm to the music.

Gibão – a leather, vest-like garment that used to be worn by northeastern cowmen and cangaceiro bandits, as protection against the thorny caatinga brushwood.

Jardineira – public transport bus

Jerimum – pumpkin

Macaxeira (also aipim) – manioc

Mangar – to make fun of

Maracatu – 17th century Pernambuco folklore that blends Indian and African cultural and religious expressions.

Papangu – someone who dresses up or uses a papier-mâché mask in regional celebrations, but mainly in Caruaru, Pernambuco.

PF – short for Prato Feito which is a simple, ready to eat meal served on a plate or tray, usually consisting of rice and beans, a piece of steak, chicken or fish, and a salad.

Parracho – coral reefs that are excellent for diving around and game fishing.

Pífano – an rustic fife usually made of bamboo, similar to the piccolo flute, played in the well-known and popular Bandas de Pífano and Zabumba bands.

Pitu – a large, very tasty freshwater shrimp that is very common in the Northeast and other parts of Brazil.

Quadrilha – a lively type of square-dancing that originates from the European quadrille that was introduced in Brazil in the early 19th century via the imperial court of Rio de Janeiro. Nowadays, the quadrilha is only danced in June festivals and rural commemorations.

Queijo de coalho – a cottage cheese that is very common in North and Northeast Brazil. After the curd has separated from the whey and pressed, it is salted and eaten fresh or matured, and is often grilled.

Repente – improvised music-making by singers who are accompanied or not by a guitar. Originally the Moor people took this custom to the Iberian Peninsula from where it was brought to Brazil by the Portuguese 200 years ago.

Santo-de-pau-oco – hollow saint statue; also a hypocrite or false person In the colonial days, there was contraband of gold and diamond that often was done inside hollow saints. Smugglers relied on customs officials being too superstitious to violate the icons and check for contents.

Surubim – a large, flat headed, sweet water fish, that can weigh up to 20 kg. and is excellent food; mostly roasted or grilled.

Sururu – a mussle-like mollusc that is mostly eaten with an onion, oil and vinegar sauce.

Tapioca – another type of manioc flour pancake that is served with different fillings, those with cottage cheese and shredded coconut being favorites.

Umbu-Cajá – a fruit very much enjoyed in the Northeast. It is different from umbu and from cajá which are two other types of fruit.

Xaxado – a rhythm and dance that originated in the Pernambuco hinterland. The name emulates the sound that sandals make on the dance floor. It is said that the feet of the Cangaceiro bandits spread the dance from Pernambuco to other States.

Xilogravura – engravings and printing from such engravings; a technique much used in the Northeast to illustrate the cordel literature.

Xote – northeastern music normally played by trios of accordion, bass drum and triangle players. It resembles xaxado and forró music. Very possibly this word is taken from the German word Schottisch which was a polca-like Hungarian dance.

Zabumba – bass drum that is standard in most Northeastern musical arrangements.

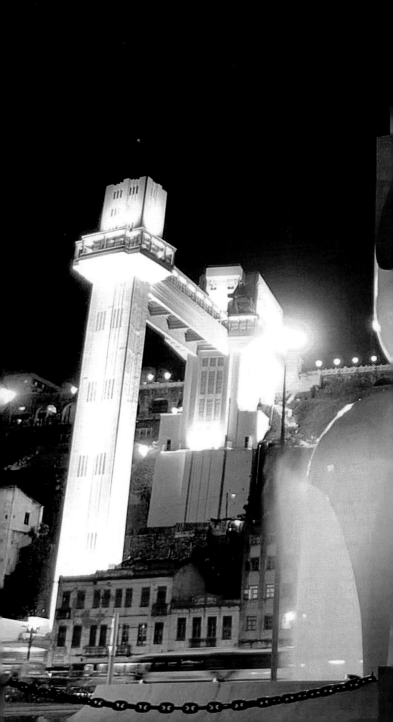

BAHIA

BAHIA

It is the biggest State of Northeast Brazil, with an area of 567,000 km². It has the most extensive coast, stretching over 1,103 km and boasts the largest cave in the entire Southern Hemisphere – the Toca da Boa Vista – of which 98 km already chartered; it boasts Brazil's biggest bay – the Todos os Santos Bay – which comprises most of the State's coastline, and, yearly, the 40 *trios-elétricos* (sound booster trucks), that send 2 million people reeling during carnival in Salvador. The first capital city of Brazil, Salvador's heritage in architectural treasures were declared national monument and Cultural Heritage of Humanity by Unesco. There are so many churches in Salvador that some say there is a church for every day of the year. It was to Bahia that the first African slaves were taken, to work the land. They brought with them their traditions which are so easily identified in the local music, cooking and religion. The main roads in Bahia are the BR-101 that crosses the State from East to West and is the main route to Brasilia, and the BA-001 highway that hugs the coastline. The Southern section is 673 km long with amazingly diverse geographical and ecological characteristics. In the Porto Seguro region, there are still untouched stretches. Near Ilhéus, where novelist Jorge Amado lived for many years, it is possible to experience life as it was when the cocoa trade reigned absolute, and follow trails that run through the mata atlântica forest as well as coastal environments. In the Southern tip of Bahia is Caravelas, from where motorboats provide transport to the most sought after skin-diving havens, refuge also for the calving *jubarte* humpback whales between July and November. Along the 230 km stretch of the Northern beaches are some of the grandest hotels. The most traditional profane and religious festivals take place from December to March. All year round Chapada Diamantina can be visited, but April through September, a remarkable lighting renders the water of the enchanted Poço Encantado. Beside rural and industrial activities, their economy is based on tourism.

◀ **Salvador: view of the Lacerda Elevator with Mario Cravo's sculpture**

LEGENDS

National Park

Paved road

Dirt track

0   120   240 km

PERNAMBUCO

SERRA DA CAPIVARA

BR 235

BA 210

Juazeiro

Paulo Afonso

Canudos

ALAGOA

BR 235

Jeremoabo

manso

Santo Sé

Sobradinho

Euclides da Cunha

BR 407

Xique-xique

SERRA DA BABILÔNIA

BR 116

SERGIPE

BA 052

Irecê

BAHIA

BR 324

Feira de Santana

BR 110

Praia de Mangue Seco

BA 099

Ibotirama

BR 242

Argoim

Alagoinhas

CHAPADA DIAMANTINA

Lençóis

Paraguaçu

Camaçari

Mata de São João

Praia do Forte

PraiaArembepe

Mucugê

SALVADOR

m Jesus da Lapa

BA 142

Baía de Todos os Santos

Morro de São Paulo

Jequié

Valença

BR 101

Contas

Camamu

Praia Barra Grande

Itacaré

SERRA DA JUREMA

BA 001

Vitória da Conquista

SERRA DO SALGADO

Itabuna

Ilhéus

Praia do Una

Praia de Comandatuba

Jequitinhonha

Canavieiras

Belmonte

PAU BRASIL

BR 367

Santa Cruz Cabrália

Eunápolis

Porto Seguro

Praia de Arraial D'Ajuda

MONTE PASCOAL

Praia de Trancoso

Praia de Caraíva

DESCOBRIMENTO

Praia de Cumuruxatiba

Prado

Highlights

❶ Salvador

❷ Chapada Diamantina

❸ Itacaré

Caravelas

MARINHO DOS ABROLHOS

Salvador

Pelourinho: complex of colonial architecture that was turned into a monument by Unesco

Aracaju: 325 km
Vitória: 1,200 km
Cachoeira: 116 km
Porto Seguro: 670 km (via Ilha de Itaparica)
 2.440.886
 71
 Bahiatursa, 202-1244
@ www.bahia.com.br

The city was founded in 1549 by the first Governor General Tomé de Souza and made capital city of Brazil, which it was for 214 years, until 1763. Its original name was São Salvador da Bahia de Todos os Santos, after the bay it's on, discovered 48 years earlier on All Saints Day, November 1. The heritage of colonization is evident in Salvador's architecture, culture and mainly in the faces of its people. Getting to know Salvador requires a certain physical fitness, as the city's topography is often extremely uneven, with myriad alleyways, squares, and steep streets. The central part is divided into Cidade Alta and Cidade Baixa. The Cidade Alta is where the Pelourinho is, and the restored building complex, as well as some of the most important churches in Brazil. In the Cidade Baixa, the Mercado Modelo, Solar do Unhão, the road that leads to other beaches of Todos os Santos Bay, the Senhor do Bonfim church and the Ribeira marina. Bahia's women selling the spicy Afro-Brazilian acarajé patty keep mainly to the bohemian district of Rio Vermelho. And between Ondina and Pça. Castro Alves is the famous carnival circuit along which 2 million revellers dance their way behind the trio-elétrico, every year.

HIGHLIGHTS

Elevador Lacerda and Praça da Sé
Pça. Municipal, Historical Center. Everyday, from 6 a.m. to 11 p.m.
The Lacerda lift was built in the late 1920's and links the Cidade Alta and the Cidade Baixa. To your right, when leaving the lift in Cidade Alta, is the Palácio Rio Branco. To the left is Pça. da Sé. The Sé Church was pulled down in 1933. Where it stood, a leaning Cruz Caída cross was erected to protest. Next to this memorial is the Belvedere da Sé, one of the oldest panoramic view spots

The first capital city

S alvador was founded in 1549 to protect the new territory from foreign invasions. Until then, since 1535, Portugal had implemented the same colonization method in Brazil, as in its Ilha da Madeira and the Açores territories. It consisted of donating vast strips of land to donees that were responsible for the administration and agricultural exploitation of their lot. The province of Bahia started off very well under Francisco Pereira Coutinho, chiefly by cultivating sugarcane. However, Indians began attacking the Portuguese, often incited by French corsairs who were smuggling brazilwood to Europe. Eventually, such continuous attacks, poor administration, the impending danger of losing dominion, as well as appeals for action from settlers themselves to D. João III, ruler of Portugal, brought about the decision to properly colonize Brazil. Tomé de Souza arrived in Salvador as Governor General with the task of building the first capital here. A fortified city was built, partly on the 65-meter above sea level highland where residential and administrative areas were centralized, and around the lower section bay, with a port. In Salvador and surroundings, sugarcane and tobacco crops were increasingly grown, and goods shipped from the port to Portugal throughout the 17th, 18th and 19th centuries. Imposing courthouses were built by the increasingly wealthy landlords. Those in the historical center of Salvador were restored and can be viewed. With a gradual shifting of the economic focus, more Southern regions of Brazil, the capital was transferred to Rio de Janeiro in 1763.

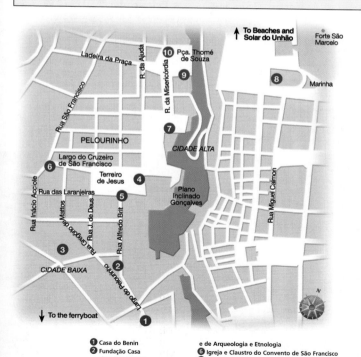

1 Casa do Benin
2 Fundação Casa de Jorge Amado
3 Museu Abelardo Rodrigues
4 Catedral Basílica
5 Museu Afro-Brasileiro
e de Arqueologia e Etnologia
6 Igreja e Claustro do Convento de São Francisco
7 Praça da Sé
8 Mercado Modelo
9 Elevador Lacerda
10 Palácio Rio Branco

History of torture

Pelourinho was once the site of the pillory, a stone column with brass rings to which slaves and criminals were tied and whipped or simply exposed to public ridicule. Originally, the pillory stood in front of the House of Representatives and Jail, on Pça. Castro Alves. Later, in the 17th century, it was transferred to Terreiro de Jesus which now is the historical center. But the cries of those being punished would disturb the ceremonies in the nearby Jesuit church, so it was transferred again, this time to Lgo. das Portas de São Bento, and then once again to where today is Lgo. do Pelourinho, officially called Pça. José de Alencar. The column was demolished but the name, after which the entire district is known, remains.

in Salvador, from where the famous Mercado Modelo can be sighted, a Navy detachment, the Forte de São Marcelo and the Bahia de Todos os Santos Bay. Also on the square are the Casa de Misericórdia buildings, the Paço Arquiepiscopal, and a monument to Tomé de Souza. A little farther on is the Plano Inclinado Gonçalves transport system that also provides a link between the low and upper cities. Next to the Sé is the Lgo. do Terreiro de Jesus, that leads to Pelourinho.

Palácio Rio Branco

Pça. Thomé de Souza, Downtown.
Monday from 2 to 6 p.m.
Tuesday to Friday, 10 to 12 a.m.
and 2 to 6 p.m. 🏛️ ⚪ ⚪
The governor generals used to live here, and the palace has undergone many changes since it was first built during the 16th century. In 1912 Salvador was bombarded by the San Marcelo fort

canyons in a conflict between State and federal troops and the palace was badly damaged. In 1919 it was grandly re-inaugurated. Its architecture mixes different styles that range from the jacaranda wood ceiling to Luiz IX furniture. Today, it houses the Fundação Pedro Calmon, the Memorial dos Governadores, and an area where exhibitions take place, in the main hall.

★ Pelourinho 🏛️ ⚪ ⚪ ⚪ 🌙

The complex of colonial architecture that makes up Pelourinho was turned into a national monument by Unesco. It consists of around 800 colonial mansions built in the 17th and 18th centuries by wealthy land-owners. The site is in the upper part of town. It was abandoned for many years, and became dangerous and decadent until 1985, when restoration work began. There are art galleries, *capoeira* (leg fighting) schools, boutiques, handicraft shops,

São Francisco Church: extensively gold-embellished interior

restaurants and places to go at night. In the internal squares **Pedro Arcanjo, Teresa Batista** and **Quincas Berro D'Água** artistic activities are intense. The first visit can begin at the **Terreiro de Jesus** and the **Catedral Basílica Church**, and then the **Faculdade de Medicina**, a building constructed in the 17th century by the Jesuits. Today is houses the **Museu Afro-Brasileiro**, the **Museu de Arqueologia e Etnologia** and the **Memorial da Medicina**. A little further on, side by side, the **Ordem Terceira de São Francisco,** founded in 1635, and the **Igreja e Convento de São Francisco** dated 1587. that form big arquitetural complexes in Salvador. On leaving, turn right along R. Inácio Acciole, then left along R. Laranjeiras and right again, on R. Gregório de Mattos. On the corner you will find a **Bahiatursa Tourist Information Center**. If you go down R. Gregório de Mattos, **Casa do Olodum** is on the left-hand side; on the right, the **Museu Abelardo Rodrigues** of sacred art is, and the **Teatro Miguel Santana**, that presents the Balé Folclórico. Finally, go to Lgo. do Pelourinho where the **Museu da Cidade**, the **Fundação Casa de Jorge Amado**, the **Restaurante do Senac** and **Igreja Nossa Senhora do Rosário dos Pretos** are all situated. The church was built over the 18th century to slaves, so

they too could go to mass as they were not allowed into churches the white elite attended. Tuesday is the day of blessing. Mass is read at 6 p.m. to the beat of African drums. After there, is a show by the **Olodum** percussion group in Lgo. de Teresa Batista.

★ Catedral Basílica

Terreiro de Jesus, Pelourinho. Monday to Saturday, from 8:30 to 11:30 a.m. and from 1:30 to 5:30 p.m. 😊 😊 Baroque concert Sunday at 11 a.m. Built between 1657 and 1672, the cathedral is covered both in and outside with Lioz marble brought from Lisbon. The altar is the largest and richest among all Portuguese-Brazilian Baroque. The cell in which Padre Antônio Vieira died can also be visited.

★ Museu Afro-Brasileiro

Terreiro de Jesus (old School of Medical Sciences), Pelourinho. ☎ 321-0383. Monday to Friday, from 9 a.m. to 5 p.m. 😊 ⑪

A collection of original African art and art inspired by African cultures can be seen there. There are also Brazilian works with an association to African art. Highlights are the 27 carved, wood panels by Rubens Carybé, with different kinds of sea shells and mirrors, that are representative of the *candomblé orixá* deities. In the same place is the

◀ The Basílica Cathedral reflects in the fountain of Terreiro de Jesus

Religious syncretism

In the 16th century slaves coming from Africa to work on the plantations brought with them African traditions that ever since have influenced religious life in Brazil, specially in Bahia. They were forbidden to practice their own *candomblé* rites, given that the Portuguese colonists also had the mission to catechise in the Catholic faith, the 'unbelieving' Indians and Africans. Slaves found a way to relate their *orixá* deities with the Catholic saints, which brought about a syncretism that permeates religious and cultural manifestations in Bahia. The slaves first held their religious ceremonies in the *terreiro* (terraces used for drying crops around their courtyard quarters), as they were not allowed into the churches. Each *terreiro* worshipped a favourite *orixá* (saint with a namesake Catholic holiday). Each orixá has a day of the week. If you wish to visit a *candomblé terreiro*, you are advised not to go

Baianas relate orixás with the saints

without a guide. The most traditional temples are Gantois and the Axé Opô Afonjá. in São Gonçalo do Retiro. Information is available from

---

Museu de Arqueologia e Etnologia with a collection of archeological findings of the Alto Xingu.

★ Igreja da Ordem Terceira de São Francisco da Penitência

Cruzeiro de São Francisco, Pelourinho. ☎ 321-6968. Monday to Friday, from 8 a.m. to 5 p.m.

The façade is the only example left of the 15th century of the Spanish plateresc style in Brazil. The main altar is completely leafed in silver, and a splendid organ was built in 1848.

★ Igreja e Claustro do Convento de São Francisco

Cruzeiro de São Francisco, Pelourinho. ☎ 322-6430. Monday to Saturday, from 8:30 a.m. to 17:30 p.m. Sunday, from 2 to 5 p.m.

The church was built in 1587, destroyed during the Dutch invasion, and reconstruction began around 1720. Because of its extensively gold-embellished interior, it is one of the richest churches in Brazil. It is an example of Baroque and neo-classical styles. Three naves lead up to the main

altar with gold-plated, Rococo figures. It has more Portuguese tiles than anywhere else in Bahia.

Museu Abelardo Rodrigues

R. Gregório de Mattos, 45, Pelourinho. ☎ 320-9383, ww.museuabelardo rodrigues.ba.gov.br Tuesday to Sunday, 1 to 7 p.m. Free entry on Thursdays.

Abelardo Rodrigues, a lawyer, compiled the largest private, sacred art collection in Brazil, with 808 works made of clay, wood, ivory and soapstone. The Solar do Ferrão, which houses the collection, was built in 1701.

Casa do Benin

R. Padre Agostinho, 17, Pelourinho. ☎ 241-5679. Tuesday to Friday, from 9 a.m. to 6:30 p.m. Saturday from 1 to 5 p.m. and Sunday from 9 a.m. to 1 p.m. Entrance: free.

The house has many objects made of metal, ceramics and pottery, woven materials and baskets, and woodwork brought from Benin, Africa, by Pierre Verger. The concrete pillars of the building have been disguised with palm leaves woven into intricate

The Modelo Market: craftmanship and *capoeira* ▶

patterns, similar to those made with leaves and fibres in African countries.

★ Fundação Casa de Jorge Amado

Lgo. do Pelourinho, Pelourinho.
☎ 321-0070, www.fundacaojorgea mado.com.br Monday to Saturday, from 9 a.m. to 6 p.m. Closed Sunday. Entrance: free . 🖰 ⬤ 🏛

Here, the works of the author, born in Itabuna (see *Ilhéus*), can be studied and are preserved. Covers of translated versions, photographs, videos, manuscripts, badges and medals, letters and documents that tell the life story of Jorge Amado, who so well knew and brought to life in best-selling novels, quintessential Bahia. Some of his characters, like Quinquas Berro D'Água and Dona Flor circulate around the Pelourinho streets. The museum also has a center of Brazilian literature studies, with a research and documentation section.

Museu da Cidade

Lgo. do Pelourinho, Pelourinho.
☎ 321-1967. Monday to Friday, from 9 a.m. to 6 p.m. Saturday, from 1 to 5 p.m. Sunday, from 9 a.m. to 1 p.m. Closed Tuesday.🖰 🏛

Images and figures of *orixá* deities in elaborate costumes and head dress, from the Afro-Brazilian *candomblé* religion. So is the collection of documents on the poet Castro Alves.

Mercado Modelo

Pça. Visconde Cayru, Cidade Baixa. Monday to Saturday, from 9 a.m. to 7 p.m. Sundays and holidays, from 9 a.m. to 2 p.m. 🖰

The customs and general warehouses used to occupy this building, that was transformed into the Modelo Market with 300 small shops selling arts and crafts, ceramics, earthenware, jewels, sweetmeats, pictures and paintings, leather-ware, *berimbaus* and other souvenirs. Items of every price can be found, and bargain you must, since it is expected. Between 11 a.m. and 1 p.m. *capoeira* groups give presentations in the back part of the Market.

Museu de Arte da Bahia

Av. Sete de Setembro, 2340, Vitória.
☎ 336-9450. Tuesday to Friday, from 2 to 7 p.m. Saturday and Sunday, from 2 to 6:30 p.m.🖰 🏛

The Baroque, mainly *jacaranda* wood entrance doors are striking, specially the Mexican masks carved into the wood. Inside, 18th-century furniture, jewels, East India Company porcelains and paintings by local artists are shown.

Museu de Arte Sacra

R. do Sodré, 276, Downtown.
☎ 243-6511,www.mas.ufba.br. Monday to Friday, from 11:30 a.m. to 17:30 p.m.🖰 🏛

This is one of the most representative collections of colonial sacred art, that has

Resistence with Capoeira leg fighting

Capoeira is a weaponless form of defense that slaves used when abused by their masters, who soon prohibited its practice. It combines dance and martial arts movements in a series of bodily contortions, that require outstanding balance, agility and strength. The *berimbau,* bow-like percussion instrument, is strung with a wire that is tapped with a small stick, over where a gourd and is attached to the bow. At the same time, with the left hand, a coin is used to modify the wire sounds, and the bow is moved against and away from the body, inflecting the sound's timbre and vibration produced by the gourd. The *caxixi,* a small wicker and dry seed rattle worn like a ring on the right hand, completes the supporting rhythmic accompaniment for the *capoeira* fighters, though hand clapping by on-looking *capoeiristas,* encircling the combatants, is another element, as is the all white attire.

The *capoeira* origins are also not clear. Mestre Bimba (1900-1973) believed that *capoeira* was a manifestation created in the slave quarters of the big plantations in the coastal regions of Bahia. Another, Mestre Pastinha (1889-1981), was convinced it came from Angola, where the blows and kicks are somewhat slower and body action is closer to ground. Both have their school and followers in Pelourinho, and every day at 11 a.m., there are *capoeira* performances in the Mercado Modelo.

Escola Mestre Bimba. ☎ 322-5082
Escola Mestre Pastinha and Associação de Capoeira de Angola. ☎ 321-3087. All in the Pelourinho.

Capoeira: from slave quarters to the street

over 2,000 items, including precious stones and silverware. The Nossa Senhora de Guadalupe and Nossa Senhora das Maravilhas, both 16th century, are leading attractions. The story goes that Padre Antônio Vieira was blessed by the latter, and was transformed into a great orator.

★ Igreja de Nosso Senhor do Bonfim

Pça. Senhor do Bonfim, Bonfim. Internet: www.senhordobonfim.org.br. Tuesday, Wednesday, Thursday and Saturday, from 7 to 12 a.m., and 2 to 6 p.m. Friday and Sunday, from 6 to 12 a.m. and 2 to 5 p.m. Closed Monday. 🕒 📷
Built in 1754, this became Salvador's most popular church, but more because of its Bonfim icons than any architectural virtues. The sea captain Teodósio Rodrigues de Faria had it build in observance of a promise made, on surviving a tempest at sea. Inside the church is the miracle chamber with gypsum, wood and even gold parts of the body, in remembrance of mercies bestowed. The washing of the church stairs on the second Thursday of January, has become very important in the Salvador calendar. The best day for visiting the church is Friday, when those who go, dressed in white, ask for peace, and pay homage to *Oxalá* (Senhor do Bonfim in the Catholic religion).

★ Solar do Unhão e Museu de Arte Moderna

Av. Contorno. ☎ 329-5551/329-0660, www.solardounhao.com.br / www.mam.ba.gov.br The external section is open daily from 9 a.m. to 10 p.m. The modern art museum opens Tuesday to Friday, from 1 to 7 p.m.; Saturday and Sunday, from 2 to 8 p.m. The restaurant is open everyday for lunch and dinner. 🕒 📷
Another colonial architecture example of the 16th century. It is like all the wealthy rural plantation complexes of its time, with the large owner's house, chapel, and surrounding slave quarters, and the sugarmill. Rail tracks, that are

still there, were also later added for wares to be pushed along, in trucks. Its hillside location offers a marvelous view over the Bahia de Todos os Santos Bay. The modern art museum collection can be seen on the main house, and includes works by Di Cavalcanti, Volpi, Portinari and Pancetti.

Beaches

Salvador has many urban beaches, along its 30 km shore, with easy access by car. Buses, that leave from Pça. da Sé, also go to most beaches and places along the coast. Starting in the city center, the first beach is **Porto da Barra** where the first Brazilian fort was built – Forte de Santo Antônio. The Barra-Ondina Carnival circuit begins here. After Porto da Barra there is a long stretch of sea which is inappropriate for bathing but very nice for walks. The water improves from the pretty **Piatã** beach with palm trees and playing courts, onward. The next is

Bands of Bonfim: amulet

Itapoã, whose lighthouse, near Cira's *acarajé* was imortalized in Dorival Caymmi songs. Then come **Stella Maris** and **Flamengo** beaches, where bathing conditions are best. Because the contour is uneven here, natural pools are formed. At this point, the center of Salvador is a one hour drive away.

SURROUNDINGS

Ilha de Itaparica

This is the largest, 240 sq km island in the bay. It still has some historical

The spicy Baiano savories

The cookery in Salvador is a trip in itself – aside everything else, it is unique insofar as combining African, European and Indian culinary ingredients and customs. From Africa, the dendê oil, extracted from the homonymous palm nut. From Portugal, the preparation and conservation procedures and seasoning, and from the Indians, the manioc flour, sea food and pepper. The rich, spicy, varied and sonorously named concoction of foods, is unrivaled: *acarajé, caruru, vatapá, bobó, abará, quindins de laiá*. *Acarajé*, from the African nagô word meaning *acará* (small cake) and *jé* (to eat), is a small ball made of a bean mixture, deep-fried in *dendê* oil, with a *vatapá* stuffing. *Vatapá* looks a little like mashed potato and has cocoa-nut milk, shrimp, cashew nut and other ingredients. When it is your turn to be served, the traditional question is hot or cold? If you prefer "hot", your

acarajé will come with lots of very hot baiano pepper, and if "cold", not quite so much. It can also be served with a *vinagrete* garnish (chopped onion and tomato in olive oil and vinegar). The baiana women who prepare the *acarajé*, are as traditional as the food they cook, and according to custom, it is done as a duty and in honor of the deities that guide them. There are many baiana women all over Salvador, but three have made a famous name for themselves, which waiting lines attest. Acarajé da Cira, in Itapoã and Rio Vermelho. ☎ 249-4170/ Acarajé da Dinha. ☎ 334-1703/ Acarajé da Regina. ☎ 363-5474. Both in Rio Vermelho.

Acarajé: in honour of the deities

buildings, and many summer houses. But it has also become a through-way for beach goers heading South (see *Morro de São Paulo*). Ferryboats, for people and cars, leave from the São Joaquim terminal, roughly every ten minutes after the hour. At the other Bom Despacho end, there are vans and buses to different parts of the island. From December to March, waiting lines at the ferry can get quite long, and the best way to avoid them is buying a ticket in advance.

North Coast

214 km by Estr. do Coco and Linha Verde, as far as the Sergipe border. ⬤
From Salvador, straight up, are some of the most important beaches of Bahia that are easily reached by car and also by bus, which leave the Bus Station. **Arembepe** is the first beach. The sea is very blue at this point, where the important sea turtle protection project, Tamar, operates. Nearby, there's a small hippie community in thatch-roof huts among the coconut trees, next to a river. During the 1960's, Janis Joplin stayed here for a while. Next is **Barra do Jacuípe**, calm waters in the encounter of river with sea. About 45 km further up is **Itacimirim.** The Linha Verde highway commences near this point and advances, often in long straight stretches, to the Sergipe border. On this part of the road, the first beach is **Praia do Forte**. On entering the village, to your right are the Castelo de Garcia Dávila ruins. A resort hotel occupies a considerable part of the beach at one end, and the other, a larger Tamar base than the one in Arembepe. It has a museum, nursery tanks, and souvenir shop. A long stretch of the beach is good for swimming, and to the left, past

Forte de Santo Antônio, in Porto da Barra

Tamar, natural pools are formed. **Imbassaí Beach** is another 10 km ahead; as yet undisturbed, with a river that runs along the water line, forming a peninsula. **Porto Sauípe Beach** follows Imbassaí and was chosen for an immense real estate project, the Costa do Sauípe. **Massarandupió Beach** some 23 km further north, has an area reserved for nudists. The last beach on the Linha Verde stretch is **Mangue Seco**, immortalized by Jorge Amado in his *Tieta do Agreste* novel. and to reach it, one is ferried across the Real River. From the small hamlet there, a buggy car ride over the dunes can be arranged. It takes around 40 minutes to walk from the village to the beach.

TIPS

– When you get to Salvador, buy yourself the *Guia do Ócio*, a monthly guide for the leisure seeking lazy, with information on restaurants, cultural activities and night-life.
– Bahiatursa is the official Bahia tourist agency with many booths in Salvador.
– Don't miss the sunset from Solar do Unhão. The best way there is by taxi.

The Carnival routes

On Ash Wednesday, *trio-elétrico* sound trucks meet on Pça. Castro Alves; the most extraordinary and unforgettable part of the Salvador Carnival, with higher-than-decibel-counter music and incredible light displays. There are the busts of the trio-elétrico inventors, Dodô and Osmar, in Pça. Castro Alves. Dodô was always trying to find better ways to use music for the Carnival parades. In 1950 a frevo dance company came to Salvador from Recife and impressed him greatly, so he and Osmar, with their amplifiers and instruments, took to the streets a top a 1929 Ford, playing Pernambuco frevos. The innovation was called *pau-elétrico*. The following year, their two friends took turns in forming a more effective musical threesome, and the trio-elétrico was born. There are two main routes through the streets of Salvador. The first, taken Thursday to Saturday, goes from the Barra to Ondina. The other starts in Campo Grande and goes to Pça. Castro Alves, from Sunday to Tuesday. It is the longest and most traditional, and can take up to 8 hours to complete. Apart from the

trio-elétricos, each parade has many different percussion groups, the chief ones being Timbalada, Ara Ketu, Olodum, Cheiro de Amor, Beijo and Eva, and are famous throughout Brazil. Other, more traditional *blocos*, include Tapajós and Filhos de Gandhy. The best way to take part in the Carnival is to buy the *abadá* smock, which will allow you to enter the area isolated by cords around all the *blocos*. Each provides its revellers with beverages and has its own security personnel. It is more economical to stay outside the isolating cords – but take extra care if you do, and don't carry anything valuable. You can buy an *abadá* smock to dance in the same *bloco* every day, or else a passport into a different *bloco* each day. The Central do Carnaval sells both. (www.central docarnaval.com.br, 372-6000). In the Pelourinho, the old-time street Carnival, with small music bands leading hosts of dancers in fancy costume, is much calmer. As animated as the seven days of Carnival, are the rehearsals of the *blocos*, since October. The most well-known are Timbalada (245-6999), on Sunday, and Ara Ketu (247-6784),on Thursday, Olodum has year-through rehearsals on Tuesday, in Pelourinho.

Yearly, 2 million people reeling during the carnival in Salvador

◄ Barra do Jacuípe: calm waters in the encounter of river with sea

Bom Jesus da Lapa

Senhor Bom Jesus cave: the final point for the pilgrims

Salvador: 821 km
Belo Horizonte (Minas Gerais): 894 km
Brasília (Distrito Federal): 636 km
👤 54,421
🌐 77
ℹ️ Bahiatursa, ☎ 481-5399

Situated on the banks of the São Francisco River, in the back country of Bahia, Bom Jesus da Lapa is a famous pilgrim center, that over 800,000 people visit every year, chiefly in July.

In caves, requests for miracles or thanks

The shrines and sanctuaries people come to revere are inside 15 caves in the surrounding hills. The larger, maze-like caves, that are most visited, are Senhor Bom Jesus, Nossa Senhora da Soledade and Santa Luzia. Curiously, the stalactite and stalagmites formations inside of the caves provide supports for statues and images, and even for the baptismal font. Most pilgrims come to Bom Jesus in buses or trucks from other parts of the Bahia interior, and from Minas Gerais. The streets are lined with dozens of booths where Bom Jesus wristbands and T-shirts are sold, as well as replicas of body parts. These are taken into the caves with requests for miracle, or in thanks for divine favors. Intermingling with the sacred item stalls, gaily decorated, brilliantly lit booths selling, apart from religious memorabilia, plastic toys, flowers and other inexpensive souvenirs.

The typical Northeastern musicians and poets complete a scenario into which profane aspects have increasingly been incorporated. Visitors also can have their pictures taken. Many also climb the hill higher, above the cave, for the view over the city and the São Francisco River. At these times, the town administration also organises shows and presentations with regional bands and theater groups. Hotels and guesthouses are packed. The Bom Jesus religious tradition began in the early 17th century. Now, from July to September pilgrims from several parts of Brazil dominate the streets of the city. The populace is very proud of the São Francisco River. A big bridge spans it near Bom Jesus. The pier under it has become a meeting point for fishermen, and also visitors, who can go for boat rides. Life there is directly connected to the river all the time. The economy of Bom Jesus is based on irrigated subsistence farming, and water is taken from the São Francisco, and also the Corrente River which crosses the Sitio da Mata district, near Bom Jesus. Cattle and pigs are also raised on a small scale. A common sight when on a boat ride will be men fishing, women washing cloths and children playing along the banks.

TIPS

– Take the BR-324 road to Feira de Santana; from there BR-116 up to Paraguaçu and then continue on BR-242 toward Lençóis and on to Ibotirama from where, by the BA-160 road you reach Bom Jesus da Lapa.
– Praça da Bandeira is the town's chief meeting place where, aside from July/September, people come together every day to hear forró music and drink beer in the bars around it.
– From July to September, book your hotel well in advance.

A life of preaching

The religious tradition of Bom Jesus began in 1690 when the Portuguese Francisco de Mendonça Mar crossed the backlands of Bahia in a life of preaching and penitence, after renouncing the comfort of Salvador, where he worked as a goldsmith. He changed his name to Francisco Soledade and, on arriving at the banks of São Francisco River, he chose a grotto on a hillside as his hermitage, where he had a divine vision: He should build his home there and dedicate the rest of his life to helping the suffering people of the backlands. He lived there in isolation for years whilst the fame of his great virtue started to spread among the *sertanejos*. In 1706 he was ordained priest. Since 1722, when he died, the number of faithful who visit the area increases every year. From the interior of Bahia and Minas Gerais, they thank an attained grace or ask for blessings.

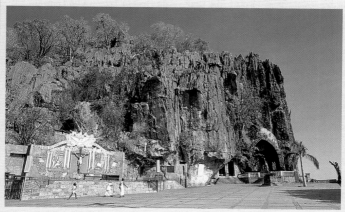

Caves are transformed in churches

Cachoeira and São Félix

Igreja da Ordem Terceira do Carmo: baroque of the 18th century

Salvador: 116 km
Feira de Santana: 46 km
30,416
75
Centro de Turismo ☎ 425-1214

The surrounding regions of Salvador are known as the Recôncavo Baiano and were of strategic importance in colonial Brazil. The land along the Paraguaçu River was excellent for planting sugarcane. The gold was brought into port, along the river, and then shipped to Portugal. It also was the battle ground for brave men fighting for independence of Bahia and of Brazil. After Salvador, Cachoeira has the most significant Baroque and architectural heritage in Bahia, and for this reason was made a national monument and is protected by the National Historic and Artistic Institute. It's a country of brave fighters, where battles for the independence of Bahia and Brazil took place. Once, the unarmed population took a Portuguese man-of-war by force, which spurred other conflicts for the independence of Bahia. Two important Cachoeirense women took active part in the struggles:

Ana Nery, who had been a nurse in the Paraguay war, and Maria Quitéria, who dressed as a soldier in order to participate.

HIGHLIGHTS

★ Historical Center
The best way to know Cachoeira is on foot. A good starting point is the **Igreja da Ordem Terceira do Carmo** baroque church. Its richness is comparable to São Francisco Church in Salvador. On leaving the church, turn right and pass the Town Hall, which was originally the **House of Representatives** and the Jail, and also served as seat of the Bahia government on two occasions: once in 1822, during the war of independence, and in 1837, during the Sabinada uprising. Continue straight ahead until you reach a house with a white façade where **Ana Nery** (1815-1880) was born. She was a nurse who became famous for her work, nursing wounded soldiers during the war with Paraguay. Next to this house is the **Igreja Matriz Nossa Senhora do Rosário do Porto de Cachoeira**. At the corner, a left turning will lead you to Rua 13 de Maio street where the

Railway Station: a museum, a restaurant and a tobacco shop ▶

Fundação Hansen Bahia stands. It houses the collection of works by Karl Hansen, a German artist whose woodcuts portray the life and misery of prostitutes in Pelourinho, where he used to live. To the left, in the next block in a corner building, is the **Irmandade da Nosa Senhora da Boa Morte** association, responsible for the celebrations that honor the Virgin Mary which take place in the second half of August. This fraternity of women descendants of slaves is considered to be the oldest of its kind in Brazil, and this ceremony too, combines *candomblé* and catholic divinities. On the next block to the left, are the **Filarmônica de Cachoeira** headquarters.

At the end of Rua 13 de Maio and to the right, is Praça Dr. Milton where the **Chafariz Imperial** (1827) fountain and Santa **Casa de Misericórdia** (1734) building can be seen.

SURROUNDINGS

São Félix 🌐 🧑 🌑

Another important monument is the **Dom Pedro II**, a 365 m steel bridge linking Cachoeira to São Félix, that cars and trains still cross. It was imported from England by Dom Pedro II to improve transport of wares and goods to the port of São Félix, which at a time was the Republic's greatest cigar exporter port.

In the **Centro Cultural Dannemann** delicate works by women artisans are on display. The city architecture is contemporary with that of Cachoeira. The **Matriz do Senhor Deus Menino** and the Senhor **São Felix** churches, as well as the **Market** and the **Town Hall,** are specially prominent examples. Also visit the **Casa da Cultura Américo Simas**, and the old **Railway Station** where there is now a museum, a restaurant and a tobacco shop.

TIPS

– Access: from Salvador, take BR-324 as far as junction with the BA-420 road, which will take you to Cachoeira .
– Most places of interest in Cachoeira are open Tuesday to Friday from 9 a.m. to 5 p.m. and on weekends from 9 a.m. to 2 p.m.
– A good opportunity to visit Cachoeira is during celebrations that merge profane with religious. During these numerous festivities, local folklore is exhibited, like *samba-de-roda, trança-fita, terno de reis*, the *afoxê* Carnival troups, Bumba-Meu-Boi, and *capoeira* contests. Easter Week is in March or April; celebrations that combine Feira do Porto, São João and Independence Day happen at the end of June; Nossa Senhora da Boa Morte is celebrated in the second half of August; Nossa Senhora do Rosário (patron saint), in the first half of October and Nossa Senhora D'Ajuda in the second half of November.

Caravelas

Igreja Matriz de Santo Antônio: neo-classical style

Prado: 50 km
Salvador: 865 km
Porto Seguro: 272 km
Vitória: 470 km
👤 20,096
🌐 73
ℹ️ Secretaria de Turismo ☎ 297-1404
@ www.abrolhos.com.br

The small town of Caravelas, in the Southern tip of Bahia, practically on the Espírito Santo State border, used to be a trading port. Its importance grew enormously when a railway was built in the second half of the 19th century linking it to inland Minas Gerais State. Its historical site dates from those times, and, although neglected, still displays some good examples of the neo-classical style of its day, and façades decorated with tiles brought from the Portuguese territory Macau, in China. The railway was abandoned in the 1960's because of the bad state it was in, and the vast, national unification road building project that was underway. In latter years, its proximity to the Abrolhos Archipelago has turned it into a tourist center. From Caravelas, boats also leave for some of the most popular snorkelling places in Brazil.

HIGHLIGHTS

Parque Nacional Marinho de Abrolhos

Tourist agencies in Carvelas take visitors to the Park, in outings of one whole day. It takes 4 hours to go and come back in a fast boat. But there are excursions that can last 2 or more days which, specially divers, prefer, and the boats that take them are used as lodgings. In bad weather, boats do not leave Caravelas.🐚

The coral reefs made sailing in those parts extremely difficult in the olden days, and accidents and shipwrecks were not unusual. So when navigators neared the archipelago, they would be alerted with an 'abre os olhos' or 'keep your eyes open' warning, which gave origin to the name Abrolhos. It is formed by five islands: Siriba, Redonda, Guarita, Sueste, and Santa Barbara. Approaching tourist boats are met by Ibama staff, and escorted to the Siriba island, which is the only one where visitors can disembark. The *atobá*, which is the most numerous bird

Monte Pascoal: the first sign of firm land that Cabral had seen ▶

Atobas in Abrolhos Archipelago: the best place to dive in Bahia ▶

here, can be seen from close quarters; so can its nesting places that a trail leads through. While the island is covered mostly in grassland, life in the waters is impressively abundant with fishes, corals, turtles and squid.

From July to November, humpback whales arrives here from the cold Antarctic waters, to give birth to their young, in warmer waters. Some get to be 16 m long and weigh 40 tons.

In high season, and when whales can be sighted, you might have to wait several days before boarding. In low season, boats don't leave without a minimum of 6 persons.

SURROUNDINGS

Prado

50 km from Caravelas by BA-001 highway 🏖️ 🦐

The Caí River, near which it is said that Portuguese explorers first came into contact with Indian people, is in the Prado district. Prado has a well kept courthouse; also good restaurants. Its main attraction is a 33 km sea coast that heads north to Cumuruxatiba, with rugged cliffs rising high alongside most of the way. **Viçosa**, **Paixão**, **Tororão** and the **Ostras** beaches are all along this stretch. After Cumuruxatiba, there are two ways to reach the Caí River sand bars. By car, 18 km along a very bad, dirt road, best negotiated by 4-wheel vehicles that can be hired. The meeting of the dark river waters and the blue sea is spectacular, and worth the bumpy ride. By boat, the journey is longer, as it passes Ponta do Corumbau (*see Porto Seguro*) with Monte Pascoal mount visible most of the way.

Parque Nacional do Monte Pascoal

85 km from Caraíva by dirt road or 30 km from Itamaraju via BR-101 road. ☎ 294-1110. Daily from 7 a.m. to 5 p.m. 🚫 🦐

The Monte Pascoal mount was the first sign of firm land that Cabral, who discovered Brazil, had. The Park was created in November 1961 and covers 2,250 sq km. The vast forest with majestic, centennial trees such as the brazilwood, jequitibá, maçaranduba and jacarandá, is home to many birds and animal species. Around 500 remaining Indians of the Pataxó tribe live inside the Park. A short 700 m path leads to a visitation center were handicrafts can also be bought. Another, a little longer leads to the foot of the hill. To reach the summit takes around two hours, and the wood trail is steep. But specially on a clear day, the magnificent view from the top, over miles of precious forestland and the ocean beyond, is very rewarding.

TIPS

– Some of the special spots between Cumuruxatiba and the Caí River estuary, such as inlets forming natural pools, and refreshing streamlets crossing the usually hot sands before reaching the sea, can only be observed by hikers or cyclists.
– For those who prefer long distances, the Prado-Porto Seguro or 'discovery' trek, is an interesting hiking option. It takes an average 12 days to complete and is organized by a guide of Prado ☎ 298-1514.

Chapada Diamantina

Lençóis had its apogee in the gold cycle, in the 19th century

Salvador: 427 km
Feira de Santana: 297 km
Ibotirama: 286 km
🚶 8,910 (Lençóis)
🚶 75
😀😀😀

The park comprises the Mucugê, Andaraí, Lençóis and Palmeiras districts. Lençóis was turned into a national monument and is the town most travellers choose as their base from which to visit the Chapadas. It offers the best lodging facilities, restaurants and excursion agencies. With its 400 m gorges in the valleys and peaks ranging up to 1,200 m, the impressive Chapada, with its over 100 registered caves, 70 waterfalls, ravines and rocky cliffs, separates the valley of the São Francisco River from the Bahia coastline. The Park is on the east border of the State, and is crossed from North to South by the Sincorá mountain range. Lush green vegetation emerges in the arid Sertão of Bahia due to the high peaks that obstruct the clouds, causing abundant rainfall all year round, specially between November and January.

Palmital: trail to"Fumaça from the Bottom" ▶

The mosaic-like plant growth in the Park includes the stunted *caatinga* vegetation, and lush woods that line the water courses and tree groves. The park's wild life includes the 'mocó' guinea pig which is typical of the *caatinga* environment, pig-like capivaras, rabbit-sized cotia rodents, a smaller variety of anteater and the large tapir. Encounters, however, are more common with snakes and birds.

HIGHLIGHTS

Waterfalls 🌀 🌀
Cachoeira da Fumaça is one of the most traditional Chapada attractions. The water falls 340 m with the vapours forming a smoky-looking cloud, which gives the fall its name. It can be reached at the bottom from Lençóis, or at the top

from Capão, following a 12 km trail. The Fumaça por Cima (Fumaça from the Top) trail, involves a steep 2 km climb to reach the plain, where cattle used to be raised. The view from up there, also of Capão, is amazing. In the valley, there are three small 'alternative' communities whose members resort only to natural medicines, ecological farming methods and home-grown produce, and keep honey bees. The Fumaça por Baixo (Fumaça from the Bottom) is one of the most traditional Chapada treks. There are two options

to this waterfall is 7 km long. It crosses very slippery, riverbed terrain and takes about 2.5 hours to do. This part of the Park is least visited. Access to the trail is from the BA-014 road, from Andaraí. The dark waters of the **Cachoeira do Sossego** drop 15 m in stages of lovely, variegated, sandstone formations. To reach it, there is a 7 km trail (2.5 hours one way), alongside the river. In the district of Itaetê, a succession of cataracts forms the **Bom Jardim, Roncadeira, Herculano** and **Encantada waterfalls**, with heights

Spetacular view from Morro do Pai Inácio: main atraction for visitors

and a hired guide is essential.
The 3-day option is strenuous and recommended for very fit hikers, who also like camping. The **Cachoeira da Andorinha** is near the town of Mucugê. The trail is approximately 4 km long and passes several falls and natural swimming pools along the way.
The **Cachoeira do Buracão**, in the Ibicoara township at the Southern tip of the park, drops almost 120 m in the middle of a canyon. In water volume terms, it is the region's largest.
In a **Capivari River** tributary, there is the **Cachoeira Capivari** that descends the high walls, past colorful pebble shelves of green, red, pink and white into a dark pool, which is perfect for swimming in. The trail there is strenuous, so it's best if done in more than one day. **Cachoeira do Ramalho** is 110 m deep and forms a very large swimming pool too. The trail that leads

ranging around 100 meters.
To reach them is difficult, and when it rains, positively adventurous. The Herculano Waterfall is specially magnificent with its three cascades tumbling into a large lagoon.

Vale do Pati

To traverse this valley takes up to 4 days (40 km) from the Caetê-Açu village, to Andaraí, at the other end. The Castelo and Lapinha quartzite caves, with an entry and exit, are well worth visiting on the second day. From there, the Gerais do Vieira plains, in all their vastness, spread before the traveller. To swim in, there are several rivers as well as the Funis, Altina and Cachoeirão waterfalls with drops of over 150 m. The 1,580 meters. Morro Branco mount is in the Pati valley, but the presence of an experienced guide is necessary to climb it.

The Gold Rush

The Chapada Diamantina plateau lies in the central region of Bahia. Its geological history goes back 1.8 billion years when the remote backcountry *sertão*, used to be covered by the sea. Layer upon layer of sediment has been built up, one over the other. Tectonic movements, 800 million years ago, moulded the chapada which, ever since, wind and weather have forged into high cliffs, steep gorges, canyons and valleys. In Chapada, colorful sandstone, quartz rock and limestone configurations cover an area of 1,520 sq km. In the early 19th century, after the discovery of precious stones there by the German naturalists, Spix and von Martius, the region began to be populated. Gold and diamonds were the most sought-after minerals in those days. From 1980, a massive exploration of other minerals and ore began, with the use of huge, earth-moving machinery. Many river courses were diverted, leaving behind craters that can still be seen. In 1996, authorities closed mining activities.

Caminho do Serrano, Salão de Areias Coloridas e Cachoeiras 🌑🌀

A short walk from Lençóis, known as the Caminho do Serrano trail, following the Lençóis River, passes the Salão de Areias Coloridas (colored sand chambers) and takes you to the Paraíso water hole. It passes several pebbly bathing spots, and also leads to the charming Cachoeirinha and Primavera waterfalls that are both on the Grizante River, and to the Halley well.

Grutas da Lapa Doce, do Sol e da Torrinha
70 km from Lençóis 🌑🌀

The Lapa Doce cave has over 30 m underground chambers. From it, only a few-minutes walk takes you to the Sol Cave with its pre-historic cave drawings. The Torrinha cave, with competent, on-site guides, is considered one of the richest and most rare in cave ornamentation. A perfect way to recover from the *sertão* heat is in the shade, under the *umbuzeiro* tree that can be found by the snack bar, just above the Lapa Doce cave.

Gruta do Lapão
4,5 km from Lençóis. 🕐 Three hours. 🌀
The 3 km hike through dry and stony terrain (don't forget to take water

Next to Pratinha cave, a lake of transparent waters

along) leads to one of the biggest quartzite caves in Brazil, extensively used by the miners, years ago. Its opening is 20 m high from where, through a 1 km tunnel, the exit on the other side can be reached. But do not go in without an experienced guide.

Grutas da Pratinha e Azul

75 km from Lençóis.
🕐 Three hours. 🍃🏊

In the Pratinha cave, visitors can swim in the underground lagoon with the aid of headlights, and view the limestone formations on the walls. Look for turtles, freshwater shrimp and traira lung fish that often find their way in from the outside lagoons. The water is cold even in summer. The Gruta Azul is worthwhile visiting in the morning when a ray of sunshine lights up the underground ceiling.

Marimbus

18 km from Lençóis. 🕐 Three hours. 🛶
Marimbus is the generic name given to the waterlogged areas between the Lençóis and Andaraí districts. They are also known as the 'Pantanal da Chapada', due to the large amount of water that has accumulated on the plains, probably as a result of river redirections and drainage systems of prospects. Marimbus of Lençóis is located along the Santo Antônio River. Throughout

its over 1,254 sq km extension, a rich variety of flora and fauna have made their home, and is now protected by the Marimbus wildlife preservation organization, called Itaquara. Among other things, it forbids motorboats in the area. A good excursion alternative, therefore, is the Roncador ranch, with many beautiful waterfalls. Marimbus of Andaraí is also well prepared to receive visitors.

Morro do Pai Inácio

28 km from Lençóis.
🕐 Two hours. 🐎🏊

Pai Inácio Mount is located on private property in the Sincorá hills and can be reached by an old 18 km mining trail. By car, take the BR-242 road toward Seabra. From the top of the hill, one of the best views of the Chapada Diamantina can be enjoyed. The legend has it that Pai Inácio, who was a slave, ran away with his master's wife. In Lençóis, excursion agencies organize outings on horseback to Pai Inácio.

Poço do Diabo

20 km from Lençóis 🍃🏊
The Poço do Diabo, or Devil's Well, is in the Mucugezinho River and takes a 20-minute walk to be reached. Its waters are dark, but good for swimming and jumping into, from the 20 m bank.

◀ Gruta da Torrinha: rich in cave ornamentation

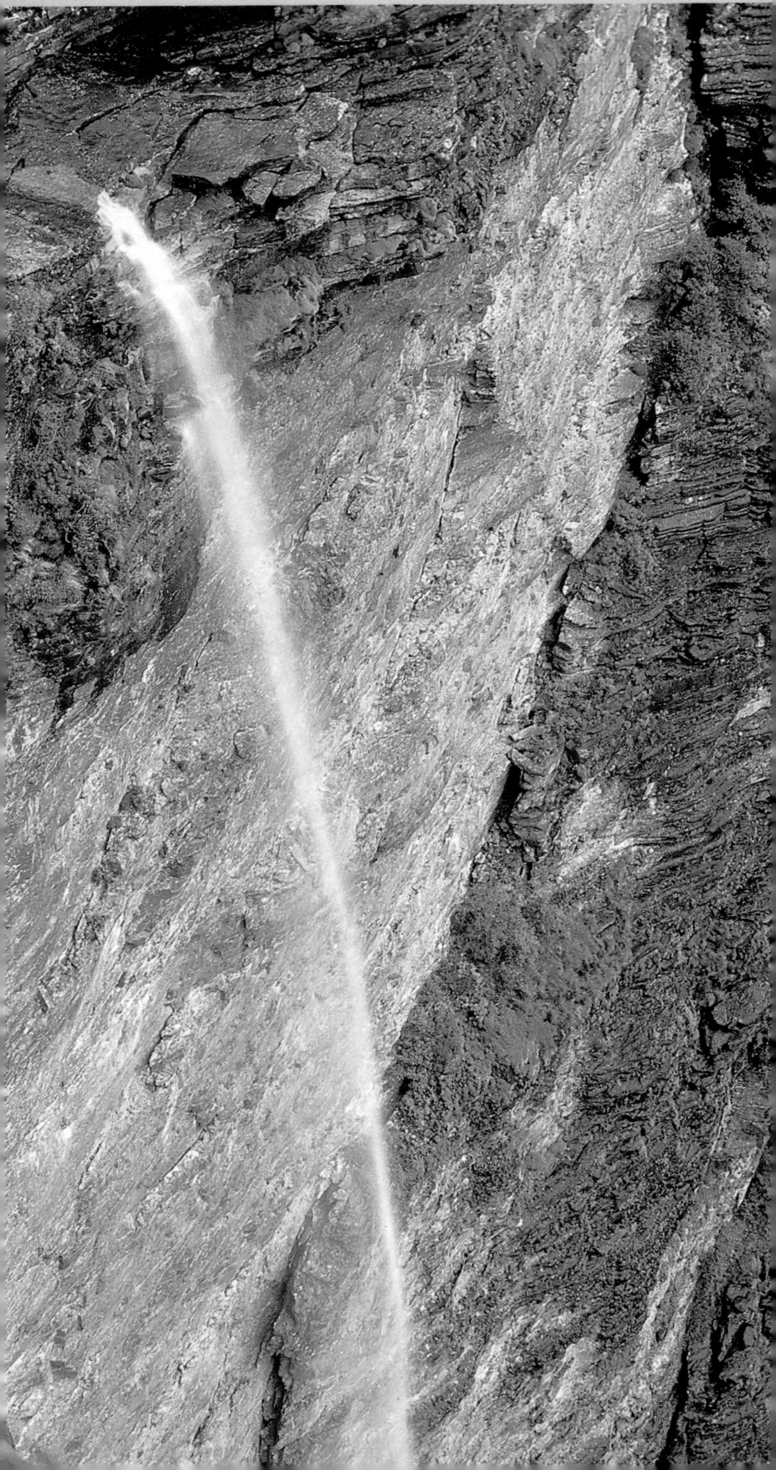

Poço Encantado e Azul
150 km from Lençóis

To get to know these favorites among the lakes, it is best to stay somewhere in Andaraí, Mucugê or Xique-Xique de Igatu. Poço Encantado, the Eenchanted Well, is 64 m deep and 98 m wide, and its water is crystal clear. According to how the light enters the shaft, its tonality changes dramatically. Specially between April and September, when light reflected from the mountain side hits the water, the rainbow-like effect is spectacular and extraordinarily beautiful. Bathing is not allowed to protect a rare species of albino fish found in this well. In the Poço Azul waters, however, some 40 km away, near Nova Redenção, a refreshing dip can be had.

Xique-Xique de Igatu
114 km from Lençóis 🛶

The official name of this town is Igatu de Andaraí. It used to be an important mining center during the second half of the 19th century, but was abandoned when its resources were exhausted. Everything there is made of stone; the houses, gardens, paths and walls. It rests atop a hill from where views are gorgeous. The walk down the trail is delightful and smooth.

Poço Encantado: special from April to September

TIPS . . . .

– Access. There are several regular flights into Lençóis. The airport is 25 km from the city. By car from Brasilia, take BR-242, a road that passes Lençóis. From Salvador, follow BR-324 up to Feira de Santana and from there, take the BR-116 link to Argoin, from where, proceed via the very poorly maintained BR-242 road, until you reach Lençóis. During the night, assaults are common on this stretch. Several bus companies have services to Lençóis: from Salvador (Viação Real Expresso), from São Paulo, Volta Redonda and Uberaba (Emtram), from Feira de Santana, Aracaju, Maceió, Recife and Palmas (São Geraldo). Always use a local guide: Associação de Condutores de Visitantes de Lençóis and Associação de Guias e Condutores de Ecoturismo – also in Lençóis. In Andaraí and Palmeiras, look up the visitor guide associations. Authorization from the local Ibama unit is necessary to visit the Park.

– Chapada Diamantina can be visited any time of the year. In the summer, from December to March, rivers and falls swell. Between April and September however, the Poço Encantado lighting spectacle happens; one of the greatest attractions, and highly recommendable.

– The roots of most local dishes are in the early mining days. Typical dishes include goat tripe ragout, stewed chicken in gravy, kale with coarse manioc flour farofa, chicken with saffron, and the exotic, stewed palma cactus; all well worth a try.

– Despite being in the back country, the crystal clear waters of the Chapada Diamantina rivers are wonderful for snorkelling in; so bring the equipment.

– Banco do Brasil is the only bank in the region and few places accept credit cards, so bring cash.

◀ Cachoeira da Fumaça: a 340-meter waterfall

Ilhéus

Ilhéus inspired books of writer Jorge Amado

Itabuna: 36 km
Itacaré: 65 km
Salvador: 458 km
Porto seguro: 315 km
👤 221,883
🌐 73
ℹ️ Bahiatursa, ☎ 231-8679.
Ilhéustur, ☎ 634-3510
@ www.ilheus.com.br

The history of Ilhéus has very strong
ties with the past cocoa trade of
Brazil. Although the first seedlings
were brought from the Amazon
regions already in 1746, production
only peaked in the 1920's, when
Brazil became the greatest cocoa
exporter in the world. In 1926, for
instance, over 47,000 sacks of cocoa
were shipped to New York from
Ilhéus. Misfortune struck in 1989,
when plantations were devastated by a
parasite named *vassoura-de-bruxa*.
The local economy and livelihood of
the people were very badly hit;
moreover, other countries in Africa
and Asia were successfully growing
the fruit and taking over the market.
An idea about what the golden years

in Ilhéus were like, during which,
even fashion was being copied in
other cities, can be found in the
ostentatious architecture of those
times, and in the imaginary world
that became the background in four
novels by its most illustrious citizen,
Jorge Amado: *Cocoa, The Violent
Land, São Jorge dos Ilhéus and
Gabriela, Clove and Cinnamon*.
Although born in Itabuna in 1912,
Jorge lived in Ilhéus until 1930.
Much of his writing is set in the
environment of the Ilhéus streets, bar
life, and churches. An entire block,
that inspired the author particularly,
is now named after him.

HIGHLIGHTS

★ Bar Vesúvio
Pça. Dom Eduardo, 190. ☎ 634-2164.
Open daily from 11 a.m. to 2 p.m.
Jorge Amado is supposed to have
inspired his Gabriela on a clove-
scented, cinnamon colored cook who
used to work in this bar. Nacib,
another character in the book, is in
love with her. It is a place of
obligatory visitation, where a *quibe*
and *cacaurosca* juice are served.

Bataclã

Av. Dois de Julho

This used to be an old cabaret –
the most scented in Ilhéus, as only
French girls danced there. It also is
featured in the *Gabriela* novel. The
rich colonels came in through a
secret passage so as not to be caught.
Today, all you see is a painted front
with reflection glass panes that hide
the debris inside.

★ Casa de Cultura Jorge Amado

R. Jorge Amado, 21, downtown.
Monday to Friday, from 9 to 12 a.m.
and 2 to 6 p.m. Saturday, from 9 a.m.
to 1 p.m. Closed Sunday.

This house was bought by Jorge
Amado's father in 1926 and Jorge
wrote some of the chapters of his first
novel, *Land of Carnival*, there. In this
handsome, two-story house, the
author's books, cloths, trophies, and
many photographs of him in Ilhéus,
are on display.

Catedral de São Sebastião

Praça Dom Eduardo, downtown.
231-2374.

Built in honor of one of the three
patron saints of city. The other two
are Nossa Senhora da Vitória and
São Jorge. Its immense vaulted
ceilings are Roman; otherwise it
combines Baroque and more
classical styles. It's also mentioned
in the *Gabriela* novel, the Vesúvio
bar being just opposite.

Teatro Municipal

R. Jorge Amado. 231-8164.
Monday to Friday, from 9 to 12 a.m.
and from 2 to 6 p.m.

Many grand operas, concerts and
plays were staged in this once famous
theater that opened in 1932. It was
rebuilt in 1986 and its acoustics are
said to be among the best in Brazil.

The Catedral: present in *Gabriela* novel

Cocoa land

In 1534, when Brazil was
divided into hereditary
provinces, Jorge Figueiredo
Corrêia became donee of the
Ilhéus region. Although he never
ventured into his fortune's
hinterlands, he named it São
Jorge (his name) and dos Ilheus
(of the islands), because
of three rocky islets called
Itapitanga, Itaipins and Rapa,
visible from the Alto São
Sebastião highland, where the
village was founded. From there,
not only the river could be
watched and the town protected
from Indian attacks, but ships out
on the open sea, identified, and
made welcome or not.
Before cocoa, the basis of
the economy was
sugarcane, planted on
big stretches of also
donated land, called
sesmarias. One stretch

belonged to Mem de Sá who
later became governor general
of Brazil. In Rio do Engenho, the
center of his farm, the Nossa
Senhora de Santana Chapel,
built in 1537, can be visited. It is
considered the third oldest church
in Brazil. The cocoa trade became
specially profitable in 1890,
and the hot and humid climate
of Ilhéus was taken maximum
advantage of. It is around this
time that the figure of the rich,
almighty cocoa colonel emerges.
These men rose to powerful
positions on the local political and
economic scenes, but they too, are
now part of the cocoa legend.
After 1989 the local
economy and livelihood
were badly hit when
plantations were
devastated by a parasite
named *vassoura-de-
bruxa*.

Cocoa: black gold

SURROUNDINGS

Fazenda Primavera

24 km along the Ilhéus-Itabuna road.
Book in advance. ☎ 9983-7627/
613-7817.

On this ranch, an old-time *fazenda
de cacau* (cocoa plantation) routine
can be followed; from planting the
seedlings to harvesting and
processing the fruit. It has been
turned into a national monument,
and keeps important documents,
such as a letter bestowing on the
landowner, the title of tenente-
coronel (which were the cocoa
colonels) signed by the first
president of Brazil, Marechal
Deodoro. Visitors can also go for a
pony ride, drive around in a horse-
pulled wagon and drink cocoa juice.

Museu Casa Verde

R. Miguel Calmon, 123, downtown,
Itabuna. ☎ 680-5020. Tuesday to
Sunday, from 9 a.m. to 5 p.m.
This green façade residence of
cocoa colonel Henrique Alves dos
Reis shows us how the wealthy
lived and furnished their homes. On
display, baccarat crystal, Luiz XV
furniture, and chinaware.

Estância Hidromineral de Olivença

R. Lúcio Soub, Olivença. Tuesday
to Sunday, from 9 a.m. to 6 p.m.
For a fee, you can spend the day
bathing in the pools's ferric waters.
The iron, magnesium and iodine
they contain are good for skin and
stomach troubles. The town of
Olivença is 20 km south of Ilhéus
and also has some nice beaches like
Cai n'Água, **Batuba** and **Back Door**.

Eco Parque de Una

Ilhéus-Canavieiras (BA-001) 45 km
from Ilhéus. Cidade Sol buses
there, leave from the Ilhéus and
Canavieira terminals. Visits between
9 a.m. and 2 p.m. must be
booked in advance. Closed Monday.
☎ 633-1121. Internet:
www.ecoparque.org.br.
English and German-speaking
guides.
The Una park borders the Reserva
Biológica de Una, and is known as
a private nature conservation
monument. It was only recently
opened and is among the best-
preserved remaining Mata
Atlântica forest environments. Its
wildlife is extraordinarily diverse.
Jeep transport is provided from the
bus stop on the road to the park. A
visit lasts around 3 hours and the
paths along which guides lead
visitors are easy. All trees are
identified along the way. Specially
fantastic are the suspended
walkways up to 22 meters high,
from which specially bromelias
and orchids can be seen at close
range, in their natural splendour.
With a little luck, it is still possible
to see a golden-headed lion
tamarin, or even a sloth may also
come into view. Special, prior

Façade restored in front of Canavieiras port

Praia de Serra Grande, in the route between Ilhéus and Itacaré

arrangements can be made for bird-watching excursions - over 200 species have been identified. The outing usually ends with a swim in the Maruim River. In May of 2002 a self-explanatory, 5-km trail was completed for experienced hikers.

Canavieiras

Ilhéus-Canavieiras (BA-001) road, 110 km from Ilhéus. From Porto Segura, take BR-101as far as Santa Lúcia, and from there, the BA-270 road for another 79 km.

The Pardo River, which begins in the North of Minas Gerais State, with its Cipó and Patipe tributaries, forms the island of Canavieira; population is around 35,000. The symbol of the island is the crab. In September the crab festival with shows, talks on crab cultivation and its importance for the region, and many stalls selling crabmeat-based dishes. Such abundance is drawn from the 90 sq km swamplands around the island, the ideal breeding place for crabs.

Visitors are also surprised with the main transport, which is the bicycle. The city is very flat, so it's the perfect way of getting acquainted with it. Start with the **historical site Governador Paulo Souto**, with its well-preserved, neo-classical, colonial court where today restaurants and handicraft shops function. Carry on alongside the port, toward the square. There you will find the

ruins of mansions, and also a display of panels with photos of marlin fishing. They were taken not far from the coast there, where marlin fish is not uncommon. Carry on along the wharf and into Rua 15 de Novembro that will take you to the **Town Hall** built in 1899, and the 1718 **São Boaventura Church**, in honor of the city's patron saint.

From the historical site dock, boats leave for the Garça island, where mud baths are very popular, as a treatment for skin problems and rheumatism. In the late afternoon, the flight of the herons and the seagulls circling overhead are very striking. Next can be over the Lloyd Bridge to Atalaia island and to the city's long, palm-treed beaches but rather murky sea, due to the swamp and river waters.

Near Canavieiras are the **Lapão Caves** and the **Três Marias** belvedere, with a picture-postcard view. Rafting is also done on the **Una River, another tributary of the Pardo River**. Travel agencies in Canavieiras organize both cave and rafting outings.

TIPS

– The times of events in Ilhéus can change. Check in advance.
– In Canavieiras, an unwritten rule gives cyclists right of way always, so drive carefully!
– Also drive carefully on the road to Ilhéus and BR-101 road, on which animals often roam.

Itacaré

From top of Vila de Itacaré, view of the Praia de Pontal, in Península de Maraú

Ilhéus: 65 km
Porto Seguro: 380 km
Salvador: 420 km
👤 18,120
🌐 73
@ www.itacare.com.br
😊 😊 😊 (through Ilhéus)

Itacaré is one of the rare places left where deserted beaches meet untouched Mata Atlântica forest, probably owing to its relative isolation, as it used to take over 4 hours to get there from Ilhéus by a dirt road. With the newly built BA-001 road, access is easy and takes less than an hour by car, and around 1.5 hours by bus.

On foot or bike, Itacaré, with its few streets and restaurants and bars that only open during summer, has five beaches. By the mouth of the Contas River, on the left-hand side, canoes can be taken to cross over to Pontal and Piracanga beaches. Jeeps going to Maraú peninsula are also ferried across at this point.

HIGHLIGHTS

Urban beaches 🏖 📷
On Rua Caminho da Praia, on the right side of the village, shops are open all year round. It leads to Concha Beach, where most guesthouses are concentrated. Bars also dot the coastline, on the right end of which, called Ponta do Xeréu, is a beacon to signal the rough ocean front. Sunsets from this point are magnificent.

Farther on from Conchas, four small bays that form the **Resende**, surfers' favorite **Tiririca, Costa** and **Ribeira** beaches. When the tide is low, you can also reach **Siriaco**, a small stretch of sand with trees that nearly reach the waterfront.

A different trail through the woods goes to **Prainha**, another small bay flanked by hills and covered in palm trees. The walk is well worthwhile and unforgettable!

After Prainha is **São José**, where a resort was built. If you are not staying at the hotel, the only way to reach this beach is by taking a strenuous path over the right end hill.

Distant beaches from Itacaré and Tijuípe Falls
By car or bus via BA-001 in the direction of Ilhéus. 🏖 🌳 📷 😊

Tiririca, the best waves ▶

Prainha: small bay covered in palm trees ▶

Along side Mata Atlântica woodland, are the more distant beaches. Visitors mostly leave their cars parked along the road and in makeshift parking areas. From Itacaré, the first beach 9 km beyond, is **Jeribucaçu**. To reach it, a 40-minute walk with some rather steep patches. Yet the magnificently blue sea into which runs a transparent river, and the palm tree covered beach, more than justify the effort. By another trail, to the left, is the **Arrud**a reef. Be careful not to step on any corals!
A gateway gives access to **Hawaizinho Beach** which is 15 km away from Itacaré and suitable for bathing only at low tide, because of the rocky sea bottom. Before reaching it, another trail which is very slippery when it rains branches off to the left, and winds its way through the thicket to **Engenhoca Beach**, another surfers' delight. One more short walk, also leftward, will take you to a natural pool formed along the rocky shore, and good for bathing.
Itacarezinho is 18 km away from Itacaré. From this point on, the beach reaches as far as the eye can see; deserted, flat and ideal for a 5-km walk to where the **Tijuípe River** flows into the sea.
The **Tijuípe waterfall,** is 22 km from Itacaré, where there are snack-bars and toilets. The water is crystal clear, clean and perfect for bathing.

Also for a trip down the river in rubber canoes called 'duckies', which can be arranged in Itacaré – a program all ages can enjoy.

Rio de Engenho and Pancada Grande waterfalls
From the left side of the Contas River mouth, boats take off for these two waterfalls. 🚤 🐦 🏊
The Engenho fall, also known as Cleandro fall, is 30 minutes away by boat, and its two falls form a pool. An interesting alternative to get there is the swamp route, along which, despite the noise of motor, birds can be heard. Pancada Grande is farther away and takes one hour by boat, and another 40-minute trek, to reach. Its 40-meter drop is one of the highest in the region.

SURROUNDINGS

Península de Maraú
235 km from Itacaré to Camumu, via Ilhéus. 🚤 🐦 🏊
One of the few places left in Bahia where, even in the high season, miles of deserted beaches and palm groves can be found. Warm-water lagoons, natural vistas, trails through Mata Atlântica forest and restinga marshland. To get there, the Camamu Bay must be crossed, in the direction of the **Barra Grande** community where most of the guesthouses and restaurants are. **Taipus de Fora Beach** is a one-and-half-hour walk or a

half hour tractor and trailer drive away. Check when the tide is low and natural pools are formed. From the **Morro da Bela Vista** hilltop, also known as Morro do Celular, people spend hours drinking cocoa water, simply enjoying the **Lagoa do Cassange** scenery. For those wishing to stay somewhere in the most unspoiled spots of the peninsula, like Algodões, Saquaíra and Casange, it is best to contact guesthouses there, and make the way across from Barra Grande.

TIPS . . . .

– The road between Ilhéus and Itacaré is called Estrada Parque. Much care was taken to minimize impact on the eco-system it cuts through, and which was declared a biological reservation by Unesco. At certain points, nets connect tree-tops on both sides to allow monkeys to cross unharmed, in their search for food. There are also many "go slow – guaiamum crab crossing" signs.
– On the way to Itacaré there are signs that indicate a sightseeing belvedere. Check it out and take some photos with Serra Grande Beach for a backdrop.
– Hire one of the guides on Ribeira beach if planning the Prainha trek. The trail parts in some places and does not always follow the coastline.

– Getting know more distant beaches does not necessarily require a guide. But the AGIR guide association organizes excursions that leave Itacarezinho and go to Engenhoca, via the beach, and with some rockclimbing.

– The rapids on the Contas River are good for rafting with one and a half hour, level 4 and 5 drops. Outings start in Taboquinhas, and travel agencies in Itacaré organize them, including the hour's drive there.

– Access: there are two ways to get to Maraú peninsula. The first from Valença, 90 km along south-bound BA-001 toward Camamu. From there, the boat ride to Barra Grande. From Ilhéus, it's 130 km on the BR-101 and another 40 km along BA-001 to Camumu. Monday to Saturday, boats usually leave Camumu at 11:20 a.m. and 5 p.m. and on Sunday, at 8:30 and 11 a.m. The timetable can vary however, and therefore it's good to check it at the guesthouse. From Itacaré one simply crosses the Contas River to arrive on the peninsula, but the road is precarious. In Itacaré, travel agencies organize one-day jeep outings around the peninsula and its points of attraction.

– The dirt road across Maraú peninsula is very precarious. Cars get stuck easily; 4-WD jeeps are the best.

Morro de São Paulo

From a belvedere behind the lighthouse, view of the first three beaches

Salvador: 120km from Salvador
(throught Itaparica)
Boipeba: 40-min boat ride
👤 11,410 (Cairu)
🌐 75
@ www.morrodesaopaulo.com.br

Morro de São Paulo, Boipeba and
Cairu are the biggest among the some
30 islands of this archipelago. Cairu is
the district that governs them, and is
the second oldest city in Brazil. A
walk along its not many streets with
some old mansions and the Santo
Antônio Convent, opened in 1650.

HIGHLIGHTS

The village and the 4 beaches

A small village on the Tinharé Island,
Morro, as it is known, has become
popular, specially among the younger
people. Many Brazilian and foreign
tourists flock there all year round.
Apart from the four beaches that bear
the unusual names: **Primeira** (First),
Segunda (Second), **Terceira** (Third)
and **Quarta** (Fourth). Parties and

beaches are the main attractions. The
first three beaches are most urbanized;
the Second being popular for its luau
moonlight parties. From the Fourth
onward, shores are still fairly deserted
with palm-trees looking out over the
endless, blue ocean.
The only way to get to Morro is by
boat. A small, hilltop church is a
reference for fishermen and
navigators on the sea. On leaving the
old waterfront, is an **arcade** built in
1630, that leads to the **Morro de São
Paulo Fort**. It was built to protect the
new territory against invasions. Ruins
of the fort can be visited, and from it,
a steep way leads to a small village.
To get your breath back, rest a while
on the steps of the **Nossa Senhora da
Luz Church**. The beach sand covers
streets, where cars are not allowed to
circulate. Stalls are erected toward
evening time, that sell handicrafts and
beverages, including the all popular
batida cocktails. On the main Rua
Caminho da Praia are the restaurants,
snack bars, post-office, shops and
travel agencies.At the highest point is
a lighthouse, where many gather in
the afternoons, to observe the sunset.
Behind the lighthouse there is a

Fortaleza: protection against invasions ▶

belvedere and panoramic view of the first three beeches.

SURROUNDINGS

Boipeba

40 minutes by boat from Morro de São Paulo, or 150 km from Salvador. www.ilhaboipeba.org.br 🌀 🌀 🌑 🌍

Adjacent to Tinharé Island is Boipeba and its tranquil villages that differ completely from the vibrating Morro life-style. Some 4,000 live in the small Moreré, Monte Alegre and São Sebastião communities, and in **Velha Boipeba**, where lodging can be found. Velha Boipeba was started in 1565 by Portuguese fleeing attacks by the Aimoré Indians. The Inferno River crosses the island and where it converges there is a calm, river beach called **Boca da Barra,** where boats that transport people and visitors lands, and take the children to school, in a neighboring village.

On leaving Boca da Barra, the first beach is Tassimirim, with a few dwellings and a guesthouse. A well marked trail amidst the trees leads to a place called **Cueira,** where natives prepare and sell lobster, steamed over an open fire. From there on, palm trees stretch as far as the eye can see. A two-hours walk along the coast line at low tide, or one hour by boat that leaves from Boca da Barra, brings you to peaceful **Moreré,** with some houses, a hostel, and a few restaurants. It is the chosen spot for those who love nature and take pleasure from eating juicy mangaba and mango fruit straight off the trees. It is also possible to take a boat ride to the natural pools. At the end of the day, from the Inferno riverbank, watch out for a magnificent sunset. Concern with the preservation of its ecosystem has brought Boipeba under the State's Environment Protection Act.

TIPS

– Access: from Salvador there are three ways to get to Morro de São Paulo. By plane, in a 20-minute flight from the Luís Eduardo Magalhães Airport, with Aero Star ☎ 71 377-1763; via a catamaran boat that leaves from the Mercado Modelo marine and takes two hours ☎ 71 326-3434. The third alternative is to cross over to Itaparica Island and take a bus to Valença in 2.5 hours. Then from Valença to Morro, a half-hour boat ride. It is best to travel lightly when going to Morro, as porters can be rather a nuisance. If you do need help, set a price beforehand.

– Access: from Salvador to Boipeba, cross over to Itaparica Island, go to Valença and on to Torrinhas. Hire a boat for the 30-minute ride ☎ 75 229-6182.

Another option is to go from Valença to Graciosa from where there is regular boat service that leaves at 2 p.m. It takes two hours. One-day excursions leave Morro de São Paulo, and on the way back, boats follow the Tinharé Island coastline and go in among the mangroves, even stopping in Cairu. Another option, albeit uncomfortable, is the tractor that leaves Quarta Praia in Morro and rumbles along a trail for two hours before it reaches the Boca da Barra.

Paulo Afonso

Paulo Afonso Hydroelectric: energy and radical sports

Salvador: 480 km
Aracaju (Sergipe): 294 km
👤 96,499
🌐 75
ℹ️ Secretaria de Turismo
☎ 281-2757
🌀 🌀 🌀

The Paulo Afonso district borders on
the States of Alagoas, Sergipe and
Pernambuco. It is actually more easily
reached from the capital of Sergipe,
Aracaju, that is 260 km away.
The city expanded with the
hydroelectric power plants that were
built along the São Francisco River.
Today, five plants operate in Bahia
and one in Sergipe. Because of the
rocky formations, steep cliffs and
precipices, the city has become a
favorite meeting place of radical
sports enthusiasts. From the steel
Dom Pedro II bridge, bungee jumpers
dive down into the 85-m chasm. The
steep banks are ideal for rappelling,
and abysses crossed on ropes, with
block and tackle, Tirolese-style.Near
the Paulo Afonso power station, a
cable car crosses the shaft. Half-way
across it, the Furnas de Morcegos Bat

filled cave can be seen best.
The legendary bandit, Lampião,
and his gang, are supposed to
have taken refuge there.
For those who enjoy hiking, the
Umbuzeiro hill in the district of
Riachinho has trails surrounded by the
caatinga vegetation with *umbuzeiro*,
xique-xique and *mandacaru* trees (see
Ecological Scenario). The top of the
hill is a place of pilgrimage, and from
it, the entire city of Paulo Afonso, as
far as Raso da Catarina, can be seen.

SURROUNDINGS

Raso da Catarina 🌀
In Raso da Catarina, more remote
parts of the *caatinga*, which were
other favorite hiding places for
Lampião and his group, given their
difficult access, can be visited. An
experienced guide must be present
though, for some of the ways are
very precarious and unmarked.
Temperatures can reach up to
43°C during the day, dropping
to 15°C at night. The Baixa do Chico
canyon trail is one of the best -known
in the Raso da Catarina and from it,
unusual formations moulded by the

Raso da Catarina: hiding place for Lampião ▶

wind out of the rocky, dry land, can be seen. Typical *caatinga* fauna, such as the armadillo, chameleon-like iguanas and small, wild pigs, live here. May to August is the best time to visit the Raso, when it rains most, and the foliage is greenest.

From Paulo Afonso it is 58 km to the Baixa do Chico, where the trek to Brejo do Burgos starts off, usually in the early morning hours. It takes all day and water must be taken to avoid dehydration.

Parque Estadual de Canudos

287 km from Paulo Afonso to Euclides da Cunha. Take BR-110 southward, and BR-235 westward.

The main sites of the Canudos battles described by Euclides da Cunha are still recognizable. The area was transformed into a park in 1997 by the State University of Bahia. Even though it is still afflicted by endemic poverty and suffers endless droughts, there is some beautiful scenery, specially near the Cocorobó lake, which now covers the original town of Canudos, after the Vaza-Barris River was damned in 1970. Its inhabitants were moved to surrounding towns. When the droughts are very bad, the Second Canudos, built after the war, emerges from the water, like the Santo Antônio Church, the cemetery, and the concrete pedestal used as the *matadeira* (killer) canon base. On the Alto do Mário hill, from where there is also a good vista over the old Canudos site, trenches dug during the war are still distinguishable. For those who appreciate silence and contemplation, the evenings are beautiful. Most days of the year, the sun beats down mercilessly, and one cannot help thinking about the desolation of Canudos. But in April, it usually rains and the scorched vegetation turns green again for a while. At such times, the animal world also seems to come alive; armadillos and the shy deer can more easily be sighted; but also snakes. During the first two weeks of June, the Santo Antônio celebrations take place in Canudos. Many booths selling regional food, drinks and other knick-knacks are erected, and animated *forró* music is played everywhere. The town of Euclides da Cunha, which is 70 km from the Park, offers slightly better, but also simple, lodging options. The important event in this town are the Saturday fairs in Praça Rui Barbosa, where it is possible to learn a little about the life, culture and customs of the peasant people. On sale are rubber tire sole sandals, *ouricuri* palm leaf and liana baskets, and of course, cow and goat leather hats – the trade mark ornament of the man of the backland.

Tips

– A good opportunity when visiting Paulo Afonso is getting to know the Museu de Arqueologia de Xingó in Canindé de São Francisco (*see Sergipe*) Penedo, in Alagoas.
– In Paulo Afonso, the Mangaio Atelier de Turismo organizes hikes, rapel expeditions and the trek to Raso da Catarina.

Porto Seguro

Beaches for all tastes in Porto Seguro

Arraial D'Ajuda: 60 km via BR-367 or
15 minutes by ferryboat
Caraíva: 120 km
Salvador: 776 km
Trancoso: 80 km
👤 95,665
🌐 73
ℹ️ Secretaria de Turismo ☎ 288-4124
@ www.portonet.com.br/guia
😊 😊 😊

Porto Seguro is on the left margin of
the Buranhém River and is the central
point of a region known as the
Discovery Coast or Costa do
Decobrimento, that stretches from the
mouth of the Caí River, where
Portuguese colonizers made their very
first contact with native Indians, to
Santa Cruz Cabrália, where navigator
Pedro Álvares Cabral landed his fleet
and the first Mass in Brazil was
celebrated, in 1500. It was declared
a National Monument to Humanity
in 1999, by Unesco. The building
of Porto Seguro followed the same
formula used in most coastal
townships founded by the Portuguese,
with the higher grounds reserved for
the colony's local administrative
center and upper-class dwellings,
and a lower with the port. More
recently, the city has become one of
the most accessible and popular
tourist centers in Brazil. To cope with
the massive year-round influx of
visitors, it has developed an
extraordinary infra-structure. Most
visitors come and stay within the
confines of the Porto Seguro
excitement, but in Arraial D'Ajuda,
Trancoso and Caraíva there are places
nearly peaceful and untouched.

HIGHLIGHTS

Cedoc - Documentation and Memorial Center
R. da Matriz, 76, Historic Town.
🌐 288-2499. E-mail: cedoc@uesc.br.
From Friday to Tuesday
from 8 a.m. to 6 p.m. 💳
The Center is a public library with
mostly books and documents that are
related to colonial Brazil. It has a copy
of the letter that the scribe Pero Vaz
Caminha wrote to the king of Portugal.
A framed copy of this "birth certificate"
of Brazil can be purchased there, as
well as a history book about the
discovery published by the University

In the Historic Town, the mark, the church and the museum ▶

of Santa Cruz in Itabuna, Bahia, that includes an analysis of this letter.

Igreja Matriz de Nossa Senhora da Pena

Pça. Pero Campos Tourinho, Historic Town. From Tuesday to Sunday from 2 to 6 p.m.
This church was built in 1535, when Pero Campo Tourinho was still donnee of the province. Inside are images of São Francisco de Assis, which was the first sacred statue brought to Brazil from Portugal, and Nossa Senhora da Penha.

Igreja Nossa Senhora da Misericórdia

Pça. Senhor dos Passos, Historic Town.
This 1526 church has Baroque elements in the front and a life-size image of Jesus on the Cross.

Marco do Descobrimento

Pça. Pero Campos Tourinho, opposite the Porto Seguro museum, Historic Town.
Erecting landmarks was the standard procedure of the Portuguese, to indicate possession of new found lands. This mark is of white limestone, with 1.5 m. high and is inscribed with the Portuguese coat of arms and a cross.

Museu Casa Colonial

Pça. da Misericórdia, 30, Historic Town. 288-0660. From Tuesday to Sunday from 9 a.m. to 5 p.m.
The typical home and life of a colonial civil servant or the small shopkeeper is

The brazilwood business

After the discovery, came a long period during which the Portuguese had to effectively take possession of their vast new land which was not so simple, as the only attraction then, for their navigators, was a tree from which was extracted a red die greatly coveted by European cloth makers at the time. This was the *caesalpinia* brazilwood or *pau-brasil* tree, which gave the country its name. Soon, Spanish and French seamen learned about the availability of this commodity, and began coming here more frequently after it. In 1535, donnee Pero de Campo Tourinho inaugurated the village of Porto Seguro. Then Aimoré Indians started to attack and the village soon began to decline. For many years, its economy was based on logging, fishing and salt businesses. In 1968, Porto Seguro was declared a national monument.

portrayed: furniture, hammocks, cutlery and even domestic animals.

Museu de Porto Seguro

Pça. Pero Campos Tourinho, Historic Town. 288-2285. Daily, from 9 a.m.

View from the Historic Town: 14 kilometers of beaches

to 5 p.m. 📧 ⑩
The building is dated 1772 and was the town assembly and jail. It personifies the power and constant vigilance of the Portuguese Crown over the colony.

Beaches
14 km of beach along BR-367 North 📍
All Porto Seguro beaches are famous for the action and fun that beachgoers are allured into by the animation leaders atop the huge waterfront platforms. In **Mundaí** and **Taperapuã**, 7 km from downtown, there are many beach stalls, snack bars, restaurants, shops, even a helicopter pad, and unfailingly, the stage from which animators conduct gym and aerobic exercises, dancing, gymkhanas, and loads of fun for all to join. The more tranquil beaches, with coconut trees and quiet surroundings, are **Ponta Grande** and **Mutá**, that are

Pataxós: identity and cultural affirmation

"Their faces are dark and a little reddish, with handsome features and good, well-made noses. They go naked, and don't cover themselves in any manner. They are not concerned about showing their private parts, and do so with the same innocence as they show their faces." This is what Pero Vaz Caminha wrote to the Portuguese government after the first contacts with Tupi natives had been made, in the land then called Vera Cruz.

According to estimates, in 1500, the native population was around 8.5 million. By 1822, it had dropped to 4 million and today declined to a mere 500,000 individuals. In the region of Porto Seguro, attempts by some of the Pataxó tribes to save the customs and traditions of their people are quite apparent.

Natives: keeping traditions

12 km from downtown, and not far from Santa Cruz Cabrália.

Parque Marinho do Recife de Fora

Schooners leave from the Cais da Tarifa wharf in front of the Passarela do Álcool, for the 45-minute boat ride out to this marine park. The outing lasts 4 hours.

This outing is made during low tide when reefs form natural pools out in the open sea.

The marine park covers an area of 17.5 sq km and in some places, snorkelling is allowed. Through the masks, the most beautiful corals, colored fish, molluscs and algae can be observed. At times when

can get to know the daily routine of the villagers, walk along their forest trails, watch the setting of traps, shoot with a bow and arrow, and eat roasted fish.

SURROUNDINGS

Santa Cruz Cabrália
23 km North via BR-367.
The road that leads to the beaches north of Porto Seguro also goes to Santa Cruz Cabrália. Here, beaches are less crowded than in Porto Seguro. In Coroa Vermelha is a cross on the site where the first Mass was read in Brazil by Frei Henrique de Coimbra. An engraved stone was put there in 2000 to register the meeting between the presidents of Brazil and Portugal, during the commemorations of

Arraial: quiet life of the citizens when there is no tourists

the tide is very low and the reef is even more exposed, the trip out is even more worthwhile.

Reserva Pataxó da Jaqueira
Access via BR-367 in direction of Santa Cruz Cabrália: 8 km after entering left, on the Mangue River Beach, another 2 km to the reserve. Visits must be arranged beforehand. ☎ 9991-5653/ 9991-4560.

Pataxó Indians administrate this reserve, where the customs and cultural identity of their people are reclaimed and safeguarded. In an important reforestation project, they planted many native trees, such as the caesalpinia pau-brasil and arapari species, rue trees, and many other indigenous plants. Visitors

500 years of discovery. Here is also a handicraft center with many booths selling Pataxó Indian art and work, such as necklaces, rattles, attractive wooden bowls and dippers. Nearby is the Museu Indígena with objects, photos and posters that tell their history. In the historic center of Cabrália, 8 km beyond Coroa Vermelha, the assembly hall, jail and **Nossa Senhora da Conceição** church are located in the upper part of town. Here, the patron saint is celebrated on December 8, which is also when the Chegança or Marujada folklore street pageant takes place, telling of the sailors saved during a very bad storm out at sea.

Arraial D'Ajuda
60 km via BR-367 or 15 minutes by

Beaches in Cabrália are less crowded than in Porto Seguro ▶

ferryboat from Porto Seguro.
www.arraial.com.br 🌐📧📷📞📧
In Arraial, as it is known, there are
three well-defined areas of activity: the
village, the beach trail, and the beaches.
In the upper village, there are a few
historical buildings around a square that
also has shops, handicraft stalls,
restaurants and a market. Nossa
Senhora D'Ajuda patron saint church
built in 1549 at one end of the square
and behind it, the people discovered a
small spring with water they believed
healing and miraculous. For a long
time, it was a place of pilgrimage.
Nowadays, the fresh spring is simply
appreciated as good drinking water that
people take home. On the opposite side
of the square, is Bróduei street that
leads to Caminho das Praias or Mucugê
beach road. And along this not very
wide road and off it, are the most
popular bars, restaurants, shops,
boutiques and the small commercial
center of Arraial, which from December
to March are all open until very late into
the night. Farther down the road is a
steep slope to Mucugê Beach, with
many waterfront stalls that usually get
packed with people, specially during the
summer months. Along this beach, on
the right, is **Parracho Beach** that
gets lively and crowdy at night time,
specially when there are moonlight
beach parties. A 10- minute walk
farther is **Pitinga Beach**, where the first
cliffs begin to rise. The last and most
peaceful beach is Taípe, which is a 50-
minute walk from Pitinga. To the left
side of Mucugê are beaches that even in
summer are not overcrowded. From

them, one can see Paradise Waterpark.
www.paradisewaterpark.com.br,
☎ 575-1500.

Trancoso
80 km from Porto Seguro via BR-367
or 40 km via Arraial D'ajuda,
southward. Internet: www.transcoso
bahia.com.br 🌐📷📞📧Ⓜ
In Trancoso, the main center of
convergence is the Quadrado square, on
a plateau some 40-meter high over sea
level. Actually, Quadrado is a large
rectangular area with pretty, colorful
houses all around it, where artists have
ateliers and restaurants, bars and
guesthouses are concentrated. Trancoso
was put on the map again in the 1960's
when a hippie community moved there
and shared the square with the Indians
who lived around it. In front of the bars
are immense fig trees. São João Batista
Church is the only building in the centre
of the square. Its back is to the sea. In
front of it are two masts with flags – one
for São Sebastião, celebrated on January
20, and the other for São Brás, whose
holiday is February 3. The main beaches
in Trancoso are **Coqueiros**, which is
closest, **Nativos** to the right of the square
with its river, and **Pedra Grande Beach**,
where one can go for long walks.

Espelho and Curuípe
105 km from Porto Seguro
or 25 km from Trancoso, southward
via the Entry to the Outeiro das
Brisas Condominium. 📷📧
www.outeiro.com.br 📷📧
A combination of coconut groves,
semi-deserted beaches and tide water

São João Batista church in Trancoso: the only building in Quadrado

To get to Caraiva village one must cross the river in a canoe

pools along the reefs rank Espelho and Curuípe among the finest and most beautiful beaches on the Brazilian coastline. Looking out to sea, on the left, when the tide is low, one can get over the cliff and onto **Setiquara Beach**, which is also known as the **Outeiro Beach**. Above these cliffs is the Outeiro das Brisas estate. To get to **Espelho and Curuípe beaches**, leave Trancoso Beach and follow direction signs to Outeiro das Brisas. The road is not paved and not very good. There is a sentry at the entrance to Outeiro, where visitors must identify themselves. To the right, and 6 km beyond are Espelho and Curuípe; to the left and 4 km farther, the Outeiro das Brias condominium, with guesthouses, restaurants, and a polo club. It also has a landing strip for small aircraft. Coaches and buses are not allowed in.

★ Caraíva

120 km from Porto Seguro and 30 km from Trancoso, southward. Internet: www.caraiva.com.br 🐟 🏠 🍴
Isolation is one of the greatest appeals of Caraíva, which is on a peninsula, with **Caraíva River** on the north, and the Atlantic Ocean on its west side. The district's southern border is the

Misfortune strikes Caraíva

For a long time, Caraíva was a busy place, that used to supply Porto Seguro and also Salvador with agricultural products that were grown in small farms along the river. Canoes would be used to carry the palm leaves, manioc flour, bananas, sugarcane, beans, meat, cocoa and coffee down to Porto Seguro. Eventually, progress came to these parts too, and a sawmill was installed in 1940. Then an accident happened and changed things dramatically for Caraíva. One of the sawmill's cauldrons exploded, killing one person and causing a lot of destruction to the mill.
It caused all wood processing activities to cease and people left in large numbers. In the late 1970s, Caraíva was discovered once again, and then an economic cycle based on ecological tourism began.

Parque Nacional do Monte Pascoal.
To get to Caraíva village one must leave
the car or get off the bus on one side of
the river and cross it in a canoe. Caraíva
streets are of sand and their taxis are
donkey carts. In some homes and also
guesthouses there, electric light and hot
showers are not available. Electricity
should arrive there in the next years,
under the condition that cables are laid
underground. There are two Caraívas:
one during the high season (July, and
December to February) and the other
from March to November. Despite all
odds, in the high season, the population
trebles; guesthouses and restaurants are
full and *forró* gigs and partying carry on
into early hours of the morning. In the
low season, many guesthouses close.
From Trancoso, the road to Caraíva
passes the Outeiro das Brisas sentry. It
is a dirt road, with some slippery parts
and rudimentary plank bridges over
streams. Its 30 kilometers takes about
two hours to negotiate. The Águia Azul
company has buses that do the Porto
Seguro-Caraíva route, with stops in
Arraial D'Ajuda and Trancoso.

Rio Caraíva and Aldeia Pataxó

Outing organized by Casa Barra Velha,
☎ 9985-0241; and Pousada Lagoa,
☎ 9985-6862. 🅐🅑🅒

A visit to Caraíva should include a trip
up the river. On the way up, there are
stops for bathing, and to observe the
flora and fauna along the swamps and in
the rainforest. It ends late afternoon, with
a last pause at one of the small rural
clearings from where a spectacular
sunset can be seen, with Pascoal
mountain in the background A different
excursion includes, apart from the boat
trip up the river, a ride on horseback as
far as the Barra Velha hamlet, where
Pataxó Indians live. On the way back,
the horses go along the beach. Another
fun option, when the tide is going out, is
to go up the river in a boat and drift back,
inside buoys made from the inner tubes
of truck tires.

Ponta do Corumbau

145 km from Caraíva by a dirt road
🅐🅑🅒🅓

Situated on the Corumbau River, this
small town gets its name from a
phenomenon that happens at very low
tides, when a long sand bank is exposed

that one can walk along. One of the
nearby places that specially divers like are
the Itacolomi reefs where between
December and March the crystal clear
waters allow lobsters, groupers, mackerel
and many other fishes to be observed.
Corumbau has only a few houses, and
kilometers of sandy beaches that are
practically deserted. It gets a little more
lively in summer and for the São
Benedito festivities in April. The rest of
the year round, only fishermen can be
seen, either going out to sea to put out
their nets or bringing back their haul.
Corumbau is rich in marine life and for
a long time was visited by industrial fishing
boats. This has changed. It is a region
with one of the richest bio-diversities in
the Southern Atlantic, but with endemic
species that are now threatened with
extinction. To save this variety, the
Reserva Extrativista Marinha do
Corumbau was created. From Corumbau
one can go out to sea to get the same view
and impression that Cabral had, when

first sighted Monte Pascoal in 1500.
Ponta de Corumbau can be reached in
two ways. By sea, in outings that begin
in Caraíva and also Cumuruxatiba, with
stops for a swim in Itacolomi or in the
Patoxó reserve. Or by way of road that
starts well in Prado and passes Guarani,
and then turns into a 60- km stretch of
difficult and precarious going, before
Corumbau is reached.

TIPS

– The Passarela do Álcool, or Alcohol
Promenade is one of the most popular
night programs in Porto Seguro. It
runs all the way down R. Portugal, and
also in the colonial courthouses where
there are many bars. At night, things
get even more colourful with all the
stalls where cocktails are prepared.
– Expresso Brasileiro buses do the
route that connects the center of Porto
Seguro with its Northern beaches and
Santa Cruz Cabrália beaches.

– In Arraial D'Ajuda, most bars,
restaurants and shops open mid
afternoon and stay open until early
morning hours.
– From Arraial square, vans take
tourists to different beaches, along not
very well -kept dirt roads.
– From Arraial one can walk to
Trancoso along the beach.
It takes about three hours and is an
interesting way to know all the lovely
beaches on the way. However, it is
important to do this trek while the
tide is out so that the Taípe
Beach cliffs can be got over, and some
rivers can be crossed.
– In the high season, going from
Porto Seguro to Arraial via BR-367
can be a better option than waiting
in the long line to cross with the ferry.
– A now traditional event in Arraial is
the Cultura Mix that takes place
in the Espaço de Arte Galápagos in
January, with handicraft exhibitions,
music and theater shows.

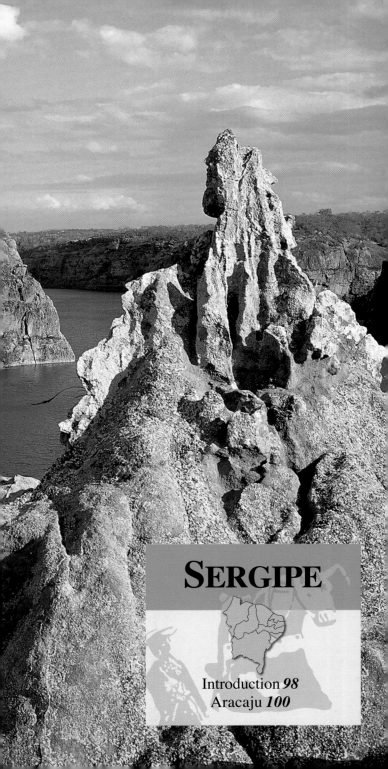

SERGIPE

SERGIPE

Sergipe, that covers 22,050 sq km, is the smallest Northeastern State. The name derives from the native Tupi language and means 'crab river'. Aracaju was founded in 1855 and was planned to be the State's capital, as the old one, São Cristovão, did not have the adequate shipping facilities to handle Vale do Cotinguiba sugar exports. Sergipe's history tells us of French invasions during the years of discovery, that were mainly after brazilwood, and a brief Dutch take-over between 1637 and 1645 of São Cristóvão, which was practically destroyed when they were expelled. Today, this fourth oldest city in Brazil still has a lot of unspoilt 17th and 18th century architecture. The town of Laranjeiras is considered the cradle of Afro-Brazilian traditions in Sergipe. In this region, the State's sugarcane plantations were concentrated, and many cultural expressions, forgotten in other Northeastern states, are kept alive here.

Aracaju has a 30 km sandy coastline, dotted with stalls from beginning to end. Many traditional dishes on menus in the State, are based on crab meat, abundant in the region's swampland. To take advantage of the festivities, the best time to visit Aracaju is during the local festivals, the first being the so called 'pre-caju' a 15 day revelry that precedes Carnival. Then in June, there are the Santo Antônio, São João and São Pedro celebrations, so popular throughout all Northeastern States and here, accompanied by the authentic and contagious *forró* music. The immense São Francisco River runs into the Atlantic Ocean at the Northern border with Alagoas, and the meeting of the waters is a spectacle that attracts many visitors. The river is navigable as far as where the river was damned, submerging a canyon, for the Xingó hydroelectric power station in the district of Canindé do São Francisco.

The most important road links are BR-101, which runs North to South, and BR-235, that crosses from East to West. Sergipe is the fourth major oil producer in Brazil. It also boasts the highest maracujá passion fruit exports, and is second in the orange and coconut processing sectors.

Poço Ve

Tobia
Barre

Highlights

❶ Aracaju
❷ Cânion de Xingó
❸ São Cristóvão

◀ Cânion de Xingó: inundated for construction of the hydroelectric

etrica de Xingó
Canindé de São Francisco

2

São Francisco

Gararu

1

SE
206

Sergipe

Carira

SERGIPE

Neópolis

Brejo Grande

SE
304

Cabeço

Dias

BR
101

Itabaiana

agarto

BR
235

Areia Branca

Rosário do Catete

Praia de Pirambu

Vaza-barris

Laranjeiras

✈ **ARACAJU**

Praia de Atalaia

A DO
MBA

BR
101

São Cristóvão

Estância

Praia de Mosqueiro
Praia de Vaza-barris

3

SE
318

N
W   E
S

0   72   144 km

LEGENDS

National park

Paved road

Dirt track

Aracaju

Aracaju is a planned city and lies on the banks of the Rio Sergipe, close to the sea

Salvador: 347 km
Maceió: 287 km
Canindé do São Francisco: 200 km
João Pessoa: 631 km
👤 461,534
🌐 79
ℹ️ Emsetur ☎ 214-0976
@ www.emsetur.com.br
◉ ◉ ◉

Aracaju became capital of the State in 1855 due to its strategic location, close to the sea, on the banks of Sergipe River, which made it an ideal outlet for sugarcane goods produced in the interior of the state. Because it was founded for this purpose, Aracaju is a planned city with chessboard-like streets and squares. Even for someone visiting for the first time, it's easy to get around the well signed streets and avenues. The seafront, with Atalaia Beach, which is 30 km long has many bars, restaurants and hotels. The crab is also symbol of this region, and crab meat appetisers are served in most restaurants.

HIGHLIGHTS

Catedral Metropolitana

Pça. Olímpio Campos, Downtown.
☎ 214-3418. Monday from 12 a.m. to 6 p.m. Tuesday to Friday: 6 a.m. to 6 p.m.. Saturday from 6 a.m. to 9 p.m. and Sunday from 7 a.m. to 9 p.m. ◉
The Igreja Matriz de Nossa Senhora da Conceição was completed in 1875, and in 1910 was turned into a cathedral. It combines neo-gothic and classical styles, and the dome was painted by Orestes Gatti, an Italian painter, and Rodolfo Tavares, from Bahia.

Calçadão da Av. 13 de Julho ℹ️

This extensive pedestrian promenade that edges the avenue, links downtown to the beach, and further. It is more popularly known as Av. Beira Mar and is perfect for walks and jogging. Along it, there is a Tourist Information Center, and also a view place, from where the island of Santa Luzia and the marshland can be seen.

Colina de Santo Antônio

Pça. Siqueira de Menezes, Downtown ◉ ◉
This hill, on which stands the neo-gothic Santo Antônio Church, is Aracaju's highest point, with a view

Land of sugar

◄ São Cristóvão: first capital

In 1535, with the division of Brazil into hereditary provinces, the region of Sergipe, where native, Tupinambá Indians lived in some 30 tribal settlements along the coast, was donated to Francisco Coutinho. First, the Jesuits went there, around 1575, and built churches near the Piaui and Vaza-Barris rivers. When government officials under Luís de Brito arrived, the Indians fled. This was understood to be a breach in the so far friendly relations, and attacks against the Indians began, and became constant, until some of the tribes had been decimated. Colonization of the region became strategic to repress French contraband of brasilwood, and to catch slaves that had escaped from plantations in the region known as Reconcavo Baiano. Years later, the town of São Cristóvão became the seat of government, and colonisers pushed inland and up the rivers. In an offensive by the Dutch, three towns were taken; one of them was São Cristóvão. The occupation lasted from 1637 and 1645 and resulted in its almost entire destruction. When power was regained by the Portuguese, São Cristóvão was rebuilt and sugarcane planted. Its products became the basis of the Sergipe economy for nearly three centuries. In 1855 the capital was transferred to Aracaju.

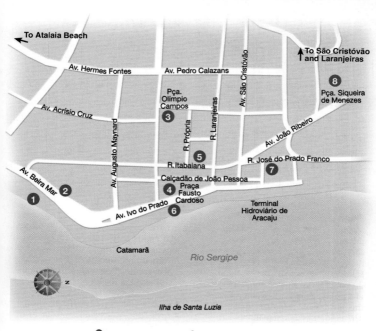

1 Mirante para Santa Luzia
2 Memorial de Sergipe
3 Catedral Metropolitana
4 Palácio Olímpio Campos
5 Centro de Turismo
6 Ponte do Imperador
7 Mercados Thales Ferraz e Antônio Franco
8 Colina de Santo Antônio

over most of the city, Sergipe River and the Santa Luzia Island. This is where a meeting of the Assembléia Provincial took place when it was decided that the capital was to be transferred there, from São Cristóvão.

Centro de Turismo and Rua 24 horas

Travessa Benjamin Constant, Downtown. ☎ 214-5023. Daily from 9 a.m. to 11 p.m. 🅰 🅰
Originally a school, built in 1911, the building was refurbished and today houses the Museu do Artesanato (handicraft center) that is open Monday to Friday from 8 a.m. to 6 p.m., and a Tourist Information Center that is open daily from 8 a.m. to 8 p.m. Around the internal courtyard there are stalls, that sell regional handicrafts, mostly leather,

Centro de Turismo: art and craft are sold

sisal hemp and lacework. There is also a platform where late evening shows are staged. The 24-hour Street is next to the Tourist Information with lots of clothes shops and boutiques; there's also Internet bar.

Memorial de Sergipe

Av. Beira Mar, 626. ☎ 211-3579. Monday to Friday from 10 a.m. to 4:30 p.m. and Saturday from 8 to 12 a.m. 🅰
The 6,000 piece display arranged in different rooms, with photos and everyday objects, give a good insight into Sergipe's history, since the colonial days. Costumes and weapons used by gangs in the era of cangaço banditry are shown, as well as fossils found in some State regions. There is also a collection

of hand-painted ceramics by Rosa Faria.

Mercados Thales Ferraz and Antônio Franco

R. José do Prado Franco, Downtown. Daily from 6 a.m. to 6 p.m. 🅰
These market buildings, that are near the Terminal Hidroviário, were completely restored and offer an excellent option for visitors to get acquainted with regional cookery, herbs, an infinity of condiments, fruits, drinks and snacks, handicrafts and souvenirs. The breakfast served there is lavish and varied.

Palácio Olímpio Campos

Pça. Fausto Cardoso, Downtown. ☎ 216-8000. Entrance: free; visits by appointment only. 🅰
Concluded in 1863 and seat of the State government, this palace was originally built in a neo-classic style. Italian architects changed the façade and interior, conferring eclectic characteristics that were so fashionable in Europe at the beginning of the 20th century.

Ponte do Imperador

Av. Ivo do Prado, Downtown. 🅰
This portal was built in 1860 as a gateway into the city for Emperor D. Pedro II and his wife, Dona Tereza Cristina, when they visited Aracaju. Originally it was built of wood, which over the years was replaced for a steel structure. It stands on the banks of the Sergipe River and faces Pça. Fausto Cardoso.

Beaches 🅰

The shoreline of Aracaju is very long. The distance between the downtown and **Mosqueiro Beach** at the mouth of the Vaza Barris River is around 17 km. The most urbanized stretch, where bars, restaurants and hotels are concentrated, is between the **Artistas** and **Atalaia beaches**. Along this extension, is a place called **Passarela dos Caranguejos**, or crab walk. From Atalaia on, beach stalls dwindle and neighboring areas become increasingly residential. From Mosqueiro, catamaran tours can be arranged along the Vaza-Barris River. At this point one can also cross over to **Caueira** by ferryboat, to where dune-flank **Abaís**

Lagoa Redonda in Pirambu: a swampy region

and **Saco do Rio Real beaches**. On the way, there are signs indicating Porto N'Angola, from where the crossing to **Mangue Seco** in Bahia, is made. The Sergipe River separates the capital from the Santa Luzia Island. The crossing is done from the Terminal Hidroviário. On the other side are the **Atalaia Nova**, **Costa** and **Jatobá Beaches**. It is a swampy region, and boats can be hired for a ride up the Pomonga River. An excursion into the swamps, arranged and accompanied by a biologist, can also be arranged. ☎ 276-1201. Another bridge over the Rio

Ponte do Imperador: homage

Japaratuba leads to the **Praia de Pirambu** that is 45 km long and has another base of the Tamar Project.

SURROUNDINGS

Cânions do Rio São Francisco, and Museu Xingó ⓜ ⓧ

213 km from Aracaju. Via BR-101 North, as far as Nossa Senhora das Dores district. From there, take SE-206 to Canindé do São Francisco.

The São Francisco River Canyons, in inland Sergipe, are 100 meters high in some places and 60 km long. They were inundated when the river was damned for the over 5 million kilowatt Xingó power plant.

The depth of the water varies from 15 to 160 meters. Further inland along the river, in the State of Bahia is another dam and the massive Paulo Afonso power complex. Catamaran rides on the river, that leave from the Bar Karranca's, with a stopover at **Gruta do Talhado**, can be hired.

These tours pass places that herons have chosen for nesting and rearing their young. Such outings present a worthwhile opportunity to visit the **Archaeology Museum of Xingó**, where many specimens are kept of the thousands of vestiges such as skeletons, ceramic, stone and bone instruments, remains of fires, and ornaments, that were found there, of the people that lived along the São Francisco basin over three

Ponta dos Mangues, northern Sergipe ▶

Cânion de Xingó: 100 m high in some places and 60 km long

thousand years ago. These fragments were collected in an extensive archaeological salvation project before the canyons were flooded. The area of the museum (827 sq m) is divided into theme rooms; flint and stone utensils, graves, cave drawings, ceramics, and depictions of the fauna and human activities of those times. The museum is open Wednesday to Sunday, between 9 a.m. and 4:30 p.m. ☎ 212-6448. A different tour goes along hat part of the river that was not damned, to a place in the caatinga brushland called **Grota de Angicos** where the police finally managed to surround and kill the famous bandit Lampião and 9 members of his gang. These tours leave Xingó Parque Hotel. ☎ 346-1245.

Estância

69 km from Aracaju via BR-101 South.📷
Located in Southern Sergipe, Estância is one of the oldest towns in the State and still has well-preserved court houses; some with Portuguese tile façades and gardens with many trees. Here, writer Jorge Amado is to have finished his novel *Terras do Sem Fim* and started another, *Tieta do Agreste*, to which the backdrop is **Mangue Seco**, not far

from there. Estância is famous throughout Northeastern Brazil for its very lively and animated Festa Junina, with grand pyrotechnical displays. These shows include the traditional fire boats made of bamboo and wood, filled with gun powder, that shoot along an iron cable propelled by a rocket.

Foz do Rio São Francisco

137 km from Aracaju. Follow BR-101 North. Turn right at SE-304 and continue to Brejo Grande. 📷 📷
At the end of a 2,700 km journey that passes five states, São Francisco River marks the borderline between Sergipe and Alagoas states. Its riverhead is in Serra da Canastra in Minas Gerais. At the mouth of this lifeline for thousands of people, boat rides can be arranged either with fishermen that dock in Brejo Grande, or with the catamaran people, that leave from Propriá. The boats go as far as Cabeço from where one can see Alagoas on the other side, with a stopover for a swim in a lagoon that lies between the river and the sea. A light beacon built in 1876 on the Sergipe side to assist navigators can be seen on these tours. But not for much longer it is feared, as wear and tear from the sea waves is ruining the

São Francisco Square, São Cristóvão: 17th century ▶

foundations. In 1995, when the danger of collapse became very evident, the top part was removed by the Marinha and taken to Rio de Janeiro. Meanwhile, the main construction resists and can be viewed by all those navigating there.

Laranjeiras

23 km from Aracaju. From the old bus station, São Pedro buses or vans leave every half hour. ⑩ ❷ ❸

Around Laranjeiras most of the sugar cane plantations of Sergipe were concentrated. The slave presence in the region is very evident from what is shown in the Museu Afro-Brasileiro (R. José do Prado Franco, ☎ 281-1297). There is a good collection of every day items in a typical colonial courthouse and sugar mill, as well as religious artifacts, and also instruments of torture. Afro-

Brazilian folklore expressions and traditions are kept alive by the people of Laranjeiras and every January, the Cultural Conference of Laranjeiras takes place, in which related issues are discussed and performances for visitors put on. The Museu de Artes Sacras, opened in 1980 in a 19th-century building, houses one of the State's most important collections (Pça. Heráclito Diniz Gonçalves, 39, ☎ 281-1297). There are seven churches in Laranjeiras, some at the top of a hill with a beautiful vista over theVale do Cotinguiba. The **Bom Jesus dos Navegantes** and **Senhor do Bom Fim Beaches** are two of these churches. The **Sagrado Coração de Jesus Church** has a German 19th-century organ. The painting on the dome is said to be by José Teófilo de Jesus, from Bahia. The **Nossa Senhora da**

Life and death of the Cangaço

Cangaceiro bandits were groups that roamed the backlands, united around one leader. They assaulted, invaded, destroyed and sacked property, murdered, and spread terror and panic among all those who would not take part in their negotiations. They were independent, and mostly against the government They were mercenaries, and killed for money. The word cangaceiro comes from canga, which means yoke or bond. The most famous group was lead by a Virgulino Ferreira da Silva from Pernambuco, nicknamed Lampião, and his woman, the famous Maria Bonita. They adopted a different kind of clothing that included bordering and adornments that resisted the arid caatinga conditions. Their leather hat rims were turned up in front and decorated with gold and silver coins and stars. This so-called king of cangaço and his followers terrorised Alagoas, Rio Grande do Norte, Paraiba, Pernambuco, Sergipe, Bahia and Ceará, between 1917 and 1938. In their long fight to defeat cangaço bands, the government began dealing with coiteros, who had to

Lampião and Maria Bonita: the end in Angico

give shelter to gangs on the run, in fear of retaliation. This tactic forced Lampião into increasingly remote hiding places and finally culminated with the police encircling and killing him, Maria Bonita and nine other members of the gang on a farm in Angicos (Sergipe) on July 28, 1938, after a tip-off. With the group, the police found cash and five kilos of gold, which was the equivalent then, to the price of 120 brand-new cars. After the ambush, they were all beheaded and their heads exposed in a Salvador museum until 1968, when they were buried. Soon, the heads will be transfered to the future Museu do Cangaço.

Comandaroba Church was built by the Jesuits in 1734. The underground construction is of limestone and there are escape passages. One tunnel leads to the **Gruta da Pedra Furada** which was a retreat for prayer. All places of interest in Laranjeiras are open Tuesday to Friday from 10 a.m. to 5 p.m. and Saturday and Sunday from 1 to 5 p.m. ☎ 281-1297.

São Cristóvão
23 km from Aracaju via BR-101 South. From the old Bus Station, São Cristovão buses leave every half hour.
São Cristóvão, considered to be the fourth oldest city in Brazil, was founded in 1590 by Cristóvão de Barros. It was the capital of Brasil between 1820 and 1855. There is a courtyard of the 17th and 18th centuries which is very well preserved and was made a national historical monument. The best way to view its unspoilt architecture is by walking from the first to the third square. The walk could start in Pça. São Francisco, named after the convent located there, built in 1693. In its left wing, is the **Museu de Arte Sacra** (Sacred Art Museum) with over 500 pieces of art; censers, sacred icons, furniture and hollow saint statues. It opens Tuesday to Sunday from 12 a.m. to 6 p.m. ☎ 261-1240. The convent was made into army headquarters during the raids against Antônio Conselheiro in 1897 (see Canudos Uprising, Bahia).

In the same square is **Casa da Misericórdia**, the first hospital built in the province of Sergipe, and the **Museu Histórico** (Historic Museum), which is in the old palace where D. Pedro II and Dona Teresa Cristina stayed. Visiting times are from 1 to 5 p.m., Tuesday to Sunday. ☎ 261-1435. In Pça. da Matriz is the **Nossa Senhora da Vitória Church** in colonial Baroque, that dates back to 1608. It was practically destroyed when the Dutch were banished, after their short take-over. There is also the old jail, and a colonial **Sobrado do Balcão Corrido** that has Moorish traits. In the Pça. Senhor dos Passos is the **Carmo Church and Convent**, and the **Museu dos Ex-Votos**, where blessings bestowed on

believers are represented. The Benedictine sisters bake and sell delicious biscuits there. On the second Sunday after Ash Wednesday, Senhor dos Passos is celebrated.

TIPS

– One day van excursions to the São Francisco Riverbed and Xingó Canyon are organized by tourist agencies in Aracaju. Catamaran tours are conditioned to a minimum number of passengers.
– Check schedules in São Cristóvão and Laranjeiras before going to places of interest.
– Traditional Festa de São João de Paz e Amor in Sergipe is in Areia Branca, 36 km from Aracaju.

ALAGOAS

ALAGOAS

Alagoas is the second smallest of the Northeastern States, and most of its beauty spots and points of interest can be found along a 230 km coastline of dazzling blue seas, fringed by countless coconut groves, and also plantations. There are exceptions though, in small towns of historical importance, that are in the hot, dry, sertão hinterland. The grand São Francisco River provides the natural Southern border with Sergipe and Bahia and is navigable for 180 km upstream, as far as the Xingó hydroelectric power station, which is on

the Sergipe side. In Alagoas, the river passes two historical towns before it flows into the Atlantic Ocean. These are Piranhas and Penedo. All riverbank communities are permeated in old customs and traditions characteristic and unique of the lower São Francisco River basin. Some of Brazil's colonial history can also be traced into the semi-arid backlands of Alagoas, most importantly that which tells of the first run-away slave dominion, that was started in the early 17th century, called the Quilombo dos Palmares nation, and the countless mucambo villages that came under its rule. The Northern coastline, all

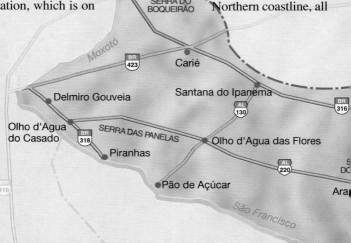

▼ The rafts are trade mark of view of Alagoas

the way up to Pernambuco, is quite different, and has long stretches of coral reefs that act as barriers against the waves which makes for the calm and warm waters on those shores, ideal for bathing and other recreational opportunities. Specially the natural pools, formed by the reefs, are greatly enjoyed by sun and sea lovers.

Highlights

❶ Maceió
❷ Penedo
❸ Maragogi

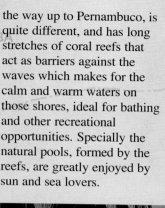

SERRA DO CAFÉ

Camaragibe

União dos Palmares

SERRA D'ÁGUA

BR 104

BR 101

Maragog

Japaratinga

São Miguel dos Milagres

Passo de Camaragibe

Barra de Santo Antonio

eira dos Índios

Manguaba

Messias

Paripueira

MACEIÓ

Mundaú

Marechal Deodoro

AL 215

ALAGOAS

Praia do Francês

Cururipe

Roteiro

AL 101

Barra de São Miguel

BR 101

AL 105

Jequiá da Praia

Cururipe

N
W   E
S

0   35   70 km

nedo

AL 225

Piaçabuçu

LEGENDS

National Park
Paved road
Dirt track

Maceió

In the Capital, the urban beaches one leading onto the other

Aracaju: 294 km
Recife: 285 km
Salvador: 610 km
👤 797,759
🌐 82
ℹ Secretaria de Estado de Turismo e Esportes ☎ 315-1600.
@ www.visitealagoas.com.br.

An avenue runs along the urban beaches of Maceió, which are Jatiúca, Ponta Verde, Pajuçara and Sete Coqueiros, one leading onto the other. There are many food and drink stalls along the wide sidewalk, as well as restaurants and bars, where live music is played. Pratagy, Guaxuma, Ipioca and Riacho Doce beaches are a little farther away. In order to see the old colonial buildings, around which the city first developed, take a walk in Jaraguá and downtown.

HIGHLIGHTS

Mirante São Gonçalo
Praça Rosalvo Ribeiro 🌐🌐
From here is a panoramic view over Pajuçara and over the docks of Jaraguá Port. Next to the belvedere, there are handicraft stalls, and the small São Gonçalo Chapel.

Praça Dom Pedro II
Downtown 🌐🌐
The buildings around this square were constructed for the visit of Emperor Dom Pedro II to Alagoas. The original characteristics of several have been changed. Imperial palm trees adorn the square, on which there is also the Cathedral, the Public Library and Archives, a mansion that used to be belong to the Baron of Jaraguá, and the State assembly hall.

Praça dos Martírios
Downtown 🌐🌐
In front of the square stands the beautiful Bom Jesus dos Martírios Church in blue and white Portuguese tiles. Next to the church is the Fundação Pierre Chalita, with a big collection of mostly 17th to 19th century paintings and religious art. On the same square is the seat of the Alagoas government.

Teatro Deodoro
Pça. Deodoro, Downtown. ☎ 326-5353.
@ www.ipedal.com.br/cultura/teatro.

Jaraguá, lakes and coconut trees

Gogó da ema: a symbol until the 1950s

In Tupi language, Maçayó, which became Maceió, means "that which covers the swamp" in reference to the land bank formed by the sea, which surrounds the lagoons. In early colonial times, boats would harbor in a bay that they called Jaraguá. Gradually, a proper port began to develop, specially after the sugar business was also brought to the region. In 1815 the settlement became a village, and in 1839, the Alagoas province capital, which up to then had been the neighboring town of Marechal Deodoro. Maceió city expanded into new areas, and the district of Jaraguá began to lose its hegemony and glamor to more recent and modern developments in these new districts. The value of property and business there declined rapidly, which eventually led to abandonment. But in 2000, a restoration project rebuilt houses and recovered original architectural charms. Maceió beaches also have their little stories. In the 1940s and 50s one of the most popular places of visitation was an old palm tree on the Ponta Verde Beach, that had a downward curve before it grew up again, and was nicknamed 'gogó da ema' or the ostrich neck.

This particular palm tree no longer exists, but remains one of the symbols of Maceió.

To Lagoa Mundaú

Porto

Praia da Avenida

Praia de Pajuçara

Piscinas naturais

Praia de Sete Coqueiros

Pça. Deodoro

R. do Sol

CENTRO

Pça. Rosalvo Ribeiro

R. Humberto Mendes

R. Ind. Cícero Toledo
R. Sá e Albuquerque
R. Sta. Leopoldina

JARAGUÁ

Av. Maceió

Av. Jagadeiros Alagoanos
Av. Dr. Antonio Gouveia

PAJUÇARA

Feira de artesanato de Pajuçara

Av. Robert Kennedy

Av. Prof. Sandoval Arroxelas

PONTA VERDE

Av. Álvaro Otacílio

Praia de Ponta Verde

To the north beaches

Alagoas late Clube

❶ Teatro Deodoro
❷ Pça. D. Pedro II
❸ Mirante São Gonçalo

Jangadas raft on natural pools of Pajuçara

Monday to Friday, from 8 a.m. to 5 p.m.
Entrance: free 🌐
The theater, that took five years to
build, was completed in 1910. It was
cause for controversy since, according
to the original city plan, a church was to
be built there. In 1988 it had to be
closed for repairs and was only reopened in 1999.

★ Pontal da Barra 🎯 🐚 ⛪

On the shores of the Lagoa Mundaú
lagoon are many restaurants and places
where different kinds of lace are
produced and sold. Several squares are
occupied by the lacemakers. From
Pontal da Barra boats make excursions
along Mundaú lagoon and its channels,
and to Manguaba lagoon, where it
meets the ocean, and to the many
islands that are surrounded by swamps.
Some of these islands are populated,
like Santa Rita in Lagoa Mundaú.

Beaches
🎯 🐚 ⛪ 🏄

There are many coconut trees along
Pajuçara. Jangada raft rides take

visitors out to natural pools about 2 km
from the coast. In 20 minutes the reefs
are reached and passengers can swim
among the coral reefs. Other rafts
anchor out there, selling drinks and
foods that are much enjoyed by the
visitors. Diving masks can be hired to
watch the colorful fish. This outing
should be done when the tide is low
and the reef more exposed. Most of the
city's hotels are concentrated in **Sete
Coqueiros**. On the waterfront there is a
handicraft market with over 100 stalls.
The next beach, after the Yacht Club,
is called **Ponta Verde**. In the Cheiro da
Terra complex there are over 200
stands that sell handicrafts, snacks, T-
shirts and clothing, records, and much
else. And at the end of the afternoon
there are free shows. The small
Cangaço e Folclore Alagoano Museum
has a collection of photographs and
tells the story of Lampião and his band
that used to also make forays into
Alagoas. A little farther on, in **Jatiúca**,
are stalls on the wide pavement that
sell differently flavored tapioca
pancakes. The sidewalk continues; so
do the palm trees and the great number
of hotels. Along the **Cruz das Almas**
stretch, the sea is good for surfing. In
Guaxuma there are summer homes
along this beach, and its waves are big.
Two kilometers farther is **Riacho**
Beach, where a fishing community
lives. Here, the reefs form a barrier
against the rough sea and so the waters
are calm and good for swimming.
Pratagy is not crowded and has palm
trees along some parts of it. Here the
titbits and appetizers prepared in the
beach stalls are based on crab meat.

Convent and Church Franciscano, in Deodoro

Lagoa Mundaú: on boat by islands that are surrounded by swamps ▶

From Cupuíba to logos

The jangada raft, docked in the sand, has become an icon on the Maceió beaches. They are usually made of cupuíba wood, that is also known as 'pau-de-jangada'. Seven or eight 6 m long trunks are tied together with strong rods of hardwood, to form the base. A mast is attached with only one sail, held out by a notched boom that can swivel on the mast. The jangadeiro controlling the huge cotton sail and the rudder-oar with a movement called zinga, usually stands on the stern, but there is a seat on which he can sit. Jangadas, that can carry up to six passengers used to be seaworthy for only one year. But now, technology has brought an innovation also to this ancient craft.

A seaworthy composite of spyroform and wood is replacing the expensive tree trunks in the base, improving stability and comfort, and extending its useful life to 5 years. And many companies now use the sail as advertising media for their logotypes.

An icon on the Maceió beaches

Customers can choose which one they would like out of the cages where they are kept alive in.

Ipioca Beach is the most Northern beach in Maceió. It is very quiet and rather lacking in amenities, but has many palm groves, and the reefs that are not far out, form natural pools. Floriano Peixoto, who became Brazil's second president, was born in the Ipioca neighborhood.

SURROUNDINGS

Marechal Deodoro

26 km from the capital, on the way to Porto da Barra 🚌 🏖 ♿

Marechal Deodoro is an attractive colonial town and was the former State capital. Its old buildings are concentrated in and around downtown, and can easily be visited in a single walk. The house where Marechal Deodoro's family used to live is now a **museum**, with its original furniture and decorations. (Daily, from 8 a.m. to 6 p.m.). In the same square is **Projeto Alagoas. Presente !** where handicraft produced by poor children is exhibited and sold. The Convent and Santa Maria Madalena Church took over 100 years to build, and were only completed in 1793. They have typically Baroque characteristics, and details are curved and gold plated. Lagoa Manguaba is the biggest lake in Alagoas with a 34 km perimeter. Along its shore are waterfront snackbars and restaurants that specialize in seafood. In Francês Beach all around the bay are waterfront restaurants that serve their customers at tables set along the sandy beach. When the tide is low, glass-bottom boats take tourists out to the natural pools.

Barra de São Miguel

Duas Barras: the Jequiá River slits and an island is formed

Maceió: 33 km
Aracaju: 261 km
Penedo: 130 km
👤 6,379
🌐 82
ℹ️ Prefeitura. ☎ 272-1209.

All along the Barra de São Miguel
there is a long stretch of sand. Along
some of these, standard beach stalls
are set up along the promenade.
During the week it is very tranquil,
but weekends and during high season
São Miguel gets very lively. A reef
barrier that represses the waves
makes the shore ideal for bathing.
Nearby is the Lagoa do Roteiro.
From Maceió down south, there is
Barra de São Miguel, Roteiro, Jequiá
da Praia, Cururipe and Piaçabuçu. The
entrance to Barra de São Miguel is 33
km from Maceió, via AL-101. From
Francês Beach on, in Marechal
Deodoro, it's another 12 km.
Dom Pero Fernandes Sardinha, the
first bishop of Brazil, is supposed to
have been captured and eaten by the
Caetés Indians, who where cannibals
and lived in this region.

A reef barrier represses the waves ▶

HIGHLIGHTS

★ Praia do Gunga 🏖 🚤 🏄

From Barra de São Miguel, schooner
tours cross Lagoa do Roteiro and go
to Praia do Gunga, in the district of
Roteiro. Swamps, high rugged cliffs,
beaches and reefs can be seen on the

Praia de Barreiras, in Cururipe ▶

way; so can the meeting of the lake water with the sea and beautiful houses on Barra de São Miguel. When the tide is low, the reefs that flank the mouth of the lake get more exposed. ☎ 272-1188. It is not unusual to see fishermen walking on the exposed sandbanks of the lake, called croas, when the tide is out. At Praia do Gunga there is one part that faces the freshwater lake water Lagoa do Roteiro, and another, the sea, where the Gunga lighthouse is. Snack bars there play music and have showers for bathers to use. Handicraft is also sold there. A huge coconut plantation flanks the entire coastline. Access to Gunga is also possible by land, but authorization to do this must first be obtained from Hotel Enseada. ☎ 231-2643. In this way it's 18 km via AL-101, from São Miguel. Carnival and New Year's celebrations are very lively occasions in Praia do Gunga. Transparent waters are excellent for scuba diving. From Gunga, the next beach is Jequiá da Praia, with access via AL-101 S, 29 km from Barra de São Miguel. There is a spot along the road from where there is an excellent view over Lagoa do Roteiro, Gunga Beach and the coconut plantation. The beaches are Jacarecica do Sul, Duas Barras, Lagoa Azeda and Pituba. In Duas Barras the women sell handicrafts they make out of the leaves of the ourici palm that

grows there. These they hang from the rafters of their homes and display in front of their houses, to attract customers. On the beach, Jequiá River slits and an island is formed, before either part of the river meets the ocean. This is the reason why the beach is named Duas Barras. The liveliest part of the beach is near Dunas de Marapé Restaurant, near the mouth of the river. To get to the restaurant and the beach, the restaurant has a boat that ferries customers across the river. Carapeba is a small fish and its fishing is the highlight of Pituba and Lagoa Azeda. These are tranquil beaches and Pituba Beach can only be reached from Lagoa Azeda Beach. 70 km from Barra de São Miguel is the district of Cururipe with more lovely beaches called Miai de Baixo, Miai de Cima, Lagoa do Pau and Pontal de Cururipe. The Cururipe River runs through the village of Cururipe. Ourici palm leave craftwork – hand and shopping bags, receptacles and boxes – are made at the doors of the homes, where the artisans chat and weave the dry palm leaves.

TIPS

– After Barra de São Miguel, southward, the conditions of AL-101 road get worse.

Maragogi

Walks to natural pools and nautical sports in Maragogi

Maceió: 130 km
Recife: 120 km
Tamandaré: 50 km
👤 21,832
🌐 82
ℹ️ Prefeitura ☎ 296-1130.
@ www.maragogi.al.gov.br.

Maragogi districts borders with
Pernambuco State. There are the
pretty Barra Grande, São Bento,
Maragogi and Proba beaches.
Other districts, farther south, are
Japaratinga, Porto das Pedras,
São Miguel dos Milagres, Passo do
Camaragibe, Barra de Santo Antônio
and Paripueira. They were all taken
during the Dutch invasion of the
Northeast. From Maceió to the
Northern beaches, the way to get
there is AL-101. If you are coming
from Recife, take BR101 and the
PE-60 road.

HIGHLIGHTS

Praia de Maragogi 🏊 🌊 🏖️
The catamaran boat goes to the
natural pools that are also called

galés. They are about 6 km from the
shore and a 15 minute ride out. These
outings start off at the Hotel Salinas
de Maragogi, but Frutos do Mar,
☎ 296-1403 and Pontal do Maragogi,
☎ 296-6161 tours also do the same.
The site they visit is much sought-
after for nautical sports.

Praia de São Bento 🏊 🌊
Very good place for catching clam
and shellfish. São Bento is also
excellent for bathing. Very popular
are the bolo do goma rusks, sold
there. Able craftsmen carve driftwood
and stones into the most amazing
forms and shapes, and sell them at
the Ponto do Chaves Restaurant.

★ Barra de Santo Antônio 🏊 🌊 🏖️
Japaratinga is the first Southern
district after Maragogi. Then come
São Miguel dos Milagres, Passo de
Camaragibe, Barra de Santo Antônio
and Paripueira districts. All are
protected under the APA protection
decree. Japaratinga Beach is 10 km
from Maragogi and has snack-bars
and restaurants. To get to São Miguel
dos Milagres one has to cross the

Carro Quebrado: quiet beach ▶

The corals

Corals preserved for 135 km

The waters are transparent and warm in this part of the Alagoas coast, which is the ideal for corals to form. Alongside the swamps, corals are the perfect environment for many marine species that find protection and food there. In the Northeast are the only coastal reefs formations in Brazil, and to preserve them, APA Costa dos Corais environmental protection law was created in 1997. It shelters 135 km of coastline, from Paripueira in Northern Alagoas to Tamandaré, in Southern Pernambuco, as well as the continental platform along this stretch, covering 4,135 sq km. This category of conservation unit allows the presence of human being, providing that available natural resources are used in a sustainable way. Do your part in this conservation effort: do not touch or step on the coral; dive with care and carry equipment close to your body, to avoid it from causing damage to rocks and animals; do not buy handicraft that is made of coral.

Manguaba River by ferry. There, the main beaches are Riacho, Toque and Porto da Rua. There are also excursions to the natural pools formed by the reef 1 km out to sea, and up the Tatuamunha River (Ecomariner, ☎ 295-1170). Beyond this river is Porto das Pedras, where the peaceful beaches of Patacho and Tatuamunha are, and the lighthouse, from where there is a lovely beach view. In Passo de Camaragibe are more beaches – Macineiro, Morros and Barra de Camaragibe, where the Camaragibe River flows out to sea. Some

constructions built by the Dutch in the 17th century are still found here. 60 km from Maragogi is Barra de Santo Antônio. From this beach one is able to cross the Santo Antônio River by ferry and get to Ilha de Croa, which actually is a peninsula. Along the way is Carro Quebrado with its waterfront palm leave stalls and high cliffs that follow its coastline. The rocks along these cliffs are of a purple, yellow, and blue color. In Santo Antônio, Tabuba Beach has natural pools 1 km from the shore. Its waters are protected and good for swimming. The Sapucai River runs out to sea here, and catamaran tours can be arranged (Tabuba Restaurant, ☎ 291-1391). Paripueira is a small town and its beaches are Costa Brava, Sonho Verde and Paripueira. At this point one is 100 km north of Maragogi, via AL-101. Here too, boat rides to the natural pools are available, and are best, when the tide is low. Carnival in Paripueira is among the liveliest in Alagoas, and there one more peixe boi manatee protection center was created and is open to visitation (AL-101 North, km 17, in front of the Venta Club Pratagy, ☎ 293-1100).

TIPS

– The company Atlântica has daily bus from terminal de Maceió, with stops on the main beaches, until Maragogi.

Penedo

The location, next to the mouth of the São Francisco River, was fundamental for Penedo

Maceió: 157 km
Aracaju: 120 km
Arapiraca: 70 km
👤 56,993
🏛 82
🚌 🚢 ferryboat

Penedo has two main points of attraction: the architectural complex in the historical center, and the natural beauties along the majestic São Francisco River. All of the historical center, mostly 17th century, has been turned into a National Monument. The town lies quite high in relation to the river, and its highest point is Pça. Barão de Penedo with the Nossa Senhora do Rosário Cathedral, the Oratório dos Condenados (Chapel of condemned), and the Casa de Aposentadoria (house of retirement). Penedo is on the natural Southern border of Alagoas – the São Francisco River. On the opposite side, lies Neópolis, in Sergipe (*see Aracajú, Sergipe*) and a ferry carries passengers and vehicles across. The two towns are not far from the mouth of the river, and the region is known as the lower São Francisco basin, which is navigable.

HIGHLIGHTS

★ Igreja Nossa Senhora da Corrente

Praça 12 de Abril Tuesday to Sunday from 8 a.m. to 6 p.m.
This church was built as a private place of prayer for the André de Lemos Gonzaga family, in 1765. They were abolitionists and helped run-away slaves, falsifying freedom certificates and giving refuge inside their church. The building is quite well preserved and original. The floor was brought from England and the wall tiles are Portuguese. They are unusually colorful; not only with the recurrent blue and whites, which is very rare. The front of the building and the main altar are Baroque, but the side altars are in a neo-classical style. The wood pillars inside are covered in gold, and tours around the church are guided.

Igreja de São Gonçalo Garcia

Av. Floriano Peixoto. From Tuesday to Saturday from 8 a.m. to 6 p.m. Sunday from 9 a.m. to 4 p.m.
Of the original plan, that began to be executed in the late 16th century and completed in 1770, very little is left.

Igreja and Convento Nossa Senhora dos Anjos ▶

The boulder of São Francisco

The city started during the 17th century

In 1535, one year after the hereditary provinces had been apportioned, the Portuguese Duarte Coelho took possession of the Southern limits of the Pernambuco province, along the São Francisco River. He found a place along this river that was a little higher and chose that for his base. Not only was it favored by a natural transport route, it provided a strategic command over what came and went along the river delta and that was an excellent position for the commercer. A settlement was started and named Vila de Penedo do São Francisco. Penedo means boulder and makes reference to the altitude of the chosen site, compared to its surroundings.

In 1637 the Dutch invaders, that took most of the Northeast, also arrived in Penedo under the leadership of Mauricio de Nassau and built a bulwark, called Mauricio Fort, near the river. In 1645 however, the Dutch control had declined and the Portuguese regained control of their territory, including Penedo, and also the São Francisco River while the Dutch garrison was imprisoned inside the fort, they destroyed it. But the city survived this war.

The entire ceiling had to be replaced because of damage caused by termites. The church's different styles bear witness to the long time it took to be built and other changes that were incorporated. It stands in one of the main town squares.

Igreja e Convento Nossa Senhora dos Anjos
Rua 7 de Setembro, 218. From Tuesday to Friday from 8 to 11:30 a.m. and from 2 to 5 p.m. Saturday and Sunday from 8 to 11:30 a.m. 📷
This chapel was connected to the Franciscan order and the neighboring convent, that began to be built in 1660, is also open for visitation.

Teatro Sete de Setembro
Av. Floriano Peixoto. Tuesday to Friday from 8 to 11:30 a.m. and from 2 to 5

p.m. Saturday and Sunday from 8 to 11:30 a.m. Entrance: free. ☺

This theater used to belong to the Philharmonic Society started by a Portuguese called Manoel Pereira Carvalho Sobrinho, in 1865 to motivate love for good music.

On September 7, 1884 it was inaugurated, with grand pomp and circumstance, and became the first provincial theater in Alagoas. Gradually the Society became more comprehensive and included ballet and theatrical performances in its agenda. The china statues, which probably came from Portugal, represent the four goddesses of the arts – music, poetry, painting and dancing. On the triangular front piece, the Imperial Philharmonic Society coat of arms can be found. More recently, the entire building was renovated.

Fundação Casa do Penedo

R. João Pessôa, 126. ☎ 551-2516. Tuesday to Sunday from 8 a.m. to 6 p.m. Entrance: free. ⏺

The town's history, and that of the lower São Francisco region, is kept here. There is a historic, iconography collection in the library, where old newspapers are also kept.

Paço Imperial Court Museum

R. Dâmaso Dumont. ☎ 551-2738. Tuesday to Sunday from 11 a.m. to 5 p.m. ⏺ ☺

Emperor Dom Pedro II stayed here when visiting Penedo in 1859. Imperial objects and furniture, as well as research material on that era are on show, with 18th and 19th century paintings, crystals and medallions.

The same building houses the Memorial Raimundo Marinho, where there are more recent photographs and documents that belong to the 1960s and 80s. The building stands on the bank of the river, and was only recently restored and reopened to the public.

Foz do Rio São Francisco ☺

From Penedo to the São Francisco delta it is 30 km, that catamaran boats do in a 3-hour excursion with up to 40 people, organized by the São Francisco Hotel. During the trip, passengers get to know Neópolis, Ilha das Flores and Brejo Grande, which are on the Sergipe side of the river, and Piaçabuçu, in Alagoas.

SURROUNDINGS

Piaçabuçu

25 km from Penedo via AL-101 road. ☺ ☺

Piaçabuçu in Caeté Indian language means big palm tree. And in fact, Piaçabuçu is one of the main coconut producers in Alagoas. Its privileged location also allows tourism to play an important role in the local economy. The town is on the São Francisco River margin closest to the sea – only 13 km away, and boats that do trips there leave from the city wharf. Reservations can be made with the Secretaria de Turismo, opposite the wharf, ☎ 552-1473), where the

Square sail called butterfly, is found only in Penedo

Mouth of the São Francisco: the river cross 5 States before reach the sea

rotation of guides and boatsmen is organized. The best is to form groups that can share the cost of the trip, that takes around 45 minutes to reach the open sea, and one hour to return, upstream. A lunch can be included, either in a floating restaurant on the Sergipe margin, or else in Piaçabuú itself. The tour passes Potengi village and palm huts along the banks, that fishermen live in. A typical embarkation, and exclusive, in these parts of the São Francisco River, is a log canoe equipped with a rudimentary square sail, called borboleta or butterfly. The guides that accompany visitors on these trips have entertaining little stories and anecdotes to tell about the river islands. On their margins, the swamp follows the current of the water and vegetation has adapted to these precarious and moveable conditions. At the mouth of the river are dunes on the Alagoas side. Under these dunes lies buried by the sand a small palm hut village and its church. The entire region around the river delta comes under the Piaçabuçu Preservation Statute that aims at preserving an ecosystem balance, in the dunes and in the salt marshes, where migrating birds come to mate, and sea turtles lay their eggs, not to mention a myriad of other species that would probably not survive unprotected. (*Read about the São Francisco Ecological Scenario and about Aracaju, Sergipe*).

Beaches 🏖
42 km from Penedo via AL-101 South
The first beach in the southern part of Alagoas is Peba, with a stretch of dunes that follows the São Francisco River mouth. The next one, northward, is Pontal do Peba with a long stretch of compact sand, and with summer homes, guesthouses and restaurant along the waterfront, that continues as far as Feliz Deserto Beach.

TIPS

– Access: from Maceió it's 184 km to Penedo via AL-101. Another way to get there is along BR-101; then follow the Penedo exit at the AL-225 and AL-110 junction. From Maceió, Real Alagoas buses do this route every day. ☎ 223-3931. From Aracaju to Neópolis, it's 120 km. (*see Aracaju, Sergipe*). In Neópolis, a ferry crosses São Francisco River to Penedo. Santa Maria buses go daily from Aracaju. ☎ 344-1240.
– Penedo celebrates its anniversary on April 12, when the week of popular tradition festivities also take place.
– In Penedo, artists specialize in woodwork and sculptures of saints. These can be found in the Mestre Antônio Pedro artisan market or on Praça Comendador Peixoto. Clay and palm leaves are also used a lot, in local handicrafts.
– In the Bom Jesus dos Navegantes festival that happens on the second Sunday of January, many decorated boats gather on the São Francisco River. The procession moves down the river and past Penedo, drawing others to join them on the way.
– In November, there is an event called Recita Penedo that encourages and rewards the best literary achievements of new writers.
– Also in November amateur fishermen get together for an angling contest in Pontal do Peba Beach in Piaçabuçu. The road between Penedo and Piaçabuçu is very bad and has no direction signs.

PERNAMBUCO

PERNAMBUCO

Pernambuco is located in the central-east of the Northeast region. It covers an area of 98,281 km² and as it lies in an east-west bearing, the State has large stretches of forest, an arid vegetation zone and the backlands. The coast has 187 km of beaches with reefs and cliffs. At a distance of 545 km from the coast is one of the most appreciated diving areas in the country: the Parque Nacional de Fernando de Noronha. The history of Pernambuco dates back to the times of the first colonization, in the 16th century, when Duarte Coelho became the landlord of the captaincy that extended from the Rio São Francisco to the Ilha de Itamaracá. He was responsible for establishing the first sugarmills, which made Pernambuco one of the most important exportation centers of the Brazilian colony. The wealth generated by sugarcane attracted Portuguese settlers who brought with them a great number of Africans to work in the mills.

So much wealth aroused the greed of the Dutch. After a failed attempt to take possession of Bahia, they attacked Olinda in 1630 and settled here for 24 years.

The popular culture is emblematic, marked by the rhythm of the *maracatu* and the 'mangue' beat. Luiz Gonzaga, in the song *Asa Branca*, portrays the drought in the Northeast. The novelist Ariano Suassuna, brought up in Pernambuco, is one of the greatest champions of regional culture. He founded the Armorial Quintet in Recife, a style that created a Brazilian Erudite Chamber Music and popular roots music. And from literature, the writers João Cabral de Melo Neto, Gilberto Freyre and Manuel Bandeira are distinguished. The Carnival in Recife beat its own record by uniting more than one million Carnival merrymakers in the Galo da Madrugada. In the typical cuisine, the memorable dishes are *buchada* of goat, *sarapatel* and *moqueca*.

◀ Bridges appear in several downtown points, in Recife

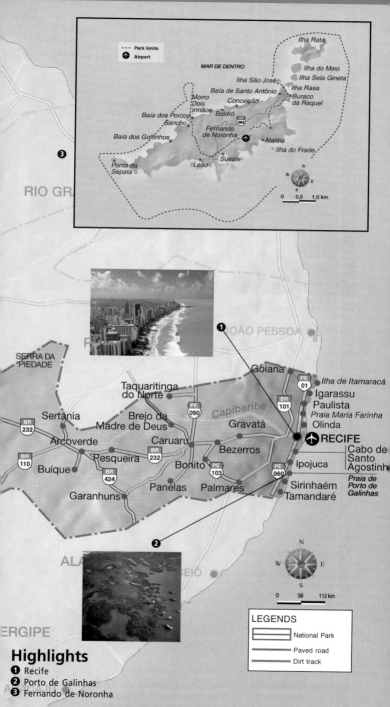

--- Park limits
⊕ Airport

MAR DE DENTRO

Ilha Rata

Ilha do Meio
Ilha Sela Gineta
Ilha São José
Baía de Santo Antônio
Ilha Rasa
Buraco
da Raquel

Morro
Dois
Irmãos
Baía dos Porcos
Sancho
Boldró
Conceição

Baía dos Golfinhos
Fernando
de Noronha
363
Atalaia
Ilha do Frade

Ponta da
Sapata
Leão
Sueste

RIO GR

0   0,5   1,0 km

JOÃO PESSOA

SERRA DA
PIEDADE

Gôiana
PE
01
Ilha de Itamaracá

Taquaritinga
do Norte
BR
101
Igarassu
Paulista
Praia Maria Farinha

Sertânia
Brejo da
Madre de Deus
PE
090
Capibaribe
Gravatá
Olinda

BR
232
Caruaru
BR
232
Bezerros
⊕ RECIFE
Cabo de
Santo
Agostinh

Arcoverde
Pesqueira
Bonito
PE
103
Ipojuca
PE
060

BR
110
Buíque
BR
424
Sirinhaém
*Praia de
Porto de
Galinhas*

Garanhuns
Panelas
Palmares
Tamandaré

ALA

CEIÓ

SERGIPE

0   56   112 km

LEGENDS

National Park
Paved road
Dirt track

Highlights

❶ Recife
❷ Porto de Galinhas
❸ Fernando de Noronha

Recife

The city view from Olinda: tradition and modernity side by side

João Pessoa: 135 km
Maceió: 245 km
Natal: 280 km
Olinda: 7 km
👤 1.422.905
🌐 81
ℹ Empetur ☎ 3427-8000
@ www.pernambuco.com

The capital city of the State of Pernambuco is surrounded by water. Constructed on three islands – Boa Vista, Santo Antônio and Recife, which also form the old center – the city is parted by the Capibaribe, Beberibe and Jordão rivers. A total of 39 bridges around the city join several points of the islands to the continent, thereby giving Recife the nickname of the 'Brazilian Venice'. The city mixes the past with the present, modernity and tradition. Detached houses and artist's studios share space with the luxurious high-rise buildings. Sophisticated restaurants exist with simple bars with tasty menus. There are many historic monuments spread around the city, which make visitors enthusiastic about wandering through the old narrow streets full of history.

The economy of Recife is based on industrial activities, commerce and principally on tourism and services.

HIGHLIGHTS

★ Bairro do Recife Antigo
🌐 🎭 ⬤ 🎿

The main-street of the suburb, Bom Jesus, has a restored mansion from the start of the 17th century. At night the scene changes: the street is closed to cars, the pavement is covered with tables and from the bars, it is possible to hear music. In the past, the place was called R. dos Judeus and in 1640 the first synagogue on the American continent was built here. Today, on the site of this old temple, is the **Centro Cultural Judaico de Pernambuco**. It was called Congregação Rochedo de Israel and functioned between 1636 and 1654, during the period of Dutch domination, but the Portuguese who did not permit the practice of other religions except Catholicism destroyed it. In 2001, the building was re-inaugurated as a cultural center and historic archives in memory of Pernambucan Jews. Opening hours are Tuesday to Friday, from 9 a.m. to 5 p.m. and on weekends, from 3 to 7 p.m.   ☎ 3224-2128.

New Amsterdam

Until the 17th century, Recife was only a village, working as the port of Olinda, at that time the most important center of the region. Its expansion began in 1630 with the occupation of the Dutch. As the heart of Dutch domination in Brazil, at that time it was baptized Nova Amsterdã. In 1637, count Maurício de Nassau arrived in the city and started the urban development. On the occasion, sanitation projects were completed on the current Ilha de Santo Antônio, and a bridge was built linking the city to the mainland. They imported pre-fabricated houses from Holland and introduced to Brazil the type of construction known as 'thin detached houses' – with two or more floors, elongated windows and staircases. The street Bom Jesus, where the bohemian lifestyle is concentrated in the old city, was the first paved street. Nassau brought mapmakers, astronomers and naturalists with him from Europe to record the conquered land.

Urbanization began in 17th century

1. Praça da República
2. Igreja da Ordem Terceira de São Francisco
3. Torre Malakoff
4. Centro Cultural Judaico
5. Marco Zero
6. Parque das Esculturas
7. Museu do Trem
8. Casa de Cultura
9. Pátio São Pedro
10. Mercado São José
11. Forte de Cinco Pontas
12. Passeio pelo Rio Capibaribe

Also in the vicinity is **R. do Apolo** and **Pça. do Arsenal da Marinha**, where on Sundays from about 2:30 p.m., roughly 120 stalls sell handicrafts and regional products. In front of the square is **Torre Malakoff.** Built in 1855 to house the first observatory of the American continent, it was also the entry gate to the city for whom came from the sea. A stairway leads to the top from where there is an ample view of the city. Take the opportunity, at the end of the day, to see the stars through the telescope that is available on the terrace. On the ground floor there are computers with internet access. Opening hours are Tuesday to Sunday, from 3 to 8 p.m. ☎ 3424-8704.

Returning by R. Bom Jesus to the corner with Av. Barbosa Lima, turn to the left and go seawards. Soon, in the center of Pça. Rio Branco, there is the **Marco Zero**, a sign indicating where the birth of the city was. From this spot, five streets go in the direction of the suburb of Recife Antigo. In one of the corners is the Stock Exchange building of Recife and Paraíba. The square and the streets were planned to symbolize a palm of a hand from where the five fingers extend. Looking towards the sea it is possible to see the sculptures of the artist Francisco Brennand, created on an extensive line of cliffs in a place known as the **Parque das Esculturas**. In total there are 70 works positioned during the celebrations of 500 years of the

discovery of Brazil, in 2000. The biggest is 32 meters tall and is called Coluna de Cristal. Access to the park can be by boat leaving from Marco Zero, or by land through the suburb of Brasília Teimosa.

Forte do Brum

Pça. Comunidade Luso-Brasileira, Recife Antigo. ☎ 3224-4620. Tuesday to Friday, from 9 a.m. to 4 p.m. and weekends, from 2 p.m. to 4 p.m. Entrance: free. ⚑

Located between Olinda and the Porto de Recife, the fort was used as a defensive base by the Portuguese in the 16th century and after by the Dutch during the invasion. With the expulsion of the Dutch the fort was rebuilt in stone and plaster. The building houses the Museu Histórico Militar where cannons and weapons are on display as well as photographs, which confirm the presence of the Brazilian Armed Forces in the Second World War.

Forte de Cinco Pontas

Pça. de Cinco Pontas, São José. ☎ 3224-8492. Monday to Friday, from 9 a.m. to 6 p.m. and weekends, from 1 to 5 p.m. ⚑ ⚑

Built in wattle and daub by the Dutch in 1630, it originally had five points. The defeat of the Dutch preceded the completion of the construction and when the fort was rebuilt by the Portuguese, only 4 points were built,

The old new suburb

A t the end of the 1930s, the economic center started to move from Recife Antigo to the neighboring suburbs. In place of the large structures of commerce, the region began to house the activities of the port and bohemian life, with nightclubs and brothels. The city centre itself became the seedy part of town, and the buildings built in the 17th century lost value and were left in bad repair. In about 1970, studies were started to recover the historic value of the constructions. The results started to become apparent from 1993, with the Projeto Cores da Cidade, created as a joint venture between the city council and private business. The main focus was R. Bom Jesus and its proximity, with revitalization of the two-floored buildings. With the new proposal, Recife Antigo would maintain the ancient characteristics and gain new activities.

Restored patrimony

Forte de Cinco Pontas: from the original five points projected, only four were built

even so the name persisted. The location, on the banks of the Rio Capibaribe, intended to guarantee the water supply for the city and impede the entry of vessels. The **Museu da Cidade do Recife** functions from inside the fort with maps drawn by the Dutch, cannons, paintings and ceramic wall tiles.

★ Rio Capibaribe Boat Trip

Embarks from the pier of Cinco Pontas, São José. ☎ 3424-2845. @ www.catamarantours.com.br Daily at 16:30 and 8 p.m. 🕐 1¼ hours. ♿
A catamaran navigates along the Rio Capibaribe and its estuary, passing under bridges and circling the islands, which form the old centre. Guides accompany the visitors telling the history of the city by its constructions and bridges. The boat trip at the end of the day has its high-point when the lights of the bridges and R. Aurora and R. Sol are turned on, creating an enchanting scene. It is an excellent option to know Recife from a different perspective.

★ Igreja e Convento da Ordem Terceira de São Francisco

R. do Imperador, Santo Antônio.
☎ 3224-0530. Monday to Friday, from 8 to 11:30 a.m. and from 2 to 5 p.m. Saturday, from 8 to 11:30 a.m. ♿ 🚹
Even though the façade is badly preserved, inside there is one of the most important sacred relics of baroque: it is the **Capela Dourada da Terceira Ordem**

from 1695, with carvings of golden wood from the 18th century. The convent built in 1606 and after restored, is open to the public and has the walls decorated with Portuguese ceramic wall tiles from the end of the 17th century. **The Museu Franciscano de Arte Sacra** is also in the same edifice.

Praça da República

Bairro Santo Antônio 🚇
There are several important constructions around the square.
The **Palácio do Governo**, also known as Palácio Campo de Princesa, nowadays houses the State government. On this same site, Maurício de Nassau built his first residence in 1641. By the side of the palace is the **Teatro Santa Isabel**, also built in the same period as Nassau and soon after, the **Palácio da Justiça**, where the law courts operate. The **Ponte Princesa Isabel** crosses the Rio Capibaribe connecting the Pça. da República to R. Princesa Isabel. It was constructed in 1643 with oil-lamps and sculptures at its two ends. Above it, on one bank is the **R. da Aurora**, illuminated by the rising sun and on the other bank, where the sun strikes the rest of the day, is the **R. do Sol**.

Bridges 🚇

The **Ponte Maurício de Nassau,** built in 1643, is the first bridge of Brazil, originally wooden, which linked the Ilha de Santo Antônio to the mainland.

Frevo and Carnival

The carnivals of Recife and Olinda are the most traditional of the State and two of the biggest in the country. The Carnival group Galo da Madrugada, considered the biggest in the world (it entered into the *Guinness Book of Records* with the mark of one million participants), starts to form on Saturday. The departure point of the group is the Forte de Cinco Pontas. The Carnival stretches along Boa Viagem with grandstands and private boxes along the edge. *Trios elétricos* (trucks carrying high-tech sound systems) play *frevo* and unite the merrymakers the entire day in the central streets. In Recife Antigo a calmer Carnival takes place.

Step of 'frevo'

The **12 de Setembro** is parallel to Maurício de Nassau and passes over the Capibaribe River. The mobility of the construction made the passage of large vessels carrying sugar possible.

★ Casa da Cultura de Pernambuco

R. Floriano Peixoto, Santo Antônio.
☎ 3224-2850 and 3224-7626.
www.cultura.pe.gov.br. Monday to Saturday, from 9 a.m. to 7 p.m. and Sunday, from 9 a.m. to 2 p.m.
Entrance: free.

The old prison of Recife functioned on the banks of the Capibaribe River, and nowadays, each cell is a shop, which sells handcrafted articles produced in different regions of the State. The building is similar to the original from 1867 in the format of a cross with guard towers and iron bars. In the courtyard there are presentations of dance and music. Four panels called *Frei Caneca*, by the painter Cícero Dias, pay homage to episodes in the history of Pernambuco. In one of the cells, the writer Graciliano Ramos was held prisoner during the Estado Novo (Dictatorship between 1937-1945).

Museu do Trem

Av. Rio Capibaribe, 147, Santo Antônio.
☎ 3424-3141, ex. 32. Monday to Friday, from 9 to 12 a.m. and from 2 to 5 p.m.
Entrance: free.

The old Estação Central Ferroviária remains in a good condition comparable to when the English built it. Inside, a large shed holds around 400 objects and documents of the railways of Pernambuco. It is also an underground railway station.

Pátio de São Pedro

Between R. São José and Av. São Jorge, São José

This is an important historical site of the

city, around which there are different buildings from the colonial period. The **Catedral São Pedro dos Clérigos**, designed by Manuel Ferreira Jácome and built between 1728 and 1782 is the symbolic construction in the center of the courtyard. The façade is elongated vertically, while the door has a baroque style and inside, the pulpit, altars and galleries are covered with embedded stones. The ceiling exhibits an exquisite work of the painter João de Deus Sepúlveda, which represents São Paulo blessing the Catholics. At the end of the day, the restaurants owners spread their tables in the courtyard in front of the cathedral. Also in the square is the **Casa do Carnaval**, which displays posters depicting the celebrations in Pernambuco. ☎ 3224-6368

★ Mercado de São José
Pça. Dom Vital, São José. Monday to Saturday, from 6 a.m. to 5:30 p.m. and Sunday, from 6 to 12 a.m.
About 500 stalls show a diversity of handicrafts from Pernambuco in this building constructed in 1875 from a pre-fabricated iron structure brought from France. There are clothes, religious articles, lace towels, ceramics, meats, herbs and fruit. In front of one of the exits of the market is the **Basílica Nossa Senhora da Penha**, with enormous marble columns.

Instituto Arqueológico e Geográfico de Pernambuco
R. do Hospício, 130, Boa Vista. ☎ 3222-4952. Monday to Friday, from 1 to 5 p.m. Saturday, from 8 to 12 a.m.
Here the halls tell the history of the State, showing photographs, maps and furniture. The highlight is the stone mark, which divided the territories of the captaincies of Itamaracá and Pernambuco in the 16th century.

Museu do Estado de Pernambuco
Av. Rui Barbosa, 960, Graças. ☎ 3427-9322. Monday to Friday, from 9 a.m. to 5:30 p.m. and weekends, from 2 to 5 p.m.
The original building had only one story but after, a second floor was constructed. Today it houses approximately 12,000 items with emphasis on Indian art, sacred art and furniture from the Imperial age. Paintings that portray the Pernambucan

wars are positioned by the side of works by artists such as the town planner Burle Marx, and the painters Cícero Dias and Rego Monteiro.

Museu do Homem do Nordeste
Av. 17 de Agosto, 2187, Casa Forte. ☎ 3441-5500, ex. 638. Tuesday, Wednesday and Friday, from 11 a.m. to 5 p.m.; Thursday, from 8 a.m. to 5 p.m. and weekends, from 1 to 5 p.m.
Permanent exhibits about the history of the occupation of the State, the cultural styles, information about religions and handicrafts. The museum belongs to the Fundação Joaquim Nabuco.

Museu do Homem do Nordeste

Oficina Cerâmica Francisco Brennand
Av. Caxangá, km 16, Várzea. Property of Santos Cosme and Damião. ☎ 3271-2466. Monday to Friday, from 8 a.m. to 5:30 p.m.
In a mixture of museum cum shop, Francisco Brennand constructed a type of temple in an area of Atlantic Forest. Part of the exhibition is displayed in a garden, another in a 15,000 m^2 shed. The artist sells sculptures and painted ceramic wall tiles.

Beaches
The main is the **Praia da Boa Viagem** with reefs that dam the water forming natural swimming pools very close to the sands. A pedestrian precinct follows the 7 km of beach, with a wide promenade for walks, kiosks and sports courts. Surfing is prohibited due to shark attacks. The hotels, buildings, restaurants and bars are found in front of the beaches. Around the **Igreja Nossa Senhora da Boa Viagem** there is a handicraft fair and also the dividing mark with the

◀ Pátio de São Pedro: Catholicism and bohemia

The polemic works of Francisco Brennand

Praia da Piedade, to the south of Boa Viagem. The stretch towards Olinda is the **Praia do Pina.**

SURROUNDINGS

Igarassu

Situated at 39 km from Recife by the BR-101 highway. 🚻🅿🚐🏨

The first landlord of the captaincy of Pernambuco, Duarte Coelho, founded the town in 1535. The historic centre, with a few other important buildings, is composed of only two streets, easy to visit on foot. The most important church of the town is **Santos Cosme e Damião**, which is considered to be one of the oldest of the country. The church holds the mortal remains of the saints that are displayed to the public during the festival of Cosme and Damião from September 20 to 27. (Opening hours: Tuesday to Friday from 8 to 12 a.m. and 2 to 5 p.m. Weekends from 8 to 12 a.m.)

The Igreja e Convento Sagrado Coração de Jesus, on the same street, were built in 1742 and 1747 respectively. At the entrance there is a small rotating door called the 'contribution circle', which was the only contact the nuns had with the outside world and where the faithful deposited their offerings to the church. In the same block, there are the ruins of the **Igreja Nossa Senhora de Misericórdia,** destroyed by the Dutch, and the detached house where **D. Pedro II** was lodged during his visit to the town in 1859. The **Igreja e Convento de Santo Antônio**, of the Franciscan order, has conserved blue and white Portuguese ceramic wall tiles, which cover part of the wall. The histories of Saints Bernardino, Diogo, Pedro and Nicolau were painted by Rabelo, one of the baroque masters, on the ceiling of the nave. The convent has a cloister open to the public and an art gallery. The original building was concluded in 1588, destroyed by the Dutch and restored in 1693.

TIPS

– During the visit to Recife Antigo, take a break in the bar known as *As Galerias* and try the 'maltado', a mixture of chocolate ice cream, milk and chocolate syrup served cold and frothy. The bar was established in 1928 at R. Marquês de Olinda, 58. In R. Aurora, visit the **Cine São Luiz**. The hall was built in 1952 and has 790 seats. When the lights go out, two stained-glass windows light up displaying colored flowers.

– The Pólo Pina on R. Herculano Bandeira, between Pina and Boa Viagem beaches is where some of the most traditional bars and restaurants are to be found.

– There are about 17 shipwrecks in front of the Porto do Recife. The best time for diving is from October to April when the waters are more transparent and there is less wind.

◄ Praia de Boa Viagem: restaurants, bars, hotels and natural swimming pools

Caruaru

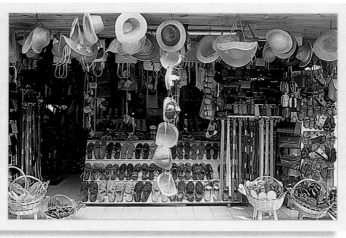

Markets of Caruaru are famous for the variety and size.

Recife: 130km
Campina Grande (PB): 160km
Maceió: 187km
♙ 253.634
⊕ 81
ℹ Fundação de Cultura e Turismo de Caruaru
☎ 3721-1633.
@ www.caruaru.com.br
☎ ☎

Located in the Pernambucan *agreste*, Caruaru is famous for its Festas Juninas (a traditional religious festival in June) and for its clay modelling. The local clay has supplied the artistic production of Pernambuco since the start of the 20th century and is based as a family activity. The women were apt to modelling utility earthenware: pans, jugs, pots and bowls, whereas the men had the job of producing bricks, roof tiles and ceramic drainage pipes. A handicraft production center formed by followers of the master Vitalino is found in the community of Alto do Moura, a rural area of Caruaru. He was the creator of the distinct style of Caruaru clay dolls, which portray scenes from the day-to-day life and northeastern folklore.

HIGHLIGHTS

Alto do Moura

7 km from the center of Caruaru ⭕ �🚍 ⊕
The suburb is a national reference for the production of ceramics and is considered by Unesco "the biggest center of figurative art work of the American continent". The production method is always the same: the clay is extracted from Ipojuca riverbanks. After drying, the works are baked in wood-fired kilns for up to ten hours. One of the more traditional articles is the chess set made by Marliete, the daughter of craftsman Zé Caboclo, where the pieces of the set represent northeastern characters: Padre Cícero is the bishop, Lampião and Maria Bonita represent the king and queen, Mestre Vitalino's house in the place of the castle and *sertanejos* represent the pawns. In the main street of Alto do Moura, the **Casa-Museu Mestre Vitalino** exhibits personal possessions including the furniture of the craftsman. Opening hours: Monday to Saturday, from 8 to 12 a.m. and 2 to 6 p.m. and on Sunday until midday.

Feiras de Caruaru

Parque 18 de Maio. @
www.feiradecaruaru.com.br

The open-air market served to provide supplies to travelers who came from the backlands on their way to Recife. It was just one market but was split into several, according to the types of goods. The **Feira de Artesanato** operates every day, and is the most famous, with standard stalls, which sell carved wooden objects, leather, clay items and embroidery. The **Feira do Paraguai** sells electronic goods. The **Feira da Sulanca**, on Tuesdays, is economically the most important for the region as it is where textile articles produced in the city are sold. The market covers 20,000 m² – and the locals are sure to tell that it is the biggest open-air market in the world.

SURROUNDINGS

Bezerros

Situated at 20km from Caruaru by the BR-232 highway.

The main highlight of Bezerros is the Parque Ecológico located in Serra Negra, 10 km from the town. The heart of the park is a cultural and tourist centre, which has exposition halls and simple rooms to accommodate visitors (☎ 3728-1960). In the park there are waterfalls, caves, trails and vantage points spread over the *agreste* vegetation.

Bonito

Situated at 60 km from Caruaru by the PE-103 highway

Located in the *agreste*, in the

'Cordel' and xylography

Cordel of J.Borges

The 'cordel' or 'market booklet' initiated at the end of the 19th century and served to express social disapproval and to tell stories. It was given this name as the leaflets were displayed on 'cordels' (twines) similar to those of a washing line. At the start of the 20th century, some books started to have designs on the covers printed using xylography. This technique uses a square or oblong block of wood and a pointed instrument. The wood is customarily *pau d'arco*, *cajá*, *umburana* or *cedro*, which are suitable for carving; and the tool used is a sharp-bladed knife. Small grooves are cut in the wood to form the desired design. Similar to a rubber stamp, ink is spread over the entire carved surface, and the engraved picture is reproduced on paper or fabric.

mountainous land of Serra de Borborema, Bonito is notable because of its waterfalls that bathe the municipality, which are found about 20 km from downtown. It is necessary to hire a guide to visit them.

The master of Caruaru

In the 1940s, Vitalino Pereira dos Santos (1909-1963) moved from the countryside and set up residence in the city. He developed a technique of producing clay dolls and passed it on to his children and friends. In the years that followed, more than 30 craftsmen specialized in modelling clay. Among them are Zé Caboclo, Manuel Eudócio and Mestre Galdino. The first piece of Mestre Vitalino was of a hunter with a dog aiming at a cat. He left a legacy of 118 clay characters, which today are studied and reproduced by the heirs of his technique. The most repeated theme of the clay dolls is the daily life of the north-eastern people – scenes from popular culture, such as men on horseback, pregnant women and people dancing.

Vitalino left a great legacy

Fernando de Noronha

Morro Dois Irmãos in Noronha: unforgettable sunset

Natal: 365 km
Recife: 545 km
🧍 2051
🌐 81
@ www.fernandodenoronha.tur.br

The Archipelago de Fernando de Noronha is protected by two Conservation Units: a Parque Nacional and an Área de Proteção Ambiental. The national park of Fernando de Noronha is formed by 21 islands, with a total area of 112 km². Approximately 85% of it is sea. The biggest island, where the principal attractions and infrastructure for the visitor are located is 17 km². Located at about 4° south of the Equator, the park belongs to the State of Pernambuco; although it is nearer to Rio Grande do Norte. The largest islands are: Fernando de Noronha, Rata, Rasa, Meio, Lucena and Sela Gineta. The others are practically inaccessible crags. Renowned for being one of the most beautiful places in Brazil, it is a paradise for divers. The beaches can be visited on boat trips departing from the Porto de Santo Antônio, by buggy, circling the island or on foot to the closer beaches.

HIGHLIGHTS

Projeto Tamar
Alameda do Boldró.
☎ 3619-1171.
Since 1984 Green Sea Turtles and Hawksbill Sea Turtles, more commonly found on Leão, Americano and Bode beaches, have been the target of researchers on the archipelago. In the visitor's center of the Projeto Tamar, facts about the species, information about studies and tanks with animals can be found. Lectures take place every day at 9 p.m. and are very enjoyable. Some beaches such as Sancho and Cacimba do Padre are out of bounds during the night from January to July, as it is the turtle egg-laying season.

Vila dos Remédios
The Ruins of the **Forte Nossa Senhora dos Remédios,** which was built in the 18th century by the Portuguese, and has already protected the island from invaders and housed prisoners, are located here. The site has been listed by the Instituto do Patrimônio Histórico e Artístico Nacional since 1961. Nearby there is the **Igreja Nossa Senhora dos Remédios,** from 1772.

Fish and corals: paradise for divers

Morro do Pico ⊘

Located on the main island and at 322 meters, it is the highest peak of the archipelago. On the summit there is a lighthouse but it is prohibited to climb to the top. Morro do Pico is a reference point for visitors, as it can be seen from many places throughout the archipelago.

Mar de Dentro ⊘ ⊘

On the continental side of Fernando de Noronha is the Mar de Dentro (Inside Sea). Here is one of the only places in Brazil where it is possible to see the sunset over the sea, as almost the entire Brazilian coastline faces east.
Conceição Beach is one of the longest stretches of sand of the archipelago and is where the ruins of **Nossa Senhora da Conceição Fort** are to be found. From November to March there are good waves for surfing. The **Boldró,**

Americano, Bode and **Cacimba do Padre** beaches follow one after the other and can be crossed by foot at low tide. Still on this side of Mar de Dentro, the **Porcos Beach**, and its natural swimming pools are located in front of **Morro dos Dois Irmãos**, one of the crags of the archipelago.The **Sancho Beach**, a symbol of the park, is a good place to dive and to swim. Access is gained by means of a stairway descending in the middle of a cleft in the cliffs on the trail that leaves the Praia da Cacimba do Padre Beach. In the extreme south of the island, one of the unique areas of preserved forest is **Ponta do Sapata,** where there are interesting rock outcrops and pools for diving.

Mar de fora ⊘ ⊜

In the **Buraco da Raquel** there are natural swimming pools with rock outcrops. It is normally inhabited by

Spinner dolphins

S pinner Dolphins choose Fernando de Noronha as a place to rest, breed and escape from predators. With a little luck, the visitor who dives in the waters of the archipelago can see and swim beside some of them. Others can be seen jumping and pirouetting – justification for its name as spinner. The somersaults and the sounds, which they emit, is the way that they communicate. The **Baía dos Golfinhos** has the greatest numbers of Spinner Dolphins, which can be seen from the top of the mountain that borders the bay. Dawn is the easiest time to see them and it is prohibited to enter the water. In 1990 the Projeto Golfinho Rotador was created, which monitors the area. ☎ 3619-1295.

Dolphins in a preserved area

Praia do Sancho: access by means of a stairway descending in the middle of a cliff ▶

Birds like the atobá-de-pata-vermelha are found in Noronha

turtles, which can be seen from the neighbouring vantage point at the top of the rocks. It is not permitted to dive here. In front of **Morro do Frade** is **Atalaia Beach**, which forms an enormous natural swimming pool at low tide. Diving expeditions must be scheduled, in order of arrival, with Ibama on the Praia do Sueste. On the calm beach of **Baía do Sueste** there is a mangrove and the Forte de São Joaquim. The shallower stretches are delimited by buoys to protect the corals and it is excellent for free diving.**Leão Beach** is the favourite place of turtles for egg laying.There are reefs bordering the entire stretch of beach.

TIPS

– Be prepared for the steep costs of

hotels and food, on average higher than in other northeastern beaches. It is necessary to pay a daily charge to stay on the island, which increases progressively after the seventh day.

– Access can be achieved from Recife or Natal. Longer routes are also possible; there are flights that leave São Paulo. The boat trip takes one ou two days.

– The dry season occurs from August to December, when the waters are more transparent and better for diving.

– The BR-363 highway, which crosses the main island, is the shortest federal highway in Brazil with 7.5 km.

This is considered one of the best places in Brazil and in the world for diving. There are prep courses for beginners. The waters are warm and clear with excellent visibility.

– Within two hours it is possible to cover the **Trilha Caieira** on foot, passing over all the hillside of Mar de Fora to Pedra Alta. The **Trilha Costa Esmeralda** requires six hours of trekking during the lowest tides. The departure point is the Boldró Beach and the finish is Cacimba do Padre Beach.

Old History

The archipelago was already shown on maps in 1502. In 1504 it was donated to Fernando de Noronha, the sponsor of an exploration expedition, which reached Brazil. In the 17th century it was invaded by the Dutch; and subsequently by the French and even Charles Darwin visited here. The Portuguese built fortifications all over the main island to guarantee possession. In 1938 a prison was installed and the forest was devastated in order to better monitor escape attempts. In the 1940s, during the Second World War, the archipelago was transformed into a military area and used as a base by the navy to support the allied forces.

Finally, in 1988, to assure protection and balance of the ecosystem, the Parque Nacional Marinho de Fernando de Noronha was created and it was reintegrated to Pernambuco.

Ilha de Itamaracá

The island view from the top of Forte Orange

Recife: 50 km
João Pessoa: 122 km
Caruaru: 184 km
👤 15.858
🌐 81
@ www.pernambuco.com/turismo/
itamaraca.html

Ilha de Itamaracá, which in the language of Tupi-guarani Indians means "stone that sings", gave its name to the hereditary captaincy that encompassed the region between Itamaracá and Paraíba. In the 17th century the Dutch, who at that time had captured Pernambuco, built the Forte Orange here, thus named as a tribute to the Dutch royal family. Today Itamaracá is the most important tourist spot on the State's northern coast, and includes from the Centro de Proteção e Pesquisa do Peixe-boi Marinho to churches and baroque constructions from the era of colonial Brazil. To reach Forte Orange there is an access bridge to the island following the only road. The old village settlement was a strategic watchtower of the island during Portuguese colonization. Located at the highest point of Itamaracá, it has a view of the Canal de Santa Cruz between the island and the continent.

HIGHLIGHTS

★ Forte Orange
Estr. do Forte, Praia do Forte.
☎ 3544-1666.. Daily from 9 a.m. to 4:30 p.m. 🏛 🍴
The Dutch originally built it in wattle and daub in 1631. Seized by the Portuguese, it was reformed 23 years later using stonewalls and 13 cannons were installed. The building is in an excellent state of conservation, there are also handicraft shops, a museum telling the history of the fortress and exhibiting objects found during excavations at the fort. From the top of the ramparts there is an observation point of the Ilha Coroa do Avião and the beach.

★ Coroa do Avião
Leaving by the side of Forte Orange ✪ This is a sandbank in front of Ilha de Itamaracá, where the Jaguaribe River meets the sea. It is a resting point for migrating birds and a habitat rich in wildlife. Kiosks sell fish and oysters.

Centro de Preservação do Peixe-boi

◀ **Fernando de Noronha: one of the most beautiful places in Brazil**

By the side of the Forte Orange ☻ 3544-1056 and 3544-4937. ◉ This Ibama Center of Aquatic Mamals cares for manatees, threatened with extinction. The amenities for visitors were increased in 2002 to create a fauna theme park, called Eco-parque Peixe Boi & Cia. There are tanks with animals, explanatory posters and a shop.

Manatees: protected in Itamaracá

SURROUNDINGS

Paulista

25 km from Itamaracá by the BR-101 highway to Maria Farinha enter Igarassu and take the ferry in the village of Nova Cruz. Maria Farinha, Conceição, Pau Amarelo, do Ó and Janga beaches belong to the municipality of **Paulista**. The town is situated between the sea and the Timbó River, which is used for nautical sports. **Maria Farinha** is one of the most traditional summer resorts for Pernambucans, and its name was inspired from a species of crab that is abundant in the region. There are several luxury condominiums along the Canal de Santa Cruz, which cut the beaches into two parts. Veneza **Water Park**, a theme park between the beach and the Timbó River, has water toboggans, swimming pools, river of rapids, saunas and sports courts (Av. Cláudio Gueiros Leite, 10050. ☻ 3466-8845. @ www.venezawaterpark.com.br) The **Praia da Conceição** has a

small chapel that was built in a sugarmill in 1842. In **Pau Amarelo**, a fort from 1719 marks the spot of the first landing of the Dutch in Brazil. It still preserves the original cannons. There is a line of large stalls on the seafront.

TIPS

– Access: To reach Itamaracá by car, follow the BR-101 highway north to the municipality of Igarassu. Subsequently take the secondary road. By bus, Itamaracá Bus Company makes the route departing from Santa Rita – Itamaracá is very close to Recife. For this, on weekends, the town receives many visitors. If you're looking for tranquillity, visit the island during the week. It is possible to fly a microlight between Itamaracá and Maria Farinha with a quick stop at Coroa do Avião.

Forte Orange: tribute to the Dutch royal family

Olinda

Churches, handicrafts, tapioca and frevo: Olinda is history and partying

Recife: 7 km
Caruaru: 150 km
João Pessoa: 120 km
367.902
81
Secretaria de Turismo
3439-9434
www.olinda.pe.gov.br

For its historical wealth, both architectural and cultural, Olinda became protected by the federal government in 1968 and was included in the list of World Heritage Cities in 1982 by Unesco. Since the 1930s, the Instituto do Patrimônio Histórico e Artístico Nacional (Iphan) started the registration process of isolated properties. The buildings from the 17th century conserve their beauty but are adapted to the current Pernambucan culture: the houses are artist's studios, conservatories, bases for Carnival groups, museums, shops and restaurants. It is worthwhile to wander through the narrow streets of the historical center on foot. The tourist guides, principally the children, spread out in search of visitors who wish to know about the

history of the city, taking them to the most important spots. Handicrafts sold in the stalls of the streets represent the scenery of the region: using small slivers of timber, the craftsmen create highly coloured semi-detached houses. The municipal beaches are developed and polluted, at some points, because the coast receives an intense load of waste coming from the Rio Beberibe – even so, at the weekends, the beaches are very busy. Olinda is located 6 km from Recife and 12 km from the Aeroporto de Guararapes.

HIGHLIGHTS

Centro Histórico
The best way to see the historic center is on foot. The start can be from the **Carmo Church**, in the flat part of the city. Be prepared to climb the steep slope of R. de São Francisco and see, on the right, the **São Francisco Church.** On the left, the **Travessa de São Francisco** gives access to R. da Palma and, subsequently there is a gradual slope to the top where the **Sé Church** is located. Take advantage by trying the tapioca prepared in kiosks. The **Nossa Senhora da Graça**

Church is found on R. Bispo Coutinho, the highest point in Olinda, from where there is a view of the entire city and the sea. Continuing down the street to the bottom is Lgo. do Amparo. Here there is **Amparo Church** and soon after **São João Batista dos Militares Church**. Seize the opportunity to visit the artist's studios. The continuation of R. do Amparo is Treze de Maio where the **Contemporary Art Museum** is situated and further on the Square of the city office and **São Bento Monastery**. From there go down the back street on the left, 15 de Novembro and arrive at **Eufrásio Barbosa Market.** Returning along R. do Amparo, turn left on R. Prudente de Moraes and take the second on the left, Bernardo Vieira de Melo to visit **Ribeira Market**.

★ Igreja da Sé

Alto da Sé. Daily from 8 to 12 a.m. and 1 to 5 p.m. ☎ 3429-0627.
The city blocks are organized in circles around the Sé Church and the façades of the other churches face this church too. Founded in 1537, it was the first parochial of the Northeast and since 1676 it is the cathedral of the archdiocese of Olinda and Recife. It was torched and has been rebuilt on several occasions. From the top of Sé it is possible to see the cities of Olinda and Recife together. It is also called Igreja do Senhor Salvador do Mundo. Surrounding, in the **Pça. do**

The Old City

"Oh what a delightful setting to build a citadel", Duarte Coelho, the first Portuguese landlord of the captaincy of Pernambuco, is reported to have said, on seeing the site for the first time in 1535. With the establishment of convents, monasteries and a Jesuit College, the settlement continued to grow, stimulated by the wealth generated by sugarcane. Here the first Law school of Brazil was founded. In 1630, Olinda was invaded and torched by the Dutch, remaining inactive for 24 years. In 1676 the diocese of Olinda was established, thus creating a city, which was the State capital until 1827.

Buildings from the 17th century

Convento de São Francisco, the oldest in Brazil

Giant puppets announce the arrival of the "frevo" dance groups

The extended Carnival of Olinda

Olinda Carnival begins one week before the official starting date. On the Saturday before the start of the festival, the merrymakers are already on the streets to 'brincar o carnaval' as it is normal to say. The partying only finishes on the Friday after Ash Wednesday. Craftsmen become involved in the production of the Carnival costumes and the adornments during months, decorating the streets and houses. *Frevo* dance groups and the Afro-Brazilian dance groups of *maracatus* are traditional. The slopes are occupied by people dressed in gigantic costumes of about 3 meters in height made from papier mâché on wire frames, which draw the *frevo* dance groups. There are traditional groups such as the Virgens do Bairro Novo, in which the men dress up as women, as well as the Elefante, Potombeira dos Quatro Cantos, Vassourinhas, Homem da Meia Noite and Saudade. On Wednesday it is the turn of the waiters of Olinda who parade in Bacalhau do Batata. The so-called 'quatro cantos de Olinda' is on the corner of Ladeira da Misericórdia with R. Prudente de Morais. It is here that the groups meet to warm up for the party. Near Eufrásio Barbosa and Ribeira markets the attraction is the *maracatu* nation. Also called 'baque virado' the rhythm emerged from the influence of the Negroes, Indians and the Portuguese. A variation, which occurs in the interior of Pernambuco, is the rural maracutu, also called 'orquestra' or 'baque solto'. The men, normally farmhands, use bright-colored clothes.

Alto da Sé, there are handicraft shops and kiosks that sell tapioca.

★ Igreja e Convento Nossa Senhora das Neves

R. de São Francisco, 280. ☎ 3429-0517. Monday to Friday, from 8 to 12 a.m. and from 2 to 5 p.m. and Saturday from 8 to 12 a.m.
The construction of the convent was initiated in 1585. The building was destroyed by the Dutch and restored by the Portuguese in the 18th century.

Notable are the São Roque, Noviços, Santa Ana and Capítulo chapels. The entire Franciscan complex calls the attention due to the perfection of the detailsand peculiarities.

Igreja e Mosteiro de São Bento

R. São Bento. ☎ 3429-3288. Monday to Friday, from 6:30 to 11:30 a.m. and from 2 to 6:30 p.m. Weekends, from 6:30 to 11:30 a.m. and from 2 to 5:30 p.m.

Bright colors, perukes and 'batucada' in 'maracatu' of Olinda ▶

This was the second Benedictine Monastery built on Brazilian soil dating from the 16th century.
The church is known as one of the richest of Olinda and it has on its façade a majestic coat of arms, as well as the bell tower from the 18th century. On Sundays at 10 a.m. there are presentations of Gregorian Choir Singing.

Igreja Nossa Senhora da Graça e Seminário de Olinda

R. Bispo Coutinho. ☎ 3429-0627. Monday to Friday, from 8 to 12 a.m. and 2 to 5 p.m. Entrance: free. ⬤
Situated at the highest point of the city, from where all the churches and buildings of the historic center can be seen and, in the background, the sea and Recife. The seminary was the old Jesuit royal college and it conserves the architecture of the 16th century.

Mercado da Ribeira

R. Bernardo Vieira de Melo. Open daily from 9 to 12 a.m. ☎ 3231-7128. ⬤
This was where slave trading took place. Today stalls sell handicrafts such as carnival masks, parasols used in the *frevo* dance and T-shirts.

Mercado Eufrásio Barbosa

Av. Sigismundo Gonçalves. ☎ 439-1415. Monday to Saturday, From 9 a.m. to 6 p.m. ⬤
This is also called Mercado do Varadouro and it brings together handicrafts and has cultural presentations. This building was the first customs house of Pernambuco.

Museu de Arte Contemporânea de Pernambuco (MAC)

R. 13 de maio, 149. ☎ 3429-2587. Tuesday to Friday, from 9 a.m. to 1 p.m. weekends, from 2 to 5 p.m. ⬤ ⬤
The building was constructed to house the ecclesiastic prison, where prisoners served sentences for religious crimes. Since 1996 it lodges a permanent art exhibition of Pernambucan artists.In front, in the **São Pedro Advíncola Chapel**, masses for the convicts were held.

Sete Nichos ⬤

During Easter week, large gates, called recesses, which exist between the houses are opened. There are seven of them in diverse points of the historic center, where chapels used on procession days are situated.

TIPS . . . .

– The taxi fare from Recife to Olinda can turn out to be more expensive than you would imagine. It is considered an inter-municipal trip, which is a higher rate (bandeira 2), than the normal rate, within city limits.

Carnival: only a giant puppet can hide the façade of Igreja da Sé

Petrolina

Petrolina is one of the world's most important fruit producers

Recife: 760 km
Salvador: 500 km
Feira de Santana: 441 km
218,538
87
Prefeitura
3862-2001.
www.petrolina.pe.gov.br
ferry from Juazeiro

Petrolina is blessed with the São Francisco River. The tourist activities and the economy are based around it, which has made Petrolina the biggest city of the Pernambuco backlands. One bridge spans the river and links Pernambuco with the municipality of Juazeiro in Bahia. The dry soil and high temperatures of the backlands changed after the arrival of irrigation technology. The water, drawn from the São Francisco River, is taken by canals to the farms. Data from 2001 reveal that the region is one of the world's most important fruit producers with a cultivated area of 12,000 km².

HIGHLIGHTS

Catedral de Petrolina

Pça. D. Malan. Monday to Friday, from 6 to 12 a.m. and from 3 to 6 p.m. Saturday, from 6 to 11:30 a.m. and from 6 to 9 p.m. Sunday, from 6:30 to 10 a.m. and from 4:30 to 9 p.m.
Inaugurated in 1929, it has a large set of French stained glass windows and a clock tower given by Father Cícero (*read Juazeiro do Norte, on Ceará*).

Museu do Sertão

Pça. Santos Dumont. 3862-1943. Open daily from 10 a.m. to 6 p.m.

The billy goat on the table

The goat is part of the scenery of the backlands. Be it on the roads, in the *caatinga*, or the sound of the bell hanging from its neck, it is an image from the *sertanejo's* life. Billy and nanny goats and kids are also present in the cuisine. In Petrolina the 'Bodódromo' is a place, which brought together restaurants specialized in goat dishes.

Established in 1973 and reconstructed in 1996, the exhibits include a portrait of diverse aspects of the Sertão: fauna, flora, household utensils, old photographs of the city.

Rio São Francisco ◐

Av. Cardoso de Sá, which runs alongside the river, became one of the main neighborhoods of the city. Besides the bars, restaurants and a promenade, there is the so-called 'gate to the river', an event center that brings together restaurants, bars and venues for shows. High-rise buildings are beginning to be constructed.
The Presidente Dutra Bridge unites the cities of Petrolina and Juazeiro. The crossing can also be made by ferry.

Centro de Arte e Cultura Ana das Carrancas

R. Barão de Boa Vista, 115. BR-407, 500, Cohab Massangano. ☎ 3863-6061.
Monday to Friday, from 8 a.m. to 5 p.m. Entrance: free 🅲
The artist known as 'Dama do Barro' innovated the art of sculpturing figureheads. Instead of using wood, Ana Leopoldina dos Santos uses clay. Her husband, who is blind, is entrusted with preparing the raw material, removing the impurities. In his honor, Ana makes the eyes of the images hollow, a registered mark of her work. In the Center there are also sculptures from other artists of the region.

Ilha do Rodeadouro

The vessels depart from the Estr. da Tapera ◐ 🚢
One of the islands on the São Francisco

Grape, one of the most successful cultures

River, Rodeadouro has bars together with a fluvial beach. To reach the island it is necessary to catch a boat – the trip takes only ten minutes.

TIPS

– Do not forget to try the *surubim*, a freshwater fish prepared with coconut sauce and butter, which is served with rice and puree. It can be smoked, dried or fresh; baked or barbecued.
– The roads near to Petrolina suffer from a high rate of hold-ups.
It is preferable to arrive by aeroplane so as not to be inconvenienced.One of the worst stretches is between Cabrobó and Petrolina, on the BR-428 highway.

The figureheads of São Francisco

Between 1880 and 1950 figureheads were fixed on the bows of vessels, which navigated along the São Francisco River. They had two functions: the first was to keep away the bad spirits and so protect the trip, and the second was to attract fish to the shade that the carvings produced on the water. To keep away the evil, the figurehead required strong features, with enormous teeth and a frightening look. They were painted in red, black and white, or left in the natural color of the wood used for the carving.

The tradition of putting them on boats was slowly lost and with time, they started to be used as ornaments. Sculptured in wood or clay, in all sizes, they are found in Petrolina and in many other northeastern cities.

To keep away the bad spirits

Porto de Galinhas

Rafts at high seas: ten minute to arrive at natural swimming pools

Recife: 60 km
Maceió: 230 km
Caruaru: 194 km
 59,281 (Distrito de Ipojuca)
 81
 Secretaria de Turismo. 3552-1480.
@ www.portodegalinhas.com.br

The south coast of Recife is one of the best-equipped areas to welcome visitors. Cabo de Santo Agostinho, Tamandaré and Porto de Galinhas beaches are part of a region christened the Costa Dourada. The best-rated stretch is that of Porto de Galinhas, the most famous beach of the municipality of Ipojuca. Maracaípe, Cupe, Muro Alto and Serrambi beaches are also included.
In 1850 it was prohibited for the slave ships to land in the Porto do Recife. To escape inspection, the smugglers found a nearby landing site to the south. The ships carried both guinea fowl and slaves. The password used to notify everyone of the arrival of the 'goods' was: there is 'galinha nova' (new hen) in the port! And so the old settlement of Porto Rico or Praia do Porto became known as Porto de Galinhas.

HIGHLIGHTS

★ Porto de Galinhas
In front of the beach there is the **Pça. do Artesanato,** with stalls that sell clothes, accessories and souvenirs.
In the same place there is a stall of the Associação dos Bugueiros where trips to the neighboring beaches are organized (3552-1160). The trips are best at low tide as the buggies go very close to the sand. The raft sailors are also present and provide trips to the natural swimming pools. The trip itself takes about ten minutes by raft to the reefs, which form natural pools, and included is a stop for swimming and wandering over the corals. It is possible to swim to some pools. Check the times of the tides and only go at low tide. The pools and the band of sand practically disappear when the level of the sea is high. At the weekends and during the high season the beach becomes busier. In the main streets of the village there are galleries with shops and restaurants.

Vila de Nossa Senhora do Ó
Situated at 9 km from downtown Porto de Galinhas
The village has as its main charm the

Nossa Senhora do Ó Church, built in 1780 in the baroque style and a 350-year-old baobab tree *(Adansonia digitata)* of 15 meters in diameter brought from Africa by slaves.

Praia de Cupe

Located 5 km to the north of Porto de Galinhas.

Reefs run alongside of some stretches and coconut trees follow practically the entire seafront. Most of the beach, however, is unprotected and is thus good for surfing. There are many hotels.

Praia de Muro Alto

Found 8 km to the north of Porto de Galinhas, after the Praia de Cupe.
Access is gained by buggy or on foot by a dirt track passing the Praia de Cupe. There are natural swimming pools formed by the reefs and a high wall of white sand, which gives the beach its name. It is delightful and good for swimming. It also gives access to Gamboa Beach, which has pools too, and mangroves.

★ Praia de Maracaípe

Situated at 3km to the south of Porto de Galinhas
The name, in the language of the Tupi Indians, means 'river that sings'. However, the river, which sang when it hit the roots of the trees, was diverted for the construction of roads. Much

less bustling than Porto de Galinhas, the beach is well visited by surfers. In **Pontal de Maracaípe** there are natural swimming pools and it is where the mouth of the Rio Maracaípe is located surrounded by mangroves.

Praia de Serrambi

Found at 15km to the south of Porto de Galinhas.
To reach this beach it is necessary to enter in closed condominiums where there are holiday cottages. Access is gained by a dirt track in good condition surrounded by sugarcane plantations. A headland splits the **Ponta do Serrambi** in two parts: on one side the sea is calm and on the other it is good for surfing. In front, Santo Aleixo Island completes the view. In 1998 the first deliberate shipwreck of the country happened near here. The scrapping of the 50-meter long tug Marte was performed 12 km from the coast of Serrambi.

SURROUNDINGS

Tamandaré

Situated at 75 km from Porto de Galinhas by the PE-60 highway to the south.
Tamandaré beaches have a promenade with kiosks near to a small ribbon of sand and reefs. The **Casa do Artesão**, established in the old meat market sells local handicrafts. **Santo Forte Inácio de**

At low tide, a buggy trip to the north beaches is the best option

The discovery of Pinzón

The Cabo de Santo Agostinho competes with Porto Seguro for the title of the first Brazilian soil to be touched by European feet. According to some documents, on January 26, 1500 – and so before the arrival of the Portuguese – the Spanish navigator Vicente Pinzón, commanding three caravels disembarked in this part of the continent and carved his name on several tree trunks, as proof of his presence. Because of the Tratado de Tordesilhas, from 1494, these lands belonged to Portugal, obliging the Spanish to give up their claim of the lands. In April, Pedro Álvares Cabral and his fleet arrived on the coast of Bahia and officially discovered Brazil. The municipality today is investing to recover the history of Pinzón. At the access of the PE-60 highway there is a Pinzón monument.

Loyola and the **Farol** are found on the **Boca da Barra Beach**. The municipalities of Tamandaré, Sirinhaém, Rio Formoso and Barreiros compose the Environmental Protection Area Guadalupe. The objective is to guarantee the preservation of the reefs, mangroves, Atlantic forest, and *restinga* forest by teaching both locals and visitors, with lectures and other information. (Av. José Bezerra de Melo Sobrinho, 1009, Alvorada, Tamandaré. ☎ 3676-1177). Notable is the **Carneiros Beach** where Formoso River flows into the sea, favoring swimming both in the river and sea. There are a few bars, many holiday homes and small farms nearthe beach. Coconut palm-trees are found along all the stretch of sand and the water is green and very clear. After Formoso River starts the municipality of Sirinhaém and following this is Santo Aleixo Island.

Cabo de Santo Agostinho

Located at 50km from Porto de Galinhas by the BR-101 and PE-60 highways. 🏖️🍴🏨🅿️

The oldest buildings are found in the suburb of Nazaré. The **Nossa Senhora do Nazaré Church** was built at the top of a hill in 1597. Masses are celebrated on Saturdays at 7:30 p.m. At the side are the ruins of a convent of the Carmelite Order, built in 1692. At this spot there is a panoramic view of the sea and the ruins of **Castelo do Mar Fort**, built of granite stones in the 17th century. **Paraíso Beach** is a spot of fishermen, warm transparent waters and a panoramic view of the Enseada de Suape and Tatuoca and Cocaia Islands. More rustic and more difficult to reach are **Gaibu** and **Calhetas** beaches, with access by a dirt track with many slopes and the final stretch is covered on foot. **Calhetas** is a small beach with a narrow band of sand, formed of two coves separated by a line of rocks. It is good for fishing and diving. In the past it served as a safe port for the Portuguese troops who fought against the Dutch. It has white sands, warm transparent water, natural swimming pools and it is good for surfing.

TIPS

– Access: to reach Porto de Galinhas follow the BR-101 highway south and take the PE-60 road. Buses leave from the bus station in Recife directly to Porto de Galinhas passing by the airport. ☎ 3527-9118.

Ruins of the Forte Castelo do Mar

PARAÍBA

PARAÍBA

In South America, the sun rises first in Paraíba. Ponta do Seixas is near the State capital, João Pessoa, and is the most easterly point of continental Brazil. To the north, Paraiba, (56,584 sq km) borders with Rio Grande do Norte; to the south, with Pernambuco. Ceará is on the west border and the Atlantic Ocean washes its 147 km against the eastern shoreline. Tourism is still very incipient; lucky Paraibanos, who have to themselves some of the nicest urban beaches in Brazil, the jolliest São João celebrations and the first, officially recognized, nudist beach in Northeastern Brazil. In Barra de Mamanguape is one of Projeto Peixe-boi manatee protection centers, where the most endangered aquatic animal in Brazil is cared for and studied. Recently, the last stretch of PB-008 road was opened. It runs along the south coast from João Pessoa. BR-101 goes north. Some parts are not in good condition, and maybe for this reason, beaches along those stretches are still relatively unspoiled. In Cabedelo, not far from João Pessoa, the Transamazônica highway (BR-230) begins. It cuts through Paraíba from east to west, and up into the Northern parts of Brazil. Vegetation throughout Paraíba is predominantly brushwood. It is a flat State with altitudes that vary from sea level in Cabedelo, to a maximum 1,197 m on Pico do Jabre, in Teixeira. Because the Equator is so close, it is very hot, and there are no great thermal variances. Average yearly temperatures are around 25°C. Rainfall is irregular, and the heaviest showers happen between February and July. In the early days of colonization, Paraíba was part of the province of Itamaracá, which now is the name of a town in Pernambuco. Sugarcane was the State's first large scale crop and still plays an important role in the economy.

◀ Grand June Festival in Campina Grande: considered the liveliest in northeastern Brazil

SERRA DA
ARARUNA

PARAÍBA

PLANALTO DA BORBOREMA

Mataraca
Praia Barra de Camaratuba
Baía da Traição
Mamanguape
Lucena

Rio Tinto

Cabedelo
Ponta do Seixas
JOÃO PESSOA
Conde
Praia de Tabatinga

Praia de Coqueirinho

Praia de Tambaba

Areia

Campina Grande

Ingá

Queimadas

Cabaceiras

Paraíba

Gramame

QUEBRADA

MACEIÓ

N
W   E
S

0   64   126 km

Highlights

❶ João Pessoa
❷ Tambaba
❸ Campina Grande

LEGENDS

National park
Paved road
Dirt track

João Pessoa

Tree lined streets and quite beaches in João Pessoa

Recife: 115km
Natal: 180km
Maceió: 351km
👤 597.934
🌐 (83)
ℹ️ Pbtur ☎ 226-7078.
@ www.pbtur.pb.gov.br

The city has a well-preserved colonial court and housing complex and is the perfect destination for those seeking nice, quiet urban beaches. Beach-goers are mostly locals and people who live inland. Trees line practically all the streets and provide friendly and welcome shade from the hot sun. João Pessoa was recognized by the United Nations as being the greenest city in the Americas. Its tree-planted parks and what is left of the State's tropical rainforest reserves also contributed to such a distinction. Moreover, a municipal decree disallows any building within 150 m of the shoreline to be over four stories high. Thanks to the fertile land the region was ideal for sugarcane planting which began in the 16th century.

HIGHLIGHTS

Capela de Santa Teresa, Igreja do Carmo, Palácio do Bispo

Pça. D. Adalto, Downtown.
🌐 221-7817. Monday to Saturday from 2:30 to 5:30 p.m.

The Order of the Carmelite temple became a convent in the 19th century. Its Baroque façade has limestone details. On the opposite side of the square, stands an old mansion with a Portuguese tile front that used to belong to an important citizen.

Casa da Pólvora

Ladeira de São Francisco, Downtown.
Monday to Friday from 8 to 12 a.m. and from 1 to 5 p.m. Entrance: free.

Baroque Santa Teresa church

Built in 1710 to store gun powder and weapons belonging to the Paraíba troops. It was restored in 1979 and now houses the Walfredo Rodrigues Photography Museum with many pictures of João Pessoa of the past.

Catedral Basílica Nossa Senhora das Neves

Av. General Osório, Historic Center. 221-2503. Monday to Friday from 2 to 6 p.m. Saturday from 2 to 8 p.m. and Sunday from 6 a.m. to 8 p.m.
João Pessoa's first church was built in 1586 and has undergone 4 restoration projects. It stands near Pça. Antenor Navarro, where some of the town's best restaurants are concentrated.

★ Convento e Igreja Franciscana de Santo Antônio

Pça. São Francisco, Historic Center. 218-4505', wwwsaofrancisco@uol.com.br. Monday from 2 to 5 p.m. Tuesday to Sunday from 9 to 12 a.m. and from 2 to 6 p.m.
This beautiful monastery was built in 1589 and since 1636 is the seat of the government. In 1734 the church plaza was tiled with pictures of the 14 stations on the way to the cross. The biggest cross in South America also stands in this plaza. The ceiling of the church is painted in strong blues, reds and gold. Inside the church is the Gold Chapel, the São Benedito Chapel, and a religious art collection.

Igreja São Pedro Gonçalves

Lgo. São Pedro Gonçalves, Historic Center. 221-6393. Tuesday to Saturday from 2 to 6 p.m. Sunday from 8.30 to 12 a.m.
Situated in the upper section, along the passage that connects Porto do Capim and downtown. The saint this church is named after is the protector of all seafaring men. On the same square, the old Globo Hotel was built

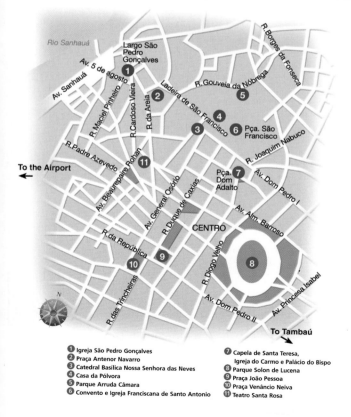

1. Igreja São Pedro Gonçalves
2. Praça Antenor Navarro
3. Catedral Basílica Nossa Senhora das Neves
4. Casa da Pólvora
5. Parque Arruda Câmara
6. Convento e Igreja Franciscana de Santo Antonio
7. Capela de Santa Teresa, Igreja do Carmo e Palácio do Bispo
8. Parque Solon de Lucena
9. Praça João Pessoa
10. Praça Venâncio Neiva
11. Teatro Santa Rosa

João Pessoa is assassinated

The first name of João Pessoa was Filipéia, after the head of the then joint sovereignty Spain and Portugal, King Philip. St. Philip is also the town's patron saint. It was the third township in Brazil to become a city, after Salvador and Rio de Janeiro. When the Dutch invaded Northeastern regions of Brazil in 1630, they also took Filipéia and changed its name to Frederica, in honor of their own monarch. After they were expelled, a few years later, its name was changed again; this time to Parahyba, which in the Tupi language means 'river not easy to navigate'. Then it was renamed again, this time after João Pessoa, the popular State Governor assassinated in 1930. He had became prominent on the national political scene in 1928, when he was indicated by his uncle and ex-President Epitácio Pessoa, to be Getúlio Vargas' Vice-President in the 1929 elections, in opposition to the candidate Julio Prestes of the São Paulo and Minas Gerais oligarchies, which had always won the elections. Getúlio Vargas was from Rio Grande do Sul. He lost the elections, but the alliance that had backed him challenged the outcome. The time was ripe for confrontation; and the murder of João Pessoa, who was in Recife at the time, ignited the fuse of a military revolt that quickly spread from the south, where it began, all over the country, that brought Getúlio Vargas into power. The era of the New Republic had begun and Getúlio kept himself in office for 15 years.

◀ Statue of João Pessoa

at the end of the 1920s, but was transformed into the João Pessoa Historical Center Revitalization Committee headquarters.

Praça Venâncio Neiva and Praça João Pessoa
Historical Center. 🖰
On one of the corners of Venâncio Neiva square, stands what is known as the Pavilhão do Chá or tea pavilion that was built, with oriental architectural touches, in 1928. In the middle of the square is a bandstand. Next to this square is another that was named after João Pessoa, but is also known as Praça dos Três Poderes as this is where the state Legislative Assembly, the Governor's Palace and the Palace of Justice are concentrated.

Teatro Santa Rosa
Praça Pedro Américo, Historic Center.
☎ 218-4384. Daily from 2 to 5 p.m. Entrance: Free. 🖰
This theater, still used, was built in 1887. In the center of the square is the bust of painter Pedro Américo.

Parque Solon de Lucena
In the center of João Pessoa there is a lake around which imperial palm trees were planted. It is one of the most traditional and characteristic picture postcard scenes of the city.

Espaço Cultural José Lins do Rego
R. Abdias de Almeida, 800, Tambauzinho. ☎ 244-1360. Monday to Friday from 8 to 12 a.m. and from 2 to 5 p.m.; Saturday and Sunday from 2 to 6 p.m. 🖰
In this imposing complex, homage is paid to Paraibano writer and novelist José Lins do Rego. It is built on three levels, and has a planetarium, two theaters, a cinema and art gallery and a library. Also a museum with a good collection of the writer's memorabilia.

Mercado de Artesanato Paraibano – MAP

Av. Rui Carneiro, 241, Tambaú.
☎ 247-3135. Monday to Saturday
from 9 a.m. to 7 p.m.;
Sunday from 9 a.m. to 5 p.m. 🏛 ⬤
Over a hundred stalls fill this three
story building, that offers visitors an
excellent infrastructure and great
variety of handicrafts, lace and stitch
work, pottery and ceramic artefacts.

Parque Arruda Câmara

R. Gouveia Nóbrega, Roger.
☎ 241-1382. Daily from 8 a.m. to 5 p.m. ⬤
This park has a mini-zoo, short trails
and is where the municipal
horticulture and tree nursery are kept.
Legend has it that the spring of
Tambiá fountain, built in 1782, from
which the park gets its nickname
"Bica" was started because of the
many years of tears shed by an Indian
girl, after the loss of her beloved.

Beaches ⬤ ⬤

Starting from Av. João Maurício, the
first beach to the north is **Bessa**. It is
not as urbanized as other beaches.
The next beach is **Manaíra** with sports
courts and standardized beach stalls.
A small part of it is appropriate for
bathing. A little further on is **Tambaú**,
from where boats leave for
Picãozinho, where there are natural
pools when the tide is very low. On
Av. Almirante Tamandaré, in front of
the Tambaú Hotel, is a handicraft
market. Av. Epitácio Pessoa separates
Tambaú from **Cabo Branco**. Every
day, between 5 and 8 a.m. Cabo
Branco Ave. becomes exclusively
pedestrian. When the tide is out,

Pça. Antenor Navarro: Historical Center

natural pools are formed along the
beach. To the south and on a hill,
the black and white Farol do Cabo
Branco can be seen. From up there
is the best view of **Ponta do Seixas**.
From here, via PB-018 road south and
a dirt road, one reaches the last João
Pessoa district beach called **Barra de
Gramame** and its fhishing village.
The river that runs into the sea at
this points, changes the shapes of the
sand banks that are formed there.

SURROUNDINGS

Cabedelo

25 km to the north of João Pessoa
by BR-230. ⬤ ⬤
The first beach in Cabedelo, 10 km
from João Pessoa, is **Intermares**, good
for surfing and also known as Praia
dos Macacos. A little further on is
Areia Vermelha. At ebbtide, sand
banks that look like red tinged island
because of coralline and calcareous

Camaçari Beach: before the river reaches the sea, it runs along the cliffs

algae are left behind. **Camboinha Beach** is one kilometer further on, with a little anchorage. A narrow dirt road leads on to the next beach, **Formosa**, a fishermen's haunt, from the beacon of **Cabedelo** can be seen. **Jacaré**, on the mouth of the Paraiba River is the best river beach in Cabedelo. But because the many marinas along this stretch of the river, and so the water is not good for swimming. At the point where the Paraiba River waters join the sea, is the **Santa Catarina** fort, built in the 16th century. Due to its strategic location, both French and Dutch garrisons tried to take it in the early colonial days. There is also an escape tunnel, and visits are monitored by guides.

Lucena

58 km north of João Pessoa or a 25-minute ferryboat ride from Cabedelo.

Carapibus: sea cliffs and natural pools

Not far from Santa Catarina Fort is the Cabedelo Port, from where one can get across to Lucena. **Nossa Senhora da Guia Church** is the first place of interest there. It was built in the 16th century atop a hill from where there is a fantastic view of the Paraiba and ocean waters meeting out at sea. Next come the **Fagundes** and **Gamaleira** beaches, and **Ponta de Lucena**, where, when the tide is low, one can walk out seaward, on long sandbanks. Then comes Lucena, with its weekend houses and fishermen's huts. At **Camaçari Beach**, two rivers meet before they join the sea: Miriri and Camaçari. They are outlined by high cliffs and crags, and the dark water flows along the shore and then out to sea. **Nossa Senhora do Bonsucesso Church** ruins can be reached via a trail that starts in Camaçari, or by car, along a very precarious dirt road. The next beach is **Oiteira**, with high cliffs all along it.

Barra de Mamanguape

84 km north of João Pessoa. As far as Km 51 of BR-101 and then another 30 km along an earth road. From Campina, it is the next beach. The highlight is the Manatee Project and research center which shelters animals that have run aground or were injured. They are kept in tanks at the base until they are well enough to return to their natural environment. Visitors can see them during jangada

Fortaleza Santa Catarina: 16th century building ▶

raft rides around the river mouth. ☎
228-3865, peixeboipb@uol.com.br.

Rio Tinto

80 km of João Pessoa on BR-101. ✺
Half way up the north seacoast, Rio
Tinto was founded by Germans after
World War II. They started the Rio
Tinto textile company and built the
Santa Rita de Cassia Church. The
brick houses contrast sharply with the
rest of the scenery and neighbouring
town infrastructures. Another 20 km
ahead is **Tramantaia**, an Indian
reserve with small villages along the
banks of the Mamanguape River.
Their hamlets are separated one from
the other also by the passages that
lead to the neighboring beaches. In
Trincheira, known as Prainha as
well, sand islands appear at low tide,
and at one point, the reef prevents
land erosion by the sea. **Baia da
Traição** is the biggest town in these
parts. Next comes **Praia do Forte**
with its cliff barriers. In **Barra do
Camaratuba** the river flows into a
sea which is good for surfing.

Conde

22 km of beaches. Access via PB-008
that runs along the coast. ✺
Rugged cliffs are the main
characteristic all down the Southern
shoreline. Crossing the Gramame
River to Conde, there is a short stretch
of hard dirt road that leads to **Mirante
do Gramame**. It continues to **Praia
do Amor**, where reefs, not far out,
form the shape of a heart. A little
further on is **Jacumã Beach** and the
cliffs disappear. A river, which is not
perennial, marks the beginning of the
next beach which is **Carapibus**.
Along this stretch the cliffs begin to
rise again. Small natural pools are
formed along the reefs. In **Tabatinga**
the scenery changes. There are two
bays; in one, the water of a lake flows
into the sea and in the other, cliffs
fringe the shoreline. **Coqueirinho
Beach** has a long stretch of sand and
is good water for swimming. The
cliffs that rise up in some stretches
are covered in vegetation and
sometimes canyons have been
formed. At one point on the cliff's
edge is Dedo de Deus (God's finger)
with a beautiful view over both
Coqueirinho and Tabatinga.

TIPS

– In João Pessoa, on the Wednesday
that precedes Carnival, a band called
Muriçocas do Miramar opens the
street dancing known as Folias de
Rua. It is known as Fire Wednesday.

Campina Grande

Stalls and Forró of the Grand June Festival in Campina Grande

João Pessoa: 120km
Caruaru: 160km
Recife: 180km
👤 355,331
🌐 83
ℹ️ City Hall ☎ 321-7717
@ www.pmcg.pb.gov.br
🚗😊😊😊

It is located in the barren, rocky, hinterland of Paraíba, on the Borborema plateau. In the 1930's, when art déco was fashionable, it also reached the backlands of Northeastern Brazil where it was given a local dressing. It was nicknamed déco sertanejo or déco for the countryman. Several houses built in this style can still be seen in Campina Grande. The highlight in the Campina Grande calendar are the festivities in June. They attract a public of over one million during the 30 days of fun and dancing.

HIGHLIGHTS

★ Festa Junina 🎪
The commemorations last from the first to the last day of the month, and are concentrated around a huge 42,000 sq m. area called Parque do Povo's inaugurated in 1999. Around 300 stalls sell regional food and beverages. Everything is decorated in the typical peasant fashion. *Forró* music provides the rhythm and entertainment throughout the festival and is made by small bands that have basically three instruments: a big bass drum called zabumba, the triangle and an accordion – that can also have a singer. Couples dance all night long to the two by two step. From the original *forró* music, many variations sprung, such as the *xote*, *xaxado* and the *baião*. In Campina Gande, as popular and characteristic as the *forró* is the quadrilha (square dance) where couples form a circle and then follow in the steps of a leader. On certain days of the festival, there is a train called 'Trem do Forró' that does the 1 hour and 15-minute trip between Campina Grande and Galante, a neighboring town. At the end of the day, the train returns to Campina, always to the sound of *forró* music. www.forronet.com.br

Lajedo do Pai Mateus: nature's rock sculptures ▶

Tabatinga: two kinds of bay ▶

SURROUNDINGS

Cabaceiras

69 km from Campina Grande or 183 km from João Pessoa, via PB-148.

The first settlers arrived in Cabeceiras during the 17th century. Downtown houses is the same as they used to be in the 18th and early 19th century. It is one of the most arid regions in Brazil and the economy is based on palm trees and goat breeding. Because this animal is so important for the livelihood of the population, a special commemoration was introduced in 1999 called Festa do Bode Rei or billy goat king festival. It is commemorated for 3 days in June, when people decorate their goats and sheeps. In Ribeira, about 14 km from Cabeceiras, artisans have formed a tannery cooperative called Arteza (☎ 356-9035, artezaribeira@bol.com.br; Monday to Friday from 8 a.m. to 5 p.m) to make hand-made hats, bags and carpets of the leather they produce. Lajedo do Pai Mateus is 22 km from Cabeceiras via an unmarked dirt road. There is a granite slab with over 100 boulders on it, that have been sculptured by wind and weather. Between one boulder and the other, there are beautiful views of the green and brown hues of the Borborema valleys. Prehistoric rock drawings found around this area are being studied. One can get to the foot of the hill by car and then walk up, in around 15 minutes. Another way to get up there is taking the 3 km trail that starts at the Hotel Fazenda Pai Mateus.

★ Pedra do Ingá

50 km from Campina Grande, at the Km 118 exit of BR-230.

It is a rock slab that is 23 m long and 3 m high with prehistoric inscriptions that are believed to have been made 2500 and 6000 years ago. They are in low relief and research on them has only recently begun. Some figures seem to resemble people, fruit and animals. Other figures are believed to be forms to measure time, like calendars. The Ingá River runs pastthese inscriptions and in its rock bed, are circular cavities with different depths and sizes that the water flows over. Areas surrounding the rock and the river are fenced in, and there is a museum that shows fossils, extinct mammals like the giant sloth and armadillo, and also Indian artifacts made of stone, that were all found around there. ☎ 394-1216.

TIPS

– Campina Grande has a Carnival (Micarante) which happens in April, not necessarily at Carnival time.
– In the town of Souza, 325 km from Campina Grande, there are vestiges of dinosaurs. In the Rio do Peixe Valley there is a 50-meter strip where dinosaur tracks, that date back 120 million years, can plainly be seen. Access is via BR-230.

Tambaba

The first official naturist beach to get State support

João Pessoa: 25km
Recife: 121km
Campina Grande: 148km
👤 16,413 (cidade do Conde)
🌐 83
ℹ Secretaria de Turismo de Conde.
☎ 290-1886
@ www.tambaba.com.br
🚌

Tambaba Beach is a reference along the south coast of Paraíba ever since a naturist society was officially formed and made it their refuge. It is the first of its kind to get State support. The beach is in the Conde district and is reached via PB-008 road, that links João Pessoa with all south-end beaches.

HIGHLIGHTS

Tambaba 🗸
On the way to Tambaba is a view spot that overlooks the ocean. Tambaba itself, is divided into four parts; area "A" is basically a car park: in area "B" nudism is optional; "C" and "D" areas are exclusively for naturists, with a few more sentries to ensure order and that

rules are followed. Regulations are especially strict when there are many visitors, like on weekends and during the summer months. Short trails running along the embankments link one area with another.

South shores
Access via PB-008 🗸
Many rivers flow into the sea south

Green-blue sea along the south shores ▶

Naturism

Beautiful and secluded Tambaba Beach started to be visited by naturists in 1991, and later became the first official naturist beach in the Northeast, and the second of its kind in Brazil. More than being a place where everyone walks around naked, naturism involves a philosophy and intends to encourage respect for oneself, for one's fellow people and respect for Nature. Naturists also believe that their way of behavior leads to a greater harmony with man's natural surroundings. To organize and defend the interests of its members, a society was formed in 1996, known as Naturist Society of Tambaba (Sonata). For such an enterprise and

Naturists follow rules

its facilities, the beaches and their surroundings are ideal; the hills and cliffs that stretch off the coast act as a shield from curious on lookers and unwelcome visitors, and safeguard the privacy of the society's members.

of **Tambaba Beach**. That entire coastline has ideal spots for those seeking a quiet refuge. These rivers cannot be crossed and there are still no ferries. For this reason it's best to go further along PB-008. At **Barra de Garaú**, the dirt road is very bad and only jeeps and buggies get by. It is a 15-minute ride. The **Garaú River**, which is winding and dangerous for swimming, separates Conde and Pitumba districts. Pitumba village, with some summer homes, is about 30 km south of Tambaba and has a central beach; also **Bela**

Beach which is deserted, and has many coconut trees. A little further down is the mouth of the **Mucatu River** and **Mucatu Beach**. Its waters are dark. The few snack stalls there only open during the summer months. This beach is also called Barramares. The main beach at **Pitimbu** is downtown, around 30 km after Tambaba. The local community lives off fishing. Artificial stone-block barrriers called "gabião" stop the sea from encroaching on the land. The next beach is **Barra do Abiai,** with high cliffs all along it.

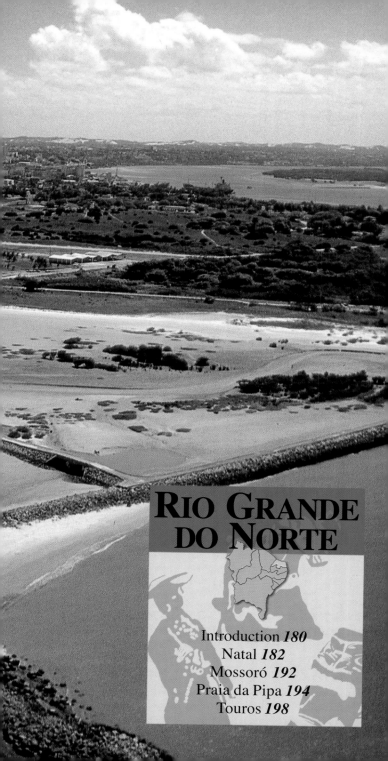

RIO GRANDE DO NORTE

RIO GRANDE DO NORT

Situated in the extreme northeast of the country, Rio Grande do Norte is the closest State to Europe. For this reason, many international excursions choose the Potiguar capital city as the entry gate to Brazil. The strategic location of the State was fundamental during the Second World War (1939-1945), for the Americans to set up a base for observation and to attack the Axis countries.

The State covers an area of 53,306 km² and to the west borders with Ceará, to the south with Paraíba and to the north and east it is bathed by the Atlantic Ocean.

In the 16th century, the captaincy of Rio Grande included the area from the Baía de Traição (Traitors Bay) in Paraíba to the Jaguaribe River in Ceará. This huge territory was vulnerable to foreign invasion. The constant attacks of the Dutch and the French who were looking for brazilwood, besides the resistance of the native Indians – the Potiguares – against colonization, were only decided when the Portuguese built the Reis Magos Fort in Natal in 1599. The fort served as an important support point for the conquest of the northern lands. The BR-101 highway, which starts in Rio Grande do Sul and cuts through all of the Northeastern States finishes in Rio Grande do Norte. The other access routes are the BR-304, which leads to the northwest and the BR-427 that goes to the southwest. Tourism on the 410-km coastline plays an important role in the economy of the State. The landscape ranges from the colored cliffs in the south, like those found in Pipa, and dunes to the north, in the region of Genipabu. Currently, the economy of the State is based on petroleum exploration – it occupies the second place in the national production – and the production of salt, responsible for 95% of the total consumption in Brazil.

◀ Forte dos Reis Magos: protection against foreign attacks

Praia de
Grossos

Praia da Pontal do Mel
Praia do Rosado

Areia
Branca

Macau

Praia de Galinhos
Praia de Caiçara do Norte

RN
221

Praia do Marco

Praia de São Miguel
do Gostoso

RRA DO MEL
soró

CHAPADA DA
SERRA VERDE

Touros

❸

Maxaranguape

Rio do Fogo

Assu

BR
406

Lages

João Câmara

Ceará Mirim

Genipabu

Piranhas-açu

BR
304

RIO GRANDE DO NORTE

Potengi

✈ NATAL

Praia Ponta Negra

SERRA
QUEIMADA

Serra Caiada

BR
226

Nísia Floresta

BR
101

Parnamirim

Praia de Búzios

SERRA AMARELA

ó

Currais Novos

Goianinha

Tibau do Sul
Praia da Pipa
Praia do Madeiro

Carnaúba dos Dantas

Canguaretama

Praia de Barra
do Cunhaú

SERRA DAS
MELANCIAS

Praia de
Baía Formosa

❶

N

W   E

S

0   88   176 km

❷

Highlights

❶ Natal
❷ Praia da Pipa
❸ Touros

LEGENDS

National park

Paved road

Dirt track

Natal

Twenty kilometers of coastline link the main highlights

Fortaleza: 530km
João Pessoa: 180km
Recife: 300km
 712,317
 84
 Secretaria Estadual de Turismo.
 0800-841516
@ www.setur.rn.gov.br

Rio Grande do Norte capital celebrated its 400-year anniversary in 1999 and, over the last few years, works such as the reform of the airport, redevelopment of the seafront, and the building of new hotels and restaurants have been executed. Morro do Careca, the Center of Tourism, the biggest cashew tree in the world and the Reis Magos Fort are the main attractions of the city. The State's capital city has 20 km of seafront that has different names depending on the suburbs. The principal access to all of the beaches is the Via Costeira, an avenue connecting Ponta Negra Beach, in the south of the city, to the center of Natal. The best access to the northern coast is to cross the Potengi River by ferry, which departs from the borough of Ribeira.

HIGHLIGHTS

Capitania das Artes
Av. Câmara Cascudo, 434, Downtown.
 232-4948. Opening hours: Monday to Friday from 8 a.m. to 6 p.m. Entrance: free.
The old Harbour Master building and former city hall today houses a cultural centre. Inside there are three galleries with temporary photography, sculpture, video and cinema exhibitions.

Coluna Capitolina
Pça. Carlos Gomes, Downtown.
A construction from the same time as the Roman Empire is on show in the centre of this square. The column was donated by Benito Mussolini for the reception given by the city to the pilots Carlos del Prete and Arturo Ferrarini in 1928. They crossed the Atlantic Ocean in an aeroplane in 3 days.

Igreja de Santo Antônio, Convento and Museu de Arte Sacra
R. Santo Antonio, Downtown.
 211-4236. Opening hours: Monday to Saturday from 6 a.m. to 7 p.m.

The Springboard of Victory

Roosevelt and Vargas: agreement in Natal

On January 28, 1943 the presidents Getúlio Vagas and Franklin Roosevelt met in Natal and decided to build an air base in the State as part of the strategy to defeat the Germans in the 2nd World War. In Natal a ramp for submarines was built and in the neighboring Parnamirim, an observation base – the present launch center of Barreira do Inferno. At that time it was known as 'the Springboard of Victory', as due to its proximity to the European continent it served as a platform for planes to 'spring' heading for action in the war. Originally, around 15,000 North American soldiers came and with them they brought customs and influenced the habits of the locals. One version for the origin of the word 'forró' appeared at that time, when the Americans organized dances at the door, a sign was displayed indicating that the party on that night was 'for all' – forró. The true source of the word remains controversial. According to folkloric expert Câmara Cascudo, 'forró' would be a corruption of 'forrobodó', which in an African dialect means party. The only certainty is that forró, the dance music, is very popular in Natal.

1. Igreja Matriz Nossa Senhora da Apresentação
2. Instituto Histórico e Geográfico
3. Museu Café Filho
4. Memorial Câmara Cascudo
5. Igreja de Santo Antônio, Convento e Museu de Arte Sacra
6. Teatro Alberto Maranhão
7. Centro de Turismo

From the Fort

The construction of a fort to protect the region of the estuary of the Potengi river started on 6th January 1598, the day of the Reis Magos (the three wise kings), the name given to the fort. Around the fortress, designed as a five-pointed star, the city started to develop. On 25th December 1599, Natal was founded. However the Portuguese did not settle down in the region but used the fort only as a base to re-conquer what are currently the states of Maranhão and Ceará, which were dominated by foreigners. Between 1633 and 1654, the Dutch invaded and took control of the city - that became known as New Amsterdam – and the fort, which received the name of Keulen Castle,

The fort impeded French attacks

a tribute to the commanding officer of the battle. On that occasion the captaincy of Pernambuco was also under the domination of the Dutch who saw the neighbouring captaincy as a strategic point for the supervision and supply of Pernambuco. The Dutch were only ousted in 1654 by the uprising of Pernambuco. The concentration of the population around the fort gave origin to Ribeira, the first suburb to emerge. The commerce

Sunday from 10 to 12 a.m. , 5 to 8 p.m. The convent opens daily from 8 to 11:30 a.m. and from 2 to 5:30 p.m.
The museum opens Tuesday to Sunday from 8 a.m. to 5 p.m. ☎ 211-9068. 🖥 🛗
The construction was concluded in 1766. It became known as Galo (Rooster) Church when one of the faithful brought a bronze rooster from Portugal to put on the top of the church tower. The Sacred Art Museum is housed in the annex. It has objects,

Igreja Matriz: the first mass in Natal

clothes, oratories and furniture from the 17th and 18th centuries.

Igreja de Nossa Senhora da Apresentação

Pça. André de Albuquerque, Downtown. ☎ 222-2245. Opening hours: from 2:30 to 6:30 p.m. The Instituto HIstórico e Geográfico opens on Monday to Friday from 8 to 12 a.m. and 2 to 5 p.m. ☎ 221-1228. Entrance: free. 🖥 🛗
The first mass was celebrated on this site. It was occupied during the Dutch occupation to house a Calvinist temple. The Dutch destroyed it themselves when they were defeated by the Portuguese. Rebuilt, its architecture followed the same Baroque style of the 17th century. In the centre is the sculpture of the mark of the foundation of Natal and soon after, the **Historic and Geographical Institute Building**, which is the oldest cultural institution of the state (1902). The patrimony includes books, periodicals and other documents.

★ Memorial Câmara Cascudo

Praça André de Albuquerque, 30, Downtown. ☎ 211-8404. Opening hours: Tuesday to Sunday from 8:30 a.m. to 5 p.m. Entrance: free. 🛗
The aim of this space is to preserve and to divulge the life and works of Câmara Cascudo. His private library is on

exhibition with photographs of his trips around the world and other documents. The building, in the neo-classical style, housed the tax office in the 18th century.

Museu Café Filho

R. da Conceição, 601, Downtown. ☎ 212-2496. Opening hours: Tuesday to Sunday from 8 a.m. to 6 p.m. 🕭 🏛

The furniture, documents and objects used by the only president of Brazil to be born in Rio Grande do Norte are on display here. Café Filho took office in 1954 after Getúlio Vargas committed suicide. The construction is known as 'Brides veil' due to its sloping roof.

Palácio da Cultura

Pça. Sete de Setembro, Downtown. ☎ 211-4620. Opening hours: Monday to Friday from 7 a.m. to 5 p.m. Weekends and bank holidays from 8 a.m. to 5 p.m. Entrance: free.🕭

The building was concluded in 1872 to house the state government offices. In 1996 it became the site of the art gallery of the state. Surrounding the Praça Sete de Setembro there are the legislative, executive and judicial government offices of the state.

★ Centro de Turismo

R. Aderbaldo Figueredo, 980, Petrópolis. ☎ 211-6218. Opening hours: daily from 9 a.m. to 7 p.m. Entrance: free. 🕭 🛍

Constructed in the 19th century as a residence, it also housed an asylum, an orphanage, an American base during the World War II and finally a prison. Since 1976, 36 stands sell handicrafts, pottery, lace and the traditional bottles

with coloured sand. On Thursdays starting at 10 p.m. the traditional 'Forró with tourists' takes place. ☎ 211-6218. Internet: www.forrocomturista.com.br

Rua Chile 🕭 🕓

Located in Ribeira suburb on the banks of the Potengi River, the principal buildings dating from the 19th century are found. At that time, the two-storey buildings and warehouses were intended to receive various products. Many of the buildings were restored and today stage musical, dance and theatrical presentations. In the vicinity it is possible to catch a ferry and goes to Redinhas Beach.

Praia da Redinha

Access by Estrada da Redinha (RN-302) or by ferry in Rua Chile going northwards 🕭

One of the greatest highlights of Redinha is the Public Market, which opens daily from 8 a.m. to 5 p.m. The market is in a simple large shed with some stalls that exist since the middle of the 19th century. It is worth visiting to eat 'Ginga with Tapioca', a fish dish invented by Dalilia, the wife of a fisherman.

Aquário de Natal

Av. Litorânea, 1091, Redinha Nova. ☎ 224-2177. @ www.aquarionatal.hpg.com.br. Daily from 8 a.m. to 6 p.m. 🕭

This is an ideal activity for families and for those interested in marine wildlife of the Potiguar coastline. There are seahorses, sea cucumbers, starfish, etc.

Teatro Alberto Maranhão: elements of French architecture from the end of the 19th century

Cascudo: passion for Folklore

The illustrious son

Câmara Cascudo was born in Natal in December 1898. He was a journalist, writer, professor and researcher. But his true passion was the stories and legends that involved the Brazilian imagination, and he left a legacy of roughly 150 books about folklore, history, geography and ethnology. His most important works are the *Brazilian Folklore Dictionary*, *Vaqueiras e Cantadores* (Rodeos and Singers), *Superstitions and Customs* and *Oral Literature of Brazil*. He traveled around Brazil and the world always trying to understand the African and European influences on the food, dance, clothes, music, customs and culture of the Brazilian people. He studied Medicine and law and in 1941 founded the Brazilian Folklore Society. Cascudo died in 1986.

Museu da Aeronáutica–Rampa

Pça. Engenheiro José Gonçalves, Rocas. ☎ 202-7500. Opening hours: Monday to Friday from 8 a.m. to 4 p.m. Entrance: free ♿

Surveillance of the German submarines during the 2nd World War was made from this base that is located on the banks of the Potengi River. Also the maintenance and refuelling of the hydroplanes, training of Brazilian officials as well as the departure of the planes that carried the airmail happened here. Photographs, documents and one of the planes used for training are on show.

Teatro Alberto Maranhão

Pça. Augusto Severo, Ribeira. ☎ 222-3669. Opening hours: daily from 9 a.m. to 6 p.m. Entrance: free ♿ Inaugurated in 1904, the building conveys indications of the French architecture from the last century. Today it is the main venue for theatrical presentations in the city.

Museu Câmara Cascudo

Av. Hermes da Fonseca, 1398, Tirol. ☎ 215-4192, ex. 43. Opening hours: Monday to Friday from 8 to 11 a.m. and from 2 to 4:30 p.m. Weekends from 1 to 5 p.m. ♿ The exhibits include reproductions of cave environments, from the production of salt and a mini processing plant of xylite – a mineral mined in the State and used in the arms industry and in the manufacture of lamp bulbs. There is a replica of Cabugi Peak, the highest point in the State. Also there are sacred art objects, African religious articles, handicraft, fossils and animal skeletons.

★ Forte dos Reis Magos

Praia do Forte ☎ 502-1099. Opening hours: Tuesday to Sunday from 8 a.m. to 4:30 p.m.♿ Built in 1598, with the passing of time the fort received improvements such as stonewalls and other structures more resistant to attacks. Inside it is possible to visit the quarters, refectories, chapel, gunpowder house, prison, torture room and the Mark of Touros – the oldest Portuguese monument in Brazil. There are also a shop, luncheonette and temporary expositions.

Beaches

13km by Via Costeira till Ponta Negra The seafront of Natal possesses promenades, uniform kiosks, hotels and restaurants. From the mouth of Potengi River towards the south the first is the **Fort Beach**. Then **Meio Beach** arises with a great barrier reef very close to the water's edge. The **Artistas Beach** has good waves for surfing and at night the bars and restaurants on the seafront get busy. At the next, a flight of stairs goes up to a lighthouse from where there is a panoramic view of the city. It is the **Mãe Luiza** Lighthouse, and the beach was named after it. Viewing on Sundays from 2 to 5 p.m. ☎ 221-4994. **Barreira D'água Beach** borders the Via Costeira, with the Dunas Park on the other side. The promenade is agreeable for walking. The last beach on the south coast is called **Ponta**

Negra, and is accessed by Av. Eng. Roberto Freire. This is the site where the greatest concentration of services for the tourist are located, including hotels, restaurants and bars. In the right-hand corner is one of the most significant symbols of the city: **Morro do Careca** Dune. It is prohibited to go up, and visitors can only appreciate it from its foot.

★ Dunas Park
Av. Alexandrino de Alencar, Tirol. ☎ 201-3985. @ www.idema.gov.br. Visitors guided on the trails on Tuesday to Sunday from 8 a.m. to 6 p.m. 🌀 🌐 🌊
It is the second biggest urban park in Brazil – after Tijuca Park in Rio de Janeiro. It covers an area of 117.2 km^2 and adjoins the Via Costeira Avenue. At the entrance is the Namoradas Thicket, a large square with area for picnics, a research center, souvenir shop and a luncheonette. There are three nature trails through the Atlantic forest, with different degrees of difficulty. To hike on the trails it is necessary to book in advance by telephone. The treks pass the dunes and elevated spots, which provide a beautiful view of the Barreira D'água Beach.

SURROUNDINGS

Parnamirim
Access is by the Rota do Sol from Ponta Negra southwards.
Ponta Negra is the last beach to the south of Natal. Afterwards is the municipality of Parnamirim. The first beach is **Barreira do Inferno** (Hell Barrier) closed to the public, as it is a military area. It is here that **Barreira do Inferno Launch Center** is located. Currently the centre is used for research and it is from here that meteorological rockets are launched. Rota do Sol, km 11. ☎ 216-1270 / 216-1304. Opening hours Monday to Thursday from 9 a.m. to 4 p.m., Friday from 8 to 12 a.m. and weekends and bank holidays from 9 a.m. to 3 p.m. By the side is **Cotovelo Beach**. A short extension of sand is good for bathing, with an area of coconut trees and another surrounded by cliffs. The last beach in the municipality is **Pirangi do Norte**, good for swimming and nautical sports. Carnival here is one of the most traditional of the State. There is a pier from where boats depart for trips in the natural swimming pools in Pirangi do Sul. The tours are from Badauê Marina. ☎ 238-2066, www.marinabadaue.com.br. 'The Cajueiro' is located one block from Pirangi. It appears in the *Guinness Book of Records* as the biggest cashew tree in the world. Its size is the equivalent to 70 normal-sized trees and it is estimated to be between 100 and 115 years old. The tree has a genetic anomaly, which makes it grow beyond the normal. There are guides who walk with the tourists amid the trunks and explain interesting facts about the cashew tree. Around the tree there are kiosks that sell handicrafts. Daily visits from 7:30 a.m. to 5:30 p.m.

Nísia Floresta
Located 20 km from Natal with access by the Rota do Sol, continuation of the Parnamirim road southwards.
The charm is the beaches with access

possible by the same road that starts in Parnamirim. Pirangi River splits the beaches of Pirangi do Norte and Pirangi do Sul and delimits the municipalities of Parnamirim and Nísia Floresta.
By the side of Pirangi do Sul is **Búzios Beach**. A formation of reefs protects the beach from the advance of the sea. There are dunes a short distance from the beach, where buggy trips are organized. On the **Barra de Tabatinga**, the Rota do Sol road passes very near to the coast. There are bars, which take advantage of the privileged position above the cliffs, similar to a gallery in a theater, with a view over the sea and the dolphins that frequently appear in the region. Next comes **Cumurupim** and **Barreta** with natural swimming pools. Another attraction of Nísia Floresta is **Carcará** Lagoon.
The entrance is via the Rota do Sol, on the junction of Nísia Floresta in the district of Timbó.

★ Dunas de Genipabu Park
Praia de Genipabu, access by the Redinha Nova road. Opening hours: daily from 8 a.m. to 6 p.m. Entry to the park is only permitted with registered buggy drivers. 🚐
The beach is pleasant for swimming, encircled by dunes and reefs that can be visited on raft trips. The commercial activities, including the restaurants and kiosks on the seafront are only open during the day. Together with the village are the dunes, which reach 50-meters high, with an inclination of 40°.

Cashew: harvest from November to January

Buggy drivers ask a strategic question: "do you want with or without emotion?". Reply "with emotion" and the sensation, which the manoeuvres cause, is descending at an inclination of 90°. From the park there is a view of Genipabu Lagoon. On the stable dunes it is possible to go on a camel ride. Rio Grande do Norte has regulated the service of buggy drivers since 1998. The Tourist Department demandsregistration of the vehicles and a selective choice of the professionals. Before hiring a driver, ask to check the authorization.

Lagoa Pitangui
Access is by the BR-101 highway to the junction of Pitangui district. Follow the signs to the entrance to the lagoon. Opening hours: daily from 8 a.m. to 5 p.m. Entrance: free 🏊 🎯
A small and pleasant lake surrounded by dunes. The bar serves meals and barbecue. It also offers several choices of activities, including pedal boats, microlight flights and an aerial runway where the participant falls into the lake.

Genipabu dunes: 50 m high ▶

Lagoa de Jacumã

Access is only by buggy, on the trips from Genipabu.

Dunes of up to 30-meters high surround the lake. From the top, stalls offer the descent in a complex system, which involves the aerial runway, a raft and a type of train powered by a Volkswagen beetle engine. From the top of the dunes the participant slides down the aerial runway, falls into the water, is rescued by the raft and carried to the top in a cart pulled by the beetle engine. Jacumã Beach is close to the lake, with fine sand and a bay with reefs. It is busier to the north, with good seafront restaurants. There are several choices of ecological trails to reach the small waterfall of Pratagi River. The trek includes walking through the Atlantic Forest and some dunes. Follow the river to the waterfall, circle around Jacumã Lake and return by the beach. Information from Naf-Naf restaurant.
☎ 228-2228. @ www.nafnaf.com.br.

Cabo de São Roque

By the BR-101 highway, enter the municipality of Muriú and go to the north. Buggy drivers follow the beach, by a way through the dunes that intersects *gameleiras* (*V. quaxinduba*) and cashew trees.

Known as the eastern most point on the Brazilian coast from the São Roque Beach, it is possible to see a grove of coconut and palm trees and also the lighthouse. A traditional icon of São Roque is a gameleira tree, which suffered a genetic dysfunction and joined with its twin. The ellipse of the two trees creates a frame. It was christened the 'Love Tree'.

Praia de Maracajaú

Starting from Muriú follow the BR-101 to Maracajaú. From Cabo de São Roque it is 15 km along dirt tracks. Trips to the 'parrachos' are organized by the Maracajaú Diver. ☎ 261-6200. www.maracajaudiver.com.br.
This point on the coast is 70 km from Natal and 46 km from Genipabu. Maracajaú is a famous beach because of its deep-sea reefs – which are called 'parrachos'. They are located 7 km from the coastline and cover a 12 km extension. Launches and catamarans travel to floating platforms, which are permanently

Cashew tree: the biggest in the world

anchored in this place and offer bar services. The 'parrachos' are more exposed at low tide. Adjoined to Maracajaú Beach is Ma-Noa Park, an aquatic park with a water toboggan, swimming pools with jacuzzi,, a leisure area and restaurant. It is located on Anéis Beach and opens daily from 10 a.m. to 4 p.m.

TIPS

– Lodging in Ponta Negra permits good walks through the streets. It is also the best beach of Natal for swimming.
– The places with the greatest amount of nightlife in Natal are: The Chaplin Complex, on Meio Beach, Zás Trás, Taberna Pub, in Ponta Negra and Blackout on Rua Chile.
– It is possible to know the lakes and the entire northern coast in only one day by buggy. The buggy drivers can be hired directly in Genipabu. It is recommended to hire buggies in groups organized in the buggy drivers co-operative itself or through a travel agent in Natal. By car, access is by the BR-101. Coopbuggy.
☎ 219-3758. Topbuggy. ☎ 219-2820. www.bugueiros.com.br

◀ Lake between Genipabu dunes

Mossoró

Mossoró is prosperous due to salt production, petroleum and irrigated fruit crops

Natal: 277km
Fortaleza: 260km
213,841
84
Secretaria de Turismo.
316-1050.
www.prefeiturademossoro.com.br

Mossoró is the second largest city of the State and grew at the mid point of two state capitals: Natal and Fortaleza. The economy expanded with the exploitation of two mineral resources: salt and petroleum. The greatest amount of salt produced in Brazil is removed from the region's salt works – around 2 million tons per year. And petroleum occupies the first place in exploitation on land and the second place in the total production of Brazil. In agriculture the most important production is irrigated fruit such as melons, cashew, guava and *acerola* (Barbados cherry). From Natal, the best way to arrive is by the BR-304.

SURROUNDINGS

Lajedo de Soledade
76 km by the BR-405 to the

municipality of Apodi. The last 6 km are by dirt track. From Fortaleza it is about 320 km to Apodi.
Located in the municipality of Apodi, the Lajedo de Soledade is a large limestone formation of approximately 1 km². In total, there is a set of 56 pre-historical paintings and engravings that

Lajedo: inscriptions from 10,000 years ago ▶

occupy an area of 400 m². Studies indicate that they were completed in the period between 3,000 and 10,000 years ago. The paintings, in reddish shades of iron oxide, show animals and geometric designs. There are several trails as well as stairways which simplify access to areas on the steeper slopes. The area of Lajedo is divided in three parts: the richest in artwork is Araras, with representation of birds, gigantic animal bones and caves; in Urubu it is possible to see a great cleavage which is covered by water during the rainy season; and Olho d'Água, a lake around which there are pre-historic engravings as well as fossils of extinct animals. Part of this area can be covered by car on dirt tracks. Lizards, bats and typical flora of the backlands such as *macambiras* (*Encholrium spectabile*) and *maracatus* are easily observed. The visitor's attractions are found on the main street of Soledade. There are the **Soledade Museum** and **Lajedo Activity Center** where it is possible to contract a guide for the trek. In the museum, posters show the results of archaeological research in Lajedo and sell handicrafts; and the Activity Center houses a tourist information center where the craft workshops of the city operate.

TIPS

The route to Mossoró from Natal takes four hours. From the Potiguar coast follow the BR-110 to Mossoró. From Fortaleza, access is gained by the BR-116 highway to Boqueirão do Cesário and after by the BR-304. Be prepared to walk around Lajedo de Soledade under the intense *sertão* sun.

The defeat of Lampião

In a historic session in the council chambers in 1883, the city became the pioneer in the State and the third in Brazil to abolish slavery. It was the same chamber where, in 1927, the first woman in the whole of Latin America exercised her right to vote. In this same year, one of the greatest defeats in the history of banditry occurred. Led by the city Mayor and Father Motta, Mossoró resisted the invasion of the famous outlaw Lampião and his gang. It is said that about 200 armed men positioned themselves in strategic spots in the city waiting for the attack. When it happened, six of Lampião's men died, among whom was the leader Jararaca, whose grave is one of the most visited in the cemetery of the city.

Praia da Pipa

Cliffs, coconut trees and dolphins makes up the scenery of Pipa

Natal: 85km
Tibau do Sul: 8km
João Pessoa: 125km
👤 7,749 (Tibau do Sul)
🌐 84
@ www.pipa.com.br
⛴ ferry around the beaches.

It is located to the municipality of Tibau do Sul and is known for the dolphins, cliffs and for attracting foreign tourists, as it is the most visited spot on the State's southern coast. On the main street, Baía dos Golfinhos Avenue, the houses are occupied by clothes, handicraft, jewelery and decoration shops, which remain open until night, taking advantage of the business of the surrounding bars and restaurants.

HIGHLIGHTS

Beaches
The greatest highlight of Pipa and the vicinity are the beaches. All are considered an environmentally protected area that guarantees, at least by law, the unconditional conservation of the ecosystem.

Known as the principal or central Beach, Pipa is the busiest in the region due to the easy access from the village of Pipa. There are natural swimming pools, kiosks and restaurants. The strip of sand is narrow and becomes even more reduced at high tide. It is a good starting point to visit the neighboring beaches.In the north, the next beach is **Curral**. After about an hour, continuing along the sands, the **Madeiro** Beach emerges. It's also know as **Golfinhos** (Dolphins') **Cove** – even from the beach it is possible to observe them. The view is even better from the cliff top, where the dense forest lodges the **Ecological Sanctuary** – where there are 16 trails, with beautiful vantage points along the route. Access to the sanctuary is gained 2 km along the Tibau do Sul road. Opening hours: Monday to Saturday from 8 a.m. to 5 p.m. and Sunday from 8 a.m. to 1 p.m. **Cacimbinhas** is deserted and at the foot of the cliffs there is a flight of stairs, which goes to Cacimbinhas Observation Point. For those who come from Natal, the first stretch of sea that you see on the left is the

Cacimbinhas Observation Point. The next beach is **Tibau do Sul**. It is from here that the ferry leaves, crossing the **Guaraíras Lagoon**, which was formed by the estuary of the Tibau River before it meets the sea. There are boat trips organized by the Marinas Hotel departing from the lake side in Tibau do Sul to visit the mangrove areas. From the other side, on **Guaraíras** Beach, there are dunes, which go along the beach, with one area well covered by vegetation. Returning to Pipa Beach, the first beach to the south is called **Amor**, where it is only possible to arrive by walking at low tide. The waves are rough, good for surfing but dangerous for bathing. The strip of sand is narrow, more so at high tide, when the beach practically disappears. A cliff verges on the beach and its plateau is a meeting point to appreciate the view

of the beach and sunset. During the period of American presence in Natal, in The Second World War, the plateau served as an observation point. **Moleque** is a small bay with cliffs bordering the beach and stones in the sand. It is only possible to reach it at low tide. **Minas** Beach is accessed by the beach also by either walking or by buggy on a sandy track parallel to the beach. More deserted is the **Tamar Project,** that takes care of marine turtles. The last beach before arriving at the mouth of Curimataú River is called **Sibaúma**.

SURROUNDINGS

Barra do Cunhaú
From Pipa it is 15 km along the beach to Barra do Cunhaú. By the BR-101 highway it is 26 km to Goianinha and 25 km to Barra de Cunaú.

Stone in the shape of a "pipa" barrel named the beach

Once upon a time there was a fishing village....

A rock on Amor Beach gave the name to Pipa Beach. Known today as Moleque Rock, it was mistaken for a barrel by sailors and thus became a reference point for those who were passing on the high seas. As one name for a cask is 'pipa', the beach received this name. The rock is easily seen in the sand, near to the cliffs, and at high tide it becomes partially covered by the

water. Until the 1970s, the city was a peaceful fishing village. The number of tourists increased with the arrival of the surfers, and the profile of the visitors changed over the years. In the place of fishing, the economy started to be based on the construction industry, with new hotels and restaurants being built with the standards of big cities, but with the charm of a village.

www.praiabarradocunhau.com.br
Canguaretama retains marks of a
genocide that happened in 1645. In a
farm near the city, Dutch Calvinists
and Indians commanded a massacre
of Catholics in the region. During a
Mass, there was an invasion of the
Nossa Senhora das Candeias Chapel
and almost all of the faithful and
Catholic priests present were killed.
Three priests escaped. The episode
marked the start of the Dutch
domination in Rio Grande do Norte.
To visit the chapel, at the
Canguaretama road junction, take the
road to the municipality of Nova Cruz
and follow the signposts
to Cunhaú farm. Canguaretama also
has one of the most beautiful beaches
of the region: **Barra do Cunhaú**, 13
km from downtown. The beach is
bordered by the Catu River to the
north separating it from Sibaúma
Beach and Curimataú River also
known as Cunhaú to the south
separating it from the municipality of
Baía Formosa. When traveling by
buggy, both rivers can be crossed by
ferry. In Barra do Cunhaú the reefs
are very close to the sands, forming
natural swimming pools. There are
few buildings and most are summer
cottages. On Catu River there are
kayaks for rent.

Baía Formosa

From Pipa it is 30 km along the beach
to Baía Formosa. By the BR-101
highway it is 27 km to Goianinha plus
16 km until Baía Formosa.
Crossing the mouth of Cunhaú River on
a ferry, the first beach that you come to
is **Coqueiral,** in the municipality of
Baía Formosa. Access is only from
Barra do Cunhaú Beach at low tide. A
coconut farm follows the border of the
beach. The next beach, **Baía Formosa**,
the main beach of the municipality, is a
port and a fishing center. An unusual
view on the site is the old fisherman's
cemetery, with all of the gravestones
facing the sea. The beach has short
stretches of dunes split by rocks and
cliffs. The sea is particularly good for
surfing. The following beach, that of
Bacopari, has as its reference point the
black and white colored lighthouse on
the seafront – resembling the white of
the sand and the black of the reefs on
the beach. On **Cotia** Beach, a
continuation of Bacopari, is the
entrance to **Mata Estrela**. The place is
a private Reserve of Natural Heritage,
and one of the biggest areas of Atlantic
Forest preserved in the State, with short
trails among the native trees.
Inside the forest there are 19 lakes with
the best-known being **Araraquara Lake,**
also called the lake of Coca-Cola – the

Rocas Atoll Marine Biology Reserve

The Marine Biology Reserve of
Rocas is located at 267
km from the city of Natal and
108 km from Fernando de Noronha.
To arrive at the two islands that
form the reserve, the Lighthouse
and the Cemetery, it takes 26 hours
traveling from the continent. As it
became a biological reserve in 1979
– the first in the country – access is
only permitted to researchers who
study the characteristics of a
preserved and unique ecosystem,
where turtles lay eggs, the birds
reproduce and it is a shelter during
migration. The birds include atobás
(masked booby – Sula dactylatra),
fragatas (man-of-war bird –
Tachypetes aquilus), trinta-réis
(Large-billed Tern - Phaetusa

Atol das Rocas is an ecological reserve

simplex) and viuvinhas (Long-tailed
Tyrant - Colonia colonus), which are
spread over the 72 km² of the
islands. The vegetation of the atoll is
trailing and there are no sources of
fresh water.

Praia do Amor: coves form the shape of a heart

decomposition of plants and the soil rich in iron make the lake very dark. Soon after it is Junco Lake.

The last beach in Rio Grande do Norte is **Sagi**, a fishing village with dunes and the sandbar of Sagi River on the border of Paraíba State.

TIPS

- Access: distance between Natal and Pipa is 90 km. From Natal, it is 64 km till Goianinha by BR-101 and more 26 km by a paved but narrow road. It is a very dangerous road. There are some private minibuses that drive you from Natal. From Paramirim Airport, there are also taxis.
- It is easier to see the dolphins when the tide is coming in, as it is when they arrive closest to the beach to feed. The highest numbers can be found on the Curral and Madeiro beaches. A good choice for a trip is to visit by schooner the Curral, Enseada dos Golfinhos, Moleque and Amor beaches, which takes one hour and a half. The schooner belongs to Aventureiro Company, which is located in Passarela do Sol, Pipa Beach. ☎ 246-4206.
- During the turtle egg-laying season from November to May, much more care is required when walking on the beach. The passage of vehicles at this time is prohibited.
- The nearest gas station to Pipa Beach is 4 km away.
- In Pipa, the Pipatour Company organizes whole-day buggy trips to Barra do Cunhaú and Baía Formosa along the beach. The ideal would be to make both trips on different days to take the best advantage of the places.
- To escape from the hustle and bustle of Pipa, a good option is to stay in Barra do Cunhaú or Baía Formosa.
- In the higher part of the city of Baía Formosa there is a good commercial area.

Touros

The Portuguese planted their mark of conquest of a new land here

Natal: 88 km
Mossoró: 309 km
Areia Branca: 356 km
👤 27,879
🌐 (84)
ℹ️ City Hall
☎ 263-2214.

Founded in 1835, Touros is a historical city on the seashore. There are cannons pointing out to sea, which served as protection in the colonization period against foreign invasion. It is the city with the best tourist amenities on the northern Potiguar coast, and so it is a good choice as a base to visit the beaches close by. The BR-101 cuts across all of Brazil and finally arrives in Touros, the place where the Portuguese established the Touros Mark, which later was taken to the Reis Magos Fort in Natal.

HIGHLIGHTS

Farol do Calcanhar
Access is by the end of the BR-101 highway. ☎ 592-5402. Opening hours: Sundays from 2 to 5 p.m. Entrance: Free

Founded in 1943, the Calcanhar lighthouse is located in a military area. It is 62 meters high, the highest in Brazil. To reach the top it is necessary to climb a total of 298 steps, but today it is only possible to observe it from the outside.

SURROUNDINGS

Barra do Rio Punaú
From Touros it is 23 km by dirt track in the direction of Natal to the municipality of Rio do Fogo. 🌿 Barra do Punaú is the spot where the waters of the Punaú River and the Atlantic Ocean meet, forming a delightful landscape which has already been the venue of several television commercials. On the beach there are kiosks, which offer microlight flights, kayak and horse-riding trips. In the direction of Touros from Barra do Punaú, Zumbi Beach, a cove of low dunes formed of soft sands and several coconut trees, and Fogo River, with reefs and stones on sands.

São Miguel do Gostoso
Located 23 km from Touros along the beach, or by the RN-221 road in the

Farol do Calcanhar: the highest in Brazil ▶

direction of Fortaleza.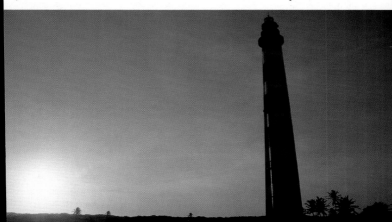
A beach with rocks on a wide band of light sand and some reefs. There is a choice of lodgings and food, but no nightlife. As it is calm it is ideal for the traveller looking for peace and quiet. Windsurfing is common, due to the calm waters and the strong winds.

Praia do Marco

Access is exclusively by the beach. There is access by dirt track to the settlement, from where it is necessary to take a trail through the middle of vegetation.
Marco Beach enjoys a cove with drifting dunes and a natural marine formed by reefs. The waters are calm and shallow with white sands. It is a breeding ground for marine turtles. Thus, on the edge of the beach, there are many nests and during the breeding season it is possible to see the spectacle of the turtles heading to sea.

Caiçara da Praia Norte

Access is along the beach, passing by dunes in the direction of Fortaleza.
On the path that gives access to the beach, on Ponta dos Três Irmãos, the visitor will cross a stretch of dunes marked with the vegetation of the *caatinga*. The region exhibits great *mandacaru*s (Pleated cereus – *cereus jamacaru*), a species of cactus abundant in the Northeast. It is possible to see the roots of plants, which entered in the process of petrifaction.

Praia de Galinhos

Access is by the RN-121 road and after a path between the dunes. It is essential

to be accompanied by a guide or buggy man who knows the route.
Situated on a peninsula, Galinhos Beach has many leisure options. A boat trip by an inlet of the sea crossing over salt lakes is one of them. For this, head to the car park in Galinhos, from where boats leave to the mangroves, with a pause in front of the Diamante Banco salt works and passing by the uninhabited Cobra and Patragil Isles. Do not be surprised if an ox cart pulled by a donkey stops by your side and the driver asks 'Taxi'? Donkey-taxis are very common on Galinhos Beach.

Praia do Rosado

Access is by the beach or dirt tracks from the municipality of Areia Branca.
From Rosado, which is found in the municipality of Mangue Port, the beaches comprise an area denominated Costa Branca, due to the high number of salt works. Extraction of salt is the fundamental economic activity for the subsistence of the population.
Rosado Beach is the geological fulfillment of the prophecy of Antônio Conselheiro (*read Canudos, Bahia*) that one day, the *sertão* would become the sea and the sea would become *sertão*. The soil of the *tabuleiro* region, reddish in color with a cracked aspect, characteristic of the *sertanejo* regions, is found below a substantial area of drifting dunes. The white sands of the dunes mix with the red soils of the *tabuleiro* forming a desert of diverse shades of pink, red and

orange. The spot also provides a panoramic view of the surrounding area, and the scenery is completed by the green forests inland and by the deep blue of the sea. The region is practically unknown. The visitor might run into a herd of goats, further adding to the rustic image. The region of the dunes is located on a plateau of cliffs, which reach a height of 20 meters. At the bottom is the beach with stones and a village.

Ponta do Mel
Access is by the beach or dirt track from the municipality of Areia Branca.
This is a calm cove with weak waves with a band of soft light sand. There are dunes with *caatinga* vegetation and high cliffs, which give a panoramic view of the horizon and the entire region. It is the only beach in the region of Costa Branca with a boarding house which even though it has a sea view, from the beach it is practically impossible to see the building, giving a really primitive sensation to the place. Together with the boarding house there is an oil well that can be visited. Ponta do Mel is inhabited only by lobster catchers from a little settlement, which holds a traditional party, when their sailors

return home from the high seas with an abundance of crustaceans. Besides fishing, they survive off subsistence agriculture in cleared fields which head inland, in a region of *sertanejo* soils.

São Cristóvão
Access is along the beach at low tide.
This is a 5-km-long beach where fishing boats are anchored. It has reefs and a coconut grove. Between São Cristóvão and Ponta de Mel there is a cemetery facing the sea on a plateau of cliffs. The next beach is **Redonda,** with reddish dunes and trailing vegetation. Following this the visitor arrives at **Morro Pintado**, also with access to the village of Benfica. It is a straight beach, with dunes and rocks over a ribbon of fine light sand. There is a fishing settlement. **Baixa Grande** has just begun to develop its fishing village, but it is peaceful. **Upanema**, on the other hand, is a developed beach and is almost a neighborhood of the municipality of Areia Branca. The beach is partitioned by cliffs and has a lighthouse.

Areia Branca
Access is by the BR-110 highway.
The municipality of Areia Branca is

330 km from Natal and has around 20,000 inhabitants. Since its foundation, in the middle of the 19th century, Areia Branca received migrants from the drought areas, who settled in the region, and started to work in agriculture. It was historically linked to the municipality of Mossoró, as it is on the estuary of the river of the same name. Mossoró represented an important economic center in the Northeast, based on the economies of sun-dried beef and salt producers. Areia Branca was the natural port, from where all the inland production was shipped. Today it has its economy based on fishing, salt, petroleum and tourism.

Sacred stone

In the times of the great conquests of the 16th century, Portugal claimed the ownership of new lands using the 'mark of a stone'. And this was not different in Rio Grande do Norte. When they arrived on the Marco Beach on the northern coast in 1501, they built a stone column of about 1.3 meters (4 feet) high on the beach registering the deed. On it a cross representing the Catholic faith, the shield of Portugal and inscriptions in Latin, Arabic and Portuguese were engraved. For a long time the sculpture was considered sacred and the Cauá indigenous community, who live close to the site until today, removed fragments of stone to make infusions which were thought to heal ills. The Mark was the venue of religious ceremonies and sacred promises, where even skeletons and bones were deposited. The monument was transferred, in 1976, from Marco Beach to the State capital where it is on display to the public inside the Reis Magos Fort. It is considered to be the oldest Portuguese registration of this type in Brazil that still preserves its original characteristics.

Symbol of possession

CEARÁ

CEARÁ

Situated in the north of the Northeast, Ceará occupies an area of 146,348 sq km. Colonization started in the 17th century and suffered from strong resistance from the indigenous tribes who lived here. The first fort of the capital, Schoonenborch, was constructed by the Dutch and seized by the Portuguese in 1654. Ceará led the slave abolition movement in Brazil and gave an end to slavery in the State four years before the rest of the country. One important name in the movement was Francisco José do Nascimento, the Dragon of the Sea, who was a *jangadeiro* (raft sailor) from Canoa Quebrada and leader of the strike of boatmen who took the sold slaves to other provinces. Ceará is the land of pilgrimages and religious processions. In Juazeiro do Norte, the priest Cícero Romão is worshipped and consecrated as a saint by the people. The devotion to him extends all over the Brazilian backlands. The main cultural events of the State are the *vaquejadas* (a type of rodeo originally following the roundup after winter), which take place principally in the countryside and the *maracatu* of Ceará (a Carnival parade to the beat of drums), with a different rhythm to all other Brazilian *maracatus*. The lobster fishing and crabbing cultures are very obvious on the State's east coast.

Ceará has important representatives in the literature world such as José de Alencar, Rachel de Queiroz, and the popular poet Patativa do Assaré. Musicians like Fagner and Fausto Nilo gained prominence in the popular Brazilian music movement. And the wit from Ceará made the characters created by Chico Anysio, Renato Aragão and Tom Cavalcanti famous in Brazil. The rainy season extends from December until April – harvest time. The dry season is from May until November. Practically the whole State is set in a semi-arid zone and the predominant vegetation is *caatinga*. The main economic activities are the production of beans, corn, rice, cotton, cashew-nuts, and the textile, food, chemical and shoe manufacturers, besides tourism.

Highlights

❶ Jericoacoara
❷ Fortaleza
❸ Juazeiro do Norte

◀ Canoa Quebrada: the second most important tourist center in Ceará

Praia de Guriú

Camocim

Jericoacoara

Paracuru

Praia de Lagoinha

Itapipoca

CE 364

Sobral

nguá

Aprazível

BR 222

SERRA DAS VERTENTES

UBAJARA

FORTALEZA

Aquiraz

Cascavel

Beberibe

Praia de Morro Branco

BR 020

CE 040

Praia do Cumbe

SERRA DA IBIAPABA

Curu

Guaramiranga

Canindé

Boqueirão do Cesário

Praia de Canoa Quebra

BR 122

Aracati

BR 304

Icapuí

de

io

Quixadá

Russas

Praia Ponta Grossa

CEARÁ

Quixeramobim

Morada Nova

Tauá

Jaguaribe

BR 116

RIO GRANDE DO NORTE

SERRA SÃO DOMINGOS

SERRA DO FRANCO

ERRA CARIRIS OVOS

Iguatu

Icó

Farias Brito

BR 230

N

W   E

S

tana do Cariri

Crato

Juazeiro do Norte

PARAÍBA

0   72   144 km

CHAPADA DO ARARIPE

BR 116

Brejo Santo

BR 232

PERNAMBUCO

LEGENDS

National park

Paved road

Dirt track

Fortaleza

In Av. Beira-Mar the main hotels and a daily handicraft market are located

São Luís: 1075 km
Natal: 523 km
Canoa Quebrada: 165 km
Jericoacoara: 300 km
A 2,138,234
⊕ 85
ℹ Secretaria de Turismo: ☎ 488-3900
✪ 😊 😊
@ www.turismo.ce.gov.br

The sun shines all the year round in the capital of Ceará where the average annual temperature is 27°C. The city possesses very peculiar characteristics as it aggregates the *sertanejo* traditions and the habits of the coastal fishermen, which results in a rich cultural mix reflected in the cuisine, the architecture, and the vernacular of its people. The population is a blend of Indians, Portuguese and migrants from the drought-ridden areas. In Fortaleza jerked beef and fish are eaten by the side of the sea.

The nightlife is intense all week long, but especially on Mondays. The bars are found in the Iracema neighborhood. The city has many cinemas, theaters, dance and folkloric music groups, a cultural center and a planetarium. The humor in Ceará seems to be present in all cultural exhibitions. Praça Ferreira, in downtown, is the stage for these pranks. On Thursdays, the bars around the square promote comedy shows.

HIGHLIGHTS

Catedral Metropolitana

Av. Alberto Nepomuceno, 339, Downtown. ☎ 231-4196. Opening hours: Monday to Friday from 8 a.m. to 5 p.m. Saturday from 8 to 12 a.m. and Sunday from 9 a.m. to 1 p.m. Entrance: Free. 🍴 🕺

Originally built of wattle and daub in 1729, the current building underwent two re-constructions. In 1854, it was converted to a stone church of simple architecture with a façade of two towers and in 1938, due to a crack, which threatened the structure of the building, the church was demolished and re-built in the Neo-gothic style.

★ Centro de Turismo

R. Senador Pompeu, 350, Downtown. ☎ 231-3566. Opening hours: Monday to Friday from 8 a.m. to 6 p.m. Saturday from 8 a.m. to 2 p.m. and

Iracema's country

In 1535 the captaincy of Siará was donated to Antônio Cardoso de Barros. But only in 1611, Martim Soares Moreno, an expert of the Indian language and customs, initiated the process of colonizing the captaincy and was named City Captain in 1619. He maintained a fraternal friendship with the natives which was fundamental in the destruction of the French and Dutch who had been trying to occupy the region. Schoonenborch Fort, which had been built by the Dutch, was taken by the Portuguese in 1654. It was re-baptized Fortaleza de Nossa Senhora de Assunção and, in 1726, the settlement around it was elevated to the category of city with the name of Fortaleza. The Portuguese Martim Soares Moreno inspired José de Alencar to write the novel *Iracema* – the story of a love affair between a Portuguese man and an Indian. From the union of the couple Moacir was born, a name, which, in the Tupi Indian language, means 'son of suffering'. There are readers of the novel who say that

Statue of Iracema in Fortaleza

Iracema is an anagram of the word America and the union of the couple symbolizes the interbreeding between the Portuguese and the Indian peoples. The current architecture of the city dates from the end of the 19th century, and was inspired from the period of French belle époque. The streets were geometrically distributed similar to a chessboard. At that time, it was customary, and considered very elegant to speak French. Fortaleza gained mansions and stately houses, buildings that until today can be seen downtown.

1. Centro de Turismo
2. Catedral Metropolitana
3. Centro Dragão do Mar de Arte e Cultura
4. Casario de Iracema
5. Museu do Maracatu
6. Cine São Luiz
7. Teatro José de Alencar
8. Igreja do Sagrado Coração de Jesus

Sunday from 8 to 12 a.m. Entrance: Free. ⬤◉Ⓜ⬤

Built in colonial style between 1850 and 1866, the building functioned as the public prison in Fortaleza until 1970 when it was transformed into a Tourist Center. On the ground floor there is an arcade with several handicraft shops. It is possible to buy different types of lace, embroidery, articles made from straw, apart from sweets and derivatives of cashew and *cachaça* (popular Brazilian white rum). The tourist center is also the venue of the Museum of Arts and Popular Culture, which is located on the upper floor. The assets include 1,500 items such as clay dolls, masks, and sacred figures. Also there is an exhibition of ox carts and fishing rafts, all with due explanations about the different types of vessels. In the Tourist Center itself there is also a museum of mineralogy.

Catedral Metropolitana: Neo-gothic style

Cine São Luiz

R. Major Fecundo, 500, Praça do Ferreira, Downtown. ☎ 226-8739. Daily sessions - check the programming. ⬤

It is considered to be one of the most delightful cinema auditoriums in Brazil. In 1958 the construction was completed, nearly 20 years after the beginning of the work. The lobby is illuminated by imported crystal chandeliers from what was Czechoslovakia and the stairway to the upper floor is lined with Italian marble. In the past the finesse of the building required the audience to wear social dress. The auditorium has a capacity for 1,500 people.

Igreja do Sagrado Coração de Jesus

Pça. do Sagrado Coração de Jesus, Downtown. Opening hours: daily from 8 a.m. to 8 p.m. ⬤⬤

It is considered to be one of the most beautiful churches in the city and the bronze statues of Christ's twelve apostles are displayed inside. The statue of Christ himself is 3 meters tall. The building used the labor of migrants escaping from the droughts inland. The church was restored in 1957 because part of the façade had collapsed. It is located in front of the Sagrado Coração de Jesus Square, where there is a bus terminal.

Museu do Maracatu

R. Rufino de Alencar, 362, Downtown. ☎ 231-5447. Open hours: Tuesday to Thursday from 8 a.m. to 5 p.m. Entrance: Free. Ⓜ

The Maracatu Museum is situated at the back of the São José theater. Its exhibits include the dresses and allegories used in the maracatu, - the Carnival processions of Ceará. The visitor can find explanations to the origin and history of the event, characterized by a slower rhythm than the *gingado* (swaying) maracatu of Pernambuco.

Praça do Ferreira

Downtown, between R. Major Facundo and Floriano Peixoto. ⬤

It was founded in 1825 by the pharmacist Antônio Rodrigues Ferreira. The square was the venue of open-air markets and a meeting place for Europeans and immigrants escaping from the drought. In 1902, trees were planted and it gained 4 large cafés. It became a haunt of the cultural elite. In 1933 a clock tower called the Coluna da Hora (Time Column) was built but was destroyed in 1966. The current architecture is from 1991. Kiosks were constructed and the column was recreated. Here, the sun was jeered, after a week of rain in the 1930s.

Teatro José de Alencar

Pça. José de Alencar, Downtown. ☎ 252-2324. Accompanied visitors. Opening hours Tuesday to Friday from 8 to 11 a.m. and from 2 to 5 p.m.

A mixture of styles characterise the architecture of the theater, whose construction was initiated in 1908. It is divided into two blocks separated by an internal courtyard. In the first block there are two floors: the ground, with the box office, the main foyer and bathrooms and the upper floor, where there is a second lobby. The entrance has a façade of ironwork imported from Scotland with stained-glass windows in the nouveau art style, contrasting with the neo-classical style of the first block. Inside there are three floors, smooth columns, neo-classical details in the auditorium and Luis XV banisters. The garden was designed by the landscaper Burle Marx, in the 1970s. The theater is a reflection of the city at the start of the 20th century, which incorporated the French culture of belle époque in its architecture.

Casario de Iracema

Around the Dragão do Mar Art and Cultural Center there are diverse coloured storehouses with colonial façades. At the beginning of the 20th century they accommodated comercial companies and the suburb where they were situated was called Outeiro da Prainha. From the 1980s the warehouses began to attract the interest of artists who started to settle here. By the end of the 1990s, 58 buildings had had their façades restored and painted in a project christened 'Colors of the City'. The majority of the depots have been transformed into bars and restaurants. It is common for live music shows to take place here.

★ Centro Dragão do Mar de Arte e Cultura

Rua Dragão do Mar, 81, Iracema Beach. ☎ 488-8612. @ www.secult.ce.gov.br/CDMAC/Cdmac.asp. Opening Hours: Tuesday to Thursday from 9 a.m. to 5:30 p.m. Friday to Sunday from 2 to 9:30 p.m.

Inaugurated in 1999, the spot is a complex dedicated to cultural activities. With 30,000 sq m of floor space, there are two museums, a theater, two cinemas, auditorium, rooms for courses, library, handicraft shop and a planetarium. The Ceará Contemporary Art Museum, which is part of this recreation center, has as its permanent exhibition paintings of Raimundo Cela, Antônio Bandeira, Chica da Silva and Aldemir Martins – distinguished names from the art world of Ceará. It also holds temporary exhibitions, as well as the Panorama de Arte Brasileira. Memorial da Cultura Cearense always exhibits themes that mirror the culture of the State. The

In Teatro José de Alencar, the architecture is a reflection of the French *belle époque*

Centro Dragão do Mar: painting, cinema and theater exhibitions

Planetarium possesses leading-edge technology, which reproduces the constellations, comets, nebulae and the natural satellites. The theater and cinemas have times and prices which vary according to the attraction. It is recommended to telephone beforehand or to acquire the programme of the month distributed free at tourist information points, in hotels and other museums of the city.

Praia de Iracema
Access by R. dos Guanacés ●

The architectonic collection is composed of small colorful houses, where bars and restaurants operate. It is famous for its intense nightlife. Near the sea is located the **Ponte dos Ingleses** (Bridge of the English), constructed in the 1920s, which is by the side of the remains of the old metal bridge from 1906. In the same place there is also a grounded ship. The bridges were constructed because Fortaleza did not have a port and the ships anchored far from the shore. With the construction of Mucuripe Port, the bridges became obsolete. At the end there is a pier with a sculpture of the Ceará artist Sérvulo Esmeraldo. Following along the seafront, there is the 6-meter high monument of Iracema made of concrete and glass fibre by the Cearense Zenon Barreto. There is another monument of Iracema on Ave. Beira Mar.

Praia de Mucuripe
Av. Beira-mar, soon after the statue of Iracema ●

This is where the port of Mucuripe is constructed. With good waves for surfing, it is very popular with the young locals. It is known as Mucuripe, but also called Pinzón Beach. It is said that months before Cabral's fleet arrived at the coastline

of Bahia, the Spanish navigator Vicente Pinzón landed in Mucuripe. The discovery did not enter in the official registers as a consequence of the resolutions of the Tordesilhas Treaty which demarcated these lands as the property of the Portuguese crown. Also attributed to Pinzón are the discoveries of the Cabo de Santo Agostinho in Pernambuco and the Jericoacoara Beach.

★ Praia do Futuro
Access by Av. Santos Dumont ● ●

The only beach in the urban perimeter suitable for bathing. Located after Mucuripe, the access to the beach is by paved roads. Along the side of the beach is an 8 km long pedestrian promenade with stalls giving an infrastructure with restaurants, public showers and varied seats and tables spread over the sands. The beach is very popular, always busy in the high season and at weekends. At night some kiosks remain open for live music shows.

Av. Beira Mar / Praia do Meireles ● ●

The most luxurious hotels are located on Ave. Beira Mar, constructed in the 1960s, connecting the east and west zones of the city. The sea is unfit for swimming, even though it is always packed with bathers. There are restaurants serving local food and a handicraft fair functions every night. Lacework, objects made from straw and small bottles decorated with sand are sold. The fair operates in front of the Othon Hotel and continues to the Náutico Atlético Cearense Club. The pedestrian precinct is well policed and there are tourist information. Here the monument that's the emblem of the city, the statue of Iracema, is located. Inaugurated in 1965, it was created by the artist Coribiano Lins.

Casa de José de Alencar, Museu de Renda and Museu de Antropologia

Av. Washington Soares. ☎ 229-1898.
Opening hours: Monday to Sunday
from 8 to 12 a.m. and 2 to 5 p.m.
Entrance: Free. ♿ ♨

This is the place where the writer
from Ceará, José de Alencar, author
of *Iracema* and *The Guarani* was
born. The 9 hectares of land, which
belonged to the father of the author,
including a simple house built of
bricks with a thatched *carnaúba* roof,
were incorporated by the Federal
University of Ceará. Inside the house
is the Lace Museum with samples of
the most popular handicraft of Ceará.
It is a good opportunity to know the
variations of lace, the different
stitches, and the instruments of work.
On the same land is the
Anthropology Museum, with articles
from the time of slavery, such as
iron rings and whips used to punish
the slaves.

Parque do Cocó

Av. Sebastião Abreu, Dionízio Torres
Created to protect a large area of
mangroves and one of the largest
urban parks of Latin America.

It is traversed by Ave. Sebastião
Abreu in such a way that it is possible
for it to be seen from several spots in
Fortaleza. It is an ecological
preservation area for typical wildlife
of the mangroves and has an area for
musical shows and a jogging track.
Another area known as Adahil
Barreto, accessible by Rua Vicente
Leite, possesses infrastructure
including a restaurant, pedal boats,
and a playground.

SURROUNDINGS

★ Beach Park

R. Porto das Dunas, 2734, Aquiraz.
☎ 361-3000. www.beachpark.com.br.
Daily from 11 a.m. 5 p.m. Check the
internet for periods the park closes
for maintenance. ♨ ◉

Aquatic park with thematic water
toboggans and swimming pools with
artificial waves. The biggest of the
slides is called 'Insane' and is 40-m
high, dropping almost in a free fall.
But there are no risks: no one has ever
fallen out of the slide. The park has
direct access to a private beach, with
kiosks at the edge of the sea. The
prices are higher than in the rest of
Fortaleza but the service is first class.

Praia do Futuro: the most famous beach of the city

★ Cumbuco

Access by the CE-085 highway to the west. Buggy drives with the Cumbuco Buggy Men Co-operative. ☎ 318 73 09.
🚗🛝

The 16-km beach belongs to the municipality of Caucaia, and it is one of the most developed on the west coast. In the left corner of the beach is the **Cauípe** lagoon, with stalls that serve food and drinks. A good option is to go on an excursion with the Cumbuco Buggy Men Co-operative who organize two trips: one of them goes across the dunes to **Parnamirim** lagoon where it is enjoyable to 'ski-bunda' – sliding down the dunes on a wooden plank - and fall into the lake. The second trip, besides Parnamirim, includes the **Banana** lagoon and **Cauípe** sand-bar, where the river meets the sea. The landscape is marvelous, a combination of coconut palm-trees, water and sands, gaining shades of colors. At Cauípe Sand-bar, even when the tide is out, never try to cross by car. There is deep quicksand and there is a high risk of becoming bogged down.

Parque Paraíso Perdido

Vale da Lua Cheia, Icaraí, Caucaia municipality. ☎ 318-1004. Friday to Sunday From 9:30 a.m. to 5 p.m.
🚗🛝

Thematic park with 600 wild animals, including monkeys, tigers and hippopotamus. Playground, rope bridge, Tarzan's house, swimming pool with toboggan.

Museu da Cachaça

30 km from Fortaleza in the municipality of Maranguape. Take the CE-O65 and after continue for 5 km along dirt tracks. R. Senador Virgílio Távora. Follow the signposts for Fazenda Ypioca. Tel: 341-0407. Opening hours: Tuesday to Sunday from 8 a.m. to 5 p.m. Closed Mondays.🅿

Ypioca Farm is situated at the foot of Maranguape Mountain Range and has an extensive green area. The Casa Grande (principal farmhouse) was built in 1846, the same year as the fabrication of its first barrel of *cachaça* (a popular Brazilian light-colored rum). The exhibition includes old machinery, documents and films. The largest cask in the world, with a capacity of 374,000 liters of firewater is one of the highlights of the farm.

Guaramiranga

Access by the CE-065 highway 91km from the capital city.
www.serraguaramiranga.hpg.ig.com.br
🅿📷🏔

Guaramiranga is a mountain city surrounded by Nature, situated in Maciço do Baturité. As it is 865 meters above sea level, the temperature is always mild, varying between 18°C and 25°C. In only one walk it is possible to visit it entirely.

Relax by the swimming pool or free fall: catering for all tastes at Beach Park

Extreme maneuvers in the sands of Cumbuco

The infrastructure is directed towards ecotourism, with trained guides. Also it is possible to fish in the Trilhas Park. Leaving Guaramiranga, in the direction of the district of Pernambuquinho, there is the second highest point of the State of Ceará, with an altitude of 1,115m, Alto Peak. From there, there is a panoramic view of the whole region including dense woods, the sea and the *sertão* of Ceará as well as an unforgettable sunset. In February, during the Carnival, it is the time of the Jazz Festival and, in September, there is the Northeastern Theater Festival. In the city there is still a total of 0.1% of the remaining Atlantic forest of the State of Ceará, transformed into an Ecological protected reserve.

Parque Nacional de Ubajara

324 km west of Fortaleza. Open daily from 8 a.m. to 5 p.m. The cable car operates until 4 p.m. 🚻 🅿️
Created in 1959, the Ubajara National Park is the smallest in the country. Situated at the top of the Ibiapaba Plateau, it has a deep-cut relief where limestone rocks are exposed and includes escarpments with unexpected drops forming abysses which shelter caves and caverns. Due to the high rainfall, and the extremely permeable soils, there are waterfalls of up to 70 metres high which fall in the middle of dense forest embedded in the Ceará backlands. The climate varies from 20°C to 26°C, and the dry period is in June and July. The park has a very good infrastructure and depends on a cable car to transport the visitors to the entrance of the Ubajara Cave. Groups leave from the main gate of the park every hour for guided treks through the forest to the caverns and waterfalls. The 3.5 km route to the cave can be made on foot. In total the cavern is 1,120 km long but only 420 meters are open to the public. The best time to visit the park is from July to December. The rainy season is from January to April and on very rainy days entrance to the park is prohibited.

TIPS

- Take the BR-222 to Tianguá, after followed by 18 km on the CE-187 to the entrance of the park. Buses leave from the bus station in Fortaleza directly to Ubajara National Park. Access from Teresina in Piauí is achieved via the BR-343 to the city of Piripiri, after the BR-222 to Tianguá.

Canoa Quebrada

The beaches of the region were discovered by the hippies and backpackers

Fortaleza: 152 km
Paracuru: 235 km
Jericoacoara: 454 km
👤 56,978
🌐 88
ℹ️ Secretaria de Turismo: ☎ 421-1006
@ www.canoa-quebrada.com
🚌🚗

For many years the region's beaches remained deserted, inhabited only by fishermen and women lacemakers. Today, Canoa Quebrada is very busy and forms the second largest tourist center of Ceará. The city suffered a process of uncontrolled urbanization and grew on top of the cliffs, which are geological areas that should remain unoccupied. An ecological reservation was created to protect the remaining cliffs, mangroves and dunes, which until now, have not been affected by the intrusion of man. The amenities of Canoa Quebrada are concentrated in the higher part of the town. On Broadway, the main street of the beach, there is a good choice of bars and it is crowded all year round. On the beach there is a series of kiosks that serve food and drink. Many

History of the name

In 1650, the Portuguese colonizer Francisco Ayres da Cunha was sailing near the Ceará coast, when his damaged ship grounded close to the Ponta Grossa Beach. As his vessel was no longer in a fit condition to continue, the commander decided to donate it to a local fisherman known as Master Simão. The inhabitants of the region – who had never before seen a boat of these proportions – were shocked with the size of the new "canoe-although-broken" of Master Simão. And thus the name of the beach came to be (Canoa Quebrada means Broken Canoe). In the 1970s, Canoa Quebrada was still practically unknown when it was discovered by young people: hippies, backpackers and naturalists from different regions.

beaches in the vicinity remain deserted. With a short walk it is possible to find fishing villages remote from the bustle of Canoa Quebrada.

HIGHLIGHTS

Aracati
Access is gained by the BR-304 highway. The bus company São Benedito operates between Canoa Quebrada and Aracati. ☎ 272-1232 @ www.aracati.com.br. 🚌 🏨

A historical city, with some of the colonial houses restored, it's situated 2 km from Canoa Quebrada. Aracati was the principal staging post in Ceará in the 18th century, when the economy was based on cattle breeding. The Mercado Central (Central Market), built in the 18th century in Rua Coronel Pompeu, houses a daily open-air market. On Rua Coronel Alexandrino it is possible to visit the colonial houses, the city council offices and jail. Still, on the same street, there is the Confederação do Equador building, the place where rebellious troops who fought against the monarchy in 1824 were lodged. Another highlight in the city is the Jaguaribano Museum, that operates in the Solar de Aracati – a three-story mansion with the front lined with Portuguese wall tiles. The exhibits include sacred artworks, fossils, and archaeological remains.

Praia do Cumbe
Circle the bus station of Aracati to the left and follow Rua Coronel Pompeu to the cathedral. From there it is 8 km by dirt tracks to arrive at the Cumbe settlement. Avoid visiting on rainy days as the track becomes precarious. 🏄 Cumbe Beach is situated at the mouth of the river of the same name. Due to the convergence of the sea, river and mangroves, historically, the locals survived on fishing and crabbing. With the creation of the ecological park, the capturing of crustaceans was forbidden. Today there is an abundance of shrimp vivariums in tanks, destined for salt production. Among the vivariums there is a seafood restaurant of seafood. It was built on a pier, in a channel of the Cumbe River, in which various fishing rafts, sailing-vessels and other crafts are moored.

Colored sand handicrafts

Phoenicians and dunes at the Lagoa do Mato

Praia de Morro Branco
From Aracati it is 72 km to the west. From Fortaleza it is 89 km on the CE-004 road to Beberibe. 🏄 🏨 🍴 ⚓

The great charm of Morro Branco are the cliffs that form labyrinths. The tour begins on the cliff plateau, where several hawkers sell small bottles decorated with colored sand, lace and other crafted articles. Afterwards, walking on for a few minutes in the labyrinth sculptured by water and erosion. The sands have varied shades of red, yellow and white. At the exit of the labyrinth is the dune that gave its name to the beach. There is a trail that leaves the beach and leads to a telecommunications tower at the top of the hill, giving a panoramic view of the region. It is a good option to go to **Barra de Sucatinga Beach**, 15 km to the east, by buggy, or by car going along CE-040 and then to the entrance of Sucatinga. On the way, there is also **Praia das Fontes** where there is the Gurta da Mãe d'Água. The cristaline water forms a pool that invites swimming. After that, there is **Diogo Beach**, where it will be needed to leave the car and go by foot to **Uruaú**, that hides among the dunes a beautiful lagoon. The buggies remain on Morro Branco parking lot and in front of the Praia das Fontes resort.

Caponga
103 km from Canoa Quebrada towards the west. 🏄

A 2 km long beach in a cove that shelters a fishing village – the community of Balbino. The community resists the speculation of developers but has already lost a great part of its lands due to a lack of land deeds. Today the inhabitants live near Caponga Beach. Their lands are passed from father to son and all the members of the community are, to some extent, related. They survive by planting crops and fishing, contributing to the fact that Caponga is an important fishing center in the region. The beach is a favorite of city dwellers from Fortaleza.

Cascavel

90 km from Aracati by the CE-040 road to the west. From Fortaleza it is 70 km along the same highway to the east.
The town of Cascavel does not have a beach. Its greatest attraction is the open-air market, which takes place downtown every Saturday morning. In the market, it is possible to check out how the coastal and backlands cultures fuse in the Northeast. Fish and sun-dried beef are sold side by side with clothes, furniture and animals.

Águas Belas

Leave Caponga by the Av. Lauriano Santana, follow the dirt track for 3 km to the Águas Belas settlement.
Águas Belas, with a landscape of coconut groves and dunes, is situated at the mouth of the Mal Cozinhado (Badly Cooked Food) River.

Lobster fishing season is from May to August

As legend goes, the river was baptized with this strange nickname several centuries ago when a priest and his servant were crossing with provisions. The potatoes fell into the river. The servant dived in to recover the potatoes. Later, when he cooked them and served the clergyman, there was something strange. They were not potatoes but the shells of shrimps. Not understanding the unintentional exchange, the priest talked about "this badly cooked food". The Mal Cozinhado River is surrounded by mangroves. It is possible to travel along it by boat. The boat trips are organized by the Village Barra Mar Hotel, in Caponga. Tel: 334-8088. On the other side of the river, in **Barra Velha**, there is a desert beach and the **Barra do Rio Choró**.

From Majorlândia to Ponta Grossa

121 km from Aracati to the east. The option is to rent a buggy in Canoa Quebrada.
Majorlândia Beach is the busiest in the region, ideal for surfing. It has good tourist attractions and an important handicraft production, especially bottles decorated with colored sand. There are white and reddish cliffs and a vast coconut grove. The cliffs at Majorlândia are similar to those in Canoa Quebrada and are seen at intervals on route to the border with Rio Grande do Norte. The only different cliffs are those on the short stretch which belongs to the Refúgio Dourado Hotel, where the cliffs were completely sculptured by the craftsman, Toinho da Areia Colorida. The next beach, **Quixaba**, with white cliffs is where shrimp fishing takes place. **Lagoa do Mato** Beach, 10 kilometers away, is completely deserted and one of the most beautiful of the region. It is surrounded by cliffs and dunes that are crossed by waterways that replenish the lake. The sea has coral reefs and it is possible to dive. Twenty-four km farther, **Fontaínha** is on a private property with access only from the sands. It is situated near the foot of vast crags, dunes and a primitive fishing village. These cliffs were nicknamed the Garganta do Diabo (Devil's Throat). It is said that the mud originating from them has

Cliffs and dunes in the landscape of Morro Branco

medicinal properties. **Retirinho** is the next beach. Situated close to colored dunes, it is near to the dammed waters of the São Francisco stream. In the hamlet there are bars and holiday homes. At the top of the crags is the **Som das Águas** watchtower, a little cliff by the sea, which has at its base a foot of rocks with designs formatted by the coming and going of the tides. And, finally, **Ponta Grossa** is where the vessel of Francisco Ayres da Cunha was shipwrecked. Arriving at the beach it is possible to have a good idea of the difficulties that would have been imposed on any navigator. The left point has peculiar rock outcrops, evident at low tide, creating scenery of outstanding beauty. At the same point there is a cliff of several colors. At its top there is a gigantic dune, from where it is possible to see in every direction. Historic archives reveal that the Spaniard Vincente Pinzón disembarked here in Ponta Grossa in February 1500. Ponta

Grossa is inhabited by 250 people who live off lobster fishing. The oldest residents have biblical names such as Josué (Joshua), Jeová (Jehovah) and Canaã (Canaan). Ponta Grossa is one of the most beautiful beaches of the region. The boarding houses are simple and the meals may be prepared in kiosks on the sands.

Redonda

Access by the CE-201 to the junction to Icapuí. The last 6 km are by dirt track. Leave Caponga by Av. Lauriano 🐠 🔃
This beach is visited by surfers and inhabited by lobster fishermen. From May to August, the catching of crustaceans is permitted by Ibama. In the other months, however, during the breeding season, capture is illegal. So as not to stay without a source of income during the breeding season, the fishermen created a lobster vivarium in the sea. The beach is 2 km long with much algal, which attracts Peixes-boi (manatee).

Cliffs in Ponta Grossa near the colored dunes ▶

Jericoacoara

Rest or action: Jericoacoara for all tastes

Fortaleza: 305 km
Quixadá: 439 km
Paracuru: 240 km
 9,751
 88
 Secretaria de Turismo: 669-1133
 Ibama: (85) 272-1600
@ www.jericoacoara.tur.br

According to the Tremembé Indians, Jericoacoara means the alligator's resting place. But so that the literal translation does not create false expectations the traveller has a better chance of finding pigs and jackasses resting than the aquatic reptile. They say that Jericoacoara is also a word of Tupi Indian origin, and it means the Turtle Hole. Turtles are not so rare in the region. Jeri, as it is popularly know, is considered one of the 10 most beautiful beaches in the world according to *The New York Times*. The drifting sand dunes, surrounded by lakes of pristine water, and the turquoise-colored seawaters splashing over colored rocks, could only be dignified of Environmental Protection. Jeri was converted into a national park in 2002, with the aim of

protecting its wildlife. The village does not have pavements, paved roads or great buildings. Little fishermen's cottages exist side by side with both simple and sophisticated hotels. As opposed to other regions in the Northeast, it is not possible to separate the high and low seasons in Jericoacoara, and there is all-year round tourism. In some periods, such as Christmas, the New Year Easter, more visitors are attracted than an ecotourism area can really support. Because of this, for people who prefer tranquillity, it's not recommended to visit Jericoacoara on bank holidays. But for the ones who are accustomed to the bohemian lifestyle, Jericoacoara is extremely enjoyable: there is *forró* and electronic music, all of which allied to a spectacular violet dawn and sunsets over the ocean waters.

HIGHLIGHTS

★ Pedra Furada
A 15-minute walk along the beach eastwards at low tide. This stretch receives the name of Malhada (Specked) Beach. It is possible to follow a trail from the tower of the lighthouse.

The symbol of Jericoacoara, the perforated stone, has an orifice of about 4 meters in diameter, through which the visitor can enter, sit and wait for the waves to slowly advance forwards. The rocks in the vicinity have varying tones of red and yellow, contrasting with the green of the forests during the rainy season, or the aridity in the dry season, and always the scene is graced by the blues of the sky and sea. Between July and September the sun sets exactly in line with the orifice of the stone, imparting an extraordinary sight.

★ Duna do Pôr do Sol ☯

Situated in the left-hand corner of Jericoacoara Beach, the dune unites the community and visitors at sunset. With a height of about 30 meters and an inclination of nearly 80°, the dune advances to the beach and at low tide it forms a corridor between the ocean and the sand mountain.

SURROUNDINGS

Praia do Preá

At low tide heading east for 13 km. ☯ The Preá Beach is an 8-km strip of sand and the horizon is as far as the eyes can see in every direction. It is a very good spot to swim in the sea. It still shelters a peaceful fishing village, with few bars and lodges. The proximity of the Jijoca Lake is the reason for the active tourism.

★ Lagoa Azul and Lagoa Paraíso

Via the municipality of Jijoca de Jericoacoara or across Preá Beach. There

Lagoa Azul: the paradise of Jijoca

The Sleeping City

On the way to Pedra Furada, there is a sort of cave, in which it is only possible to enter crouched. There is no way to advance inwards. As legend goes its interior is protected by an iron door behind which there is an enchanted city where a beautiful princess lives. She is perfect except for the curse that she is under: the beauty woman has only human feet and face. The body is of a serpent with golden scales. To break the spell, human blood must be spilt on the door, and thus the door will open. Then, a cross of human blood drawn on the serpent's tail will free the princess of her viper's body. At this moment, the enchanted city of Jericoacoara will reappear. According to the expert in folklore, Câmara Cascudo, a venerable old man called Old Queiroz, risked his life trying to break the spell of the serpent. He took his people to the cavern and the snake-princess appeared, but nobody wanted to be sacrificed.

are *jardineiras* (type of tourist coach) which leave Jericoacoara stopping at the two lakes or buggies to rent. ☯ The two lakes are, in truth, stretches of one bigger lake that is officially known as **Jijoca Lake**. With an area of 30 sq km, the lake starts in the municipality of Jijoca and only ends in Caiçara. The banks of the Azul Lake are the least inhabited and with a beautiful view. Paraíso is more developed and has more stalls. Ideal for windsurfing, it is prohibited to pilot motorboats. There is also a pleasant ride on a seagoing raft.

Praia de Guriú

11 km west of Jericoacoara along the corridor formed between the sea and the Pôr do Sol Dune. ☯ On the way the visitor will have to pass by the **Mangue Seco** Beach, which is deserted and exotic. Following this, take the ferry across the mouth of the Guriú River. On the other side, **Guriú** is a wide beach with light soft sand that is surrounded by dunes, reefs and coconut palms. On the buggy trail, there are the remains of what used to be the fishing village of **Tatajuba**.

The interesting formation and red tones of Pedra Furada

Camocim

From Fortaleza, by the BR-222 highway to the Aprazível road junction, turn right on the CE-364 road. This is a hundred-year-old city, and an important fishing center of Ceará. It is encircled by old stonewalls. There are several natural beauty spots, such as the **Barrinhas Beach**, with its narrow strip of sand, weak waves and pristine waters. The **Cangalha** and **Boqueirão** lakes are situated here. At the top of the cliff there is an observation point with a view of the sea where it is possible to observe the comings and goings of the fishing boats and the sunrise. For a pleasant dip in fresh water in **Seco Lake**, the visitor should follow Rua 3 de Outubro in Camocim to the end, turn left on the Rua Rodagem do Lago. Seco Lake has several bars.

Nova Tatajuba

36 km west of Jericoacoara. It is also possible to visit it by going along the beach starting from Camocim. Tatajuba village moved to another site due to a very common phenomenon in the coastal communities near dunes: the action of the winds makes the dunes drift over the houses forcing the inhabitants to move to places farther from the sea. Nova Tatajuba is an isolated settlement, on the left side of the Lago Grande effluent.

Bitupitá

From Camocim, follow the dirt track westwards, going past Curimã. The last beach on the coast of Ceará, Bitupitá is very calm. It has dunes, coconut palm-trees, a lighthouse and a simple fishing village. From there, the visitant can go to the estuary of the Timonha River, on the **Pontal das**

Por-do-Sol dunes: 30 m high ▶

Almas. This is a piece of land where the river and sea meet, with soft sands and a coconut grove. **Curimã** is a primitive village of 'jangadeiros' (fishermen who use rafts) without electrical energy. The trip must be made along the dirt roads but not when it is raining.

TIPS

– **Access**: From Fortaleza take the CE-085 highway to Itapipoca and from there follow the CE-179 to the municipality of Jijoca de Jericoacoara. In Jijoca it will be necessary to leave the car in a car park and catch a *jardineira* (type of coach) or a jeep to Jericoacoara. Some hotels offer this route.
– To arrive in Jericoacoara by bus, it is recommended to choose the bus at 6:30 p.m. that makes few stops. The bus at 9 a.m. stops many times and exceeds the total carrying capacity with people standing in the corridor.
– To arrive at Jericoacoara by motor vehicle or buggy, it is important to be always aware of the timetable of the tides or to be accompanied by a driver who knows the route, as the stretch along the beach can be dangerous, particularly at night.
– The Parnaíba Delta in Piauí and the Lençóis Maranhenses in Maranhão are geographically near Jericoacoara. The visitor who has already arrived at such a distant beach could visit these two other tourist spots. The company Jeri – Off Road offers a service of buggies. To make an economic trip, it is recommended to catch the jeep that leaves from Sunday to Thursday to Camocim at 3:30 a.m. From Camocim there is a bus, which leaves every day from the bus station to Parnaíba in Piauí. In the port at Parnaíba, take a passenger boat that crosses the delta to Tutóia. It is a very interesting ten-hour trip among the mangroves and the delta islets. The passenger boats go on one day and return on the next, and so, departures from Parnaíba are only on Mondays, Wednesdays and Fridays. It is recommended to take a nylon or cotton hammock, which can be bought in the street market near to the port of Parnaíba. In Tutóia the visitor should rent a Toyota ☎ 98 349-0016 to travel to Paulino Neves or Caburé – entrance of the little Lençóis Maranhenses –, or go directly to Barreirinhas, the entrance to the Lençóis Maranhenses Park.

Juazeiro do Norte

Faith conducts thousands to Juazeiro to praise "Father Cícero"

Crato 12 km
Fortaleza: 587 km
Petrolina: 356 km
👤 211,858
🌐 88
ℹ️ Secretaria de Turismo: ☎ 532-1495

The city is situated in the Ceará backlands, in the region of Cariri and the Chapada do Araripe. It was the chosen city of Father Cícero Romão (1844-1934) for him to preach and perform his supposed miracles, which are not recognized by the Catholic Church. Pilgrims and devotees travel to the city to contemplate the 25-meter high statue built in his honor, and to visit his tomb. A museum unites his personal belongings. Juazeiro do Norte grew and developed at the start of the 20th century by the determination of Father Cícero.

HIGHLIGHTS

Estátua do Padre Cícero
Serra do Horto, 7 km from Juazeiro do Norte.
It is the third biggest concrete work of art of the world. The first is the Statue of Liberty in New York, and the second, the Cristo Redentor (Christ the Redeemer), in Rio de Janeiro. With a height of 27m and a base of 8m, it was put up on the site where the clergyman spent his religious retreats.

Museu do Padre Cícero
R. São José 242. ☎ 511 2876.
Opening hours: Tuesday to Sunday from 8 to 11 a.m. and 2 to 5 p.m. Entrance: free. 🏛
This was the last house of Father Cícero. It is a permanent exhibition of the personal possessions of the priest, the sacred images, sermons, the priest's cassock, books and paintings.

Memorial do Padre Cícero
Pça. do Socorro. ☎ 512-2240. Opening hours: Monday to Friday from 8 a.m. to 6 p.m. Weekends from 8 to 12 a.m. Entrance: Free of charge. 🏛
Founded in 1988, it possesses an auditorium for discussions about popular religiousness. The library has books about Father Cícero's life.

Casa dos Milagres
Praça do Socorro. Opening hours:

Daily from 8 a.m. to 5 p.m.
Entrance: free 🏛
This is a hall with hundreds of ex-solemn promises of people who received graces from Father Cícero and wooden, plastic and chalk pieces representing feet, legs, arms, hands and heads. Photographs and documents signed by people who attest to the powers of the priest.

Capela de Nossa Senhora do Perpétuo Socorro

Pça. do Socorro. Opening hours: from 7 a.m. to 7 p.m. Entrance: free. 🧑
The chapel was built in 1908. On the day of Father Cícero's death, July 20, 1934. His coffin was escorted by 80,000 devotees to the high altar of the chapel, where he is buried. It is a meeting point of the faithful, chiefly on the 20th of every month.

Santuário de São Francisco

Pça. das Almas. ☎ 511-1332.
Open for masses and events. 🏛🧑
It was built in the 1950s and holds more than 30,000 people comprising the greatest religious ministry of the region.

Gráfica de Literatura de Cordel Lira Nordestina

Pça. dos Ourives, railway track.
Opening hours: Monday to Friday from 7 a.m. to 5 p.m.
This establishment offers workshops of xylography and demonstrates the process of the manual framing of this popular form of literature.

SURROUNDINGS

Chapada do Araripe

CE-292 road in the direction of Crato. The road is irregular and interrupted. It is recommended to go accompanied by guide. ☎ 571-2668/571-1854 🏛🌿
This is a large plateau in the semiarid Northeast, which was transformed into an Ecological Protection area in 1947. Its height at 970 meters blocks the cold fronts that come from the south and the air masses from the north. With the collision of the masses of air the rainfall rate reaches 1,360 mm annually forming 307 springs and waterfalls at the foot of the plateau.

Museu de Paleontologia de Santana do Cariri

Santana do Cariri, 65 km from Juazeiro do Norte. Rua Dr. José Augusto, 326. ☎ 545-1206. Access by the CE-292 road in the direction of Crato. Opening hours: Tuesday and Saturday from 8 a.m. to 4 p.m. Sunday from 8 a.m. to 2 p.m. 🏛
The arid region constitutes an important archaeological site due to the geologic formations. The backlands, which hundreds of millions of years ago was sea, preserved its fossils from the Cretaceous period more then 100 millions of years old.

"A lazy mind becomes the workshop of the devil"

Father Cícero died on July 20, 1934 and until today thousands of his followers meet in Juazeiro do Norte to honor him. His fame as a saintliness grew on the March 6, 1889, during a celebration of a mass, when he transformed Host into blood in the mouth of the beatified Maria Araújo. The Catholic Church did not accept the miracle, but people from the Northeast had no doubt. In fact, when he was alive, Father Cícero was almost excommunicated. He was a polemic man. Father Cícero gave support to the rebel troops who deposed the president of Ceará, Francisco Rabelo in 1914. For this he managed to bring together approximately 50,000 volunteers in a mini religious war, which invaded the towns of Crato, Barbalha and Quixadá. In this violent land, he was respected by rebels and colonels. He believed in the motto "a lazy mind   becomes the workshop of the devil", and because of this preached 'productivity'.

Model of Father Cícero

Lagoinha

The sunset brings out the golden tones of the dunes

Fortaleza: 85 km; **Jericoacora:** 120 km
Paracuru: 53 km
👤 20,803 in the municipality of
Paraipaba
🌐 85
ℹ️ Secretaria de Turismo: ☎ 363-1341
😊😊

Lagoinha Beach is famous for
its golden dune, which advances into
the sea, with some coconut palm-
trees in the right-hand corner of
the beach.
It is really a prized vision, especially
at sunset, when the sun brings out the
golden tones of the dune. Lagoinha
is a tranquil and quiet retreat, without
many tourists, few bars and
restaurants. It is possible to visit
lagoons, mangroves and *restinga*
forest using a combination of methods
of transport, tractor, 'jardineira' (a
type of coach) and buggy. Otherwise,
everything can be seen on foot. The
hamlet was built on the cliff top and
there are excellent boarding houses
on the seafront. The watchtower is
the ideal point to observe the sea and
the fishermen's rafts.

SURROUNDINGS

Lagoa de Almécegas
Access from Lagoinha Beach going to
the west. Day trips leaving from Pousada
O Milton. 🕐 3 hours
With a length of 2,500 meters and a
maximum depth of 8 meters, the
freshwater lake is the place fishermen
cast their nets. The communities on its
shoreline live off subsistence farming
and a small number live off tourism.
The beaches and the entire tourist
infrastructure are controlled by the
hotels, making the lake the base for
excursions. Outings, which leave
from Lagoinha, traverse areas of
restinga forests, mangroves and pass
by local settlements. Transportation is
accomplished in the back of a truck,
bound for the rural regions of
Lagoinha, passing by an old flourmill.
Arriving at the Almécegas Lagoon,
there is a break for bathing. It is a
good opportunity to try the grilled
'coalho' cheese (a Brazilian white
cheese), steamed shrimps and to drink
some coconut water in the kiosks. The
crossing of the lake is made by
catamaran. The return trip is along the
beach by buggy, passing by Jegue Lake.

Lagoa de Mundaú: catamaran trips ▶

Paracuru

From Lagoinha, at low tide, it is possible to go to Paracuru along the beach to the east. From Fortaleza follow the BR-222 to Umarituba. Turn right before the settlement and continue 7 km to São Gonçalo do Amarante. Turn left, continue for another 15 km, turn right and follow the road for 14 km.

Paracuru is the only municipality in Ceará with its downtown on the seashore. It has a vast coconut grove, a large bay, reefs, 'fish corrals', natural swimming pools, and fishing rafts along the beach. The 'fish corrals' are a type of trap which is set at sea, taking advantage of the outgoing tide. In total there are 17 km of beaches: Bica and Canto beaches have calm seas; Manguba, Ronco do Mar and Boca do Poço have good waves for surfing.

Fleixeiras

From Lagoinha at low tide, it is possible to arrive at Fleixeiras by the beach going eastwards.

With a large strip of sand, dunes and coconut trees, the Fleixeiras Beach belongs to the municipality of Trairi. The sea is rough with immense reefs. The fishing village is centered around coconut trees, surrounded by high dunes. It is a good opportunity to visit a fishing raft workshop, where it is possible to follow the craftsman's manufacturing process. At low tide a good option is to make a trip to Trairi River, in the direction of Lagoinha, passing by Guajiru Beach. It is possible to go to Guajiru along paved roads, leaving Rua São Pedro, in Fleixeiras. Continuing ahead it passes by Pedra Chata, Palitô and Pedra Rasa beaches. Another possibility is to go in the opposite direction (west), going past Emboaca arriving at Mundaú.

Mundaú

From Lagoinha, at low tide, it is possible to reach Mundaú along the beach to the west, passing by Fleixeiras. Or, also leaving from Lagoinha, go along the CE-085 for 41 km to the district of Barrento.

The road reveals a beautiful landscape starting at Trairi village. At Peixinho it is possible to see women lace makers with their cushions and lace bobbins, braiding handiwork. The dirt track, which proceeds to Mundaú Lake, crosses dunes, which advance over the trail, and sometimes the road is blocked. The lake is located where Mundaú River enters the sea forming delightful scenery with coconut trees. It is possible to make catamaran trips on the lake or cross it by ferry to Baleia Beach. Then following the beach, to the west, to arrive at Icaraí de Amontada, a very popular beach for windsurfers.

PIAUÍ

PIAUÍ

The State is the only in the Northeast whose capital, Teresina, is not located on the coast. Also it is the northeastern State that possesses the shortest coastline, with an extension of just 66 km, which was given up by Ceará more than 120 years ago, in exchange for a larger area farther inland on the border between the two States. This question is still controversial and, until today, there is a disputed area which officially does not pertain to any State. The inhabitants of Piauí compare the shape of the state, which has an area of 252,300 km², to the shape of a stocking. This format is due to the fact that Piauí was colonized from the *sertão* (the dry interior) seawards – another characteristic which distinguishes it from the rest of the Northeast. The first colonizers arriving in the region in the 17th century, coming from Bahia and Pernambuco, occupied the Canindé and Piauí River valleys. The first settlements were built in the region to combat and eliminate the most hostile Indian tribes, such as the Tremembé, and to advance cattle herding. The cities of Oeiras – the first capital city of the State –, Amarante, Floriano and Teresina are the main colonial reference points.

The Parnaíba River is the most important link in the identification and integration of the State. With a length of 1,480 km, its source is in Chapada das Mangabeiras, on the border with Maranhão, Bahia and Tocantins and it flows unto the Atlantic Ocean creating the only deep-sea delta of the American continent, which is one of the most beautiful spots on the Brazilian coast. The majority of the 70 islets that form the delta belong to Maranhão, but the tourist excursions depart from Piauí. In July 2002, President Fernando Henrique Cardoso signed a decree transforming the area of the Parnaíba Delta into a national park. Piauí enjoys four national parks. The most famous is called Serra da Capivara in São Raimundo Nonato, declared a cultural heritage site by Unesco in 1991. The conservation unit is one of the most important in Brazil for archaeology and prehistoric rock paintings. The State is one of the greatest producers and processors of cashew nuts of the country. But the principal agricultural products of Piauí are sugarcane, manioc, corn and soybeans.

Highlights

❶ Delta do Parnaíba
❷ Parque Nacional da Serra da Capivara
❸ Parque Nacional de Sete Cidades

◀ Pedra Furada: Serra da Capivara National Park

❶

Ilha do Caju

Praia Pedra do S

Praia de Maca

Parnaíba

Parnaíba

Área de litígi

❷

PARQUE NACIONAL
DE SETE CIDADES

BR
222

Esperantina

Batalha

Piripiri

● Pedro II

BR
343

Timon

✈ **TERESINA**

PIAUÍ

● Amarante

BR
316

BR
343

Floriano

BR
230

Oeiras

Picos

❸

BR
135

PI
140

Eliseu Martins

Canto do Buriti

BR
020

Caninde

BR
407

SERRA DA
CAPIVARA

SERRA DO URUÇUI

Piauí

São Raimundo Nonato

Caracol

BR
324

SERRA DAS
CONFUÕES

N

W ✦ **E**

S

CHAPADA DAS
MANGABEIRAS

0   120   240 km

Corrente

São Franc

LEGENDS

▭ National park

━━ Paved road

━━ Dirt track

Teresina

The city is situated on the Parnaíba River, far from the ocean

Floriano: 355 km
Parnaíba: 340 km
Piripiri: 183 km
São Raimundo Nonato: 525 km
714,318
86
Empresa de Turismo do Piauí (Piemtur)
222-6202
www.teresina.org.br

Piauí has the only non-coastal capital city of all the northeastern States. In spite of this, the city has the heat and smell of the seashore. This is noticeable driving along Av. Frei Serafim, the main street of the municipality, where the best shopping malls and restaurants are to be found. The average annual temperature is around 28°C, but it can easily reach 40°C in summer, during the months of December and January. Teresina is the only Brazilian capital which is located on the frontier of two States, maintaining a strong economic and social relationship with the city of Timon in Maranhão. It is enough to cross a metal bridge over the Parnaíba River – which, along with the Poti River, composes the hydrological reference of the municipality – to step into the State of Maranhão. In the outlying suburb of Velho Poti, where Teresina was founded in 1852, there are the many pottery and ceramic workshops responsible for the majority of the artistic production of the city. Here it is possible to buy crafted pieces from the manufacturers. And, in downtown, there are the churches and buildings from the 19th century, such as the 4 de Setembro Theater from 1894 and São Benedito Church from 1886.

HIGHLIGHTS

Oficina da Palavra

R. Benjamin Constant, 1400.
223-4441. Opening hours: Monday to Friday from 8 to 12 a.m. and from 2 to 8 p.m. Saturday from 8 to 12 a.m. A cultural center with a library and classroom which encourages meetings among artists, exhibitions of sculptures and paintings, and courses. Cinéas Santos, creator of the center, is the author of the official anthem of the city. He organizes the 'Cara Alegre' (Happy Face), a caravan of local artists who promote cultural activities.

Parque Ambiental Encontro dos Rios

Av. Boa Esperança, Poti Velho, ☎ 271-9514. Opening hours: Monday to Friday from 8 a.m. to 6 p.m. Saturday from 8 to 12 a.m. 🌐 ❶ ♿ This park found at the fork of the Poti and Parnaíba rivers has charming gardens, kiosks, crafted articles and a tourist center. The tambaqui fish stew in the floating bar is tasty. There is a monument that honors the Cabeça de Cuia (head of a gourd). Some children accompany visitors to tell the tale of poor young Crispim, who killed his mother because he was famished and she had not made his dinner. Before dying she cursed him, condemning him to live as a monster with a big head, for six months on the Poti River and the other six on the Parnaíba, unless he devoured seven virgins called Maria.

Museu do Piauí

Pça. Marechal Deodoro da Fonseca, Downtown. ☎ 221-6027. Opening hours: Tuesday to Friday from 8 a.m. to 5 p.m.. Weekends from 8 to 12 a.m.

Closed on Mondays. 🌐 ♿ Of the two thousand objects on display, there is a baptism basin used by the Jesuits to baptize the Indians in the 16th century. Also notable is a three-thousand-year-old tomb with the body of a child inside. The most famous work of art is a painting of D. Pedro II, by Victor Meirelles de Lima in 1875. The building was originally built in 1934 to accommodate one section of the Public Archives of Piauí. Since 1999 it is called the Odilon Nunes Museum of Piauí, honoring the most important historian of the State.

Casa da Cultura

R. Rui Barbosa, 348. ☎ 221-1755. Opening hours: Monday to Friday from 8 a.m. to 5:30 p.m. Saturday from 8 to 12 a.m. Entrance: free. ☐ All the artistic presentations of Teresina pass through here, both the fixed or itinerant programs. On the fixed programs it is possible to watch the rehearsals of the municipal orchestra, watch movies with daily showings presented by the video library or see the

❶ Casa da Cultura
❷ Palácio de Karnak
❸ Igreja de São Benedito
❹ Teatro 4 de Setembro
❺ Igreja Matriz Nossa Senhora do Amparo
❻ Museu do Piauí
❼ Oficina da Palavra

Tribute to an Empress

The city of Teresina was founded in 1852 specifically to function as the administrative seat of the province of Piauí. The then governor, José Antônio Saraiva wanted a capital with planned urban growth and, because of this, after much controversy, moved the seat of government from Oeiras, to benefit the other city. Known before as Vila do Poti until it became the capital, Teresina was bestowed this name as homage to Empress Teresa Cristina, wife of the Emperor D. Pedro II. As it was a planned city, it is easy to navigate through its streets, which resemble a chessboard. The reference points are always the banks of the Parnaíba and Poti Rivers, which embrace the centre of the city.

exposition of geology and palaeontology. There are nearly five thousand items, books, photographs, paintings, films and sacred artworks available to the visitor. The center offers dance, theater, music, art and photography courses. Founded in 1994, the Casa da Cultura is located in a 19th-century building, originally belonging to João do Rego Monteiro, the Baron of Gurguéia. Over the years the place was also a seminary, Episcopal residence, the seat of the diocese of Teresina and the National Works Department against Drought offices (Dnocs) in Piauí.

Parque Zoobotânico
Access by the PI-112, Km 5. 🍃 🎯

Handicrafts: ceramics, laces, embroidery

The park has an area of 137 hectares with dense vegetation, trails, lakes and more than 150 species of animals. One of the most important is the lizard *Coleodactylus meridionale*, the smallest in Brazil.

Catedral de Nossa Senhora do Amparo
Pça. Saraiva. Visiting hours: Monday to Sunday during office hours. 🔆
The building of the church was started in 1851. It was finally finished in 1952 and transformed into the capital's principal church during the centenary of the city. On the high altar, there is an image of the patron saint of the municipality, which was brought from Portugal during the first year of construction. The church towers have already become landmarks on the skyline of Teresina.

Igreja de São Benedito
Av. Frei Serafim. Monday to Sunday during office hours. 🔆
Situated on the main avenue of Teresina, the building completed in 1886 is protected by the National Historical and Artistic Heritage Institute (Iphan). It is the third biggest Catholic temple of the capital and is located a few meters from the Karnak Palace. The principal avenue of Teresina is named after friar Serafim, a highly esteemed personality in local history.

Palácio Karnak
Pça. da Liberdade, Downtown. ☎ 221-7061. Visiting hours: Monday to Friday during office hours. 📷
The palace has been the seat of State government since 1926. This official building, with gardens designed by

Burle Marx, has a façade inspired in the architecture of the temple with the same name from ancient Egypt.

Teatro 4 de Setembro

Pça. D. Pedro II, Downtown.
☎ 221-7100. ♿

The historic construction dates from 1894, inspired by the European style of the age. It was built to substitute the old theaters of Santa Teresa and Concórdia. However, at the inauguration, on April 23, 1894, the 4 de Setembro was unable to hold the planned party because it did not have stage sets, furniture, decoration or bathrooms. The inauguration spectacular could only be performed one year later in May 1895. Today, with a seating capacity of 582 and 10 dressing rooms, it is the venue of the principal theater plays and also political and social events of Teresina.

TIPS

– With available time, downtown Teresina is a place to be visited on foot. The D. Pedro II, Saraiva and Marechal Deodoro Fonseca squares, where the main attractions are found, are four blocks from each other. The problem of the downtown area is the heat and the excessive number of street hawkers in the pedestrian-only

Palácio Karnak: like an Egyptian temple

areas. It is by walking that you can come across the curious 'climatized street', an arcade cooled by air-conditioning and fans. It is situated behind the N.Sra.do Amparo Church.
– Do not leave Teresina without seeing the sunset over the Parnaíba River. Cross the metal bridge which spans the river to the city of Timon in Maranhão by car or on foot.
– To know the regional music, visit the Toccata CD store. Here one can find recordings by the guitarist Erisvaldo Borges and the Bandolins de Oeiras musical group comprising ladies who play *chorinho* (typical style of music).
R. Anfrísio Lobão, 922, Jóquei.
☎ 233-2151

The local menu

Inhabitants from Piauí do not pass a single day without eating 'beiju'. It is dough very similar to tapioca from Bahia, but without coconut, in the shape of a disc. Made from a gum produced from manioc flour, it is served with meat, eggs, butter, and desserts or even on its own. Also typical from Piauí are the dishes of 'Maria Isabel', seasoned rice mixed with jerked (salted sun-dried) beef, and 'paçoca', flour with jerked beef pounded in a mortar. The local cuisine, almost always, includes the basic ingredients of spring onions, parsley, coriander, coconut milk, pepper-de-cheiro (type of chilli pepper) and urucum (*Bxa orellana* - annatto). All can be accompanied by 'cajuína' a juice extracted from the cashew fruit with *tiquira* (a

Beiju: tastes good with anything

beverage made by fermenting manioc). Try one of the two best dishes from Piauí: 'Capote' which is guinea fowl with seasoned rice and 'capão' which has this name because a *capado* (castrated) rooster is the principal ingredient.

Oeiras

Igreja N. Sra das Vitórias: the oldest in the state, concluded in 1733

Floriano: 131 km
São Raimundo Nonato: 269 km
Teresina: 324 km
Parnaíba: 672 km
👤 33,890
🌐 89

The first capital city which emerged from the settlement on the Cabrobó farm, was also known as Vila do Mocha because of its location on the banks of a stream of the same name. On December 26, 1717, D. João V officially established the site as a village by way of a royal decree. It was chosen as the seat of the government until 1852, when Teresina became the province's capital. The current name originated only in 1761 and is a tribute to the municipal's namesake in Portugal. With the transference of the capital, the importance of the city diminished. The colonial buildings can be found around the principal church, N. Sra das Vitórias, raised in 1733. Three events mark the local calendar: the Festa do Vaqueiro (cowboy party), in May; the celebration of the city's patron saint, N. Sra.das Vitórias, in August; and the festival of N. Sra. da Conceição, in December.

HIGHLIGHTS

★ Igreja Nossa Senhora das Vitórias
Pça. das Vitórias 🌐
From this square it is possible to visit the principal church, Nossa Senhora das Vitórias, the oldest of the State, finished in 1733. Inside there are some 18th-century images which remain intact until today. Around the square are colonial buildings, currently occupied by commercial firms, among which are the Cine-Teatro (theater), from the start of the century and next door is the Chambers of Commerce from 1840, which today lodges a government institution that supports small and micro businesses (Sebrae).

Museu de Arte Sacra
Pça. Visconde de Parnaíba.
📞 462-1250. Visiting hours: Tuesday to Friday, from 8 to 12 a.m. and from 2 to 5 p.m. Saturday and Sunday, from 8 to 12 a.m. closed on Mondays. ⑪
More than 150 years old, when Oeiras was the capital city, the building was the residence of the province's governors. It is also known as the João Nepomuceno Palace. It exhibits sacred

Espaço Cultural Maria Bonita: the former site of the generating plant ▶

works of art from colonial Brazil, including religious artifacts.

Pé de Deus e Pé do Diabo
R. de Cruzeiro.

In front of the Casa da Pólvora (Gunpowder House) there is a rock with the Pé de Deus and the Pé de Diabo (God's foot and the Devil's foot). Those believers, who pass by it every day, throw flowers towards a mark which, it is thought, was left by Christ and throw stones at a dog's footprint which symbolizes the devil (frequently 'the Devil' is called 'the Dog').

SURROUNDINGS

Floriano
131 km from Oeiras via BR-230 🚌 🏠 ⛪

This small city played an important socio-economic role in Piauí. It was in the Terminal Turístico (Tourist Terminal) building that, in 1874, Francisco Parentes, taking advantage of a workforce of 714 slaves, opened a large agricultural establishment. He had recently arrived from France and presented progressive ideas for the time. The building housed the first agricultural college of Brazil. In the Terminal Turístico, the visitor will find ceramic and embroidery handicraft shops and also a restaurant. It is located next door to the **Espaço Cultural Maria Bonita**, the former site of the city's electrical generating plant, which still preserves the colonial architecture from the 19th century. Take the opportunity to visit the **Igreja São Pedro de Alcântara** from 1922, a major reference point for the

Arab community of Floriano. The Islamic profile of the church differs from the European influenced styles of Piauí. The carnival of the city is famous throughout the State. Merry-makers and *trio elétricos* (trucks carrying high-tech sound systems) traverse the Av. Esmaragno de Freitas, on the banks of the Parnaíba River. The river has a strong current, but this does not impede the crossing of small boats to **Barão de Grajaú**, on the Maranhense bank. The boats constantly embark from piers along the avenue.

Amarante
219 km from Oeiras. Take the BR-230 highway to Floriano and then take the BR-343. 🚌 🏠

A small town which is situated 88 km from Floriano. It is the birthplace of important personalities from the history of Piauí, such as the poet Antônio Francisco da Costa e Silva and the historian Odilon Nunes. The house where Nunes was born in 1889 has become a cultural center. During the first week of August, when his birthday is celebrated, the city becomes packed due to the festivities. From December 25 to 31, there are also celebrations in honor of the patron saint São Gonçalo. The city is part of the historic tour of the State and it carries the name of another city in Portugal. A visit downtown reveals narrow streets, sidewalks in colonial Portuguese style and walls lined with original European glazed wall tiles. On the route from Floriano is the **Quilombo de Mimbó** (community of runaway slaves).

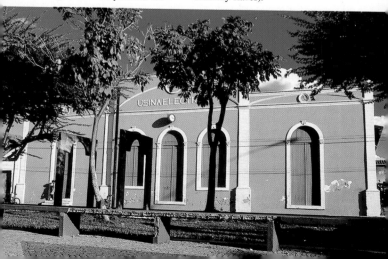

Parnaíba

The city of Parnaíba is the embarkation point to visit the river delta

Teresina: 335 km
Piripiri: 182 km
Pedro II: 240 km
Sobral (Ceará): 237 km
👤 132,235
🌐 86
ℹ️ Prefeitura ☎ 321-3016
🍴🏨

The second biggest city of Piauí, Parnaíba is a landmark on the State's coastline. The city limits reach only one branch of the Parnaíba River, which is that of the Igaraçu River. Leaving Parnaíba in the morning, it is possible to spend the entire day visiting places suchlike the Pedra do Sal (Rock of Salt), in the municipality of Ilha Grande de Santa Isabel, and the Macapá Beach, 13 km from Parnaíba in Luís Correia.

Of the Brazilian States bordering on the sea, Piauí is the one with the shortest coastline: 66 km of extension. The coast of Piauí has white sands, is covered by drifting dunes and has several confluences between ocean and river waters. The landscape is sculptured by the dancing of the sands and waters. On the eastern side, for example, one branch of the sea hits head-on with the Cardoso and Camurupim rivers, forming the small isle of Camaleão (Chameleon) off Macapá Beach. The dunes, which drift from the coast inland with the uninterrupted forces of the wind, have already formed two large natural swimming pools: the lakes of Portinho and Sobradinho. This is also a departure point to visit the Parnaíba Delta which takes its name from the city and the biggest river of Piauí. Embarkations leave from Porto das Barcas (Ferryboat Port), a historic area from the 18th century where the best restaurants and handicraft shops are to be found.

HIGHLIGHTS

★ Delta do Parnaíba
🏖️🚤🏕️🦜🌊🐚🐟

After flowing 1,480 km the Parnaíba River reaches the Atlantic Ocean forming the only deep-sea delta of the American continent. It is responsible for the presence of 70 islets. The region which starts at Parnaíba and continues to the city of Tutóia in Maranhão, was transformed into an ecological reservation. The majority of the territory belongs to the State of Maranhão. As it includes mangroves, coastal *caatinga*, dunes and beaches, the delta provides a very rich ecosystem in terms of marine and land wildlife: herons, toucans, monkeys, alligators, crabs, turtles, shrimps, a variety of fishes and the endangered West Indian manatee. **Ilha Grande de Santa Isabel** is the largest island of the archipelago. It is here that the **Pedra do Sal** Beach is located, a favorite of beach-goers. **Ilha do Caju** is perhaps the only one with a tourist infrastructure directed to ecological awareness and is the best conserved isle. It is private property, formerly inhabited by the Tremembé Indians, who were converted to Christianity by Father Antonio Vieira in the 17th century. Comprising an area of 100 km², Caju Island harbors several types of vegetation: mangroves, restinga forest, grassland and coastal

Porto das Barcas: 18th-century buildings

A historical river

The history of Piauí is mixed up with the history of the Parnaíba River, whose waters flow 1,480 km, from the Chapada das Mangabeiras (on the border with Maranhão, Tocantins and Bahia) to the Atlantic Ocean. The hydrological basin is the second most important of the Northeast, only losing to that of the São Francisco River. The majority of the first European colonizers, at the end of the 17th century, entered Piauí by the Gurguéia and Uruçuí rivers,

tributaries of upper Parnaíba. The riverside towns of the middle and lower Parnaíba – such as Floriano, Amarante and Teresina – prospered. During the age of colonization and throughout the 20th century, the river was an important trading route for the surrounding municipalities, which needed to transport grain produced in the *cerrado* (savannah) and receive fish catches originating from the sea. The river is showing signs of deep erosion, due to the obstruction of its bed. Sand banks appear along its course, even serving as beaches.

The waters of the Parnaíba form the second most important northeastern river basin

Ilha do Caju: seawater lake surrounded by 20-m dunes ▶

vegetation. Horse-riding in the flooded areas conveys a feeling of the marshland landscape. In the coastal portion, dunes and lagoons create a small replica of the Lençóis Maranhenses. Kayak trips through the mangroves are worthwhile because of the profuse flora. The local tourist guides collect oysters which are served with lemon juice. The island is private property and entrance is permitted exclusively to the guests of the only hotel which is equipped with chalets and two very comfortable secular buildings. Boat and horse trips and the guides are linked to the hotel, but are paid separately.
www.ilhadocaju.com.br ☎ 321-3044.

Porto das Barcas

Av. Presidente Vargas, on the banks of the Igaraçu River. 🏢 🌐
From the old port, built in 1768, boats carried agricultural products daily from Piauí to the ships anchored at sea, by way of the Parnaíba and Igaraçu rivers. Today the area has been restored and offers good options of restaurants and handicraft shops. Also in the vicinity are the tourism agencies which organize boat trips around the Parnaíba Delta.Another interesting feature of the Porto das Barcas is the historic pharmacy of Raul Furtado Bacellar, who died in 1996 at the age of 106 years. Born in

1891, Bacellar worked until he was 90 years old. For the people of Piauí, he was the oldest pharmacist of Brazil. In his old workplace, photographs, remedies and laboratory products from the beginning of the 20th century are on display.

SURROUNDINGS

Luís Correia
18 km east of Parnaíba 🌀 🚍
Of the 66 km of beaches which belong to Piauí, 42 km are found in the municipality of Luís Correia. The city is peaceful in the low season, but in July, December and January it is packed with holidaymakers. As they are small, all of the beaches merit visiting, from **Atalaia** to **Barra Grande**, passing by **Coqueiro** and **Macapá**. The lakes of **Portinho** and **Sorradinho** are also well worth a visit, formed by the same phenomenon as the Lençóis Maranhenses.

TIPS

– In Parnaíba the services of motorcycle taxis are commonplace.
– In Porto das Barcas, it is possible to find boats that have been grounded for a century, when there was a port busy hipping the production.

São Raimundo Nonato

Nighttime illumination of the inscriptions of the Boqueirão of Pedra Furada

Caracol: 88 km
Teresina: 534 km
Parnaíba: 865 km
Petrolina (Pernambuco): 341 km
♙ 26,880
⊕ 89
●●

The city is accustomed to being called
the "Capital of Prehistory" due to the
archaeological remains found in the
Serra de Capivara National Park. It is
also the best place in Piauí to see the
caatinga and its typical wildlife. The
typical life of the *sertão* (dry bush
countryside) is everywhere. It is enough
to wander around the outskirts of the
city and see the *casebres* (shacks) made
from mud and bamboo, the *sertanejos*
(inhabitants of the backlands) looking
for small reservoirs of water and
donkeys carrying water cans. From
October until March, which is the rainy
season, the landscape is greener. The
torrential rains during this time of year
can disrupt excursions. During the rest
of the year it is easier to observe the
regional fauna, despite the hot and dry
climate. Try to visit São Raimundo
Nonato in the last week of August, when
there are festivities to honor the patron

saint after whom the city is named.
The economy of São Raimundo Nonato
is mainly based on ecotourism, but also
on the production of cashew-nuts and
cashew-fruit. In the rural areas which
surround the municipality there are
dozens of cashew tree orchards.
Typical food and northeastern
handicrafts are preferably bought in the
downtown street market.

HIGHLIGHTS

★ Serra de Capivara National Park

Ibama: Praça do Rotary, via PI-140.
⊕ 582-2031/2085.
Time required to visit: one and
a half days. ●●●●
Declared a Cultural Heritage Site by
Unesco in 1991, the park possesses
important palaeontological specimens.
It is only permitted to visit with the
authorisation of Ibama (Brazilian
Institute of the Environment) and
accompanied by a tourist guide.
Use light clothes and boots because
it is very hot and the trails are stony.
Noteworthy is the varied scenery
with different types of relief, plateaus,
plains and canyons – locally
boqueirões. Ideally one and a half days

Boqueirão do Rodrigues, in Capivara: entry point of the different sites ▶

should be reserved to visit the park, as
the route is long: there are 14 beauty
spots to visit. About 60,000 years ago a
humid tropical rainforest covered Piauí.
With the start of the dry period, 10,000
years ago, some species disappeared
and others survived only in more humid
refuges. Nowadays there are no
permanent rivers in the park and water
accumulates in *caldeirões* (large kettles)
– holes naturally carved out of the
rocks. The variety of vegetation stands
out: from the plateaus and plains – there
is *caatinga*, also called *carrasco*, which
can have more bushes or more trees;
from the *boqueirões* – high forests
which do not completely lose their
leaves; from the hillsides of the sierra –
angicos, a type of tree, grow; and from
the Tabuleiros, trees such as the
umbuzeiro and juazeiras grow. Thorny
species such as cacti are abundant in the
landscape. The fauna includes several
endemic species such as the *mocó* (rock
cavy), the *besourinho-de-cauda-larga*
(Broad-tipped Hermit hummingbird),
and the *lagartixa-da-serra* (a type of
lizard), registered only in the park.
Also *preás* (wild cavies), rattle snakes,
sloths, armadillos, and iguanas are
common, along with the endangered
onça-vermelha (red mountain lion). At
5 p.m. visit the 'Baixão das
Andorinhas': punctually everyday, a
spectacle of birds awaits the visitor.
After searching for food all day, this is
the return of the flocks of swallows to
their nests which are incrusted on the
rock faces. The principal highlight for

Painting on the rocks: prehistoric records

visitors are the prehistoric rock
paintings: already more than 540 sites
have been identified, some with
paintings which could be 35,000 years
old, depicting scenes of day-to-day life,
as well as human and animal dancing
figures. Also polished stone and
ceramic artifacts and fossils of
prehistoric animals have been found.
Research in the region by the
archaeologist Nième Guidon indicates

A museum tells the story of man

that man could have lived in this part of the continent 60,000 years ago, although the data is contested by other archaeologists. The most famous halt on the treks is at the Boqueirão da Pedra Furada (perforated stone). It is a cliff face with more than 1,000 designs. The park has a visitor's center, luncheonette and public conveniences.

★ Fundação do Homem Americano Museum

R. Abdias Neves, 551. ☎ 582-1612 and www.fumdham.com.br Opening hours: Tuesday to Friday from 9 a.m. to 4 p.m. Weekends from 9 a.m. to 5 p.m. Closed on Mondays. Sale of tickets ends one hour before closing time. ⏲
The museum holds a complete exhibition of prehistoric man, flora and fauna of Brazil, in particular from the Serra de Capivara region. The visitor follows a guided tour accompanying professionals. In the first room there is a presentation on the national park and a display of the evolution of

Riacho dos Bois grotto in Confusões

mankind. In the next room, the regional geological formation is exhibited, along with details of the rock-paintings and the climatic evolution. The third room displays the characteristics of the fauna, and in the mezzanine there are prehistoric crafted pieces. Before going to the national parks, visit the museum. At the exit there is a gift shop with souvenirs.

SURROUNDINGS

Serra das Confusões National Park

Visits only with the authorization of Ibama in the municipality of Caracol. R. Luís Ribeiro. ☎ 589-1208/1118. ⏲ ⬦
Even though it is not yet officially open to the public, the Serra das Confusões National Park is frequently visited by residents of the region. The most important attraction in the park is the Riacho dos Bois (Ox stream) Grotto. It is a gigantic 3-km-long gorge formed by two cliffs. With an area of $5,000 \text{ km}^2$, it is one of the biggest parks and includes the greatest *caatinga* reserve in Brazil. *Caatinga* can take several forms, sometimes more open zones and others with more trees which is called *carrasco*. A total of 87 species of plants were recorded in the park, the most common being *jatobá (Hymenaea stignocarpa)*, *feijão-brava (Capparis cynophallophora)*, *camaçari (Caraipa densifolia Mart.)*, *cipó-branco (Clematis campestris)*, *grão-de-galo (Cordia superba)*, and *cangalheira (Lamanonia ternata)*. The sierra is the habitat of many species of animals like the *tamanduá-bandeira* (giant anteater), *tatu-canastra* (giant armadillo), the *tatu-bola* (three banded armadillo), the *veado-campeiro* (swamp deer), *onça-vermelha* (red mountain lion), *macaco-guariba* (howler monkey) and some birds. To arrive at the park it is necessary to leave São Raimundo Nonato by the PI-144 road towards the municipality of Caracol. It is almost 100 km along a hazardous dirt track. In Caracol it is necessary to go to the local Ibama office. After, follow a minor road for another 20 km to the entrance of the park in a vehicle of the institution or a 4-WD. Go well prepared with a packed lunch and water as the park has inadequate amenities for visitors.

The bright sun would confuse anyone who looks up at the vast cliffs, hence the name

TIPS

– Reserve three to four days to visit the region. One or two to visit the Serra de Capivara National Park; another to buy souvenirs downtown and to visit the Homem Americano Museum; and another to go to the Serra das Confusões National Park.

– Don't miss the open-air market in the center of S. Raimundo Nonato. It is possible to find many handcrafted articles from Piauí, such as hammocks made from twine of the caroá plant, and from the local cuisine like the requeijão cardoso, a type of cream cheese.

– Many travellers who decide to go to Serra da Capivara National Park by plane prefer to disembark in the city of Petrolina in the State of Pernambuco. It is where the nearest airport is located. Otherwise, if the visit starts in Teresina, Piauí, the distance is an extra 200 km. If you prefer to drive till the park, remember that the BR-235 and BR-324 highways that connect the two cities are dangerous and have high rates of accidents.

– Be sure to use light clothes and boots, as the park is very hot and the trails are dangerous.

Capivara: rock formations and a concentration of prehistoric sites ▶

Sete Cidades

The park is divided in seven cities; this is the Turtle stone at the 6th city

Esperantina: 106 km
Parnaíba: 182 km
Teresina: 183 km
Sobral (Ceará): 208 km
♙ 60,151
⊕ 86
ℹ Prefeitura
☎ 276-1377

The Sete Cidades (Seven Cities) National Park is one of the main attractions of Piripiri, which is a reference point in the north of the State. The municipality is an intersection for whom travels on the east-west route along the Brazilian coastline between Ceará and Maranhão, or on the south-north trajectory, the course from Teresina to the coast. Using a good travel itinerary it is possible to make the best of the attractions spread around the region. The park is very well prepared for the reception of visitors. Using this as the starting point, it is possible to arrive at the other two attractions in the north of Piauí: the weaving and opal handcraft shops in the town of Pedro II; and the Urubu Waterfall in Esperantina.
Two interstate highways pass through

Piripiri. The BR-222 highway from Fortaleza passes by the city of Sobral and the Ubajara National Park both in Ceará and the BR-343 comes from Parnaíba in the direction of Teresina. Along the highways it is possible to observe the changes in scenery between the *caatinga* and *cerrado*.

ATTRACTIONS

★ **Sete Cidades National Park**
Ministro Vicente Fialho highway, Piripiri, 163 km from Teresina.
☎ 343-1342. Open daily from 8 a.m. to 5 p.m. Time required to visit: 1 day. ⓘ ♨ ⚘
It provides an excellent infrastructure, including protection for visitors. There is an on-site hotel with 12 rooms to accommodate guests. With an area of only 62 km^2 and created in 1961, the ecological park is predominantly *cerrado* with transition belts to caatinga. It is a sanctuary for species of plants such as *jatobá* (*Hymenaea stignocarpa*), *murici* (*Byrsonima sericea*) and *pequi* (*Caryocar brasiliense*) and animals such as *veado-mateiro* (red brocket), *tatu-verdadeiro* (long-nosed armadillo), *onça-suçuarana* (mountain lion or

Phoenicians and ETs

The priest Francisco Domingos de Freitas founded Piripiri in 1777. But it was the journalist Jácome Avelino who, for the first time, called the rocks of the current national park 'the Seven Cities'. In 1886, he described the region for the newspaper *Constituição* from Fortaleza, in a report entitled "The Petrified City of Piauí", thereby arousing the attention for the region of the Brazilian Historic and Geographic Institution (IHGB). Avelino reported the strange rock shapes, such as the Canhões (cannons) rock, Arco de Triunfo (Arc of Triumph) – an 18-meter-high doorway – and the towers of the Grande Muralha (great rampart), among other formations. Although impressed, the journalist was careful and wrote "all of which constitutes a true imitation of a construction but it is the pure work of Nature composed of rough rock, where neither human art nor science played any role". The more esoteric theories surfaced when, in 1928, the Austrian historian Ludwig Schwnnhagen declared, in his book *The Old History of Brazil*, that Sete Cidades was a city constructed by the Phoenicians in America 3,000 years ago. The origin of the place was also attributed to the Vikings and even to extraterrestrials. Geological studies reveal that Sete Cidades is a natural formation sculptured by rainwater and by the winds.

Origin of the formations: work of nature or extra-terrestrials?

puma), mocó (rock cavy), jacu (white-browed guan), iguana (*iguana iguana*), paca (paca - *agouti-paca*), tamandua-mirim (lesser anteater – *Tamandua tetradactyla*) and cutias (red-rumped agouti - *Dasyprocta aguti*). All the species benefit from the presence of 22 water springs and a tropical climate with average annual temperatures of around 25 °C. The dry season is from June to December. From January to June the scenery becomes greener and the waterfalls have a greater flow of water. Sete Cidades encompasses rock formations created 400 million years ago when the area was very humid and the rocks started to be moulded. There is a great concentration of rocky outcrops of different colors and sizes, which resemble the ruins of walls and towers suggesting the possibility that they had been built by man. There are

Geological cities: this is the third

12 km of trails and each 'city' is a unique highlight. The second is most notable as it is possible to find prehistoric rock paintings – among which is the 'six-fingered hand' – and the natural watchtower with a height of about 40 m. In prehistoric times, the region was occupied by natives who registered their presence. The inscriptions exhibit geometric figures in red, black and yellow paint. The paintings are on smooth sandstone rock faces, in natural shelters or in concavities. Some estimates suggest an age of 6,000 years. Appreciate the sunset from the highest point in the park and observe wild *papagaios-verdadeiros* (blue-fronted parrot) flying freely in the treetops.

Mocó: typical rodent of the caatinga

SURROUNDINGS

Pedro II
46 km from Piripiri 🏙
The small town of Pedro II is considered to be the production center of hand-woven articles in Piauí. Since the 19th century, articles have been produced here using manual weaving-looms; the best articles are bedspreads, shawls, blankets, rugs, bedclothes, and hammocks. The main source of income for the municipality is from the exportation of these items to all of Brazil. Pedro II is also well known for its opal prospecting. This stone, when polished, is used in the production of jewelery and costume jewelery which is sold in the little stores of the city.

Parque Ecológico Cachoeira do Urubu
Access by the BR-113 and BR-110 highways between the municipalities of Esperantina e Batalha, approximately one hour from Piripiri. ☎ 383-1500. Open daily from 7 a.m. to 10 p.m. Entrance: free. Time required to visit: 3 hours. 🌀🏚🛖🔄
It is located on the way between the Sete Cidades National Park and the Piauí coastline. It is 20 km from the center of the municipality of Esperantina. The beauty spot has cascades, which resemble the Iguaçu Cataracts in Paraná, but in a much smaller proportion. The best time to visit the falls is in winter, from May to July, when the Longá River reaches its highest capacity in terms of water volume. In the other seasons, natural swimming pools appear and the rocks sculptured by the water current become visible. The park has amenities for the reception of visitors, restaurant, accommodation and also an ecotourism complex with campsites, fishing, bathing and a walkway above the falls.

TIPS

– Be prepared to encounter bad roads and high temperatures, always around 30°C. Use light clothes and pay much attention to the potholes and animals which wander onto the roads.
– Time required to visit Cachoeira do Urubu park: one afternoon
– Sete Cidades National Park has an on-site hotel with breakfast. Visit requires a car and a guide.

Fleeting Waterfall in Sete Cidades: only in winter ▶

MARANHÃO

MARANHÃO

The name Maranhão comes from low marshland, which is the dominating feature of the State's 640 km of winding coastline; myriad of bays, waterways, swamps, dunes and sandbanks, reefs and islands. The Maranhense culture is portrayed in many rich manifestations taken from African, Indian and European customs. But the fascination of Maranhão is not only in its cultural heritage; the State has many other attractions; some of them ideal for ecological and adventurous tourism. In days gone by, the local economy did very well in the world cotton trade, which Maranhão entered in 1755 with a company started by the Portuguese marquis and minister, Pombal. It was the famous Companhia Geral do Grão Pará e Maranhão, a private concession that gained access to special government grants in form of credits, slave labor and equipment, that were bestowed on the region's cotton growing land-owners. Moreover, great advantages were had through conflicts taking place in other cotton growing countries and for some time, Maranhão was the only cotton exporter in the world. Brazil, then, was divided into two States. Each had an independent government, and a direct link with the Portuguese Crown. They were the State of Brasil and the State of Grão Pará and Maranhão, the latter extending over a region now comprising the States of Ceará, Piauí, Maranhão, Pará and Amazonas. With this division it was hoped that development and progress were also brought to the northern regions. The sons of the elite were sent to Europe for their education. Some were later to play an important role in forming the first intellectual groups in Brazil, like the Azevedo brothers, Arthur and Aloísio; also Gonçalves Dias, Humberto de Campos, Souzândrade. By such academic circles, the nickname 'Brazilian Athens' was conceived, for São Luís. At the end of the 19th century, when slavery was abolished in Brazil, the Maranhense economy collapsed, since cotton plantations were run exclusively on this type of labor. A very long period of economic stagnation set in and lasted into the 1960's. A slowly recovering economy is now more dependent on Vale do Rio Doce Co. iron ore shipments from the Itaqui Port, and some aluminum foundries. But *babaçu* palm products also play an important role; so does the timber trade, the soy bean exports, and manioc, rice and maize crops. Cattle farming has also been on the rise in the last decades.

◄ Portuguese tile façades of houses in R. da Praia Grande

Highlights

1 São Luís
2 Carolina
3 Lençóis Maranhenses

Reentrâncias Maranhenses

Bacuri
Cururupu

SERRA
PIRANHINHA
Alcântara

Baía de São Marcos

Baía de São José

Lençóis
Maranhenses

3

SÃO LUÍS

São José
do Ribamar

Santo Amaro

Tutóia

MA
006

MA
402

Barreirinhas

Rosário

SERRA DO TIRACAMBU

Gurupi

Santa Inês

Santa Luzia

BR
222

BR
135

BR
222

Brejo

MA
020

Prejuleá

Pamaíba

Açailândia

BR
316

Coroatá

Codó

BR
10

Bacabal

Caxuxa

Caxias

343

Grajaú

Mearim

Imperatriz

Presidente Dutra

Timon

TERESINA

BR
226

Barra do Corda

SERRA
BRANCA

Grajaú

MARANHÃO

Porto Franco

Chapada das Mesas

Orozimbo

316

arolina

BR
230

Riachão

N

SERRA DO
GADO BRAVO

Balsas

PIAUÍ

W   E

S

0   112   224 km

SERRA DO PENTENTE

NS

2

LEGENDS	
▭	National park
───	Paved road
▧▧▧	Dirt track

São Luís

Aerial view of São Luís focusing Historical Center

Fortaleza: 1,075 km
Belém: 833 km
Brasília: 2,246 km
👤 942,000
🌐 98
ℹ️ Sectur ☎ 217-4065/217-4073
@ www.ma.gov.br
🚗🚌🚢

São Luís is an island with the São Marcos Bay on its west side; the São José Bay to its east, and the Atlantic Ocean to the north. It lies two degrees south of the Equator and covers 1300 sq km. Four districts share the island, which are São Luís, Raposa, Paço do Lumiar and São José do Ribamar, and two rivers cross São Luís:; the Anil and Bacanga. Both flow into the São Marcos Bay. The city also has many beaches; not all suitable for bathing. The rainy season goes from January to July. Apart from the Portuguese, the island was also occupied by the French and Dutch for short periods. With the arrival of the African slaves and through the incorporation of the native Tupinambá Indian customs and culture, São Luís became multicultural. This heterogeneity is explicit in all the region's artistic, musical and religious manifestations.

The liveliest time in the local festive calendar is May and June, with the Divino Espírito Santo and São João festivities. This is when the religious procession of the Divino, and the Bumba-Meu-Boi presentations take place, among many others happen, but many others, such as the Tambor de Crioula, Tambor de Mina, Cacuriá and the São Gonçalo dances. In São Luís, there are still many buildings and houses, with well-preserved façades in Portuguese tiles.

HIGHLIGHTS

The main attraction in São Luís is the Historical Center. A walk along cobbled streets among the many centennial manor houses with their Portuguese tile fronts is a journey into the past. Each street and alley has a story, either about some important individual, or a mythical character. Most of the popular manifestations happen in the Historical Center; it's also the site for the rehearsals for the Bumba-Meu-Boi street pageants and the Tambor de Crioula samba-like music circles.

Convento das Mercês
R. da Palma, 502, Downtown. Tuesday

Saint Louis, for the French

In 1535 when King D. João III of Portugal divided the new territory into hereditary provinces, the island of São Luis was made part of the Maranhão province. However, it was never occupied or marked in any way, either by the military commander in charge João de Barros, or by any other Portuguese authority. For another 100 years or so, it kept its original name Upaon Açu, which means "Big Island" in the native, Tupinambá Indian language. In 1612, French navigator Daniel de la Touche planted a big wooden cross roughly where the city center is now and held mass to celebrate the formal occupation of Saint Louis, named after King Luis XIII, in equinoctial France. A wall, near where the Historic Center of São Luís begins and a fort, by the Palácio dos Leões,

Palácio dos Leões: the beginning

are legacies of this short French period. In 1615, the Portuguese took back their forgotten land, only to lose it again to the Dutch in 1641. But its definite take-over, by the Portuguese, happened in 1641. Throughout the long economic crisis that plagued all northern Brazil from the end of the 19th century into the 1960's, even cultural expressions, so often entangled in the wheels of time, remained unchanged in Maranhão. But stagnation also thwarted urban modernization; and ironically, it is due to this that so much of the beautiful colonial architecture was spared in São Luís.

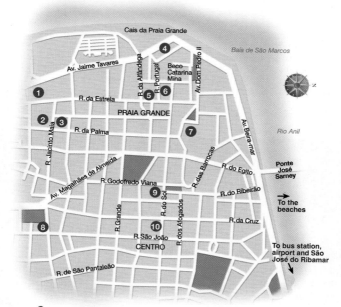

1 Solar dos Vasconcelos (Salão das Maquetes)
2 Convento das Mercês
3 Cafuá das Mercês
4 Casa do Maranhão
5 Mercado da Praia Grande
6 Museu de Artes Visuais
7 Igreja da Sé
8 Fonte das Pedras
9 Teatro Arthur Azevedo
10 Museu Histórico e Artístico

Convento das Mercês: remarkable for its colonial architecture and pavillion outlooking docks

to Friday, from 8 a.m. to 8 p.m. Entrance: free. 🚻 ⑩

This convent was founded in 1654 and has been altered several times. It was transformed into Army Headquarters and the Fire Brigade throughout most of the 20th century. In 1987 it was renovated again, and most of its original characteristics restored. Even the convent's first well, which was closed during the military occupation, was opened. Its architecture is colonial, with arched columns, and there is also a lovely view over the docks. Today the convent houses the Fundação da Memória Republicana, a collection of documents and pictures dating from Brazilian former president José Sarney's days in office. There is also a library with rare books and documents, including original sermons written by the famous priest Padre Antônio Vieira (1608-1697).

Cafuá das Mercês / Museu do Negro

R. Jacinta Maia, Centro. Tuesday to Saturday, from 2 to 5:30 p.m. Entrance: free. ⑩

A colonial style building with internal courtyard covered in masonry brought from Portugal, as was the custom in colonial days. There is also a replica of the pillory that used to stand in Largo do Carmo. In 1888 it was the jail and slave market. In 1975 the Museu do Negro was created with a collection of items donated by Afro-Brazilian cultural centres. Among its many items are manually operated mill stones, a replica of a torture chair, and photographs of Debret's slave market scene engravings.

★ Igreja da Sé

Av. D. Pedro II, Pça. João Lisboa, Centro. Daily, from 9 a.m. to 6 p.m. Free

Igreja da Sé, dedicated to N.Sra. da Vitória: neo-classical façade added in 1922

monitored tours on Tuesday, 4 p.m.
Igreja da Sé was first built in 1626 in honor of Nossa Senhora da Vitória, patron saint of São Luís. The story goes that two years after the French occupied São Luís, Portugal tried to regain control. In the ensuing battle, their men ran out of ammunition and defeat was imminent. A beautiful woman appeared and transformed sand into gunpowder. The fight was won! Many centuries of history and countless rebuilding projects separate this once humble chapel from the sumptuous metropolitan cathedral it has been turned into. In 1922, a neo-classical front was put on. Its main altar is gold plated and the ceiling was painted by João de Deus in 1927.

Museu de Artes Visuais

R. Portugal, 273, Praia Grande.
231-6766. Tuesday to Sunday, from 9 a.m. to 5 p.m.
This typical three-story, 19th-century mansion, with Portuguese tiles covering its front, is well worth a visit, not only for its style, but also the collections inside. On the ground floor, many 18th, 19th and 20th-century Portuguese, French and German tiles are shown. On the first floor, 17th-century sacred art; on the second, paintings and other works by 19th and 20th-century artists, including Alfredo Volpi, Tarsila do Amaral and Picasso. The museum also exhibits engravings that used to belong to the Arthur Azevedo important art collection.

Museu Histórico e Artístico

R. do Sol, 302, Downtown.
221-4537. Tuesday to Sunday, from 9 a.m. to 6 p.m. Closed on Sundays.
This is an especially fine, colonial manor house, built in 1836 and restored in 1973. Inside, a typical, early 19th-century, wealthy family residence is emulated, with many photos, old coins, sacred art, furniture and household items.

Casa das Minas

R. de São Pantaleão, 857, Madre de Deus.
A place of Afro-Brazilian ceremonies and worship, where 'daughters of saints' live. It was founded in the early 19th century and became a center for Afro-Brazilians, their culture and customs. It then also developed into a nucleus of political and social activities.

Woodcut representing local legend

Jansen's carriage

Ana Jansen (1787-1869) has become part of Maranhense folklore. She lived in a mansion on 240, R. Grande, and was the widow of a wealthy merchant who died in 1825. She and her family, who owned vast plantations, mills, and many slaves, became extremely powerful and influential in the region. Ana Jansen dominated the São Luís political scene, and also the local society. Men of power cow-towed to her every whim, and it was said that nothing was decided without first being scrutinized by "Donana", as she was called. She was also famous for treating her slaves badly. It was said that she used to walk on them, so as not to soil her satin slippers when leaving the carriage. Her ghost is said to wander around São Luís, and Friday nights, her tormented soul is supposed to leave the cemetery in a coach drawn by headless horses and driven by a likewise decapitated driver. On meeting the vagrant "Donana", nightwanderers are given a candle, which, when morning comes, turns into a dead person's bone.

The house is open to visitors during the Festa do Divino Espírito Santo, in May. The Tambor de Mina ritual prevails. It was originally brought to Brazil by *jejês-nagôs* Africans, who were forbidden to practice their religious rites by the Portuguese colonizers. So they simply incorporated their African gods and deities into the official, Catholic

Teatro Arthur Azevedo: neo-classical style and chandelier that is raised when lights go out

religion. Tambor de Mina chants are mostly in the jejê language, but have some Latin and Portuguese words.

★ Casa do Maranhão

R. do Trapiche, Praia Grande.
Monday to Friday, from 9 a.m. to 9 p.m.
Sundays, from 9 a.m. to 6 p.m. Guided tours. Entrance: free. 💻
On the first floor, the manifold Maranhense folklore is exemplified; Bumba-Meu-Boi characters and scenes, the Espírito Santo procession, and other popular festivities are very well illustrated. Costumes and ornamentation used in all the different sotaque versions of the pageant are displayed, and all the dolls, oxen, sculptures and musical instruments seem to come to life with the typical background music and scenery. On the ground floor, a multimedia version of all these attractions, as well as films on the ecological riches of Maranhão.

Solar dos Vasconcelos (Salão das Maquetes)

R. da Estrela, 562, Praia Grande.
☎ 231-9075/221-2760. Daily, from 9 a.m. to 7 p.m. Entrance: free 💻

Renovation of the Historical Center

Tile façade restauration

In 1979 the state government began a massive renovation program. It began in the streets of the Praia Grande district, which now are exclusively pedestrians. The project also included modernising all public services, with the rebuilding of water, sewage and drainage networks, and the grounding of electricity and telecom cable systems, allowing the defiling concrete posts to be removed. New street lamps, emulating old-time gas lanterns, replaced the so uncharacteristic fluorescent lighting. The Program also restored public market places, squares, parks and stairways. Many government buildings underwent restoration and are now being used as schools, museums, cultural and art centres, representing the social and economic attributes to the aesthetic revitalisation of the Historical Centre. In acknowledgement of the ongoing work that has been done, the Historical Centre of São Luís was declared a world monument by Unesco.

Photographs and models of the colonial houses in Praia Grande, of the Teatro Arthur Azevedo, and the old textile mills, give visitors a very good idea of the different stages involved in the extensive Historical Center of São Luís restoration project. There is also a section dedicated to another project, called Embarcações do Maranhão, which is promoting a return to traditional and inexpensive boat-building techniques. A variety of watercraft is on display; the fundamental locomotion and integration means for the Maranhão populace, on which the program is based. A family of artisans make miniature boats in a shop.

★ Teatro Arthur Azevedo
R. do Sol, 180, Downtown. ☎ 232-0299/

Albuquerque and his troops built their camp base, during the expeditions to drive out the French invaders, lead by the lord de La Ravardière. Later, during the Dutch invasions of 1641 and 1643, the fountain began to be built. It faces R. São João and is flanked by upward slopes, which are the beginning of the Mocambo and Inveja streets. The fountain is made of stonework, and the water runs from colonial Portuguese gargoyle spouts. On the entrance door to the underground water gallery network that criss-crosses the old center, is a bronze, five cornered plate of arms.

Mercado da Praia Grande
R. da Estrela, Praia Grande.
Daily, from 8 a.m. to 6 p.m.
Entrance: free. 🖐 🈺

Fonte das Pedras: stone gargoyle water spouts

232-8163. Guided tours daily, at 3 p.m. 🖐
The imposing Teatro Arthur Azevedo dated from 1815, was founded by two Portuguese shopkeepers. The original plan was to built on a square like other capital city theatres in Brazil, but the clergy objected as it would come into too close quarters of their churches. So it had to be built elsewhere. In 1948 it was made into a cinema. Based on photographs, it was restored completely in the 1990's. Neo-classically styled, its main audience, boxes and galleries seat 750 spectators. When lit, the crystal chandelier is lowered over the audience.

Fonte das Pedras
R. Cândido Ribeiro and Lucas Baldez, Madre Deus. 🖐
In 1615, around the spring that feeds the fountain, commander Jerônimo de

The market building was constructed in 1855 over the old Casa das Tulhas warehousing complex, used before as the public granary. Now its stores and sells every kind of commodity; from *tiquira* manioc rum, to sweets made from the *buriti* and cashew nuts, murici cherry, medicinal herbs, grains, spices, shrimp, dried fish, live fowl (and dead), tobacco and much more. Handicrafts are also sold there. It was modernized in 1982 and so its general and sanitary conditions are good. It's surrounded by shops and boutiques, many of which also sell T-shirts and handicrafts.

Beaches
The beaches of São Luís stretch over 22 km. The water is always warm and calm, and much enjoyed by the local population, but visitors find its coloring

São Luís beach: rapid flows of the tide

than an hour, as much as 1 km of sand. Certain parts are reserved for sports activities, chiefly soccer, competitions, with several matches being played simultaneously. **Ponta da Areia**, close to the centre, is well known for its dancing places mostly animated by reggae bands. There is also the **Iate Clube** and the **Forte Santo Antônio**, a circular edification surrounded by a stone wall. The **Ilha do Medo** is in front.
The **Praia de São Marcos** is specially busy at night because of its bars and disco joints; also its waves are good for surfing. The ruins of a small 17th century fort called São Marcos, are on the hill nearby. 17 km from the Centro, is the **Praia do Aracagi**, via Av. dos Holandeses. Its waters are clear and attractive to swimmers. More 30 km along Estr. da Raposa, is the **Praia da Raposa** where one can find bobbin lace work for sale in the big, local fish market.

SURROUNDINGS

São José do Ribamar
32 km from São Luís, Rod. São José
São José do Ribamar is a place of pilgrimage, which happens chiefly during September, in honour of the town's patron saint, São José. There is an enormous statue of him, second only to the Cristo Redentor in Rio, and the priest Cícero Romão, in Ceará (*read more in Juazeiro, Ceará*), and it stands in the Pça.

not as enticing. The big, muddy rivers running into the sea around São Luís give the sea its murky hue. The 8 km avenue that follows the coast goes to all the bars and restaurants that dot the shoreline. These are good options for an evening out, or dinner with live music and shows. Because the island of São Luís is so flat, an unusually far reaching ebb tide can uncover, in less

Bumba-meu-boi*

Bumba-Meu-Boi is a popular pageant in the North and North-east regions of Brazil. Its origins are in local cattle-raising traditions, and its main characters represent the Indian, African and Portuguese elements in the ethnic profile of the North Brazil people. The story is always the same: Catirina, a girl working on a farm, is pregnant and gets an uncontrollable craving for ox tongue. She persuades her husband (who is Pai Francisco, a kind of medicine man) to kill the most beautiful ox on the farm. The animal doesn't die but is badly wounded. In a native healing ritual called "pajelança" the Indians bring it back to life. Pai Francisco is trialed for attempting to kill the ox and found guilty, but in the end, forgiven. Apart from these characters, there is a small female donkey, many cowboys, and *caboclo* Indian-Portuguese peasants, wearing feathered costumes.
The Bumba-Meu-Boi troupes begin rehearsing in April, and the final pageants take place in June.

* *Meu* signifies my, *boi* means ox or bull, and *bumba* is a folcloric word indicating the sound of a drum, as in boom-boom.

The citie's radiolas play reggae

Brazilian Jamaica

One of the most popular types of music in São Luís is reggae. Some enthusiasts like to believe it was played in Maranhão long before becoming the craze in Jamaica. But in actual fact, it only became a mania in the 1970's after someone called Riba Macedo pestered radio stations to air it. He was the first to play reggae records in the all popular radiola dance sheds with booming amplifiers, where until then, mostly merengue, carimbó, lambada and disco was played. In a short time, reggae took over musical preference in São Luís; even a dance, that tightly clinging pairs do together, was invented. Nowadays, there are many radiolas on the island. The main ones are: **Espaço Aberto**. R. Epitácio Cafeteira, Bairro do São Francisco. Saturdays. **Tombo da Ladeira**. R. do Trapiche, Praia Grande. Wednesdays. **Bar do Nelson**. Av. Litorânea, Bairro do Calhau. Tuesdays and Saturdays. **Creole Bar**. Av. Ana Jansen, Ponta da Areia. Every day.

da Matriz. Next to it, is a life-size, masonry crib scene. The people of Maranhão are devoted to São José. According to the legend, the saint prevented a Portuguese galleon from shipwrecking in the São José Bay, which is on the continental side of the São Luís island. The survivors built a humble chapel facing the bay, and had a São José statue sent out from Portugal. At one time, the statue was removed from the little church, but it came to life as São José himself, and walked back to where it had been taken from. The word Ribamar comes from "em riba do mar" meaning on/ by the sea, and the church had to be built facing the sea, because São José likes being "ribamar". José do Ribamar is one of the most common names in Maranhão. Usually every family has one boy named in the saint's honor.

TIPS

– One of the best ways to get to know the historical center of São Luís is by joining the cultural walk that takes place Tuesdays at 4 p.m. It's organized and sponsored by the Fundação Municipal de Turismo, on Av. D. Pedro II, opposite Pça. Benedito Leite. In January, February and July (vacation months), these walks happen more

São José Ribamar statue: local saint

often: every Tuesday, Wednesday and Thursday. They take around two hours and pass Pça. Benedito Leite, Igreja da Sé, Casa Graça Aranha, Forum Episcopal, Palácio La Ravardière, Palácio dos Leões, Capitania dos Portos (port authority building), Rampa Campos Mello, Pça. dos Catraieiros, R. Portugal, Beco Catarina Mina and Casa das Tulhas. Each place is explained. ☎ 231-9086 or www.saoluis.magov/fumtur

Alcântara

Alcântara mansions on Praça da Matriz: facing them, the pillory

São Luís: 1 h by motorboat;
2,5 h by car
21.291
98
Tourist information ☎ 231-9086

The city was founded in 1648 and became a National Historical Monument in 1948. It experienced the glory days of colonialism and was also the first capital of the state. The sugar industry and salt pans, that over 8,000 slaves and Indians laboured on, were the backbone of local wealth. Like in São Luís, the abolishing of slavery ruined the economy and the city became decadent. Today, Alcântara lives on tourism. People like its many ruins old mansions, churches, museums, celebrations and also its well-preserved nature. There is a rocket and satellite launching site nearby that belongs to the Aeronautic Ministry. The Festa do Divino Espírito Santo happens in May. This is the main festival throughout Maranhão, but Alcântara is particularly proud of its own being the most traditional of all.

HIGHLIGHTS

Casa Histórica do Iphan
Pça. da Matriz. Daily,
from 8 a.m. to 12 a.m. Entrance: free.
Colonial, two-story building. The collection it houses is of domestic objects and working tools that the slaves used. Furniture, paintings, Chinese glassware chinese are very representative of the opulence that landowners enjoyed during the best colonial times.

Casa do Divino
R. Grande, 88
Colonial building built in the 18th century with a tile-covered front. It used to belong to an affluent Alcântara family, and was donated in 1980, to be used during the Divino Espírito Santo festivities. The kitchen's original clay oven is still intact. It has acommodation for all scenery used in the procession as well as the musicians. There is even room for artists to display and sell their work, during the celebrations.

Fonte da Miritua
End of R. Miritua, 1 km from

Pça. da Matriz
It is a colonial fountain, build out of cobble stones.

★ Museu Histórico

Pça. Gomes Castro, 31, Dowtown.
Tuesday to Sunday, from 8 a.m.
to 2 p.m.
Two-story building, with a blue and white tiled front. It belonged to Barão de São Bento, an important representative of the Alcantarense elite. The entire first floor has been kept as it was originally furnished and decorated for Emperor D. Pedro II, who said he would visit the city, but never did. Beautiful chinaware, furniture, and many 16th and 17th century objects are on display. The ground level of the house exemplifies a typical courthouse setting of those days. The floor surfaces and well are of ballast stones that were used, specially on slave ships, to alleviate its rolling in rough seas. They were unloaded together with the slaves, and used in civil construction. Examples of hollow saints, as those used by gold smugglers, are also on show. There are many iguanas in the gardens of this house.

Igreja and Convento Nossa Senhora de Carmo

Lgo. do Carmo, R. Grande, Dowtown.
Mass held on Sundays at 6 p.m.
This is the best preserved religious complex in Alcântara and dates back to 1665. The high altar, vestry, and balconies were recently restored, vitalizing their Baroque aesthetics, and the main nave has Portuguese tiles. There are many old graves and tombstones on the church floor.

Pelourinho

Pça. Principal, opposite the Igreja da Matriz
The 4 m high stone column used to stand in the middle of the square until 1888, when it was knocked down because slavery had finally been abolished. Many years later, a former slave woman indicated its whereabouts, and it was erected once more in its original place. Pillories used to symbolize colonial power. Around them, all official letters and Crown decrees were read to the public, but they were mostly used to publicly punish

Divine party

During the 13th century, the queen of Portugal, D. Isabel had a temple built in honor of the Divine Holy Spirit. Her admirers brought the faith to Brazil in the 16th century. May celebrations begin on Pentecost Sunday (Whitsun), 50 days after Easter, and are very popular in many Northeastern towns and cities of Brazil. They also involve choosing a committee consisting of an emperor, an empress, a butler and the "caixeira" women who keep the accounts, and allocation of "cargos" or duties to each member. Already in August, the committee starts its rounds of surrounding towns and villages, by order of either the emperor or empress, on fund-raising missions with the following year's celebration in mind. However, the custom is gradually dying out. Donations often don't cover the committee's travel costs, and observance of such manifestations is also declining. So, May celebrations are now mostly confined to a single city or town, whose people enjoy whatever refreshments offerings have made possible, and a new committee for the following year is chosen.

Procession from house to house

Arc of Igreja de S. Francisco ▶

and humiliate slaves, that were fastened to the pillory's steel rings. Slaves were also traded there.

Centro de Lançamento de Alcântara

Av. dos Libaneses, 29, Tirirical. ☎ 216-9233. Visits require authorization from the Aeronautical authorities.

Alcântara is very favourably situated for satellite-launching activities, in more than one way. The earth's maximum rotation can be taken advantage of, fuel saving being one; the region's low demographic density, the nearby city and its facilities; local weather conditions, that are relatively well defined with reasonably accurate forecasts. Moreover, should something go wrong, the proximity of the ocean could mitigate harm.

Beaches 🌳 ➲ Ⓜ ◖

The beach of **Itatinga**, 3 km from the town center, is 5 km long, with mostly fine, white sand, though mud and stone debris get washed ashore in a few places. Good for swimming, surfing, and also fishing. **Baronesa**, one and a half km from downtown, does not allure sun bathers. When the tide is high, swimming is possible. Bar da Madalena is on this cliff-surrounded beach, where reggae music is played Sundays from 12 a.m. to 12 p.m.

Ghost city

Alcântara has many derelict buildings, which contrast greatly to those that have been preserved or restored. Many ruins have been invaded by a jungle of undergrowth. The dark remains of what used to be the São Matias Church can be seen opposite the Town Hall, invaded by all kinds of weeds and creepers. Mass was held there for the last time in 1884. A little further on, toward Lgo. do Carmo, are two more ruins with a little story attached to them. Two equally wealthy and prominent families built these once luxurious palaces to receive the Brazilian emperor D. Pedro II, who had announced his intention to do the trip. In the end, he stayed in neither because he never got round to visit the city.

Glory and decadence of the city

Ilha do Livramento

A 15 minutes boat ride, that can be arranged in the Jacaré Port. 🌀⛰️🏕️

There is no infrastructure on the island, so only rudimental camping is possible. But it has a calm beach surrounded by big rocks. There is a small, 16th-century Nossa Senhora do Livramento chapel, which pilgrims used to visit. In the 1950's, Canadian monks made the island their home for a few years.

TIPS
. . . .

– **Access:** The best way to go to Alcântara is by boat. From São Luís, they leave from the rampa Campos Melo (☎ 222-8431), near the Historic Center, to Jacaré Port (☎ 337-1258), in Alcântara. To cross the São Marcos Bay takes about 1 hour. Three boats do the service: Imperial Penedo (☎ 9968-4584/231-0096). Bahia Star (☎ 232-0692). Diamantina (☎ 232-6929). Pay attention to schedule. From São Luís to Alcântara, by car, involves taking the ferryboat in Ponta da Espera, Av. dos Portugueses, Itaqui (☎ 222-8431/ 222-7378). It goes to Cajupe, on the other side of the bay, which takes 1 hour. From Cujupe to Alcântara, is another 1 hour and a half.
– To avoid finding places closed, a phone call to confirm opening time is recommended.
– Alcântara sights can been viewed in one day, so returning to São Luís the same evening is possible. By road, which includes precarious patches and a ferryboat ride, it takes 1 hour and a half longer than by motorboat.

Carolina

A typical interior Maranhão city, Carolina has many ecological attractions

Imperatriz: 221 km
São Luís: 834 km
Brasília: 1,446 km
🌐 99
👤 26,909
✈ (via Imperatriz) 🚌 🚢
@ www.carolina.com.br

The city is on the Tocantins
River. Several other rivers pass
through the district, such as the
Manuel Alves Grande, Farinha,
Lageado, Itapecuruzinho and
Lages Grande rivers, yet
despite this abundance of water,
the land is parched and vegetation
typical of the arid *cerrados* that
landscape the Chapada das Mesas
plains. Of the small villages
in the Chapada, Carolina offers
the best tourist structure and
ecological attractions. Therefore,
it has greater appeal.

HIGHLIGHTS

Cachoeira do Itapecuru
BR-230, km 30. Vila São João
da Cachoeira. 🕐 30 min. 🌐 ✈
The two 20 m high waterfalls on the
Itapecuruzinho River form
a lovely pond, with a stone and
sand covered bottom. The walk
over the rocks to get at the water
has been covered with sand sack so
visitors don't hurt their feet. Many
people from Carolina and
surrounding villages go there,
week-ends and holidays. In the
1960's, a small hydroelectric
plant was built, but later
deactivated. On its grounds,
a guesthouse with snack bar
and restaurant services
also draws many visitors.

★ Balneário de Pedra Caída
From Carolina via Estr. BR-010,
toward Imperatriz, km 35.
☎ 531-2318. Visits with local guide
aid only. 🕐 1 h. 🌐 ✈ 🌐
On this property there are 11 falls,
but only four can be visited by the
public: Média, Paredão, Pedra
Furada and Santuário. The Pedra
Caída River forms the Santuário
and Média Falls. To get there,
follow a 700 m path with 130 steps,
but otherwise straightforward.
The first fall is called **Média**. Just
another 280 m from there is the
Chapada das Mesas postcard

Cachoeira da Prata: formed by three rapids ▶

The shape of Chapada das Mesas

The rectangular form of the rocks are like tables; hence the name. The Chapada das Mesas region is in Southern Maranhão, on the Tocantins State boarder, with the Tocantins River, navigable from beginning to end. It was during Bandeirante (trailblazers) near by river excursions that the three main towns in Chapada das Mesas region were founded: Carolina, Imperatriz and Riachão. Lovely scenery, *cerrado* vegetation, waterfalls and wildlife remains untouched thanks to relative isolation of the region. Many beauty spots of Chapada das Mesas are on private land, and ecological tourism is still in very early stages.

The shape gave the region its name

Cachoeira do Santuário, that tumbles 46 m down into a turquoise lake.In July, the sun reflects directly over the well and gives the water this colour. The Brejão River has other two falls, called **Paredão** and **Pedra Furada**. A visit there requires a 2 km walk through the twisted vegetation of the *cerrado*, and a steep, 30 m descent through thick woods. Cachoeira do Paredão is a 32 m high thread of water, not far from which is the other, Cachoeira Pedra Furada, where the water gushes through a hollow rock, and down 30 m. For 3 kms, the river and its rapids are flanked by gorges with many springs that have different water temperatures.

Some are very warm. On the Balneário premises there is an area for camping, a guesthouse, snack bar and restaurant and it generates its own electricity.

Cachoeira São Romão

BR-230 toward Imperatriz km 26. It is forbidden to go to this place without a guide, because there are several bifurcations. A 4-WD vehicle is also neccessary. ● 2 hs. ❶ ✿ The Farinha River forms the 60 m of the Cachoeira de São Romão. The curtain of water is tremendously strong so one has to be careful. Walking carefully along the left flank, over slippery stones, it is possible to get behind the waterfall. There is a cave between

the water and the massive stone wall,
where otters and swallows make their
homes. In some parts of the fall,
the water is split, through which the
blue sky on the other side can be
seen – truly remarkable. The river
is perfect for bathing, but there
is a fairly strong current.

Cachoeira da Prata

BR-230 toward Imperatriz, km 26.
Turn right at the Piçarra road
and continue another 20 km.
On the road from Cachoeira de
São Romão, turn left where the
road branches in two. To find one's
way from that point on is very
difficult: a guide is indispensable.
🕐 4 h. 🚻

Cachoeira da Prata has three stages.
The first stage consists of rapids.
These can be traversed by means of a
steel cable that ends on a small island.
From it, one can see the other two
stages, each one 20 m deep. The water
volume is tremendous, but does
fluctuate during the year. It is a
popular fishing spot for the smaller
pacu fish, but also the *caranha*
snapper, which can weigh up to 15 kg.

Morro das Figuras

BR-203 toward Imperatriz, km 26.
Enter right at the dirt road and
continue 10 km. From Cachoeira da
Prata, it's 15 km, Carolina direction.
Impossible without a 4-WD vehicle
and a guide who knows the way.
🕐 3 hours. 🚻 🏊

There are pre-historic inscriptions
on the hill, 15 m high. Some
could be human figures; others
resemble animal tracks and stars.
No profound archaeological
research has yet been done,
so the period from which they
date is unknown. But they were made
by the first inhabitants of the continent.
On the way back, a strange rock
formation comes into view on
Morro Gavião Preto, of 25 m high,
at the side of Morro das Figuras.

◄ São Romão waterfall

Tocantins State can be seen from up there. The sunset is spectacular, but guide and torch will be necessary to find the way back in the dark. The trail is not well defined.

SURROUNDINGS

Balneário Parque Santa Bárbara

Município de Riachão. Exit at km 28 on the BR-230 toward Balsas.
On reaching the Rio Cocal, take a boat and cross over to the island.

It is formed by a small, 20 ha, island. The right arm of the Cocal River goes over the **Cachoeira de Santa Bárbara** that is 79 meter high. Rapel style, rope, block and tackle descents are done here. The other river arm also has falls that form natural pools at their base. The **Cânion São José** is 120 m deep, depending on how high the river is. The **Cachoeira Santa Paula** is 25 m high and the **Cachoeira do Poeta** is 20 m high. On the same side is the **Poço Azul**, a pool formed by the warm waters that spring from out of the rocky banks. These interesting formations have even been given names. One is the **Pedra do Cálice** (rock chalice) and another, **Dedo de Deus** (God's finger).
There is a snack bar, a restaurant, and also bungalows, for rent.

TIPS

– **Access**: Varig and Nordeste have flights connecting São Luís and Imperatriz. Aeroporto de Imperatriz. Av. Santos Dumont via BR-010 South (☎ 524-4666). Cia Translirio vans also connect the two cities (☎ 531-2195/531-3421); so do Açailândia buses. Both start at the Imperatriz bus station. By car from São Luís, take BR-222 to Orozimbo. From there, go till Açailândia and at traffic circle switch on to BR-10 (Belém-Brasília Highway) as far as Carolina. By bus the São Luís-Carolina journey takes 15 hours via Balsas. Empresa Transbrasiliana (☎ 243-3844).
– Cachoeira da Prata, São Romão and Morro das Figuras are not far apart, and can be visited in a one day outing.

Portal da Chapada

BR-230 toward Imperatriz, km 20.
🕐 1 hour
A 1 km long ascent leads to the top of a hill with a 5x3m vertical hole shaped in a way that resembles the map of Tocantins State. There is also an outstanding view over most of the Chapada das Mesas and the Morro de Chapéu.

★ Morro do Chapéu

BR-230 toward Extremoz. Turn off between the Carolina and Extremoz roundabouts, and continue on the dirt road for 15 km. The hill borders private property. 🕐 2 hours.
The 1,5 km trail starts at the foot of the hill and passes dense woodland, in which flora and fauna are protected. At the end of this stretch, there is another 360 m steep and difficult climb, to reach a 2 km long, 500 m wide, irregularly shaped plateau. It is one of the Chapada's highest points, and often appears on flight charts.

Cururupu

Ilha dos Lençóis dunes and lakes, similar to those in Lençóis Maranhenses

São Luís: 443 km
👤 33,686
🌐 98
ℹ Secretaria de Turismo ☎ 391-1380/
231-9086

Cururupu district is inside the protected Maranhão marshland sanctuary. It means that it is a preservation area surrounded by rivers and swamps. Because of its so many islands, bays and estuaries, it is tremendously rich in many varieties of fish, molluscs, and crustaceans. Migrating birds, such as the guará scarlet ibis, who use the area as a stop-over, have no trouble finding food here.The distant Maiaú Archipelago, although 8 hours distant, is considered the most attractive. The Ilha dos Lençóis is situated there, with dunes and lakes similar to those in the Lençóis Maranhenses. Folklore is very rich in Cururupu, where the Bumba-Meu-Boi pageant is also enacted. They have a Divino Espírito Santo procession and the tambores de Crioula and Mina musical ensembles. São João Batista, the town's patron saint, is celebrated in June and is the most important holiday.

HIGHLIGHTS

Igreja de São João Batista
Pça. João Vieira 👤
This is the main church and was built in the 1930's. Around the square it stands on, there are majestic imperial palm trees. All the São João Batista celebrations in June take place in and around the church.

Igreja de São Benedito
Pça. Siqueira Campos,
São Benedito. 👤
Built in the 1950's. Here, the town's most important religious ceremony takes place in the first week of October. The São Benedito procession is always followed by an auction.

Igreja de São Jorge
Rod. Governador Antônio Dino,
Areia Branca. 👤 🚌
The Igreja de São Jorge was built by Canadian priests, and celebrations honoring this saint are held in the last week of November. After the procession, there is also an auction, followed by a *ladainha* singsong, when sad verses are put to simple tunes. This is a popular musical custom found in many parts of North Brazil.

Islands and inlets where fishermen live ▶

SURROUNDINGS

Parcel de Manoel Luís

Visits can only be made with permission from the Gerência de Estado de Meio Ambiente e Recursos Naturais in São Luís, ☎ 218-8701. ⚡
Made into a marine park in 1991, the Manoel Luís ridge is believed to be the biggest of its kind in Latin America. It's 185 km away from the shore and only experienced divers should go there to dive. It takes 18 hours by boat, and sometimes diving expeditions have to be postponed for several days at a time, because of overly rough seas. Myriad fish and water creatures, sharks, lobsters, starfish and molluscs can be observed, swimming among dozens of shipwrecks, some dating back to the 16th century.

★ Ilha dos Lençóis

Access by boat, leaving from Apicum-açu near the district of Bacuri. Boatmen do the trip daily. ⏱ 4 h 🏺⚡🐚
The island is part of the Arquipélago de Maiaú. It has many dunes, lagoons, marshes, waterways – a haven for migrating ibises, plovers, and dolphins and porpoises.
The Ilha dos Lençóis has another name – Albinos. It all started at the beginning of the 20th century when a girl, whose mother was an albino, moved to the island. Her children were not albino, but their grandchildren all were, also through

Island is a scarlet ibis refugee

intermarriage. A population of essentially albinos came to be. Scientists from different parts of the world came to study the phenomenon; even the World Health Organizsation sent a team of researchers in 1972. Now there are not many albinos left. Most succumbed to the natural hardships, and over-exposure to sun, salt and sand.

TIPS

– **Access**: from São Luís, the best way is crossing by ferry (1h30) from the Terminal de Ponta da Espera ☎ 232-7259 to the Porto de Cujupe. The distance from Cujupe to Cururupu via MA-006 is 180 km. By car, the trip takes around 5 hours and by bus, double that time.
– There are only two places that offer lodging on the island; S. Sebastião and Céu Azul. They are quite humble, and contact with them can be made via the only public telephone in the tiny village ☎ 391-2191.

Lençóis Maranhenses

Oasis with plenty of water in which you can swim

São Luís: 272 km
Parnaíba, 441 km
👤 39.669
🌐 98
ℹ️ Prefeitura ☎ 349-1144
😊🔵❌🌀😊

Barreirinhas is a sleepy, typically interior Maranhão town, with only a few cars and many bicycles. Its main attractions are the dunes and the Preguiças River, which is the source of livelihood, and also recreation, specially for the people who live along the river banks. From Barreirinhas, tourists can take boat rides along the river, toward the environmentally protected Lençóis Maranhenses National Park.

HIGHLIGHTS

★ Lençóis Maranhenses
315 km from São Luís 🌀🟢🌀🔵🔵🔵
The Lençóis Maranhenses region was transformed into a park in 1981, and has been under federal protection ever since. Its dunes, lakes, swamps and beaches reach from the Parnaíba River delta to the Atlantic coast. The park's dunes are constantly shifting; some can get as high as 20 m. They are also

◀ **Typical boats from Maranhão**

called *morrarias* to depict the hilly landscape. Because of the wind and the evaporation of the water, the dry sand is incessantly blown about by the wind, into dunes. As unlikely as it seems, rainfall is high in the Lençóis region, and during the wet season between January and July, can be 1600 mm. This is when low-lying parts get filled with water, and is therefore the best time to explore this truly amazing park. In this Brazilian desert, instead of mirages, you have many oases with plenty of water in which to take refreshing dips.The color of the water in these lakes and lagoons varies. Some are blue, others transparent; even brown and black. The most popular are **Lagoa Azul** and **Boa Esperança**, near the end of the park. There is also **Lagoa Bonita**, one of the Park's few perennial lakes, and **Lagoa de Santo Amaro**, the park's biggest.

Crossing the Park
This is a two-day outing with the night spent in one of the village houses 🟢
The park crossing is carried out from eastward Atins village, to Santo Amaro, in the west. For this undertaking, a guide is essential; so is physical fitness. The trek, that is done between April and

June, starts off very early, around 3 a.m., and passes good lakes for swimming. The first stage, that ends in Baixa Grande, takes around 12 hours to complete. On the second day, hikers pass dunes and lakes, the hamlet of Queimada dos Britos and finish the excursion in Santo Amaro. From Santo Amaro, they return by boat to São Luís.

Rio Preguiças
Boat trip from Barreirinhas, ⏱ 4 h. 📷
The Preguiças River is a tributary of the Parnaíba River. This 4 hour boat ride takes visitors to the Pequenos Lençóis preservation, that surrounds the Paulino Neves and Caburé settlements, from where there are some of the best views of the Lençóis scenery.
At the beginning of the trip, you have the typical tropical vegetation with many palm trees, and the swampland.

Baixa Grande
Hamlet within park boundaries
Only 3 km and 1,5 km wide. Few families live here, that seem to be quite isolated from the other villages inside the park.

Sucuruju
Another hamlet within the limits of the park, on the banks of Sucuruju River.

Queimada dos Britos
A 4 hours drive in a 4-WD jeep from Sucuruju
An oasis in the sea of dunes, skirted by the Negro River. All huts are thatched with *buriti* palm leaves.

Caburé
8 km from Atins, in the most westward part of the park. 📷
This fishermen's village is on a sand trip, between a river and the Atlantic Ocean, that is only 200 m away. Canoes can be hired for short excursions up the river. The huts here are covered with *carnaúba* palm leaves.

Pequenos Lençóis
50 km from Barreirinhas or a one day trip along the Rio Preguiças. 🐚 📷
This is also an area environmentally protected. Boi, Espadarte, Vassoura and Alazão are names of hills that can be reached by walking through the sand.

Mandacaru
7 kms from Atins; a 2 hour trip 📷

This tiny village with only a few hundred houses, began with the Preguiças lighthouse, that has 160 steps and equal in height, to a 14 story building. From here, the meeting of the river with the ocean and the dunes can be viewed.

TIPS · · · · · · · · · · · ·

– **Access:** from São Luís, take BR-135 to Rosário and from there, carry on to Morros. To Urbano Santos it takes another 84 km, and to Barreirinhas, another 90 km. The last 150 km are very bad; in the rainy season, make inquiries as to how bad. The best way to get to Barreirinhas is a 10 hour trip by bus from São Luís. Private vans also do the journey; they leave São Luís at 5 a.m. (☎ 9619-4680/9976-7406-/9971-7430). From Parnaíba in Piauí, there are boats that leave Porto de Parnaíba or Porto dos Tatus on Ilha Grande de Santa Isabel, Tuesday, Thursday and Sunday.
– The best places to stay inside the park are the Queimada dos Britos, Sucuruju and Atins. Guides and transport must be arranged with agencies in the villages nearby.
– Before visiting the park, be sure to book lodgings and a jeep, specially on week-ends and holidays.
- Sunglasses are essential to walk on the dunes. Temperatures reach 40⁰C.

Lagoa Bonita: one of the perennial lakes

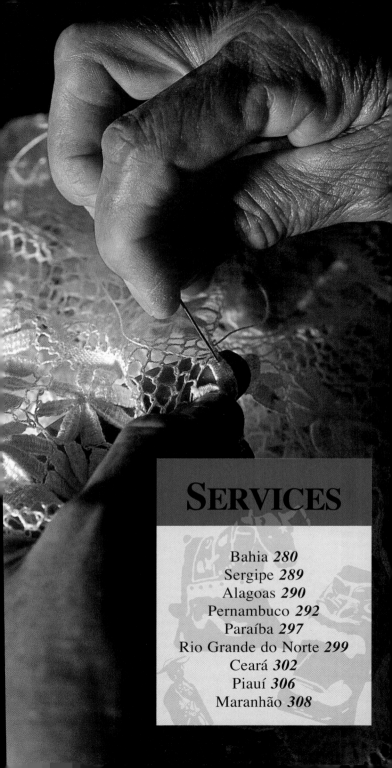

SERVICES

BAHIA

Salvador

🌐 71

USEFUL ADDRESSES

• **CITY HALL.** Pça. Thomé de Souza, Dowtown. ☎ 324-6000.
• **BUS STATION.** Av. Antônio Carlos Magalhães, 4362. ☎ 450-1332.
• **AIRPORT. LUÍS EDUARDO MAGALHÃES INTERNATIONAL.** São Cristovão district. ☎ 204-1010.
• **HOSPITAL. Geral do Estado.** Av. Vasco da Gama, Vasco da Gama. ☎ 276-8999. **São Rafael.** Ave. São Rafael, 2152, Pau da Lima. ☎ 393-3921. **Espanhol**. Av. Sete de Setembro, 4161. Barra. ☎ 246-1999.
• **BANKS. Do Brasil**. ☎ 321-9334. **Citibank**. ☎ 254-5254. **HSBC**. ☎ 320-5600. **Bank Boston**. ☎ 346-9800. **Caixa**. ☎ 319-3800. **Bradesco**. ☎ 254-7444. **Itaú**. ☎ 326-0844. **Unibanco** ☎ 243-2744.
• **CAR RENTALS. Avis**. ☎ 377-2276. **Hertz**. ☎ 377-3633. **Localiza**. ☎ 377-2272. **Unidas**. ☎ 204-1175.
• **FERRY BOAT SALVADOR-ITAPARICA. Fale-Ferry**. ☎ 319-2890.
• **EXCHANGE. Banco do Brasil**. ☎ 321-6841. **Iguatemi Câmbio e Turismo**. ☎ 450-0200; **Brasil Adventures**. ☎ 321-8896. **Olimpia Turismo**. ☎ 321-8896.
• **SHOPPING.** At Pelourinho. **ArTear**. R. João de Deus, 17. Hand-woven carpets, hammocks and spreads. ☎ 321-4728. **Coisas da Terra.** R. Gregório de Mattos, 19. Handicrafts and the famed gigantic ceramic fruit imitations. **Didara by Goya Lopes**. R. Gregório de Mattos, Shop 4. ☎ 321-9428. Afro-Brazilian culture-inspired dresses, T-shirts, shawls and bed spreads. **Projeto Axé.** R. das Laranjeiras. **Sabor dos Saberes.** R. das Laranjeiras, 5. Bookshop.
• **INTERNET. BahiaCafé.com.** Pça. da Sé, 20, Historical center. **DVD Cyber Café.** R. das Hortências, 988, Pituba. **Internet na Praça.** R. João Gomes, 88, Rio Vermelho. **NetService.** Shopping Center Iguatemi.
• **TOURIST POLICE - DELEGACIA DE PROTEÇÃO AO TURISTA.** Cruzeiro de São Francisco, Pelourinho. ☎ 322-7155. 24 hours a day.
• **TRAVEL AGENCIES. Privê Turismo**. Ave. Sete de Setembro, 2028, Vitória. ☎ 336-7522; **Tours Bahia International**. Cruzeiro de São Francisco, Pelourinho. ☎ 322-3676/322-4383; **Olímpia Turismo**. Cruzeiro de São Francisco, Pelourinho. ☎ 321-8896.

VISITOR INFORMATION

• **BAHIATURSA. Airport.** ☎ 204-1244. Daily, from 8:30 a.m. to 10:45 p.m. **Pelourinho.** R. das Laranjeiras, 12. ☎ 321-2133. Daily, from 8 a.m. to 10 p.m. **Bus station.** Av. Antônio Carlos Magalhães, 4362. ☎ 450-3871. Daily, from 8 a.m. to 9:30 p.m.
• **DISK TURISTA (COMPLAINTS AND/ OR SUGGESTIONS).** ☎ 0800-716622. **Sindicato dos Guias de Turismo** (Singtur). Cruzeiro de São Francisco, Pelourinho. ☎ 323-0360.

HOTELS

• **Albergue do Passo.** Ladeira do Passo, 3, Pelourinho. ☎ 326-1951. $
• **Albergue das Laranjeiras.** R. Inácio Accioli, 13, Pelourinho. ☎ 321-1366. $
• **Bahiamar.** R. João Mendes da Costa Filho, 125, Jardim de Alá. @ www.bahiamar.com.br. 128 rooms, air conditioning, tv, minibar. $ $ $
• **Belmar.** Av. Otávio Mangabeira, 3345, Jardim de Alá. ☎ 343-6464. 70 rooms, air conditioning, tv, minibar. $ $ $
• **Carlton Bahia Hotel.** R. Fonte do Boi, 216, Rio Vermelho. ☎ 0800-266332. @ www.pestanahotels.com.br. 433 rooms, air conditioning, cable tv, minibar, safe. Gym and games room. In the high season, packages are sold. $ $ $
• **Club Med.** Conceição Beach, Itaparica island. ☎ 681-7141. @www.clubmed.com. $ $ $ $
• **Hotel Catussaba.** Alameda da Praia, 101, Stella Maris. ☎ 0800-998010. @ www.catussaba.com.br. 256 rooms, air conditioning, tv, minibar, swimming pool, sauna. $ $ $ $
• **Hotel Fiesta Bahia.** Av. ACM, 71, Itaigara. ☎ 352-0000. @ www.fiestahotel.com.br. 244 rooms, air conditioning, cable tv, minibar, sauna. $ $ $ $
• **Othon Palace.** Av. Oceânica, 2456, Ondina. ☎ 203-2000. @ www.othon.com.br. 285 rooms, cable tv, air conditioning, minibar, sauna. $ $ $
• **Pousada das Flores.** R. Direita de Santo Antônio, 442. ☎ 243-1836. @ www.pflores.com.br. 9 rooms in an old mansion built in 1740. $ $
• **Pousada Villa Carmo.** Carmo, Pelourinho. ☎ 241-3924. $ $

RESTAURANTS

• **Casa da Dinha.** Largo de Santana,

Rio Vermelho. ☎ 334-0525. Regional. Moquecas, spicy seafood cooked in a tomato, coconut milk and dendê oil sauce. $ $ $
• **Encontro dos Artistas.** R. das Laranjeiras, 15. Pelourinho. ☎ 321-1271. Varied. $
• **Maria Mata-Mouro.** R. Inácio Acciole, 8, Pelourinho. ☎ 321-3929. International. $ $ $
• **Senac.** Largo do Pelourinho, Pelourinho. ☎ 321-5502. Regional. Buffet service with over 40 dishes and 12 desserts. $ $
• **Sorriso da Dadá.** R. Frei Vicente, 5, Pelourinho. ☎ 321-9642. Regional. One of the most traditional restaurants; a branch of the Varal da Dadá restaurant in the Federação district. Moquecas and bobó, a shrimp in yam sauce. $ $ $
• **Soho.** Av. Sete de Setembro, 384, Ladeira da Barra. ☎ 336-4455. Japanese, with a sea view. $ $ $
• **Yemanjá.** Av. Otávio Mangabeira, Armação Beach. ☎ 231-3036. Regional. Moqueca and vatapá, a seasoned manioc flour mash, with fish or meat. $ $ $

NORTH COAST
⊕ 71

HOTELS
AREMBEPE
• **Aldeia de Arembepe.** Estrada da Aldeia. ☎ 624-1031. @ www.aldeia dearembepe.com.br. $ $
PRAIA DO FORTE
• **Albergue da Juventude.** ☎ 676-1094. @ www.albergue,com.br. $
• **Pousada Ogum Marinho.** ☎ 676-1165. Alameda do Sol. $ $
• **Praia do Forte Eco Resort.** ☎ 676-1111. @ www.ecoresort.com.br. 250 rooms. Extensive, sea-side setting. $ $ $ $
IMBASSAÍ
• **Pousada Bichelenga.** ☎ 677-1122. $ $
• **Pousada Club Imbassaí.** ☎ 677-1201. $ $
PORTO SAUÍPE
• **Costa do Sauípe** (☎ 0800-569696. @ www.costadosauipe.com.br) Travel agencies arrange package tours that include lower-priced and lodging with lower than over the desk prices.
Hotels. Super Club Breezes, Sofitel Suites & Resort, Sofitel Costa do Sauípe, Renaissance Resort and Marriott Resort & Spa. $ $ $ $
Guest Houses. Pousada da Aldeia, Pousada da Torre, Pousada Gabriela, Pousada Carnaval, Pousada do Agreste and Pousada Pelourinho. $ $ $
MANGUE SECO
• **O Forte.** Praia do Rio Real. ☎ 79 9985-1217. $ $
• **Pousada Suruby.** Riverside. ☎ 79 9121-0803. $

RESTAURANTS
PRAIA DO FORTE
• **Ogum Marinho.** Alameda do Sol. ☎ 676-1165. Seafood and budget dishes. $
• **Suruby.** River-side. Fish and budget dishes. $
IMBASSAÍ
• **Restaurante da Vânia.** Alameda dos Hibiscos. ☎ 677-1040. Seafood and budget dishes. $
MANGUE SECO
• **Asa Branca.** Riverside. ☎ 9985-2580. Seafood. $ $
• **Suruby.** Beira-rio. ☎79 9121-0803. By the river. Seafood and budget dishes. $

Bom Jesus da Lapa
⊕ 77

USEFUL ADDRESSES
• **BUS COMPANY. Novo Horizonte.** ☎ 481-4117.
• **AIRPORT.** Ave. Manuel Novais. ☎ 481-4519.
• **HOSPITAL. Carmela Dutra.** ☎ 481-4714.
• **BANKS. Do Brasil.** ☎ 481-4911; **Bradesco.** ☎ 481-4016; **Caixa.** ☎ 481-4626.

HOTELS
• **Hotel Fazenda Rio Corrente.** Next to the bridge over Rio Corrente, Sitio do Mato. ☎ 481-4494. Built next to an artificial beach surrounded by palm trees. $
• **Park Hotel Panorâmico.** BR-430, Lagoa Grande. ☎481-4049. 54 rooms, tv, air conditioning, minibar, swimming pool. $
• **Saulus.** R. Francisco Magalhães, 233. ☎ 481-4105. 24 rooms, tv, air conditioning, minibar. $
• **Vale Verde.** Av. Manuel Novaes. ☎ 481-5290. 27 rooms, tv, air conditioning, minibar. $

RESTAURANTS
• **Adalto's.** Guanabara, 36. ☎ 481-5533. Variada. $
• **Oficina das Massas.** Bom Jesus da Lapa. Pizzas. $

Cachoeira and São Felix
🌐 75

USEFUL ADDRESSES
• BUS STATION. ☎ 425-1214
• HOSPITAL. São João de Deus. Pça. Dr. Milton, Cachoeira. ☎ 425-1019. Hospital Nossa Senhora da Pompéia. R. Quintino Bocaiúva, São Félix. ☎ 425-2616.
• BANKS. Do Brasil.☎ 425-2611; Bradesco. ☎ 425-1313; Caixa. ☎ 425-1916

HOTELS
• Pousada do Convento. Pça. da Aclamação, Cachoeira. ☎ 425-1716. 💲💲
• Pousada Paraguassu. Av. Salvador Pinto, 1, São Félix. ☎ 438-3369. @ p-paraguassu@uol.com.br. 17 rooms, tv, minibar. 💲💲

Caravelas
🌐 73

USEFUL ADDRESSES
• BUS COMPANIES. Águia Branca. ☎ 288-1034. Expresso Brasileiro. ☎ 297-1422.
• HOSPITAL. Regional. R. das Palmeiras. ☎ 297-1035.
• BANK. Do Brasil. ☎ 297-1211.

VISITOR INFORMATION
• TRAVEL AGENCIES. Abrolhos Embarcações. ☎ 297-1172. @ www. abrolhosembarcacoes.com.br. Abrolhos Turismo. ☎ 297-1149. @ www.abrolhoturismo. com.br. Princesa de Abrolhos. ☎ 297-1777. @ www.abrolhosdive.com.br

HOTELS
• Farol Abrolhos Hotel Iate Clube. Barra de Caravelas, Praia de Quitongo. ☎ 297-1002. 15 rooms, tv, air conditioning, minibar. Swimming pool and boats to Abrolhos. 💲💲
• Marina Porto Abrolhos. R. da Baleia, 333, Barra de Caravelas. ☎ 674-1082. @ www.marinaporto abrolhos. com.br. 34 rooms, tv, air conditioning, minibar. Swimming pool and courts. 💲💲💲💲
• Pousada Canto do Atobá. R. das Palmeiras, Dowtown. ☎ 297-1009. @ www.geocities.com/pousadacanto doatoba. 12 rooms, tv, air conditioning, minibar. Swimming pool. Cosy. 💲
• Pousada da Torre. Av. Adalico Nogueira, 115. ☎ 294-1570. @ www.abro

lhos.com.br/caravelas/pousadada torre. 12 rooms, air conditioning, tv, minibar. Swimming pool. 💲💲

RESTAURANTS
• Encontro dos Amigos. R. das Palmeiras, 370, Centro. ☎ 297-1600. Seafood. Try their catado de caranguejo crab speciality. 💲

PRADO
🌐 73

USEFUL ADDRESSES
• BUS COMPANIES. Expresso Brasileiro. ☎ 298-1273. Águia Branca. ☎ 294-1190.
• HOSPITAL. Municipal. ☎ 298-1520.
• BANK. Do Brasil. ☎ 298-2111.
• SHOPPING. Artesanato Raio de Sol. Beco das Garrafas.

VISITOR INFORMATION
• SECRETARIA DE TURISMO. Old Town Hall. ☎ 298-1123.

HOTELS
• Pousada Canto do Rio. R. Alfredo Horcades, 73. ☎ 298-1402. @ www. prado net.com.br/cantodorio 15 rooms, tv, fan. On the banks of the Jucuruçu River; also organizes boat rides into the swamps. 💲
• Pousada Guaratiba. R 6, 25, Novo Prado. ☎ 298-1514. 32 rooms, tv, air conditioning, minibar. Swimming pool, games room. 💲💲
• Pousada Lagoa Pequena. R. T, Quadra 5, Lote 2, Novo Prado. ☎ 298-1487. @ www.pradonet.com.br/lagoapequena. 10 rooms, tv, air conditioning, minibar. 💲💲
• Pousada Ponta de Areia. Av. Beira Mar, Praia do Coqueral. ☎ 298-1313. @www. pradonet.com.br/pontadeareia. 12 rooms, tv, air conditioning, minibar. Swimming pool. By the sea, surrounded by palm trees, cozy, and charmingly decorated. 💲💲💲
• Villaggio Guaratiba Resort. BA-001 (Prado-Alcobaça road), km. 10. ☎ 298-4677. A private condominium with guesthouses and summer homes. 115 beds. Swimming pool, pony, courts, shops and 8 cabins. Seafront. 💲💲💲

RESTAURANTS
• Banana da Terra. Beco das Garrafas, Dowtown. ☎ 298-1721. Sea food. Banana included dishes. Specialities: St. Martin lobster, arretado badejo grouper fish, steak and banana, and the flambéed banana with ice-cream dessert. 💲💲

- **Jubiabá.** Beco das Garrafas, Centro. ✆ 298-1503. Sea food. Jubiabá fish. $ $
- **Pizza.com.** Beco das Garrafas, Downtown. Pizza and internet. $
- **Tarrafa.** Beco das Garafas, Downtown. ✆ 298-1167. Sea food. Grilled fish with capers; shrimp in baked squash. $ $

CUMURUXATIBA
⊕ 73

USEFUL ADDRESSES
- **Bus companies. Águia Branca.** ✆ 288-1034. **Expresso Brasileiro.** ✆ 294-1144.
- **Shopping. CumuruShopping.** Av. Beira Mar. ✆ 573-1204

VISITOR INFORMATION
- **Travel agencies. Aquamar** (boats and 4x4s to Caí River and Corumbau). Ave. Beira Mar. ✆ 573-1360. @ reicigan @terra.com.br.

HOTELS
- **Pousada Axé.** Av. Beira Mar. ✆ 573-1178. @ www.portonet.com.br/ pousadaaxe. Tv, air conditioning, veranda. $ $.
- **Pousada Clara.** R. Rui Barbosa. ✆ 573-1112. @ www.portonet.com.br/ pousadaclara. 15 rooms, tv, air conditioning, minibar. $ $.
- **Pousada Sol de Verão.** R. Antônio Clinério dos Santos. ✆ 573-1042. $ $
- **Pousada Uai Brasil.** Av. Rio do Peixe, 330. ✆ 573-1130. @ www.pousa dauaibrasil.com.br. Seaside, on Rio do Peixe Beach. $ $.

RESTAURANTS
- **Catamarã Bar.** Praia de Areia Preta. ✆ 573-1124. Situated on the cliff top, also caters for people on the beach, who get their orders by means of an unusual food lift. $
- **Doce de Coco.** Av. Beira Mar. Pastries and cakes. $
- **Restaurante da Isabel.** R. Santo Antônio. ✆ 573-1186. Home cooking. $
- **Restaurante do Hermes.** Av. Beira Mar. ✆ 573-1155. Fish. Try their budião parrotfish, baked in banana leaf. $ $

Chapada Diamantina

(LENÇÓIS)
⊕ 75

USEFUL ADDRESSES

- **TOWN HALL.** Pça. Otaviano Alves, 1. ✆ 334-1121. @ pml@sendnet. com.br
- **BUS STATION.** Av. Senhor dos Passos. ✆ 334-1112.
- **AIRPORT.** BR-242 road, km 209. ✆ 625-8100.
- **HOSPITAL.** Av. Senhor dos Passos, 78. ✆ 334-1267.
- **BANK. Do Brasil.** ✆ 334-1104.

VISITOR INFORMATION
- **SECRETARIA DE TURISMO.** Av. Senhor dos Passos, Downtown. ✆ 334-1622.
- **TRAVEL AGENCIES. Cirtur.** ✆ 334-1133; **Ecotrekking.** ✆ 334-1365; **Lentur.** ✆ 334-1271; **Marimbus.** ✆ 334-1292. @marim bus@bol.com.br; **Nativos da Chapada.** ✆ 334-1314. @ nativos@sendnet. com.br; **Pé na Trilha.** ✆ 334-1245; **Venturas e Aventuras.** ✆ 334-1428. @ chapada@ venturas.com.br.

HOTELS
- **Canto das Águas.** Av. Senhor dos Passos, Beira-rio. ✆ 334-1154. @ canto dasaguas@gd.com.br. 43 rooms, air conditioning, minibar, tv, phone. Swimming pool, restaurant, bar. $ $.
- **Colonial.** Pça. Otaviano Alves, 750, Centro. ✆ 334-1114. 8 rooms, fan. Bar. $.
- **Estalagem Alcino.** R. Tomba Surrão, 139. ✆ 334-1171. 7 rooms. Bar. $
- **Hotel de Lençóis.** R. Altina alves, 747. ✆ 334-1102. @ www.svn.com.br/ lencois. 48 rooms, air conditioning, minibar, tel, tv, safe. Swimming pool, restaurant, bar, laundry, playground, leisure area. $ $.
- **Hotel Fazenda Guaxo.** Estrada da Granja, off the BA 850 road. ✆ 334-1356. 22 rooms, fan, tv. Swimming pool. River and lagoon. $ $.
- **Portal Lençóis.** R. Chácara Grota. 69 rooms, 15 bungalows (that lodge up to five), air conditioning, minibar, tv, phone, safe. Swimming pool, restaurant, bar, sauna, massage parlor, games and leisure areas. $ $ $.
- **Tradição.** R. José Florêncio. ✆ 334-1120. 78 rooms, tv, air conditioning, fans, minibar. Swimming pool. $

RESTAURANTS
- **Beco da Coruja.** R. do Rasário, 172. ✆ 334-1155. Natural foods. $
- **La Pergola.** R.. Rosário, 70. ✆ 334-1241. French and pasta. $
- **Neco's.** Pça. Clarim Pacheco, 15.

- **Neco's.** Pça. Clarim Pacheco, 15. ☎ 334-1179. Regional. $.
- **Picanha da Praça.** Pça. Otaviano, Alves, 62. ☎ 334-1248. Steaks. $

ANDARAÍ
☒ 75

USEFUL ADDRESSES
- **CITY HALL.** R. da Glória, 48. ☎ 335-2118.
- **BUS COMPANIES.** Viação Águia Branca. ☎ 335-2160. **Viação Novo Horizonte.** ☎ 335-2146
- **HEALTHCARE CENTER.** Av. Paraguaçu. ☎ 335-2129
- **CAR RENTAL. Lukdan.** Av. Alto da Bela Vista. ☎ 335-2178

VISITOR INFORMATION
- **SECRETARIA DE TURISMO.** R. da Glória, 48. ☎ 335-2056/2118
- **SERVIÇO DE INFORMAÇÕES TURÍSTICAS. Associação de Guias Andaraí.** R. Dr. José Gonçalves Sincorá, Downtown. ☎ 335-2126. @ acvandarai@bol.com.br.
- **TRAVEL AGENCIES. Andrenalina Aventura.** ☎ 334-1261. **Marimbus.** ☎ 334-1292. @ marimbus@bol.com.br

HOTELS
- **Paraguassu.** Estrada Andaraí-Mucugê, km. 2,5, Beira-Rio. ☎ 335-2073. 32 rooms, air conditioning, minibar, tv, phone. Swimming pool, restaurant, bar. $ $ $.
- **Pousada Andaraí.** Av. Paraguaçu, 550, Centro. ☎ 335-2008. 15 rooms, fan, tv, air conditioning, minibar. Swimming pool, restaurant. $
- **Pousada Ecológica.** Estrada Andaraí-Mucugê, km 3, Povoado da Passagem. ☎ 335-2176. 31 rooms, minibar, tv. Swimming pool, restaurant, snack bar, football pitch. Located in the ranch where the Poço Azul is. $ $
- **Pousada Éden.** R. Santa Bárbara, Downtown. ☎ 335-2173. 10 rooms, guides. $

RESTAURANTS
- **Lagula.** Av. Santa Bárbara, 3, Centro. ☎ 335-2246. Varied. $ $
- **Lorena.** Pça. Aureliano Gondim. Downtown. ☎ 335-2506. Varied. $

MUCUGÊ
☒ 75

- **TOWN HALL.** R. Dr. Rodrigues Lima, 10, Downtown. ☎ 338-2143.

@ pmmadm@uol.com.br.
- **BUS STATION.** Pça. Coronel Propécio, Downtown. ☎ 338-2162.
- **HOSPITAL.** R. Augusta de Madrado Matos, Downtown. ☎ 338-2112.
- **BANK. Do Brasil.** ☎ 338-2134.
- **CAR RENTAL.** Osório Motos. ☎ 338-2193

VISITOR INFORMATION
- **SECRETARIA DE TURISMO.** BA-142 road. ☎ 338-2156. @ www.vovosmilenio.pro.br/diario.
- **SERVIÇO DE INFORMAÇÕES TURÍSTICAS. Associação de Guias de Mucugê** (ACVM). Pça. XV de Novembro, Downtown. ☎ 338-2156
- **TRAVEL AGENCY. Geotur.** ☎ 3382247.

HOTELS
- **Alpina Resort Mucugê.** BA-142 road, km 40, Alto do Capa Bode. ☎ 346-1900. @ www.stn.com.br/mucuge. 32 rooms, minibar, air conditioning, tv. Swimming pool, bar, restaurant, courts, ponies. $ $
- **Pousada Monte Azul.** R. Antonino Pina Medrado, Cidade Nova. ☎ 338-2113. 5 rooms. Bar, parking. $
- **Pousada Mucugê.** R. Dr. Rodrigues Lima, 30. ☎ 338-2170. @ www.e-net.com.br/mucuje 30 rooms, minibar, tv. Swimming pool, bar, restaurant, parking. $ $
- **Pousada Santo Antônio.** R. Direita do Comércio, 114, Cidade Monumento. ☎ 338-2118. 9 rooms. $

Ilhéus
☒ 73

USEFUL ADDRESSES
- **BUS STATION.** ☎ 634-4121
- **AIRPORT.** Brigadeiro R. Eduardo Gomes, 3,5 km. ☎ 231-7629
- **HOSPITAL. São José.** ☎ 634-3233.
- **BANKS. Do Brasil.** ☎ 634-2813; BBV. ☎ 634-1023; **Bradesco.** ☎ 634-2600; **Caixa.** ☎ 634-2368; **HSBC.** ☎ 634-3115; **Itaú.** ☎ 634-2524; **Real.** ☎ 634-3365.
- **CAR RENTALS. Localiza.** ☎ 231-8007; **Unidas.** ☎ 231-8572.

VISITOR INFORMATION
- **SECRETARIA DE TURISMO. Bahiatursa.** R. Eustáquio Bastos, 308, Downtown. ☎ 231-8679. Monday to Friday, from 8 a.m. to 5:30 p.m. **Ilhéustur.** Av. Soares Lopes, 1741. ☎ 634-3510. Monday to Friday, from 9 a.m. to 6 p.m.

HOTELS

- **Albergue da Juventude.** Fazenda Toromba. R. Luiz Eduardo Magalhães, 175, Olivença . @ www.fazendaaromba.com.br. ☏ 269-1139. $
- **Aldeia Praia Resort.** Ilhéus-Canavieiras road, km 4, Praia dos Milionários. ☏ 632-7000. @ www.praia do sol.com.br. 60 rooms, tv, air conditioning, minibar. $ $ $
- **Cana Brava Resort.** Ilhéus-Canavieiras road, km 21, Praia do Sul. ☏ 269-8000. @ www.canabravaresort.com.br. 51 bungalows, cable tv, air conditioning, minibar. Swimming pool, leisure room. Lake. Surrounded by extensive greens and woodland. $ $ $ $
- **Jardim Atlântico.** Ilhéus-Canavieiras road, km 2, Praia do Sul. ☏ 632-2222. 39 rooms, tv, air conditioning, minibar. Swimming pool, sauna, leisure room. $ $ $
- **Pousada Brisa Mar.** Ilhéus-Canavieiras road, km 20, Praia de Jairi. ☏ 269-1285. 20 rooms, tv, minibar. $

RESTAURANTS

- **Marostica.** Ilhéus-Canavieiras road, km 2,5, Praia do Sul. ☏ 632-1212. Italian. $ $
- **Vesúvio.** Pça. Dom Eduardo, 190. ☏ 634-2164. Open daily from 11 a.m. to 2 p.m. $

CANAVIEIRAS
☏ 73

USEFUL ADDRESSES

- **BUS STATION. Assis Gonçalves.** ☏ 284-1201.
- **HOSPITAL. Régis Pacheco.** ☏ 284-1184.
- **BANKS. Do Brasil.** ☏ 284-1022; **Bradesco.** ☏ 284-1312.

VISITOR INFORMATION

- **SECRETARIA DE TURISMO.** Av. Rio Branco. ☏ 284-1522. Daily, from 8 a.m. to 6 p.m.
- **TRAVEL AGENCIES. Açu – Turismo e Aventura**. Historical site. ☏ 284-2248. Açu rents bikes as well.

HOTELS

- **Ilha de Atalaia Resort.** Praia da Costa Norte. ☏ 284-1510. 30 rooms, tv, air conditioning, minibar. $ $ $
- **Lugar de Kianda.** Av. Beira Mar, 1412, Praia da Costa. ☏ 284-1375. $
- **Pousada Stella Maris.** Av. Beira Mar, Praia da Costa. ☏ 284-1242. @ www.costadocacau.com.br/stellamaris. $

RESTAURANTS

- **Casa Verde.** Historical site. ☏ 284-1375. Fish, mainly cod. $ $
- **O Belvedere.** Historical site. ☏ 284-1873. Varied. $ $
- **Cantinho da Zezé.** Ave. Auguto Luiz de Carvalho, 93. Moqueca sea food. $

Itacaré
☏ 73

VISITOR INFORMATION

- **BUS STATION.** ☏ 251-2200
- **BANK. Do Brasil**. ☏ 251-2075.
- **TRAVEL AGENCIES. Ecobike.** ☏ 251-2543. @ ecobike@bol.com.br; **Itacaré Ecoturismo**. ☏ 251-2224. @ www.itacare-ecotur.com.br. **Papa Terra**. ☏ 251-2252. @ www.pap terra.com.br.

HOTELS

- **Hawaii Aqui.** Caminho das Praias. ☏ 251-3050. @ www.hawaiiaqui.com. A place with 9 guest rooms, an area for camping (30 tents). Rents bicycles and surfboards. Has tide charts, internet access. $
- **Itacaré Eco Resort.** Ilhéus-Itacaré road, km 64. ☏ 251-2233. @ www.ier.com.br. 25 rooms, tv, air conditioning, minibar. Beautiful surroundings; easy access to São José and Prainha beaches. Fee includes breakfast and one meal. $ $ $ $
- **Pousada Lobo do Mar.** R. 26 de Janeiro, 80 Passagem. ☏ 251-2031. 8 bungalows, tv, minibar, $ $
- **Pousada Refugium.** Praia da Concha. ☏ 251-2077. @ www.itacare.com/refugium. $ $
- **Txai Resort.** Ilhéus-Itacaré road, km 48, Praia de Itacarezinho. ☏ 634-6936. @ www.txairesort.com.br. 8 rooms and 16 bungalows furnished with refined taste. Swimming pool, massage parlor, reading room, yoga and ample, well-kept grounds on the seafront. For a minimum of three days with breakfast and one meal. $ $ $ $

RESTAURANTS

- **Afrânio's Food.** Caminho das Praias. Home cooking; varied. $
- **Café da Carminha.** Caminho das Praia. Mouth-watering pastries and cakes. $
- **O Restaurante.** Caminho das Praias. ☏ 251-2012. Seafood. Fish and eggplant dish, especially scrumptious. $ $
- **Pizzaria Boca do forno.** Beco das Flores. ☏ 251-3121. Good, thin dough pizza. Daily, from 6 to 12 p.m. $ $

• **Tia Deth.** Ave. Casto Alves. ☎ 251-2379. Delicious, inexpensive moqueca seafood. $

PENINSULA DE MARAÚ
⊕ 73

HOTELS
• **Pousada Lagoa do Cassange.** Praia do Cassange. ☎ 255-2348. @ www. maris.com.br/lagoadocassange. 11 bungalows with minibar, veranda & hammock, overlooking the ocean. An in-house agency organises outings. $ $ $
• **Pousada Encanto da Lua.** Praia de Taipus de Fora. ☎ (75) 9981-1244. @ www.geocities.com/TheTropics/ Beach/2610. 14 rooms with veranda. Opposite the Taipus de Fora pools. $ $ $
• **Pousada Taipu de Fora.** Praia de Taipus de Fora. ☎ 255-2276. 8 rooms, tv, minibar. Large rooms with view over the sea or a lake. $ $ $
• **Pousada dos Tamarindos.** Barra Grande. ☎ (75) 9981-2028. @ www. matemart.com.br/tamarindos. Very cosy, and excellent sushis. $ $ $

RESTAURANTS
• **A Tapera.** Barra Gande. Varied. Jerky meat, grilled fish, catado crab. $ $
• **Bar do Francês.** Praia de Taipus de Fora. ☎ 255-2225. $
• **Restaurante e Bar das Meninas.** Praia de Taipus de Fora. ☎ 71 9962-6222. $

Morro de São Paulo
⊕ 75

USEFUL ADDRESSES
• **TRAVEL AGENCIES. Batuke Services**. Caminho da Praia. ☎ 483-1280; **Morro Dive**. Terceira praia. ☎ 483-1333; **Vento Leste**. Caminho da Praia. ☎ 483-1511.

HOTELS
• **O Casarão.** Pça. Aureliano Lima, 190. ☎ 483-1022. @ www.ocasarao.net. In an old, restored mansion. $ $
• **Pousada Caravelas.** Caminho da Praia. $
• **Pousada da Torre.** Segunda Praia. ☎ 483-1038. $ $ $
• **Pousada Vila Guaiamu.** Terceira Praia. ☎ 483-1035. @ www.vilaguai amu. com.br. $ $ $
• **Pousada Villa das Pedras.** Segunda Praia. ☎ 483-1075. @ www.villadas pedras.com.br. $ $ $

RESTAURANTS
• **Ponto de Encontro**. Caminho da Praia. Varied. $ $
• **Piscina.** Quarta Praia. Seafood. $.
• **Tinharé**. Caminho da Praia. Varied. $

BOIPEBA
⊕ 75

HOTELS
• **Chalés Colibri.** ☎ (73) 9997-4354. Bungalows with cooking facility. $
• **Pousada Marina de Boipeba.** ☎ 9981-1302. Rooms and one bungalow. Excellent cooking. $ $
• **Pousada Pérola do Atlântico.** ☎ 653-6096. Rooms with air conditioning, tv, minibar. $ $
• **Pousada Tassimirim.** ☎ 9981-2378. Rooms with a fan, veranda and hammock. Excellent cooking. $ $ $

RESTAURANTS
• **Mar e Coco.** Morerá. Shrimp moqueca with banana. $

Paulo Afonso
⊕ 75

USEFUL ADDRESSES
• **BUS STATION.** Av. Apolônio Sales. ☎ 281-3365.
• **AIRPORT.** Av. Clériston andrade. ☎ 281-2136.
• **HOSPITAL.** Nair Alves de Souza. ☎ 281-3021.
• **BANKS. Do Brasil**. ☎ 281-3252; **Bradesco**. ☎ 381-4711; **Caixa**. ☎ 281-4811; **HSBC**. ☎ 281-3060.

VISITOR INFORMATION
• **SECRETARIA DE TURISMO.** Av. Apolônio Sales. ☎ 281-2757
• **TRAVEL AGENCY. Francis Tour**. ☎ 281-4488. **Mangaio Atelier de Turismo**. ☎ 282-5421.

HOTELS
• **San Marino.** Av. Getúlio Vargas, 3. ☎ 281-3026. 35 rooms, tv, air conditioning, minibar. $
• **Belvedere.** Av. Apolônio Sales, 457. ☎ 281-3814. 82 rooms, tv, air conditioning, minibar. Swimming pool. $
• **Pousada Energia.** Av. Apolônio Sales, 910. ☎ 281-5528. 20 rooms, tv, air conditioning, minibar. $

RESTAURANTS
• **Restaurante da Parada.** Av. ACM, 4

2,5 km. ☎ 281-5302. Varied. Carne-de-sol jerky, chicken cabidela giblet stew. $ $

CANUDOS
(EUCLIDES DA CUNHA)
⊕ 75

USEFUL ADDRESSES
• **TOWN HALL.** Pça. da Matriz. ☎ 494-2165
• **BUS STATION.** BR-116 road, 995. ☎ 271-1365.
• **BUS COMPANY. Gontijo**. Salvador to Euclides da Cunha. ☎ 271-1365.

HOTELS
• **Do Conselheiro.** Av. Marechal Juarez Távora, 187. ☎ 271-1093. 22 rooms, air conditioning, tv. $
• **Central.** Pça. Duque de Caxias, 82. ☎ 271-2047. 22 rooms, tv. $
• **Por do Sol.** Denox, Canudos. ☎ 494-2128. 5 rooms, fan. $

Porto Seguro
⊕ 73

USEFUL ADDRESSES
• **BUS STATION. Teminal Rodoviário de Porto Seguro**, Cidade Alta. ☎ 288-1039.
• **AIRPORT.** Estrada do Aeroporto, km 1,5. ☎ 288-3741
• **HOSPITAL. Luiz Eduardo Magalhães**. BR-367, km. 54. ☎ 288-4911.
• **BANKS. Do Brasil.** ☎ 288-2311; **Bradesco.** ☎ 288-2416; **Caixa.** ☎ 288-1288. **HSBC.** ☎ 288-2216. **Itaú.** ☎ 288-1711.
• **CAR RENTALS. Avis.** ☎ 288-4033; **Localiza.** ☎ 288-3106. **Unidas.** ☎ 288-4138; **Yes.** ☎ 288-4291.
• **EXCHANGE. Banco do Brasil.** ☎ 288-2311.
• **INTERNET. Porto Internet Bar**. R. do Cajueiro, 237, Downtown. ☎ 288-1859.

VISITOR INFORMATION
• **SECRETARIA DE TURISMO.** Pça. Visconde de Porto Seguro. ☎ 288-4124.
• **TRAVEL AGENCIES. Companhia do Mar.** ☎ 288-2107. Daily, from 8 a.m. to 6 p.m.

HOTELS
• **Oceano Porto.** Av. dos Navegantes, 719. ☎ 288-2014. @ www.porto net.com.br/oceano. $ $ $
• **Pousada do Cais.** Av. Portugal, 382. ☎ 288-2112. $

• **Portobello Praia.** Av. Beira Mar, Praia de Taperapuã, 7 km. ☎ 679-2911. @ www.portonet.com.br/portobello. 101 rooms, air conditioning, tv, minibar. Swimming pool, sports courts. The hotel is in front of the lively and popular Axé Moi stall. $ $ $
• **Quinta do Sol.** Av. Beira Mar, km 1, Praia de Curuípe. ☎ 268-8500. @ www. quintadosol.com.br. Rooms, air conditioning, cable tv, minibar. Swimming pools, sauna. $ $ $
• **Vela Branca.** R. Dr. Antônio Ricardi, Cidade Histórica. ☎ 288-2318. @ www. velabranca.com.br. $ $

RESTAURANTS
• **Amoaras.** Av. Getúlio Vargas, 245, Downtown. ☎ 288-2955. Self-service; varied dishes. $
• **Colher de Pau.** Travessa Augusto Borges, 28. ☎ 288-1763. Varied. $ $
• **Cruz de Malta.** Ave. Getúlio Vargas, 358, Downtown. ☎ 288-1763. $ $
• **Tia Nenzinha.** Passarela do Alcool, 170. ☎ 288-1846. Varied. $ $

ARRAIAL D'AJUDA
⊕ 73

USEFUL ADDRESSES
• **BANK. Do Brasil** (auto-services only). Estrada do Mucugê.
• **FERRYBOAT SERVICE BETWEEN PORTO SEGURO AND ARRAIAL.** ☎ 288-2516. 24 hour service; crossings every 30 mins. On the other side, pedestrians must take a van or bus to Arraial.
• **SHOPPING. Arcos Móveis e Objetos Exclusivos.** Estrada de Mucugê, 253; **Hecho a Mano.** Handmade paper lamp shades. Pça. da Igreja, 132; **Lambada.** T-shirts and interior decoration objects. Pça. da Igreja, 55.

VISITOR INFORMATION
• **TRAVEL AGENCY. Casarão**. Pça. Carlos Alberto Parracho. ☎ 575-1152.

HOTELS
• **Hotel Pousada Cheiro Verde.** Estrada do Mucugê, 448. ☎ 575-1066. @ www.pousadacheiroverde.com.br. $ $ $
• **Pousada Beijo do Vento.** Estrada Alta de Mucugê, 730. ☎ 575-1349. @ www.beijodovento.com.br. This hotel lies on a high cliff and overlooks the ocean. $ $ $
• **Pousada Erva Doce.** Estrada do Mudugê, 200. ☎ 575-113. Air condition-

ing or fan, tv, minibar. Swimming pool. Well located, shady and cozy. Next door is an orchid shop. 💲💲

• **Pousada da Tuna.** Estrada do Arraial D'Ajuda, 247, Praia do Apaga Fogo. ☎ 575-1333. @ www.arraialnet. com.br/tuna. 💲💲

• **Pousada Flor.** Pça. Brigadeiro Eduardo Gomes, 230. ☎ 575-1207. @ www.pousadaflor.cjb.net. Simple, but efficient. 💲

RESTAURANTS

• **Don Fabrízio.** Estrada do Mucugê. ☎ 575-1045. Italian cookery. 💲

• **Los Corales.** R. Fábio Messias Neobre, 167. ☎ 575-1760. Spanish dishes. 💲💲

• **Restaurante Manguti.** Estrada do Mucugê. Varied. Prepared plates. Their nhoque dumplings are extra good. 💲💲

• **Restaurante São João.** Pça. Brigadeiro Eduardo Gomes, 41. ☎ 575-1191. Variada. 💲

• **Rosa dos Ventos.** Alameda dos Flamboyants, 24. ☎ 575-1271. Sea food. 💲💲💲

TRANCOSO
🌐 73

USEFUL ADDRESSES

• **BUS COMPANY. Águia Azul**. ☎ 575-1170.

• **SHOPPING. Mundo Bahia**. Quadrado; **Átrium**. Quadrado.

• **INTERNET. Casarão**, Quadrado. ☎ 668-1615. Daily, from 2 to 11 p.m.

VISITOR INFORMATION

• **TRAVEL AGENCY. Candeias Turismo**. ☎ 668-1168. **Casarão**. Quadrado. ☎ 668-1615. @ www.casarao.tur.br **Trancoso Receptivo**, **Átrium**, Quadrado. ☎ 668-1085.

HOTELS

• **Cantinho Doce Chalé.** Quadrado. ☎ 668-1621. Bungalows. 💲💲

• **Capim Santo Pousada e Restaurante.** Quadrado. ☎ 668-1042. @ www.capimsanto.com.br. 9 rooms. Cozy and comfortable. Restaurant serves dinner only. 💲💲💲

• **Pousada Estrela d'Água.** Estrada de Arraial, Praia dos Nativos. ☎ 668-1030. @ www.estreladagua.com.br. This house once belonged to singer Gal Costa. Very stylish. 22 rooms, 2 bungalows, 2 master suites. 💲💲💲💲

• **Pousada do Quadrado.** Quadrado. ☎ 668-1808. @ pousadadoquadrado@bol.

com.br. Cosy. Interior decoration by famous designer, Sig Bergamin. 💲💲💲

• **Pousada Porto Bananas.** Quadrado. ☎ 668-1017. @ www.differencial.com/ portobananas. 9 rooms, 3 houses, air conditioning or fan, minibar. Rooms with a veranda. 💲💲

• **Terra do Sol.** Quadrado. ☎ 668-1036. 💲

RESTAURANTS

• **A Portinha.** Quadrado. Self-service; varied dishes. 💲

• **Atrium Doces.** Quadrado. The banana pie and the frozen peanut cream, chocolate and biscuit dessert, are delicious. 💲

• **Cabaças.** Next to a filling station on Dispersão. Varied. 💲

• **Cantinho Doce Restaurante Café.** Quadrado. ☎ 668-1410. Seafood and sweat-meats. Candle-light dinners at tables set out on square. 💲💲

• **Sandubas.** Quadrado. Snacks, sandwiches, refreshments; breakfast. 💲

• **Silvana & Cia.** Quadrado. ☎ 668-1049. Seafood and prepared plates. 💲💲

• **Yougurt's.** Quadrado. Many kinds of yoghurts; breakfast. 💲

ESPELHO AND CURUÍPE
🌐 73

HOTELS

• **Pousada Porto Espelho.** Espelho Beach. ☎ 9985-4709. @ www.helice tours.com.br/pousadaporto espelho.asp Very comfortable; a garden by the sea, with view of ocean. 💲💲💲💲

• **Pousada do Baiano.** Praia do Espelho. ☎ 9985-1767. Oceanfront. 💲💲💲

• **Gaúcho's Pousada e Restaurante.** Curuípe. ☎ 9986-2076. Ample and comfortable veranda with an enormous lawn and view of the sea. 💲💲💲

OUTEIRO DAS BRIAS

• **Bangalôs do Outeiro.** Outeiro das Brias Condo. ☎ (011) 3078-5152. @ www.outeiro.com.br Privately owned, but can be rented. The bungalows are spread over a rising, and have a vista to Setiquara Beach. They are southwest Asia inspired, sophisticated and comfortable, with microwave ovens and refrigerators. Each fits up to 6 guests, that can use condominium club facilities. 💲💲💲💲

• **Pousada Vila do Outeiro.** Vila do Outeiro. ☎ 668-5044. Coffee shop with view of sea. The comfortable rooms have a veranda. 💲💲💲

• **Pousada Vindobona.** Vila do Outeiro.

668-1482. @ vindobonapousada
@hotmail.com. Hospitable atmosphere;
the most economical option in Outeiro.
Ventilators and minibar. **$ $**
• **Pousada do Vito.** Vila do Outeiro.
9985-5414. @ www.outeiro.com.br/
pousadas_outeiro.htm Air conditioning,
swimming pool, gym, sauna. **$ $ $**

RESTAURANTS

• **Silvinha.** Curuípe. Seafood with
exotic seasoning. Reservations to be
made early; lunch is served at 12 a.m.
9985-4157. **$ $ $**
• **L'Único.** Next to Pousada do Vito.
Vila do Outeiro. 9985-5414. Italian
dishes. **$ $ $**
• **Sushiak.** Vila de Outeiro. 9985-5161.
Japanese food. **$ $ $**

CARAÍVA
⊕ 73

HOTELS

• **Pousada Cores do Mar.** Caraíva-
BA. 9993-2248. Faces sea; hot
shower, fan. **$ $**
• **Pousada da Duca.** Duca, the owner,
is very charming and makes a delicious
chocolate cake called 'nega maluca'.
Seafront. 9985-0044. **$**
• **Pousada da Lagoa.** 9985-6862.
@ www.caraiva.com.br/lagoa.htm.
Comfortable cabins; ample grounds; hot
showers, bar; candlelight. Pleasant
atmosphere; transport from and to Porto
Seguro. Internet. **$ $ $**
• **Pousada Estrela do Mar.** 9985-2032.
@ www.pousadaestreladomar.com Hot
shower and fan. **$ $**
• **Pousada Flor do Mar.** 9985-1608.
@ www.differencial.com/flordomar.
Candlelight, seafront; Mediterranean,
very comfortable. **$ $ $**

RESTAURANTS

• **Bar da Lagoa.** Next to Pousada
da Lagoa. 9985-6862. Pasta, pizzas
and snacks. Good place for warming
up before moving on to forró gig. Those
who like popular Brazilian music
(samba) and electro-pop, stay on. **$**
• **Sabor da Lua.** Next to Pousada da
Duca. 9985-0044. Vegetarian food.
Moroccan stroganoff speciality. Serves
breakfast from 8 a.m. to 4 p.m. **$**
• **Buteco do Pará.** Considered the best
fish restaurant in Caraíva. **$**
• **Restaurante Beira-Mar.** Fish, and
prepared plates. **$**

PONTA DO CORUMBAU
⊕ 73

VISITOR INFORMATION

• **BUS COMPANY. Expresso Brasileiro.** 294-1144

HOTELS

• **Canal do Pampo.** 9963-9328.
Excellent moqueca fish stews. **$**
• **Casa das Minas.** 9994-8688/
(31)3225-7859. On seafront. **$ $**
• **Jocotoca Village.** Estrada Guarani, km.
58, 55 km. 294-1244. @ www.joco
toka.com.br 20 colorful, comfortable
bungalows spread over a huge, green area.
Swimming pool, schooner outings, kayaks,
speedboat, ponies. Transport available
from and to Porto Seguro. **$ $ $ $**
• **Pousada São Francisco.** Estrada
Guarani, km 58, 55 km. 9994-4942.
@ www.corumbau.com.br 20 rooms,
air conditioning, minibar. Comfortable
and very refined decoration. Children
under 12 not allowed. Transport from
and to Porto Seguro available. Breakfast
and meals included in rate. **$ $ $ $**
• **Tocca do Veludo.** 9963-6339.
@ www.toccadoveludo.hpg.com.br **$ $**
• **Villa Segovia.** 9963-9328.
@ www.corumbaunet.com.br. **$ $**

RESTAURANT

• **Barraca Sol e Vida.** On seafront, in
Corumbau. Prepared PF meals. **$**

SERGIPE

Aracaju
⊕ 79

USEFUL ADDRESSES

• **BUS STATION.** Av. Tancredo Neves,
Novo Paraíso. 259-2848.
• **AIRPORT.** Av. Senador Júlio César
Leite, Atalaia, Km. 11. 212-8500.
• **TERMINAL HIDROVIÁRIO.** Av.
Otonel Dórea. 214-0781.
• **HOSPITAL. Hospital João Alves
Filho.** Av. Tancredo Neves, Bairro
Capucho. 216-2600; **Hospital São
José**. Av. João Ribeiro, 846, São João.
215-3864.
• **BANCOS. Do Brasil.** 212-1000.
Caixa. 211-1179. **HSBC.** 211-1040.
Itaú. 211-1380.
• **CAR RENTALS. Hertz.** 243-1776;
Localiza. 243-2811; **Unidas.**
243-3066.
• **Exchange. Banco do Brasil.** Pça.
General Valadão, Downtown. 212-1146.

- **Shopping. Centro de Turismo e Museu do Artesanato**. Pça. Olímpio Campos, Downtown. ☎ 214-5023. **Shopping Jardins Mall**. Av. Ministro Geraldo Barreto Sobral, 215. ☎ 217-1500.
- **Tourist Police Station.** Atalaia Beach. ☎ 255-2155.

VISITOR INFORMATION
- **Secretaria de Turismo. Sebrae Tourist Information Center.** Pça. Olímpio Campos, Dowontown. ☎ 214-9253; **Emsetur.** Travessa Baltazar Góis, 86, Centro. ☎ 214-6446.
- **Travel Agencies. Gold Tour.** R. Francisco Rabelo Leite, 1075, Atalaia. ☎ 226-1515; **Nativa Turismo.** Ave. Beira Mar, 1440. ☎ 243-1493; **Propagtur.** Av. Hermes Fontes, 1109, São José. ☎ 214-6703.

HOTELS
- **Aracaju Praia.** Av. Santos Dumont, 1001, Praia de Atalaia. ☎ 243-2521. Tv, air conditioning, minibar, swimming pool. $ $
- **Celi Praia Hotel.** Av. Oceânica, 500, Atalaia Nova. ☎ 226-7700. @ www.celihotel.com.br 93 rooms, air conditioning, tv, minibar, swimming pool, recreation room. $ $ $
- **Del Mar Hotel.** Av. Santos Dumont, 1500, Praia de Atalaia. ☎ 226-9100. @ www.delmarhotel.com.br. 113 rooms, air conditioning, tv, minibar, swimming pool, recreation room, sauna. $ $ $
- **Pousada do Beco Shangri-lá.** R. 7 de setembro, 219, Downtown. ☎ 297-1059. 30 beds, simple rooms. $
- **Pousada Oceânica.** Av. Santos Dumont, 413, Atalaia. Simple and comfortable. $
- **Pousada Raio de Sol.** R. François Hoald, 89, Atalaia Velha. Simple and comfortable. $
- **Xingó Parque Hotel.** Serra Chapéu de Couro. ☎ 346-1245. Canindé de São Francisco. $ $ $

RESTAURANTS
- **Carne de Sol do Picuí.** R. Manoel Gomes da Rocha, 115. ☎ 217-6850. Regional. Carne de sol, feijão tropeiro and macaxeira (jerky with beans and sweet manioc). $
- **Carro de Bois.** R. Niceu Dantas, 1040, Atalaia. ☎ 243-4800. Varied. Savory moqueca fish/shrimp croquettes. $
- **Chez Gruyère.** Av. Santos Dumont,

1500, Praia de Atalaia. ☎ 255-1000. International cookery with a north-eastern flavor. $ $ $
- **Dedinho da Iaiá.** Av. Pedro de Azevedo, 721, Salgado Filho. ☎ 246-6698. Regional. Bobó (spicy mashed beans, banana, manioc meal balls) and caruru (spicy chicken/fish, gumbo balls) $
- **Eliane.** R. Álvaro Silva, 89, Praia 13 de Julho. Sea food. The pitu shrimp with pirão fish and manioc meal purée, is famously tasty. $ $
- **O Paió.** Av. Antônio alves, 338, Atalaia Velha. ☎ 223-1460. Regional. Try their cornmeal couscous with coconut and sweet manioc). Also serve excellent breakfasts. $

ALAGOAS

Maceió
⊕ 82

USEFUL ADDRESSES
- **BUS STATION.** Av. Leste-oeste, Feitosa. ☎ 221-4615
- **AIRPORT. Zumbi dos Palmares**. Rodovia BR-104, km 91. ☎ 214-4000.
- **HOSPITAL. Santa Casa.** ☎ 221-8399. **Pronto Socorro 24 h.** ☎ 221-5939.
- **BANKS. Do Brasil.** ☎ 216-1215; **Caixa.** ☎ 326-1526; **Itaú.** ☎ 36-1085; **Bradesco.** ☎ 221-3311; **Banco do Nordeste.** ☎ 216-4600; **HSBC.** ☎ 336-3855; **Unibanco.** ☎ 221-1600.
- **CAR RENTALS. Localiza.** ☎ 325-6565; **Hertz.** ☎ 327-5712.
- **EXCHANGE. Aeroturismo.** ☎ 623-2020; **Viaggio.** ☎ 325-4681.
- **CYBER CAFÉ. Minas Café.** Av. Antônio Gouveia, 607, Pajuçara. ☎ 327-0333.

VISITOR INFORMATION
- **SECRETARIA DE TURISMO.** Av. Antônio Gouveia, 1143, Pajuçara. ☎ 315-1600. @ www.visitealagoas.com.br Monday to Friday, from 8 a.m. to 2 p.m.
- **SECRETARIA DE PROMOÇÃO DO TURISMO DE MACEIÓ.** R. Sá e Albuquerque, 310, Jaraguá. ☎ 336-4409. Monday to Friday, from 8 a.m. to 2 p.m. @ seturma@uol.com.br.

- **TRAVEL AGENCIES. Aeroturismo.** ☎ 326-2500. **Sol Maceió.** ☎ 327-9333. **Tropicana.** ☎ 221-3375. **Transalagoas.** ☎ 336-1004.

HOTELS
- **Hotel Jatiúca.** Lago da Anta, 220, Mangabeiras. ☎ 327-2555. @ www.hotel

jatiuca.com.br. 96 rooms, air conditioning, minibar, cable tv. Swimming pool, tennis court. 🪙🪙🪙🪙
• **Hotel Matsubara.** Av. Brigadeiro Eduardo Gomes, 1551, Lagoa da Anta. ☎ 235-3000. @ www.matsubarahotel. com.br. 110 rooms, minibar, cable tv. Swimming pool, tennis court and sports court. 🪙🪙🪙🪙
• **Hotel Meliá Maceió.** Av. Alvaro Otacílio, 4065, Jatiúca. ☎ 325-5656. @ www. meliamcz.com.br. 185 rooms, air conditioning, tv, minibar. Swimming pool, sauna, gym, and tennis court. 🪙🪙🪙🪙
• **Hotel Sete Coqueiros.** R. Dr. Antônio Gouveia, 1335, Pajuçara. ☎ 231-8583. @ www.setecoqueiros.com.br. 80 rooms, air conditioning, tv, minibar. Swimming pool. 🪙🪙🪙
• **Pousada da Sereia.** R. Araújo Bivar, 57, Pajuçara. ☎ 231-0231. @ www. pousadadasereia.com.br. 🪙
• **San Marino Suite Hotel.** R. Noel Nútalis, 437, Ponta Verde. ☎ 357-2255. @ www.sanmarinosuite.com.br. 126 rooms, air conditioning, cable tv, king-size beds, veranda. Swimming pool, games room. 🪙🪙🪙🪙

RESTAURANTS
• **Bar das Ostras.** R. Paulina Maria Mendonça, 153, Jatiúca. ☎ 325-8100. Fresh oysters and other specialities. Open for lunch and dinner. 🪙
• **Família Giuliano.** Av. Álvaro Otacílio, 3115, Pont Verde. Italian food. ☎ 304-3100. 🪙
• **Paraíso Lanches.** Av. Antônio Gouveia, 877, Pajuçara. ☎ 231-8446. Sandwiches prepared with different types of bread and natural fillings; natural fruit refreshments. Opens late afternoon. 🪙
• **Spetus.** Steak house. Rotating table service of different roasts; salad counter.

Barra de São Miguel
🌐 82

USEFUL ADDRESSES
• **TOWN HALL.** Pça. Miriel Cavalcanti, Downtown. ☎ 272-1209.
• **MEDICAL CENTRE. Posto de Saúde,** Pça. Miriel Cavalcanti, Downtown. ☎ 272-1719.
• **BANK. Do Brasil.** ☎272-1209, ext. 205.

ACCOMODATION
• **Pousada Aconchego.** R. João Florêncio, 79, Barra de São Miguel. ☎ 272-1011. 7 rooms, air conditioning, minibar, tv. 50 m from strand. 🪙🪙

RESTAURANTS
• **La Tablita.** R. Salvador Aprato, 30. ☎ 272-1071. Spanish recipes with Brazilian fish and ingredients. 🪙

PRAIA DO GUNGA
🌐 82

USEFUL ADDRESSES
• **BUS COMPANY. Viação Real Alagoas.** ☎ 223-3931.
• **HOSPITAL. Maternidade Cururipe.** R. Euclides Baeta, Cururipe. ☎273-1448.
• **BANKS** (in Cururipe) **Do Brasil.** ☎ 273-1086; **Caixa.** ☎ 273-1040.

HOTEL
• **Pousada Dunas de Marapé.** Praia de Duas Barras. Jequiá da Praia. ☎272-1188. 12 rooms, air conditioning, tv, minibar. Verandas. On seafront. 🪙🪙🪙

RESTAURANTS
• **Dunas de Marapé.** Praia de Duas Barras, Jequiá da Praia. ☎ 272-1188. Facing river estuary and the sea. 🪙🪙
• **Verde Mar.** Bar and Restaurant. Praia de Lagoa do Pau, Cururipe. ☎ 273-9008. Open for lunch and dinner. Seafood. Fish and shrimp stew. 🪙

Maragogi
🌐 82

USEFUL ADDRESSES
• **Bus company. Viação Atlântica.** ☎ 221-4707.
• **Bank. Do Brasil.** ☎ 296-1211.

HOTELS
• **Captain Nikolas Hotel.** AL-101, km. 40, Ilha da Croa, Barra de Santo Antônio. ☎ 291-2145. @ www.hotelcaptainni kolas.cjb.net 39 rooms, air conditioning or ventilator, tv, minibar. 45 minutes from Maceió and 100 km from Maragogi. 🪙🪙🪙
• **Fazenda Marecas.** AL-101, km. 130, and another 10 km along dirt road. ☎ 666-1600. @ www.marrecas.com.br 6 suites and 12 rooms. The main house of an old sugarcane plantation. Horse riding, pony carts. 🪙🪙🪙🪙
• **House of Lea Pousada.** R. Eugênio Costa, 1162, Paripueira. ☎ 293-1362. Air conditioning, some with tv and minibar. 86 km from Maragogi. 🪙🪙
• **Paraiso dos Coqueirais.** AL-101, Japaratinga, 96 km from Maragogi. 12 rooms, air conditioning, tv, minibar, veranda. Swimming pool, volley-ball court, play room.

Restaurant. ☎ 297-1125. $$$

• **Pousada Arco Iris.** Praia de Tabuba, Barra de Santo Antônio. Approximately 80 km from Maragogi. ☎ 291-1250. Air-conditioning or ventilator, minibar, tv. $$

• **Praia Dourada Hotel.** Sítio Bugalhão, AL-101, km 130, Maragogi. ☎ 296-6161. 117 rooms, air conditioning, tv, minibar, veranda with hammock – some facing ocean. Swimming pool and sauna. $$$

• **Salinas de Maragogi.** AL-101, km 124. ☎ 296-1122. @ www.salinas.com.br. 205 rooms, air conditioning, cable tv, minibar. Conference room, dance hall, swimming pools, spa. Restaurant. The Maragogi River flows through hotel grounds. Free laser boating, windsurfing and kayak paddling. $$$$

• **Venta Clube Pratagy.** AL-101 North, km 10, Praia de Pratagy. ☎ 218-6200. @ www.cvc.com.br/brasil/. $$$

RESTAURANTS

• **Frutos do Mar.** Av. Senador Rui Palmeira, 28. ☎ 296-1403. Serves lunch and dinner. Lobster, rice and fish sauce and manioc flour pirão puree. $$$

Penedo

⊕ 82

USEFUL ADDRESSES

• **BUS STATION.** Av. Duque de Caixias, Downtown. ☎ 551-4300.

• **BUS COMPANY. Real Viação.** ☎ 551-2602.

• **HOSPITAL. Santa Casa**. R. Getúlio Vargas, 423, Downtown. ☎ 551-2508. **Regional**. Av. Wanderley, Downtown. ☎ 551-2888.

• **BANKS. Do Brasil**. ☎ 551-2244. **Caixa**. ☎ 551-3661. **Bradesco**. ☎ 551-2627.

• **SHOPPING. Mercado das Artes**. R. Amadeu Lobo. Open daily from 9 to 11:30 a.m. and from 1 to 4:30 p.m. A centre on the dock street where artists and artisans sell their craft.

VISITOR INFORMATION

• **TOWN HALL.** Pça. Barão de Penedo, 19, Dowontown. ☎ 551-2727. @ pmpene do@ig.com.br.

• **TRAVEL AGENCIES. Opara Turismo**. R. São Miguel, 20, Downtown. ☎ 551-3740. River tours to São Francisco delta, that also start in Piaçabuçu.

HOTELS

• **Hotel São Francisco.** Av. Floriano Peixoto, 237. ☎ 551-2273. @ www.hotelsaofrancisco-penedo.com.br 52 rooms, air conditioning, tv, minibar, some with veranda and side-view of river. Swimming pool, games room. Four story building. $$

• **Pousada Colonial.** Pça. 12 de Abril, 21. ☎ 551-2355. 12 rooms, air conditioning or ventilator, minibar. An old mansion in the historical centre; a part of national monument complex. $$

RESTAURANTS

• **Forte da Rocheira.** R. da Rocheira, 2, Santo Antônio. ☎ 551-3273. On the São Francisco riverbank. Sururu mussels, rice and beans, maioc flour farofa, and manioc macaxeira purée. $

PIAÇABUÇU

⊕ 82

USEFUL ADDRESSES

• **BUS COMPANY. Real Alagoas** (daily buses to Maceió). ☎ 223-3931.

• **BANK. Do Brasil**. ☎ 552-1195.

VISITOR INFORMATION.

• **SECRETARIA DE TURISMO.** R. Coronel José Leonel, 28, downtown. ☎ 552-1473.

• **TRAVEL AGENCY. Mercator Empreendimentos Turísticos**. R. Silvério Jorge, 459, downtown, Maceió. ☎ 221-1157. @ www.mercator-tour.com.br

HOTELS

• **Pousada Chez Julie.** Av. Beira-mar, Pontal do Peba. ☎ 557-1217. @ chezjulie@ofm.com.br. Air-conditioning, minibar, tv. Swimming pool. English, French, German and Dutch spoken. $$

• **Pousada do Maninho.** Pontal do Peba. ☎ 557-1133. 29 rooms, air conditioning or ventilator, communal tv room. $

• **Pousada Santiago.** Av. Amadeu Lobo, downtown. ☎ 552-1208. 12 rooms, tv, air-conditioning or ventilator. On São Francisco riverbank. $

PERNAMBUCO

Recife

⊕ 81

USEFUL ADDRESSES

• **AIRPORT.** Recife International/Guararapes-Gilberto Freyre. Pça. Ministro Salgado Filho. ☎ 3464-4188.

• **BUS STATION. Terminal Integrado de Passageiros (TIP).** BR-232, km 15, Curado. ☎ 3425-1999.

• **HOSPITAL. Albert Sabin**. R. Senador

José Henrique, 141, Ilha do Leite. ☎ 3421-5411. **Hospital da Restauração**. Ave. Agamenon Magalhães, Derby. ☎ 3421-5444. **Real Português**. Ave. Agamenon Magalhães. Derby. ☎ 3416-1122. **Santa Joana**. R. Joaquim Nabuco, 200, Graças. ☎ 3216-6655.

• **CAR RENTALS. Avis**. ☎ 3462-5069. **Budget**. ☎ 3341-2505. **Localiza**. ☎ 3341-2082. **Unidas**. ☎ 3461-4661.

• **EXCHANGE. Anacor**. Shopping Centre Recife. ☎ 3465-3838.

• **BANKS. Do Brasil**. ☎ 3425-7111. **Bank of Boston**. ☎ 3467-4343. **Bradesco**. ☎ 3428-1500. **Caixa**. ☎ 3462-4022. **Citibank**. ☎ 3465-2314. **Itaú**. ☎ 3465-4511. **Unibanco**. ☎ 3421-4245. **HSBC**. ☎ 3217-4000.

• **SHOPPING. Shopping Center Recife**. R. Padre Carapuceiro, 777, Boa Viagem. ☎ 3464-6123.

VISITOR INFORMATION

• **TOURIST INFORMATION BY TELEPHONE.** ☎ 3425-8409

• **RECIFE CONVENTION & VISITORS BUREAU.** ☎ 3467-9984; @ recifecvb@recifecvb.com.br.

• **TOURIST AGENTS. Giro Turismo**. Av. Visconde de Jequitinhonha. ☎ 3074-5088. @ www.giroturismo.com.br. Mergulho. **Projeto Mar.** Av. Padre Bernadino Pessoa, 410, Boa Viagem. ☎ 3326-0162. @ www.projetomar.com.br.

HOTELS

• **Atlante Plaza.** Av. Boa Viagem, 5426, Boa Viagem. ☎ 3302-3333. 207 rooms, minibar, T.V., some with sea view. Swimming pool, beauty saloon. Excellent location, pleasant restaurant, with a good communal area. $ $ $

• **Bianca Praia.** R. Mamanguape, 142, Boa Viagem. ☎ 3327-0958. @ www.biancapraiahotel.com.br. 19 rooms, air conditioning, minibar, T.V., Close to Shopping Recife. $ $

• **Hotel da Praia.** Av. Domingos Ferreira, 4395, Boa Viagem. ☎ 3465-3011. 57 rooms, air conditioning, T.V., minibar. 3 blocks from the beach. $ $

• **Hotel Jangadeiro.** Av. Boa Viagem, 3114. ☎ 3465-3544. @ www.jangadeirohotel.com.br. 100 rooms, minibar, air conditioning, T.V., Swimming pool, convention hall. $ $

• **Marante Plaza.** Av. Boa Viagem, 1070, Boa Viagem. ☎ 3465-1070. @ www.marante.com.br. 119 rooms,air conditioning, cable tv, minibar, convention center. $ $

• **Mar Hotel.** R. Barão de Sousa Leão, 451, Boa Viagem. ☎ 3302-4444. @ www.marhotel.com.br. 200 rooms, air conditioning, minibar, cable T.V., fitness center, sauna, swimming pool, games room. Aimed at executives, with infrastructure for events. Amenities for the physical handicapped. $ $ $

• **Marolinda Residence.** Av. Conselheiro Aguiar, 755, Pina. ☎ 3325-5200. @ www.marolinda.com.br. 60 rooms, air conditioning, minibar, cable T.V., swimming pool, convention hall, sauna. 100 meters from the beach. $ $

• **Onda Mar.** R. Ernesto de Paula Santos, 284, Boa Viagem. ☎ 3465-2833. @ www.ondamarhotel.hpg.com.br. 140 rooms, air conditioning, minibar, cable T.V., some with jacuzzi. Swimming pool, meeting rooms. $ $

RESTAURANTS

• **Alphaiate.** Av. Boa Viagem, 1400, Boa Viagem. ☎ 3465-7588. Sun-dried beef with rice, beans and farofa (a type of stuffing). Open at lunchtime and at night. $ $

• **Buraco de Otília.** R. Aurora, 1231, Santo Amaro. ☎ 3231-1528. @ www.interativo.net/buracodeotilia. Speciality is galinha de cabidela. Open only at lunchtime, closed on Saturdays. $

• **Casa de Banhos.** Reefs of Porto do Recife, km1, Brasília Teimosa. ☎ 3075-8776. Access from Marco Zero crossing by ferry or along Ave. Boa Viagem, through Brasília Teimosa by car. Located on the reefs, a worthwhile view. Fish dishes. Open from Wednesday to Sunday. $

• **Galeria Joana D'arc.** Av. Herculano Bandeira, 513, Boa Viagem. There are several restaurants and bars in an enjoyable ambient: crepes in **Anjo Solto**, Mexican food in **Boracho**, and Japanese in **Haikai**. $ $

• **Parraxaxá.** R. Baltazar Pereira, 32, Boa Viagem. ☎ 3463-7874. Ave. 17 de agosto, 807, Casa Forte. ☎ 3268-4169. Regional. Open from 6 a.m. to 10 p.m. $

• **Restaurante Leite.** Pça. Joaquim Nabuco, 147, Santo Antônio. ☎ 3224-7977. Fish dishes. Since 1882. $ $

• **Restaurante Recife Antigo.** Pça. Comunidade Luso-Brasileira, Forte do Brum. Open only at lunchtime and during the week. ☎ 3224-1781. $

• **Spettus.** Av. Agamenon Magalhães, 2132, Derby. ☎ 3423-4122. Barbecue rodízio (type of service where different meats are offered in rotation), salad counter and hot dishes. Opens lunchtime and at night. $ $ $

Caruaru
🌐 81

USEFUL ADDRESSES
• **SECRETARIA DE TURISMO. Fundação de Cultura e Turismo de CaR.-ru. Espaço Cultural Tancredo Neves.** Pça. Coronel José de Vasconcelos, 100, Center. ☎ 3721-1633.
• **BUS STATION.** Av. José Pinheiro. ☎ 3721-2480.
• **CAR RENTAL. Nassau Veículos**. ☎ 3721-6655. **Localiza**. ☎ 3723-5566. **Unidas**. ☎ 3722-5959.
• **HOSPITAL. Regional do Agreste Dr. Waldemiro Ferreira**. BR 232, km 130. ☎ 3722-0195.
• **BANKS. Do Brasil**. ☎ 3722-1888. **Bradesco**. ☎ 3722-1222. **Caixa**. ☎ 3722-8000. **Real**. ☎ 3722-1311.

HOTELS
• **Hotel Village.** BR-232 Highway, km 135, Petrópolis. ☎ 3722-5544. @ www. hoteisvillage.com.br. 63 rooms, air conditioning, minibar, cable T.V., swimming pool, sauna, fitness center, games room. $ $

RESTAURANTS
• **Mestre Vitalino.** R. Leão Dourado, 13, São Francisco. ☎ 3721-0499. Varied. $
• **Tia Teta.** Av. Agamenon Magalhães, 925. ☎ 3721-4265. Self-service Varied. $

Fernando de Noronha
🌐 81

USEFUL ADDRESSES
• **PARK ADMINISTRATION.** ☎ 3619-1115.
• **SECRETARIA DE TURISMO.** ☎ 3619-1352.
• **IBAMA.** Alameda do Boldró. ☎ 3619-1128. @ www.noronha. pe.gov.br.
• **AIRPORT.** BR-363, near to Sueste Beach. ☎ 3619-1182.
• **BUGGY RENTALS. Pousada Morena**. ☎ 3619-1142. **Olho de Gato**. ☎ 3619-1105.
• **BANK. Real**. ☎ 3619-1415.
• **HOSPITAL. São Lucas**. Parque dos Flamboyant, ☎ 3619-1377.
• **TOURIST AGENTS. Abatur**. ☎ 3619-1307. **Atlantis**. ☎ 3619-1371.
• **DIVING OPERATOR. Águas Claras**. ☎ 3619-1225. **Noronha Divers**. ☎ 3619-1112. **Apnéia Turismo**. ☎ 3619-1247.

HOTELS
• **Hotel Esmeralda do Atlântico.** Alameda do Boldró. ☎ 3619-1255. 24 and 17 rooms, air conditioning, minibar, T.V. in the lobby. Full board. $ $ $ $
• **Pousada Atalaia.** R. D. Juquinha, 126, Vila do Trinta. ☎ 3619-1300. 5 rooms, air conditioning, T.V., minibar. $ $ $
• **Pousada Solar dos Ventos.** Road to Sueste. ☎ 3619-1347. Air conditioning, minibar, T.V., verandas. Four chalets for four people in each. $ $ $

RESTAURANTS
• **Tartarugão.** Alameda do Boldró, Cachorro Beach. ☎ 3619-1331. Meat and seafood. Daily from 5 p.m. $ $
• **Ecologiku's.** Road to Sueste. ☎ 3619-1404. Seafood. Closed Mondays. Daily only at lunchtime. $ $ $

Itamaracá Island
🌐 81

USEFUL ADDRESSES
• **CITY HALL.** Av. João Pessoa Guerra, 37, Pilar. ☎ 3544-1156.
• **BANKS. Caixa**. ☎ 3544-1186.
• **HOSPITAL. Unidade Mista de Itamaracá**. R. João Pessoa Guerra, 536, Faixa Verde ☎ 3544-1340.

HOTELS
• **Hotel Orange.** Road to Forte. ☎ 3544-1170. @ hotelorange.com.br. 52 rooms, T.V., air conditioning, minibar, swimming pool, games room. Sauna, convention centre, sports courts. $ $ $
• **Pousada Casa da Praia.** Road to Forte. ☎ 3544-1255. 14 rooms, minibar, T.V., air conditioning. Swimming pool, mini-sports hall, some with veranda. @ www.pousadacasada praia.com.br. $ $
• **Pousada de Itamaracá.** R. Fernando Lopes, 205, Pilar. ☎ 3544-1152. @ www. pousadadeitamaraca. com.br. 34 rooms, air conditioning, minibar, tv. $ $

RESTAURANTS
• **A Peti Tosa.** Road to Forte (Forte Orange Beach). Tel 3544-1081. Fish dishes. $
• **O Convés.** R. Manoel Lourenço, 126, municipality of Itapissuma. ☎ 3548-1151. The speciality is caldeirada, a dish that brings together different crustaceans, accompanied by pirão and rice, Lunchtime and night-time. $
• **Pescada Forte Orange.** PE-01 highway, km 1. ☎ 3544-1220. $
• **Porto da Ilha.** Av. Beira-Mar, 32, ☎

3544-1561. Varying dishes. $

PAULISTA
⊕ 81

HOTELS
• **Hotel Amoaras.** R. Garoupa, 525. Maria Farinha. ☎ 3436-1331. @ www.ho telamoaras.com.br. 78 rooms, T.V., air conditioning, minibar. Swimming pool. It offers water sports and a pleasant restaurant by the side of the swimming pool. $ $ $

RESTAURANTS
• **Mexilhão.** Av. Cláudio José Gueiros Leite, 1844, Janga. ☎ 3434.1389. Varied. $
• **Sea Paradise.** R. Dr. Almir B. Cunha, Maria Farinha. ☎ 3435-1740. Fish dishes $
• **Bar and Restaurant Brisa do Mar.** Av. Beira-Mar, 250. Maria Farinha. ☎ 3436.7496. Fish dishes. $

Petrolina
⊕ 87

USEFUL ADDRESSES
• **CITY HALL.** Ave. Guararapes, 2114, Downtown. ☎ 3862-2001. @ www.petro lina.pe.gov.br.
• **BUS STATION.** Av. das Nações. ☎ 3861-6007.
• **AIRPORT.** BR-235, km 11. ☎ 3863-3366.
• **HOSPITAL. Geral**. R. Honório Viana, Gersino Coelho. ☎ 3862-2700. **Regional D. Malan**. Ave. Joaquim Nabuco, Downtown. ☎ 3862-3622.
Memorial. Pça. Tobias Barreto, 2, Downtown. ☎ 3862-1122.
• **BANKS. Do Brasil.** ☎ 3035-9100. **Bradesco**. ☎ 3862-2411. **Caixa**. ☎ 3862-3511. **HSBC.** ☎ 3862-3000.
• **CAR RENTALS. Localiza**. ☎ 3862-2788. **Unidas.** ☎ 3861-1748.

HOTELS
• **JB Hotel.** R. Olímpio Virgínio, 88, Downtown. ☎ 3862-3777. 83 rooms, air conditioning, minibar, T.V., some with veranda. Restaurant with a good view of the São Francisco River. $ $
• **Petrolina Palace Hotel.** Av. Cardoso de Sá. ☎ 3862-1555. 42 rooms, air conditioning, minibar, T.V. Located on the edge of the city. $ $ $
• **Reis Palace Hotel.** R. Manoel Clementino, 1157, Downtown. ☎ 3861-2431. 27 rooms, air conditioning, T.V., minibar. $ $

RESTAURANT
• **Alvorada.** Av. Sousa Filho, 418, Downtown. ☎ 3861-4542. Varied. By weight, only at lunchtime. $
• **Bodódromo.** Av. São Francisco, Areia Branca. Goat meat and all its variations. $
• **Capivara.** Av. Cardoso de Sá, 429. ☎ 3862-2585. Fish dishes. Try the grilled filet of surubim fish, rice with carrots, farofa and caper sauce. $

Olinda
⊕ 81

USEFUL ADDRESSES
• **SECRETARIA DE TURISMO.** Pça. dos Milagres, 95. ☎ 3439-9434.
• **BANKS. Do Brasil.** ☎ 3439-1344. **Caixa.** ☎ 3439-1444. **Bandeirantes.** ☎ 3439-2211. **Itaú.** ☎ 3439-3311.
• **HOSPITAL. Pronto Socorro de Olinda**. Av. Santos Dumont, 177. ☎ 3429-4073.
• **CYBER CAFE. Olinda@.com**. Pça. João Pessoa, 15. ☎ 3429-4365.

HOTELS
• **Costeiro Olinda Hotel.** Av. Ministro Marcos Freire, 681, Bairro Novo. ☎ 3429-4877. @ www.costeiro.com.br. 41 rooms, minibar, air conditioning, Cable T.V., swimming pool, convention hall, on the seafront, some rooms with veranda. $
• **Hotel Sete Colinas.** Ladeira São Francisco, 307. ☎ 3439-6055. @ www. hotel7colinasolinda.com.br. 39 rooms, minibar, air conditioning, swimming pool, sauna. Listed historic mansion. $ $ $
• **Pousada do Amparo.** R. do Amparo, 199. ☎ 3439-1749. @ www. pousada doamparo.com.br. 12 rooms, air condi tioning, some with jacuzzi, view of the mansion and sea. Gallery sells handcrafted works of local artists. $ $ $
• **Pousada dos Quatro Cantos.** R. Prudente de Morais, 441. ☎ 3429-0220. @ www.pousada 4cantos.com.br. Minibar, air conditioning, some with veranda. Located in the historical center, in a listed building for its historical heritage. Charming decoration. $ $
• **Pousada Peter.** R. do Amparo, 215. @ www.pousadapeter.com.br. ☎ 3439-2171. 8 rooms, air conditioning, T.V., minibar. Swimming pool and an area selling handicrafts. $ $
• **Pousada São Francisco.** R. do Sol, 127. ☎ 3429-2109. @ www.pousa

dasaofrancisco.com.br. 45 rooms, air conditioning, T.V., minibar, Swimming pool, sauna, games room. $ $
• **Samburá.** Av. Ministro Marcos Freire, 1551, Bairro Novo. ☎ 3429-3466. 63 rooms, T.V., minibar, air conditioning. Sea view to the front and side. $ $

RESTAURANTS
• **Chez Georges.** R. Manoel Borba, 350. ☎ 3439-5858. French dishes with ingredients from Pernambuco. $ $
• **Estrela do Mar.** Av. Ministro Marcos Freire, 1691, Bairro Novo. ☎ 3429-7526. Beef, chicken and fish dishes. Mixed seafood Moqueca. $ $ $
• **Goya.** R. do Amparo, 157. ☎ 3439-4875. Open at lunchtime and at nighttime, closed Tuesdays. There are exhibitions of works of art in the restaurant. Seafood. Try the lobster, crab or shrimp moqueca. $ $ $
• **Kweto.** Pça. do Jacaré, Carmo Beach. ☎ 3429-2308. Closed Tuesdays. Monday open only at night. Wednesday to Sunday, lunchtime and nighttime. French, Moroccan and Indian dishes. Try the penne with lobster, shrimps and herbs. $ $
• **Oficina do Sabor.** R. do Amparo, 335. ☎ 3429-3331. Regional. Tables in the courtyard and view of city. $ $
• **Restaurant Mourisco.** R. 27 de Janeiro, sobrado 7. ☎ 3429-1390. Regional and seafood. $

Porto de Galinhas
⊕ 81

USEFUL ADDRESSES
• **HOSPITAL. São Miguel.** R. Vereador Antonio Bonifácio. ☎ 3551-1195. **Carusita Brito.** PE-38, Porto de Galinhas. ☎ 3527-9339.
• **EXCHANGE BUREAU. Norte Câmbio.** R. das Piscinas Naturais, loja 8. ☎ 3552-2125.
• **BANK. Do Brasil.** ☎ 3551-1105.
• **SHOPPING. Paulo Artesanato.** Av. Beira-mar, loja 3. ☎ 3552-1786. **Carcará.** Pça. 13. ☎ 3552-2314. Carvings made from trunks and pieces of wood. **Shopping Porto Rico.** R. da Esperança, 1. ☎ 3552-1023. **Galeria Porão By.** R. Beijupirá. ☎ 3552-2824.

VISITOR INFORMATION
• **SECRETARIA DE TURISMO.** R. Esperança, 188, Centre. ☎ 3552-1480.
• **TOURISM AGENTS. Aicá Diving.** Diving operator. ☎ 3552-1290. @ www.aica diving.com.br

HOTELS
• **Nannai Beach Resort.** PE-09, km 3, Muro Alto Beach. ☎ 3552-2100. @ www. nannai.com.br. Cable T.V., jacuzzi, air conditioning, minibar, veranda, sea view. Swimming pools circle some bungalows forming private areas. $ $ $ $
• **Pousada Beira-mar.** Av. Beira-Mar, 12, Downtown. ☎ 3552-1052. @ www.pousa dabeiramar.com.br. 12 rooms, T.V., air conditioning, minibar. On the seafront of Porto de Galinhas, some rooms with sea view and private area for sun bathing. $ $ $
• **Pousada Estação do Sol.** Condomínio Merepe III, Porto de Galinhas Beach. @ www.pousadaestacao dosol.com.br. ☎ 3552-1824. 26 rooms, air conditioning, T.V., minibar, swimming pool, bar, games room, playground. $ $ $
• **Resort Intermares.** Serrambi Beach. ☎ 3421-5177. @ www.intermares.com.br. The small resort follows the contour of the beach. Inside the resort there is a diving operator. $ $ $
• **Solar Porto de Galinhas.** PE-09, km 7, Cupe Beach. ☎ 3552-1211. @ www.so larportodegalinhas.com.br. 83 rooms, minibar, Cable T.V. Some rooms face a central swimming pool in front of the sea. Restaurant, games room, bar. $ $ $ $
• **Summerville Resort.** PE-09, Muro Alto Beach. ☎ 3302-4446. @ www. summer villeresort.com.br. 202 rooms, air conditioning, minibar, Cable T.V., swimming pool, sauna, nightclub, water sports, babysitter. $ $ $ $

RESTAURANTS
• **Barcaxeira.** R. da Esperança, 458, Porto de Galinhas. ☎ 3552-1913. manioc au gratin with sun-dried beef. $
• **Beijupirá.** Vila Porto de Galinhas. ☎ 3552-1271. Fish dishes. Try the camarulu: shrimps with sugarcane honey and passion fruit and for desert tapioca ice cream. $ $
• **Carne de Sol do Cunha.** R. Dr. Manuel Luiz Cavalcanti Uchoa, Porto de Galinhas. ☎ 3552-1340. Sun-dried beef. $
• **Peixe na Telha.** Av. Beira-mar, Porto de Galinhas. ☎ 3552-1323. Fish dishes prepared and served on telhas (similar to roof tiles). Try the filet of fish with vegetable sauce rice and pirão. $ $

TAMANDARÉ
🌐 81

• **TOURIST INFORMATION.** Av. Leopoldo Lins. ☎ 3676-1844. @ www. guiatamandare.com.br
• **BANK. Do Brasil.** ☎ 3676-1450.
• **HOSPITAL. Unidade Mista**. Av. Dr. Leopoldo Lins, Downtown. ☎ 3676-1192.

HOTELS
• **Pousada Amaragi.** Carneiros Beach, Rio Formoso. ☎ 3678-1153. @ www. pousadaamaragi.com.br. 36 rooms, air conditioning, T.V., minibar, games room, swimming pools. Located at the top of a hill in an old farm. It has an area on the beach with hammocks and water sports equipment. $ $ $ $
• **SESI Tamandaré.** R. Rômulo Gomes de Matos, Loteamento Luisiânia. ☎ 3676-1244. 50 rooms, including 20 chalets. Swimming pool, sauna, games room, playground. $
• **Sítio Gameleiro.** Carneiros Beach. ☎ 3427-1808. @ www.praiadoscarneiros.com.br. Four bungalows for 7 people each, among coconut palm-trees, set up in a former coconut farm. $

RESTAURANTS
• **Rei dos Crustáceos.** Av. José Bezerra de Albuquerque Sobrinho, Downtown. ☎ 3676-1800. Seafood. Try the large freshwater prawns in coconut sauce, rice, pirão and vegetables. $

CABO DE SANTO AGOSTINHO
🌐 81

USEFUL ADDRESSES
• **SECRETARIA DE TURISMO.** Av. Laura Cavalcanti, 69. ☎ 3522-6392. @ www.cabo.pe.gov.br
• **BUS STATION.** R. 13, 5, Aldeamento Jardim Santa Inácio. ☎ 3521-1210.
• **BANKS. Do Brasil**. ☎ 3521-1888. **Itaú**. ☎ 3521-1877. **Bradesco**. ☎ 3521-0217.
• **HOSPITAL. Santa Helena**. Ave. Presidente Vargas, 428, Downtown. ☎ 3521-0975. **São Sebastião**. Av. Presidente Vargas, 864. ☎ 3521-0430.

HOTELS
• **Blue Tree Park.** Av. Beira-mar, 750, Praia de Suape. ☎ 3521-6000. @ www. bluetree.com.br/sagostinho. 300 rooms, Cable T.V., air conditioning, fan, minibar. Swimming pool, tennis courts, sauna, fitness centre. A stretch of beach exclusively for guests. $ $ $ $

RESTAURANTS
• **Bar e restaurant da Garrafa.** Av. Beira Mar, 3, Paraíso Beach. ☎ 3522-5495. Lunch time and snacks. Try the mussels. $

PARAÍBA

João Pessoa
🌐 83

USEFUL ADDRESSES
• **BUS STATION.** R. do Varadouro, Centro. ☎ 221-9611.
• **AIRPORT. Presidente Casto Pinto**. Bayeux. ☎ 232-1200.
• **HOSPITALS. Samaritano**. Av. Santa Julia, 58, Torres. ☎ 218-2100. **Edson Ramalho**. R. Eugênio de Lucena Neiva, 13 de Maio. ☎ 218-7800. **Sta. Isabel**. Pça. Caldas Brandão, Tambiá. ☎ 214-1805.
• **BANKS. Do Brasil**. ☎ 216-1227. **Caixa**. ☎ 216-5300. **Itaú**. ☎ 241-1006. **HSBC**. ☎ 244-8611. **Unibanco**. ☎ 231-2232.
• **EXCHANGE. Banco do Brasil**. Pça. 1817, 129, Downtown. ☎ 216-1222. **Mondeo Tour**. Av. Nego, 46, Tambau. ☎ 226-3100. **PB Câmbio**. Manaíra Shopping mall. ☎ 246-2613.
• **SHOPS. Manaira Shopping mall**. Av. Flávio Ribeiro Coutinho, 805, Manaíra. ☎ 216-6000. **Terra do Sol handicrafts**.
R. Coração de Jesus, 145, Tambaú. ☎ 226-1940. **Bosque dos Sonhos**. Cabo Branco lighhouse stall where handicrafts are sold.

VISITOR INFORMATION
• **PBTUR (EMPRESA PARAIBANA DE TURISMO).** ☎ 226-7078. Ave. Almirante Tamandaré, 100, Tambaú. **Setur** (Secretaria de Turismo). Parque Sólon de Lucena, 180, Centro. ☎ 241-4414.
• **TRAVEL AGENCIES. Green Tour**. R. Irenaldo Albuquerque Chaves, 201, Sala 217, Bessa. ☎ 245-9223.

HOTELS
• **Annamar Hotel.** R. Santo Antônio, 36, Tambaú. ☎ 247-3011. @www.anmamarhotel.hpg.com.br. 58 rooms, air con-

ditioning, tv, minibar, Swimming pool. Central Tambaú, 50 meters from the beach. 💲 💲 💲
- **Escuna Praia.** Av. Cabo Branco, 1574, Cabo Branco. ☎ 226-5611. 17 rooms, air conditioning, tv, minibar. Triple and double rooms; some overlooking ocean. 💲 💲
- **Hardmann Praia.** Av. João Maurício, 1341, Manaíra. @ www.hotelhard mann. com.br. ☎ 246-8811. 120 rooms, air conditioning, cable tv, minibar. Gym, waterfront restaurant. All rooms have a small living rooms and kitchen. 💲 💲 💲
- **Hotel Casa Grande.** Av. General Édson Ramalho, 530, Manaíra. ☎ 226-5622. 100 meters from waterfront. 38 rooms, air conditioning, tv, minibar. Swimming pool and recreation room. 💲
- **Hotel Tropical Tambaú.** Av. Almirante Tamandaré, 229, Tambaú. @ www. tropicalhotel.com.br. 175 rooms, air conditioning, tv, minibar. Swimming pool, sauna, gym, recreation. ☎ 218-1919. 💲 💲 💲
- **Litoral Hotel.** Av. Cabo Branco, 2172, Praia do Cabo Branco. ☎ 247-1100. @ www.hotellittoral.com.br. 102 rooms, air conditioning, tv, minibar. Swimming pool, sauna, recreation room, and gym. 💲 💲
- **Royal Praia Hotel.** R. Coração de Jesus, Tambaú. ☎ 247-3006. @ www. royalhotel.com.br. 54 rooms, air conditioning, cable tv, minibar. Sauna, swimming pool, recreation room. On main square in Tambaú, nearby handicraft fair. 💲 💲 💲

RESTAURANTS

- **Badionaldo.** R. Vitolino Cardoso, Cabedelo. ☎ 250-1299. Crab soups. 💲 💲
- **Adega do Alfredo.** R. Coração de Jesus, Tambaú. ☎ 226-4346. Cod fish specialities. Next to the Rayol Praia Hotel. 💲 💲
- **Mangai.** Av. Édson Ramalho, 696, Manaíra. Self-service (per kilo) regional dishes. Breakfast, lunch and dinner. Tuesday to Sunday.
- **Sagarana.** Av. Almirante Tamandaré, 310, Tambaú. ☎ 226-6220. Sea food. Shrimp in pitanga berry sauce; fish in a sourish cajá sauce. Sunday to Thursday, dinner only. Friday and Saturday, lunch and dinner. 💲 💲
- **Tábua do Marinheiro.** Av. Cabo Branco, 1780, Cabo Branco. ☎ 247-5804. Monday to Wednesday, lunch only. Thursday to Sunday, lunch and dinner. Seafood. Shrimp in coconut sauce. 💲 💲

Rio Tinto
🌐 83

HOTELS

- **Hotel Pousada Tropical.** R. Oswaldo Trogueiro. Baia da Traição. ☎ 296-1223. Next to a filling station. 16 rooms, air conditioning, minibar. 💲 💲
- **Hotel São José.** R. da Mangueira, 45, Rio Tinto. ☎ 291-2357. 12 rooms, air conditioning or fan. 💲

Conde
🌐 83

HOTEL

- **Bangalôs de Carapibus.** Via PB-008 road, Carapibus Beach, Conde. ☎ 290-1436. Bungalows that fit 5 people; common eating hall. Swimming pool, recreation room, courts. 💲 💲
- **Pousada Corais de Carapibus.** Carapibus Beach. ☎ 290-1179. @ www. coraisdecarapibus.com.br. Air conditioning, tv, minibar, veranda with hammock. Seafront. 💲 💲
- **Pousada do Caju.** PB-008, Tabatinga Beach, Conde. ☎ 290-1303. @ www. pousadadocaju.com.br. 25 km from João Pessoa, 7 km from Tambaba. 16 rooms, fan or air conditioning, tv, minibar. Well located for south coast visitors. 💲 💲
- **Pousada Enseada do Sol.** Carapibus Beach, Conde. ☎ 290-1732. @ pou sadaenseadadosol@terra.com.br. 13 rooms, air conditioning, tv, minibar. Swimming pool. 💲 💲
- **Zecas.** Estrada de Carapibus. ☎ 290-1185. Air conditioning, tv, minibar. Swimming pool. Faces Jacumã Lake, 500 metres from beach. Also serves regional food. 💲

RESTAURANTS

- **Portal de Jacumã.** PB-008 road, Conde. ☎ 290-1604. @ hoteldejacuman @mailbr.com.br. Coffee shop and ice-cream parlour. 💲

Campina Grande
🌐 83

USEFUL ADDRESSES

- **TOWN HALL.** Av. Floriano Peixoto, 715, 3º andar, Downtown. ☎ 321-7717
- **BUS STATION.** Eutécio Vital Ribeiro, Catolé. ☎ 337-3001
- **AIRPORT. Presidente João Suassuna.** Av. Uberaba, Distrito Industrial. ☎ 331-1149.
- **HOSPITAL. João XXII.** Nilo

Peçanha, 83, Prata. ☎ 321-2323.
• **BANKS. Do Brasil.** ☎ 310-2200. **Bradesco**. ☎ 341-3600. **Caixa**. ☎ 321-2501. **Itaú**. ☎ 341-1545.

RESTAURANTS
• **Campina Grill.** Av. Manuel Tavares, 1900, Alto Branco. ☎ 341-6743. Regional and roasts. Pork, green beans, manioc flour and cheese purée, mint sauce. $ $
• **Tábua de Carne.** R. Vigário Virgínio, 52. ☎ 341-1008. @ www.tabuadecarne.com.br. Mainly northeastern dishes based on goat's meat and jerky. $

HOTELS
• **Hotel Ouro Branco.** R. Coronel João Lourenço Porto, 20, Centro. ☎ 341-2929. @ www.hotelourobranco.com.br. 60 rooms, air conditioning, tv, minibar, recreation lounge. $ $
• **Hotel Serrano.** R. Tavares Cavalcanti, 27, Centro. ☎ 341-3141. 59 rooms, air conditioning, tv, minibar. Swimming pool. $ $

Tambaba
⊕ 83

ACCOMODATION
• **Estalagem Aldeia dos Ventos.** Tambaba Beach. ☎ 9985-0806. 18 rooms, air conditioning or seafront; tv. $
• **Dom Quinzote.** Tambaba Beach. ☎ 246-5462. 8 rooms, suites. Caters for naturalist guest only. $

RESTAURANTS
• **A Arca do Bilu.** PB-008 road. Rodovia Abelardo Jurema, Tambaba Beach. ☎ 298-1124. Seafood. $

RIO GRANDE DO NORTE

Natal
⊕ 84

USEFUL ADDRESSES
• **BUS STATION.** Av. Capitão Morro Gouveia, 1237, Cidade Esperança. ☎ 205-4377.
• **AIRPORT. Augusto Severo**. BR-101, 15 km. ☎ 644-1000.
• **BANKS. Do Brasil.** ☎ 216-4640. **Caixa**. ☎ 215-5181. **Bradesco**. ☎ 221-1305. **Itaú**. ☎ 221-1445.
• **CAR RENTAL. Avis.** ☎ 644-2500. Hertz. ☎ 207-3399. **Localiza**. ☎ 206-5296. **Unidas**. ☎ 643-2072. Yes. ☎ 219-4001.
• **EXCHANGE. Ponta Negra Câmbio,** Av. Erivan França, 91, Ponta Negra. ☎ 232-3545.

• **HOSPITAL. Walfredo Gurgel**. Av. Salgado Filho, Lagoa Seca. ☎ 232-7500. **Santa Catarina**. R. Araquari, Potengi. ☎ 232-7700. **Memorial**. Ave. Juvenal Lamartine, 979, Tirol. ☎ 211-3636.

VISITOR INFORMATION
• **SECRETARIA MUNICIPAL DE TURISMO.** Av. Hermes da Fonseca, 515, Petrópolis. ☎ 232-9072
• **TOURISM AGENCIES. Manary Ecotours.** R. Francisco Gurgel, 9067, Ponta Negra. ☎ 219-2900. @ www.manary.com.br. Specialised in cultural and ecological tourism.

HOTELS
• **Albergue da Juventude Lua Cheia.** R. Dr. Manuel Augusto Bezerra de Araújo, 500, Ponta Negra. ☎ 236-3696. @ www.lua cheia.com.br. Architecture, decoration and illumination of the hostel are similar to a castle. At night the Taberna Pub is very busy, with live shows. $
• **Hotel Barreira Roxa.** Via Costeira, Barreira D'água Beach. ☎ 202-4097. @ www.barreiraroxa.com.br. Air conditioning, cable TV, minibar.53 rooms, minibar, cable tv, swimming pool. $ $ $ $
• **O Tempo e o Vento Hotel.** R. Élia Barros, 66, Ponta Negra. ☎ 219-2526. @ www.otempoeovento.com.br. Air conditioning, cable TV, minibar. Rooms facing the swimming pools and 100m from the beach. $ $ $
• **Ponta do Mar Hotel.** R. Skal, 2056, Ponta Negra. ☎ 236-2509. @ www. hotel pontadomar.com.br. 36 rooms, Air conditioning, TV, minibar. All with sea view. $ $ $
• **Manary Praia Hotel.** R. Francisco Gurgel, 9067, Ponta Negra. ☎ 219-2900. @ www.manary.com.br. 25 rooms. Verandas with hammock and sea view which mix luxury with the rustic. $ $ $ $
• **Ocean Palace Hotel.** Via Costeira, km 11, Ponta Negra. ☎ 219-4144. @ www.oceanpalace.com.br. 213 rooms, Air conditioning, cable TV, minibar, swimming pools, deck facing the sea, sauna, and rooms for the disabled. $ $ $ $
• **Pousada La Luna.** R. Francisco Gurgel, 9045. Ponta Negra. ☎ 236-2981. @ www.pousadalaluna.com. Air conditioning, cable TV, minibar. Pool side breakfast. Some have veranda and a sea view. $ $ $
• **Rifóles Praia Hotel.** R. Coronel Inácio Vale, 8847, Ponta Negra. ☎ 646-5000. @ www.rifoles.com.br. 110 rooms, cable TV, minibar, rooms for the disabled. $ $ $ $

RESTAURANTS

• **Pico do Mirante Bar.** Barra de Tabatinga, Nísia Floresta. ☎ 230-2226. There are hammocks with a sea view, above the cliffs. Titbits, drinks and ice creams served on rustic wooden tables. 🆂
• **Camarão do Olavo.** R. João Batista Gundim, 5, Nísia Floresta. ☎ 277-2211. Specializes in shrimps. 🆂 🆂
• **Camarões.** Av. Engenheiro Roberto Freire, 2610, Ponta Negra. ☎ 219-2424. Open for lunch and dinner. Fish dishes. The speciality is shrimps. Shuttle service. 🆂 🆂 🆂
• **Casa de Taipa.** R. Dr. Manoel A. B. de Araújo, 141, Ponta Negra. ☎ 219-5798. Regional. 30 types of tapioca, besides coffee, salads and batidas (fruit juice with cachaça). 🆂
• **Mangai.** R. Amintas Barros, 3300, Lagoa Nova. ☎ 206-3344. @ www. mangai.com.br. breakfast, lunch and dinner by weight. Food and decoration traditional sertaneja. 🆂
• **Paçoca de Pilão.** Av. Deputado Márcio Marinho, 5708, Pirangi do Norte, Parnamirim. ☎ 238-2088. The main dish has the same name as the restaurant: sun-dried beef ground with flour, rice, podded unripe beans, manioc and banana. 🆂 🆂
• **Restaurante Samô.** Av. Engenheiro Roberto Freire, 9036, Ponta Negra. ☎ 219-3669. Lunch and dinner. Fish dishes. Shuttle service. 🆂 🆂 🆂

GENIPABU AND NORTH COAST
⊕ 84

HOTELS

• **Atlântico Norte Lazer.** Av. Litorânea, 681, Redinha Beach. ☎ 224-2002. @ www. portoaltantico.com.br. Swimming pool, games room and recreation area. 🆂 🆂
• **Genipabu Spa Hotel.** Natal Road, km3, Genipabu. ☎ 225-2071. @ www.spanaturalis.com.br. It is situated at the top of the hill. It has a spa with beauty services, gym classes and treks in the dunes. 🆂 🆂 🆂 🆂
• **Pousada Caseira.** R. Projetada 1026, Maracajaú Beach. Swimming pool. Pleasant atmosphere, resembles a beach house and serves an excellent breakfast. 🆂
• **Pousada Convés de Jacumã.** Jacumã Beach. ☎ 228-2420. Simple character. 🆂
• **Pousada Três Coqueiros.** R. Ricardo Afonso, 98, Genipabu Beach. ☎ 225-2061. Pleasant surroundings with well looked after garden and small swimming pool at the bottom. 🆂 🆂
• **Pousada Villa do Sol.** On the banks

of Ceará-Mirim River, Genipabu. ☎ 225-2132. @ www.digi.com.br/villa dosol. 15 rooms, TV, air conditioning, minibar. 🆂 🆂 🆂

RESTAURANTS

• **Restaurante da Morena.** R. Vereador Ricardo Afonso, Genipabu. ☎ 961-2698. Fish dishes. Order the seafood moqueca (fish or shellfish with palm-oil and hot peppers). 🆂 🆂
• **Restaurante Maracajau Divers.** Maracajau Beach. ☎ 261-6200. Fish dishes. Try the macaroni with seafood. 🆂 🆂
• **Restaurante Naf Naf.** Jacumã Beach. ☎ 228-2228. Self service with seafood. 🆂
• **Restaurante Sinfonia do Camarão.** Anéis Beach, Manoa Park. ☎ 238-2732. Regional dishes. Try the lobster prepared with vegetables. 🆂 🆂 🆂

Mossoró
⊕ 84

USEFUL ADDRESSES

• **BANKS. Do Brasil.** ☎ 316-3300. **Bradesco.** ☎ 321-1391. **Caixa.** ☎ 315-1501. **Itaú.** ☎ 316-1099.

VISITOR INFORMATION

• **TOURISM BUREAU.** Av. Alberto Maranhão, Palácio da Resistência, Downtown. ☎ 316-1050.

HOTELS

• **Thermas de Mossoró Hotel.** Av. Lauro Monte, 2001, Santo Antonio. ☎ 318-1200. @ www.hotelthermas. com.br. The hot waters withdrawn from the 1000-meters water wells supply the ten swimming pools of the hotel. 🆂 🆂
• **Sabino Palace Hotel.** Av. Presidente Dutra, 1744, Alto São Manuel. ☎ 312-2000. 93 rooms, telephone, air conditioning, TV, minibar. 🆂

LAJEDO DE SOLEDADE
⊕ 84

USEFUL ADDRESSES

• **BUS COMPANIES. São Geraldo.** ☎ 316-7380. Jardinense. ☎ 316-2747.
• **SECRETARIA DE TURISMO.** Av. Alberto Maranhão, Downtown, Palácio da Resistência. ☎ 316-1050.

HOSPEDAGEM

• **Hotel Lajedo.** R. Joaquim Teixeira de Moura, 1161, BR 405. ☎ 333-3113. @ hotellajedo@uol. com.br. 27 rooms, TV, minibar. 🆂

Praia da Pipa
⊕ 84

USEFUL ADDRESSES
• **BUS COMPANY. Oceano**. ☎ 205-3833.
Minibuses. ☎ 217-3249/973-0353.
Coopertaxi. ☎ 643-1183.
• **BANK. Do Brasil** (Canguaretama).
☎ 241-2311. (Goianinha). ☎ 243-2220.
• **EXCHANGE. Norte Câmbio**. Ave.
Baía dos Golfinhos, 35, Pipa Beach.
☎ 246-2474.

VISITOR INFORMATION
• **PIPA TOUR**. Galeria das Cores, Av.
Baía dos Golfinhos. ☎ 246-2234.
@ www.pipatour.com.br. Tourism
agency and Internet access.

HOTELS
• **Pousada Toca da Coruja**. Av.
Baía dos Golfinhos, Pipa Beach.
☎ 502-2333. @ www.tocadacoruja.
com.br. 5 chalets and 6 rooms, air conditioning, fan, TV, minibar, sauna,
swimming pool, bodybuilding gym.
Cozy and with good taste. $ $ $
• **Pipa Hotel**. R. Praia do Amor,
Amor Beach. ☎ 246-2331. @ www.
hoteldapipa.com.br. Air conditioning,
minibar, swimming pool, TV. $ $ $
• **Marinas Tibau do Sul Hotel**. Tibau
do Sul Beach. ☎ 502-2323. @ www. hotel marinas.com.br. Chalets. On the banks
of Guaraíras Lagoon, organises boat, horse
and jeep trips. The restaurant is on a deck
on the lakeside. Swimming pool. $ $ $
• **Pousada Pomar da Pipa**. R. da
Mata, Pipa Beach. ☎ 246-2256. @
www.po mardapipa.hpg.com.br. Distant
from the bustle and near nature. $
• **Ponta do Madeiro Hotel**. Madeiro
Beach. Pipa Road, km 3, Rota do sol. ☎
246-4222. 12 rooms, 30 chalets, air conditioning, TV, veranda facing the sea. $ $ $

RESTAURANTS
• **Al Buchetto**. R. da Gameleira, Pipa
Beach. ☎ 246-2318. Italian. $ $
• **Luna Bistro**. Av. Baía dos Golfinhos, 7.
☎ 246-2240. Pasta and fish dishes. Try the
penne with shrimps and spices. $ $ $
• **Sagarana**. Av. Baía dos Golfinhos. ☎
246-2212. Seafood. The fish in 'mangaba'
sauce with mint leaves is delicious. $ $

BARRA DO CUNHAÚ
⊕ 84

HOTELS
• **Pousada Caribe Sul**. Av. do Pontal,
500, Barra do Cunhaú. ☎ 241-4225.
@ www.praiabarradocunhau.com.br/car-
ibesul. 20 rooms, 8 chalets. On the sea
front, swimming pool, bar, restaurant, TV,
air conditioning or ceiling fan. $ $
• **Pousada do Baiano**. R. da Praia,
Barra do Cunhaú. ☎ 241-4296. 12 Chalets on the sea front, air conditioning,
swimming pool, minibar, TV. $ $
• **Pousada do Forte**. Av. do Pontal,
293, Barra do Cunhaú. ☎ 241-2471. @
www.pousadaforte.com.br. The chalets
have king-sized beds, verandas with
hammocks, swimming pool. $ $
• **Pousada Vento das Marés**. Barra
do Cunhaú. ☎ 241-4431. On the sea front,
minibar, TV, air conditioning or fan. $ $

RESTAURANTS
• **Punto Máximo**. Av. Beira Mar, Barra
do Cunhaú. ☎ 241-4240. @ www.punto
maximo.com.br. Spacious hall, facing the
sea, serves pasta and fish dishes. $ $
• **Solimar**. R. da Praia, Barra do Cunhaú. ☎ 241-4242. @ www.solimar.
com.br. The speciality is the grilled dishes and seafood. $ $

BAÍA FORMOSA
⊕ 84

HOTELS
• **Chalemar**. Via Costeira. ☎ 244-2222.
@ www.chalemar.com.br. 14 chalets,
fan or air conditioning, minibar, TV.
The restaurant and the swimming pool
are near the beach and the room are on
the higher land with a sea view. $ $
• **Pousada Sonho Meu**. R. Dr. Manuel
Francisco de Melo, 143. ☎ 244-2245.
@ www.geocities.com/pousadasm. 13
rooms. It has an internal garden with
hammocks. $ $

Touros
⊕ 84

USEFUL ADDRESSES
• **CITY HALL**. ☎ 263-2214.
• **BUS STATION**. ☎ 262-2330.
• **BANKS. Do Brasil**. ☎ 263-2212.
• **HOSPITAL. Ministro Paulo de
Almeida Machado**. ☎ 263-2243.
• **CAR RENTAL**. ☎ **Josias**. 991-6624.

HOTELS
• **Punaú Praia Hotel**. Barra do Punaú.
☎ 234-1836. Chalets for families, Kayak trips, trails. $
• **Pousada Tok do Mar**. Zumbi Beach.
☎ 274-2378. $

• **Pousada Enseada dos Amores.** R. Principal, 07, São José de Touros. ☎ 206-5061. Cosy with a delightful garden and sea view. $

• **Pousada dos Ponteiros.** São Miguel do Gostoso Beach. ☎ 263 4007. Chalets facing the sea, swimming pool, games room and huts on beach. $ $

• **Pousada do Gostoso.** R. dos Corais, 2, São Miguel do Gostoso. ☎ 502-5444. Chalets for up to 5 people, which resemble fishermen's cottages. Games room, playground and swimming pool. $ $

• **Pousada Arraial do Marco.** Marco Beach. ☎ 984-6662. Rooms facing the sea, swimming pool. $ $

• **Pousada Costa Branca.** Ponta do Mel Beach. ☎ 332-7062. Comfortable chalets with king-size beds, Cable TV and air conditioning. Sea view, swimming pool. Regional cuisine. $ $ $

RESTAURANTS

• **O Castelo.** Av. Atlântica, Touros Beach. ☎ 263-2325. Fish dishes. $

• **Pousada do Gostoso.** R. dos Corais, 2, São Miguel do Gostoso. ☎ 502-5444. Fish dishes. Try the robalo fish (*Centropomus undecimalis*) with passion fruit sauce. $ $

• **Pousada Arraial do Marco.** Marco Beach. ☎ 984-6662. Regional dishes. $

CEARÁ

Fortaleza
☎ 85

USEFUL ADDRESSES

• **BUS STATION. Antonio Bezerra**. R. Hipólito Pamplona, 45. ☎ 235-1423 **Eng. São Tomé**. Ave. Borges De Melo, 1630. ☎ 256-2100.

• **AIRPORT. Pinto Martins**. Av. Senador Carlos Jereissati, 3000 (access by the BR-116 highway). ☎ 477-1200.

• **HOSPITAL. Geral de Fortaleza**. Av. Desembargador Moreira, 1500, Aldeota. ☎ 466-6200; **Santa Casa**. Ave. Barão de Rio Branco, 20. ☎ 211-1911

• **BANKS. Do Brasil**. ☎ 266-8400. **Bradesco**. ☎ 211-8266. **Caixa**. ☎ 254-4277. **HSBC**. ☎ 219-1799. **Itaú**. ☎ 252-2499. **Real**. ☎ 488-2311. **Unibanco**. ☎ 266-1212.

• **CAR RENTAL. Aldeota**. ☎ 263-5164; **Hertz**. ☎ 477-5055; **Localiza**. ☎ 477-5050; **Nobre**. ☎ 477-1355; **Unidas**. ☎ 477-1400.

• **EXCHANGE. Acctur Câmbio e Turismo**. Av. Monsenhor Tabosa, 1600, Meireles. ☎ 248-8900; **Do Brasil**. R. Barão do Rio Branco, 1515, Centre. ☎ 254-2122; **BBV**. R. Major Facundo, 322 Centre. ☎ 211-1834.

• **SHOPPING. Ceart (Handicraft Centre of Ceará).** Av. Santos Dumont, 1589, Aldeota. ☎ 268-2970; **Ceart – Dragão do Mar**. R. Dragão do Mar, 81. ☎ 226- 6917. **Tourist Center**. R. Senador Pompeu, 350, Downtown. ☎ 212-3566; **Central Market**. Av. Alberto Nepomuceno, 199, Downtown. ☎ 454-8586; **Shopping Centre**. Av. Washington Soares, 85, Edson Queiroz. ☎ 241-3577; **Avenida Shopping**. Av. Dom Luís, 300, Meireles. ☎ 264-9444; **Shopping Aldeota**. Ave. Des. Moreira, Aldeota: ☎ 458-1024.

VISITOR INFORMATION

• **TOURIST INFORMATION BUREAUS. Airport**. ☎ 477-1667; Tourist Center. ☎ 488-7411; **Mucuripe Lighthouse**. ☎ 263-1115; **Bus station**. ☎ 256-4080. **Convention Center**. ☎ 273-1622.

• **TOURISM HOTLINE.** ☎ 0800-991516.

• **TOURIST DEPARTMENT. Administrative Centre Virgílio Távora** - Edifício SEPLAN/Térreo, Cambeba. ☎ 488-3900. @ www.turismo.setur.ce.gov.br.

• **DIVING OPERATORS. Capitania dos Portos**. ☎ 254-7555. **Projeto Netuno**. ☎ 263-3009.

HOTELS

• **Albergue da Juventude.** Av. Almirante Barroso, 998, Iracema Beach. ☎ 219-3267. @ www.aldeota.com.br/albergue. 70 beds, dormitories, communal room, individual lockers. $

• **Baden Baden.** R. Silva Paulet, 188, Meireles. ☎ 248-8788. @ www. hotel badenbaden.com.br. 8 rooms, air conditioning, simple, comfortable and well located. $

• **Caesar Park.** Av. Beira-Mar, 3980, Mucuripe. ☎ 0800-852202. @ www. caesarpark-for.com.br. 229 rooms, air conditioning, tv, minibar, swimming pool, playground. $ $ $ $

• **Casa de Praia.** R. Joaquim Alves, 169, Iracema. ☎ 219-1022. @ www. hotelcasadepraia.com.br. 28 rooms, air conditioning, TV, minibar two blocks from the beach and the Bohemian life of Iracema. Simple and comfortable. $ $

• **Holiday Inn.** Av. Hist. Raimundo Grão, 800, Iracema. ☎ 455-5000. 273 rooms,

air conditioning, tv, minibar, swimming pool, playground. 💲💲💲💲
- **Hotel Beira-mar.** Av. Beira-mar, 3130, Meireles Beach. ☎ 242-5000. @ www. hotelbeiramar.com.br. 112 rooms, TV, air conditioning, minibar, swimming pool, restaurant, bar. 💲💲💲
- **Pousada Aquarius.** R. Carlos Vasconcelos, 308, Meireles. ☎ 248-0778. @ www.aquariuspousada.com.br. 21 rooms, TV, air conditioning, minibar, swimming pool. Friendly ambient, the decoration resembles a beach cottage. 💲💲
- **Pousada Feitiço do Ceará.** Av. Hildebrando Pompeu, 255, Futuro Beach. ☎ 234-6929. @ www.pousadafeiticodo ceara. com.br. 4 rooms, TV, air conditioning, minibar, games room. Chalets and rooms with hammocks on the veranda. 💲💲
- **Praia Centro.** Av. Monsenhor Tabosa, 740, Iracema. ☎ 219-1122. @ www.praiacentre.com.br. 260 rooms, TV, air conditioning, minibar, swimming pool, restaurant, bar, games room. Sea view and three convention rooms. 💲💲💲

RESTAURANTS
- **Bar 90°.** R. dos Tabajaras, 310, Iracema. Specialists in pancakes and snacks. Daily at night. 💲
- **Café Avião.** Pça. Almirante Saldanha, Centre. ☎ 219-2428. Daily from 3 p.m. Since 1931. Serves snacks. 💲
- **Ceamoara.** Av. Abolição, 3340-A, Mucuripe. ☎ 263-5501. Open daily for lunch and dinner. Try the shrimps with ementhal sauce and spinach rice, or the fish with mushrooms and tomatoes. 💲💲💲
- **Colher de Pau.** R. dos Tabajaras, 412, Iracema. ☎ 219-3605. Typical food. Speciality the sun-dried beef fried in butter accompanied with baião de dois (recipe with rice, cheese, beans and butter). 💲
- **Restaurante Dragão do Mar.** R. Dragão do Mar, Centre. ☎ 219-2954. By the side of Dragão do Mar Cultural Downtown. Daily from 6 p.m. Regional dishes. Atmosphere inspired by a fisherman's house. Try the baião de dois (recipe with rice, cheese, beans and butter). 💲
- **Vento em Popa.** Pça. Almirante Saldanha, Downtown. ☎ 219-2880. Tables outside. Live music. Gastronomic banquets with dishes from different parts of the world. 💲💲

CUMBUCO
⊕ 85

HOTELS
- **Best Western Golfinho.** Av. dos Coqueiros. ☎ 318-7444. @ www.hotel gol finho.com.br. 25 rooms, air conditioning, TV, minibar, bar, restaurant, games room, recreation room, cascade, swimming pool. Ideal for families with children. 💲💲💲
- **Pousada Dunas do Cumbuco.** Av. Central. ☎ 318-7409. 14 rooms, TV, air conditioning, minibar, restaurant, swimming pool. Localised near to the beach. Comfortable and pleasant. 💲💲
- **Pousada Lagoa do Banana.** Cumbuco/Salgado Road, km 3, Lagoa do Banana. ☎ 301-1307. 28 rooms, minibar, bar, cascade, launch, swimming pool, sailing boat on the lagoon. 💲💲

GUARAMIRANGA
⊕ 92

USEFUL ADDRESSES
- **BUS STATION.** Major Pedro Catão (Baturité). ☎ 347-1507.
- **HOSPITAL. José Pinto do Carmo** (Baturité). ☎ 321-11218.
- **BANKS.** In Baturité. **Do Brasil.** ☎ (85) 347-1011; **Caixa.** ☎ (85) 347-1616.

VISITOR INFORMATION
- **TOURISM OFFICE.** ☎ 321-1133.

HOTELS
- **Chalés das Montanhas.** Sítio Macapazinho. ☎ 321-1150. Open at the weekends. Chalets with kitchen. There is a restaurant and swimming pool. 💲💲
- **Estância Vale das Flores.** Sítio São Francisco. ☎ 325-1233. With thicket, calm and pleasant. 💲💲💲
- **Hotel Escola de Guaramiranga .** Sítio de Guaramiranga. ☎ 321-1106. Swimming pool, sauna and games room. 💲💲

RESTAURANTS
- **Hofbräuhaus.** Road to Aratuba, km 11. ☎ 9986-4925. Open at the weekends. German dishes. 💲💲💲
- **Taberna Portuguesa.** Linha da Serra, access by the Pernambuquinho road, km 9. ☎ 9983-9476. Open at the weekends. Portuguese. 💲💲💲

PARQUE NACIONAL DE UBAJARA
⊕ 85

USEFUL ADDRESSES
- **CITY HALL.** R. Juvêncio Pereira, 514,

Downtown. ☎ 634-1200. @ prefeitura-munici paldeubajara@bol.com.br.
• **BUS STATION.** Av. Dr. Joaquim Fontenele. ☎ 634-1300.
• **HEALTH POST.** R. Raimundo de Barros, Bairro São Sebastião. ☎ 634-1449.
• **TELEPHONE EXCHANGE.** R. Agapito Pereira, 163, Centre.

VISITOR INFORMATION
• **TOURISM OFFICE.** Av. Dr. Joaquim Fontenele. ☎ 634-1300, ex. 224.

HOTEL
• **Clube Pousada de Inhuçu.** R. Gonçalo de Freitas, 454, São Benedito. ☎ 626-1173. 16 rooms and 1 chalet , TV, minibar, swimming pool, sauna, restaurant, bar, sports courts. $ $
• **Pousada São Benedito.** Confi-ança Highway, km 21, São Bene-dito. ☎ 626-1592. 10 rooms and 5 chalets TV, air conditioning, minibar, restaurant. $

RESTAURANTS
• **Alô Cristina.** Av. dos Constituintes. ☎ 634-1156. snacks, pizza and pasta. $
• **Nevoar.** R. Monsenhor Gonçalo Eufrásio. Regional dishes. $
• **O Macaxeira.** Av. dos Constituintes, 296. Regional dishes. $
• **Zé Maria.** Route of the cable car. Sítio da Gameleira. Regional dishes. $

Canoa Quebrada
⊞ 88

USEFUL ADDRESSES
• **BUS STATION. Aracati**. R. Coronel Alexandrino. ☎ 421-3047
• **BUS COMPANY. São Benedito**. ☎ 421-2020.
• **BANKS. Do Brasil**. ☎ 421-1200 (Aracati). ☎ 338-1066 (Beberibe). ☎ 334-1618 (Cascavel); **Caixa** ☎ (85) 421-1444 (Aracati). ☎ (85) 334-1699 (Cascavel)
• **HOSPITAL. FSESP.** ☎ 421-1449.
• **CAR RENTAL. Josias**. ☎ (84) 991-6624 (Canoa Quebrada); **Sérgio and Júnior**. ☎ (85) 9976-9701 (Caponga); **Associação de Bugueiros de Morro Branco.** ☎ (85) 9969-5825.

VISITOR INFORMATION
• **TOURISM OFFICE.** ☎ 85 421-1006 (Aracati); ☎ 85 338-2010 (Beberibe).
• **TOURIST AGENCIES. Bhiattur**. ☎ 85 291-2030

HOTELS
CANOA QUEBRADA
• **Best Western Canoa Resort.** Av. Porto Canoa, 500. ☎ 421-9000. @ www.portocanoa.com.br. Resort with swimming pool, water toboggan, games and recreation room. $ $ $ $
• **Tranquilândia Village.** Canoa Beach. ☎ 421-7012. @ www.tranquilandia.it. Comfortable chalets which face a swimming pool on the seafront. $ $ $
• **Pousada Sete Mares.** R. Quatro Ventos, 400. ☎ 421-7109. @ www.geocities.com/pousada7mares. Quiet as it is distant from the bustle of the main street. It has a swimming pool. $ $
• **Pousada Lua Morena.** R. Principal. @ www.luamorena.com. ☎ 421-7030. Chalets for up to 6 people. Swimming pool. $ $
ARACATI
• **Pousada Bons Ventos.** R. Cônego João Paulo, 971, Aracati. ☎ 421-7093. @ www.aracati.com.br/bonsventos. TV and unheated shower. $ $
MORRO BRANCO
• **Pousada Ibitu.** Morro Branco. ☎ (85) 338-7186. @ www.ibitu.com.br. $ $ $
PRAIA DAS FONTES
• **Maresia Hotel.** ☎ (85) 338-1390. @ www.maresiahotel.hpg.com.br. Swimming pool and restaurant. $ $ $
CAPONGA
• **Village Barra Mar Hotel.** Av. Beira Rio, Caponga Beach. ☎ (85) 334-8088. @ www.barramar.com. Chalets for up to 5 people. There is a lake, pedal-boats, swimming pool with water toboggan and recreation area. $ $ $ $
• **Pousada Beira Mar.** R. Antônio Maciel, 840, Caponga Beach. ☎ (85) 334-8188. With unheated shower, TV, and private car park. $
MAJORLÂNDIA
• **Refúgio Dourado.** Majorlândia Beach. ☎ 421-8085. With colored sculptures on the cliffs. One of the buildings is a reproduction of a fisherman's cottage. Comfortable and cozy, with swimming pool and unheated shower. $ $
PONTA GROSSA
• **Pousada Canaã.** Ponta Grossa Beach. ☎ 432-5001. Simple and cozy. It is necessary to take bedclothes. $
REDONDA
• **Pousada do Zé Wilson.** Redondas Beach. Simple rooms in a fisherman's cottage. $
• **Pousada do Pescador.** Redondas Beach. ☎ 432-3018. Simple rooms in

a fisherman's cottage. Fan. $

ÁGUAS BELAS
• **Le Paradise.** Águas Belas Beach. ☎ (85) 334-8050. Rooms with unheated showed. It has a restaurant and swimming pool. On the bank of Mal Cozinhado River. $ $
• **Le France.** R. Francisco Camilo, 1376. ☎ (85) 334-8050. Rooms with unheated shower. Swimming pool, bar and cascade. $ $

RESTAURANTS
• **Barraca Mar e Sol.** Fontes Beach, near to Caponga. ☎ (85) 327-3026. Grilled fish, moquecas (fish or shellfish with palm-oil and hot peppers) and shellfish. $
• **Le France.** R. Francisco Camilo, 1376. ☎ 334-8050. Varied dishes. $ $ $
• **Village Barra Mar.** Av. Beira Rio, Caponga Beach. ☎ (85) 334-8088. Food by weight. $
• **Feitiço da Lua.** R. Dragão do Mar. ☎ 9181-5554. Delicious seviche, Peruvian recipe of raw fish marinated in lemon juice. $
• **Bistrô Natural.** R. Dragão do Mar. ☎ 421-7083. Varied. Cosy, internet access for clients. $
• **Barraca Chega Mais.** Canoa Beach. It serves à la carte and prepared plates, including sophisticated shellfish dishes. $ $
• **Tenda do Cumbe.** Canoa Quebrada Beach. ☎ 421-7252. Regional. Lobster between the months of May and December. $

Jericoacoara
⊕ 88

USEFUL ADDRESSES
• **BUS COMPANY. Companhia Redenção.** ☎ (85) 256-2728. Six and a half hours travelling starting from Fortaleza. The tickets can be bought in front of the handicraft fair on the Meireles beach.
• **BANKS.** ATMs in Jijoca de Jericoacoara: **Do Brasil** and **Bradesco**.
• **EXCHANGE. Wind Hotel:** 9982-5220 (Franchise of the exchange bureau Wall Street); **Branch of the Do Brasil** (municipality of Bela Cruz). ☎ 663-1133.
• **CAR RENTAL. Jeri Off Road.** ☎ 9961-4167. @ www.jeri.tur.br. **Microônibus do Iatã:** ☎ 669-1219/(85) 235-1967. **Pick-up from Jericoacoara to Camocim:** Sr. Odécio (collects passengers of the region who work in Camocim). Departures Sunday to Thursday at 3:30 a.m. from Rua do Forró.

VISITOR INFORMATION
• **TOURISM OFFICE.** ☎ 669-1133.
• **BOAT TRIPS.** ☎ 9952-9796 (Departures from the Izabel Restaurant).
• **Community Health Center.** ☎ 9961-2873.
• **TOURIST AGENCIES. Matusa.** ☎ 246-7354; **Hippopotamuis.** ☎ 242-9191.

HOTELS
• **Casa do Turismo.** R. das Dunas. ☎ 621-0211. 20 rooms. The second floor is a type of mezzanine with a view of the sea and Pôr do Sol Dune. $ $ $
• **Vila Calango Hotel.** R. das Dunas, 30. ☎ 9961-9364. Reservations ☎ 11-9234-8971. 3 rooms, 8 bungalows. Comfortable and quiet. $ $ $
• **Hippopotamus Hotel.** R. do Forró. ☎ 603-1616. Reservations: ☎ (85) 242-9191. 40 rooms, air conditioning, TV, bar, restaurant. Rooms around the circular swimming pool. Veranda at the entrance. $ $
• **Azul do Mar Hotel and Restaurant.** Preá Beach. 4 rooms, fan, hammock. Homely atmosphere. With a sea view, simple and comfortable. $
• **Pousada Recanto Sonhado.** R. São Francisco, 102. ☎ 9976-9460. 6 rooms, heated shower, fan. simple atmosphere, comfortable. Internet access. $

RESTAURANTS
• **Restaurante do Freddyssimo.** Paraíso Lagoon. ☎ 603-1506. Self service with pasta or pizza as entrée, choice of grilled meat as main dish and tasty liquors of cachaça with cashew pseudofruit, water melon and pineapple. Varied menu from fish to Italian food. $
• **Restaurante Azul do Mar.** Preá Beach. ☎ 9942-9352. Try the lobster grilled in butter and shrimps in garlic and oil. $ $ $
• **Restaurante da Izabel.** R. do Forró. Very simple restaurant which stands out due to the freshness and variety of fish. $ $

Juazeiro do Norte
⊕ 88

USEFUL ADDRESSES
• **BUS STATION.** R. Delmiro Gouveia. ☎ 571-2868.
• **BUS COMPANY.** Rápido Juazeiro, ☎ 571-2602; Rio Negro. ☎ 571-2854.

• **AIRPORT.** Av. Virgílio Távora. ☎ 572-0440.
• **BANKS. Do Brasil**. ☎ 512-2799; **Bradesco**. ☎ 512-2966; **Caixa**. ☎ 512-1444; **HSBC**. ☎ 512-3566.
• **HOSPITAL. Santo Inácio.** ☎ 571-2300.

VISITOR INFORMATION

• **TOURISM OFFICE.** R. Delmiro Gouveia. ☎ 512-4040.

HOTELS

• **Verdes Vales.** Av. Plácido Aderaldo Castelo (Lagoa Seca). ☎ 571-2544. @ www.verdesvales.com.br. Swimming pool, games room and gym. $$$
• **Panorama.** R. Sto. Agostinho, 58. ☎ 512-3100. Air conditioning, minibar. Restaurant and swimming pool. $
• **San Felipe.** R. Dr. Floro, 285. ☎ 511-7904. Air conditioning, TV, comfortable rooms. $$
• **Pousada Portal do Cariri.** Av. Leão Sampaio, 2120 (Lagoa Seca). ☎ 571-2399. Air conditioning, minibar. Simple and comfortable. $

RESTAURANTS

• **Giradouro.** Pça. Feijó de Sá, on the road junction to Crato and Barbalha. ☎ 571-2181. Varied. $
• **O Capote.** R. José Barbosa dos Santos, 83 (Vila Fátima). ☎ 511-4219. Varied. $
• **Restô Jardim.** Av. Leão Sampaio, 5460 (Lagoa Seca). ☎ 532-1495. Varied. $

Lagoinha

☎ 85

USEFUL ADDRESSES

• **BUS STATION.** R. Nogueira Aciole. ☎ 344-2466.
• **BUS COMPANY. Expresso Brasileiro**. ☎ 344-1300.
• **HOSPITAL.** R. Evaristo Gomes. ☎ 363-1222. Health post. R. Domingos Barroso. ☎ 363-1414.
• **BANK. do Brasil**. ☎ 344-2317.
• **BUGGY RENTALS. Coopbuggy**. ☎ 318-7309; **O Miltom**. ☎ 363-5079.

TOURIST INFORMATION

• **TOURISM AGENCY. Bahiattur**. ☎ 291-2030; **Waltur**. ☎ 219-9157; Graça Tur. ☎ 265-3944; **Ernanitur**. ☎ 244-9363; **Nettour**. ☎ 269-3099; **Beach Sun**. ☎ 248-2288.

HOTELS

• **Pousada O Milton.** Lagoinha Beach. ☎ 363-5078. 23 rooms, TV, minibar, fan, restaurant, swimming pool. $$
• **Pousada Mar à Vista.** R. Francisco Henrique Azevedo, Lagoinha. ☎ 362-1232. 5 rooms, TV, minibar, restaurant. $$
• **Isca do Sol.** R. Atlântico Sul. ☎ 315-2020 @ www.iscadosol.com 12 rooms, 3 chalets, minibar, games room, cascade, swimming pool, playground. $$
• **Pousada Volta ao Mundo.** R. Capitão Inácio Prata, 8, Taíba Beach ☎ 315-6123. 6 rooms, air conditioning, minibar. kitchen, restaurant, swimming pool. $$

RESTAURANTS

• **Chez André.** Taíba Beach, ☎ 315-6137. French cuisine. Pleasant atmosphere with a sea view. $$
• **O Milton.** Lagoinha Beach, adjoined to the hotel. ☎ 363-5078. Try the Pacu fish stew with pirão (manioc flour purée). $$
• **Volta ao Mundo.** R. Capitão Inácio Prata, 8, Taíba Beach. ☎ 315-6053. French cuisine. Sea view. $$

PIAUÍ

Teresina

☎ 86

USEFUL ADDRESSES

• **BUS STATION.** Av. Getúlio Vargas. ☎ 218-1514.
• **AIRPORT.** Av. Centenário. ☎ 225-2947.
• **HOSPITALS. Getúlio Vargas.** Av. Frei Serafim, 2352. ☎ 221-3040. **Das Clínicas**. Ave. Território Fernando de Noronha, 2566. ☎ 225-2962.
• **BANKS. Do Brasil**. ☎ 215-2100. **Do Nordeste**. ☎ 216-2600. **Bradesco**. ☎ 221-5050. **Itaú**. ☎ 221-3117. **Real**. ☎ 221-3030.
• **CAR RENTAL COMPANIES. Avis**. ☎ 232-7734. **Localiza**. ☎ 223-5800. **Unidas**. ☎ 214-1338.
• **SHOPPING. Central de Artesanato (Handicraft Center).** Pça. D. Pedro II, Centre. Notable are the wooden carvings and engravings, principally religious works of art.

VISITOR INFORMATION

• **SECRETARIA MUNICIPAL DE DESENVOLVIMENTO ECONÔMICO (SEMDEC)/DEPTO. DE TURISMO**. Pça. Marechal Deodoro, 860, Center. ☎ 221-6296.
• **EMPRESA DE TURISMO DO PIAUÍ**

(Piemtur). R. Acre. ☎ 221-6202.

HOTELS
- **Mandacaru.** R. Lizandro Nogueira, 1116, Downtown. ☎ 221-1032. Near to Pça. Rio Branco. $ $
- **Metro.** R. 13 de Maio, 85, Downtown. A few meters from the 4 de Setembro Theatre. ☎ 226-1010. $ $ $
- **Real Palace.** R. Areolino de Abreu, 1217, Downtown. ☎ 221-2768. $ $ $
- **Rio Poty Hotel.** Av. Marechal Castelo Branco, 555, Frei Serafim. ☎ 215-1500. Luxury hotel on the banks of the Poti River. $ $ $ $

RESTAURANTS
- **Camarão do Elias.** Av. Pedro Almeida, 457. ☎ 232-5025. Fish dishes. $
- **Dona Maria.** R. Prof. Joca Vieira, 909. ☎ 233-3752. Fish dishes. Try the Robalo fish (*Centropomus undecimalis*) in shrimp sauce and the black coconut dessert. $
- **Restaurante Longa.** Av. Elias João Tajra, 1139. Try the capote (castrated rooster with rice). $

Oeiras
⊞ 89

USEFUL ADDRESSES
- **CITY HALL.** Pça. Costa Alvarenga, 22, Downtown. ☎ 462-1531
- **SECRETARIA DE CULTURA E TURISMO.** Pça. da Vitória, 37. ☎ 462-1531
- **BUS STATION.** Av. Transamazônica, Bairro Rodagem de Picos. ☎ 462-2006
- **TRAIN STATION. Líder de Transportes**. ☎ 462-1040
- **BANKS. Do Brasil.** ☎ 462-1376. **Do Nordeste** ☎ 462-1144. **Caixa** ☎ 462-1112.
- **HOSPITAL. Regional Deolindo Couto**. ☎ 462-1213. **Hospital Nossa Senhora da Vitória**. ☎ 462-4100.

HOTELS
- **Bom Paladar.** Pça. das Vitórias, 44. ☎ 462-2494. $
- **Pousada do Cônego.** Pça. das Vitórias, 18. ☎ 462-1219. $
- **Velhacap.** Pça. Coronel Orlando, 366, Dowtown. ☎ 462-1252. $

FLORIANO
⊞ 89

USEFUL ADDRESSES
- **CITY HALL.** Pça. Teotônio Portela Nunes, Downtown. ☎ 522-1485.

TOURIST INFORMATION.
- **TOURIST DEPARTMENT.** Av. Eurípedes de Aguiar, 421, sala 7, Downtown. ☎ 521-3218.

HOTELS
- **Hotel Rio Parnaíba.** R. Dr. José Ribamar Pacheco, 156, Downtown. ☎ 522-1039. $ $

RESTAURANTS
- **Restaurante Flutuante.** Av. Esmaragno de Freitas, Centre. Try the fish marinated in coconut milk. $

Parnaíba
⊞ 86

USEFUL ADDRESSES
- **CITY HALL.** Pça. Santo Antonio, 643. ☎ 321-3016.
- **BUS STATION.** Av. Pinheiro Machado, Bairro Rodoviário. ☎ 323-7300.

VISITOR INFORMATION
- **SECRETARIA DE TURISMO.** Piemtur. R. Dr. Oscar Duarte, 75, Centre. ☎ 321-1532.

HOTELS
- **Pousada dos Ventos.** Av. São Sebastião, 2586. ☎ 323-2555. $ $
- **Hotel Cívico.** Av. Gov. Chagas Rodrigues, 473. ☎ 322-2470. $ $
- **Hotel das Araras.** BR-343 highway, km 5, towards Luís Correia. ☎ 323-4900. $ $ $ $

RESTAURANTS
- **Kim do Caranguejo.** Av. Nossa Senhora de Fátima, 2986. Fish dishes. Crab is the speciality. $
- **La Barca.** Av. das Nações Unidas, 200. ☎ 322-2825. Fish dishes. $
- **Rio's.** Porto das Barcas. ☎ 322-1362. varied. $ $
- **Sabor & Arte.** Porto das Barcas. ☎ 323-3616. $
- **Zé Grosso.** R. Vera Cruz, 222 (access via the bridge towards Pedra do Sal). ☎ 983-1530. Varied. $

LUÍS CORREIA
⊞ 86

USEFUL ADDRESSES
- **CITY HALL.** Av. Senador Joaquim Pires, 261, Downtown. ☎ 367-1156.
- **BUS STATION.** Av. José de Lima, Centre. ☎ 367-1217.
- **HOSPITAL. Nossa Senhora da Conceição**. ☎ 367-1123.

HOTELS
• **Pousada Macapá.** Macapá Beach. ☎ 983-1635. Rooms on the seafront facing the beach which gave the boarding house its name, in the municipality of Luís Correia. Ⓢ Ⓢ
• **Hotel Amaro.** Av. Senador Joaquim Pires, 468, Downtown. ☎ 367-1694. Ⓢ Ⓢ
• **Amarração.** R. José de Freitas, 3650, Atalaia Beach. ☎ 367-1300. Ⓢ
• **Rio Poty.** Av. dos Magistrados, 2350, Atalaia Beach. ☎ 367-1277. Ⓢ Ⓢ Ⓢ

Sete Cidades
⊕ 86

USEFUL ADDRESSES
• **CITY HALL.** Av. 4 de Julho, 280, Downtown. ☎ 276-1377.
• **BUS STATION.** Av. Estado de Pernambuco, Morro da Ana. ☎ 276-1638.
• **HOSPITAL. Regional.** ☎ 276-1325.

HOTELS
• **Fazenda Sete Cidades.** BR-222 highway, km 63. Situated a few meters from the southern gateway of the national park. Ⓢ

PEDRO II
⊕ 86

USEFUL ADDRESSES
• **CITY HALL.** Pça.. Matriz, 345, Downtown. ☎ 271-1403.
• **SHOPPING.** Artisan Association of Pedro II. ☎ 271-1635; Opala Artes Gemas. ☎ 271-1160; Opalas Pedro II. ☎ 271-1559.

Esperantina
⊕ 86

USEFUL ADDRESSES
• **CITY HALL.** R. Benjamin Constant, s/n, Downtown. ☎ 383-1232.
• **BUS STATION.** Av. Petrônio Portela, s/n, ☎ 383-1238.
• **HOSPITAL. Clínicas.** ☎ 383-1176

HOTELS
• **Hotel and Urubu Waterfall Ecological Park.** Access by the BR-113 and BR-110 highways, between the municipalities of Esperantina and Batalha. ☎ 383-1500. Ⓢ

MARANHÃO
. . . .

São Luís
⊕ 98

USEFUL ADDRESSES
• **BUS STATION.** Av. dos Franceses,

Santo Antônio. ☎ 243-1305.
• **AIRPORT.** Marechal Hugo da Cunha Machado. BR-135, km 0, Tirirical. ☎ 245-1515.
• **HOSPITAL. Socorrão.** Av. dos Portugueses, 12, Bacanga. **Santa Casa**. R. do Norte, 233, Centro. ☎ 221-5447. **Do Coração.** R. do Passeio, 400, Centro. ☎ 221-1201.
• **BANKS. Bradesco. Itaú. Do Brasil. Unibanco. Caixa. Banco Real. HSBC.**
• **CAR RENTALS. Auvepar.** ☎ 245-1283. **Avis.** 217-6180. **Localiza.** ☎ 245-1566. **Unidas.** ☎ 245-2888.
• **SHOPPING. Ceprama** (Centro de Comercialização de Produtos Artesanais de Maranhão). R. de São Pantaleão, 1232, Madre Deus. **Colonial Shopping.** R. Grande, 415, Centro. **Tropical Shopping Center.** Av. Colares Moreira, 400, Renascença. **La Ravardière.** R. do Passeio, Downtown.
• **WATERWAY PORT.** Praia Grande docks. Av. Beira-mar, Praia Grande. Arrivals and departures to Alcântara.
• **WATERWAY TERMINAL.** Rampa Campos Mello. ☎ 232-0692. Arrivals and departures to Alcântara.

VISITOR INFORMATION
• **Subgerência de Turismo.** Av. Jerônimo Albuquerque, 5th floor, Calhau. ☎ 227-5566 @ www.ma.gov.br
• **Fundação Municipal de Turismo.** Pça. Benedito Leite, Palácio do Comércio, Centro. ☎ 231-9086.
• **Tourist Information Centre. Shopping do Cidadão.** Av. Jaime Tavares, 26B, Praia Grande. ☎ 231-2000.

HOTELS
• **Brisamar.** Av. São Marcos, 12, Praia de Ponta da Areia. ☎ 212-1212. @ www.brisamar.com.br 116 rooms, air conditioning, tv, minibar, swimming pool. Ⓢ Ⓢ Ⓢ Ⓢ
• **Hotel Casa Grande.** R. das Barrocas, 94, Downtown. ☎ 232-2432. An old mansion, next to the Ribeirão fountain. Friendly atmosphere. Ⓢ
• **Pousada Colonial.** R. Afonso Pena, 112, Centro. ☎ 232-2834. 27 rooms, air conditioning, tv, minibar. Colonial, 18th century manor house. Its front is covered in high relief Portuguese tiles. Ⓢ Ⓢ
• **Pousada Victoria do Lopes.** R. do Giz, 129, Praia Grande. ☎ 222-6286. Old, restored mansion that has been very well preserved. Well located. Fan, communal toilets. Ⓢ

• **Sofitel.** Av. Avicênia, Praia do Calhau. ☎ 216-4545. @ www.accorbrasil.com.br 109 rooms, air conditioning, tv,minibar, swimming pool, court. $ $ $ $
• **Vila Rica.** Av. D. Pedro II, 299, Centro. ☎ 232-3255. @ www.hotelvilarica.com.br 210 rooms, tv, air conditioning, minibar, swimming pool, leisure room, playground. $ $ $ $

RESTAURANTS
• **Antigamente.** R. da Estrela, 210, Praia Grande. ☎ 221-7072. Daily from 6 to 12 p.m. Varied. Restored mansion in historical center. Live music/shows every evening. $
• **A Varanda.** R. Genésio Rego, 185, Monte Castelo. ☎ 232-8428. 12 a.m. to 12 p.m. Closes Sunday. The grilled shrimp is highly recommended. $ $
• **Base da Lenoca.** Av. D. Pedro II, 181, Downtown and Av. Litorânea, São Marcos Beach. ☎ 231-0599. Regional. Cuchá rice and the crab legs are good. $ $
• **Cabana do Sol.** R. João Damasceno, 24-A. ☎ 235-2586. Regional. Speciality: baião-de-dois rice and green bean mixture with jerky, mashed yellow manioc and fried banana. $
• **Vovó Chica.** R. Portugal. Daily, from 12 a.m. to 12 p.m. Simple cookery, bar-like atmosphere. Best ready-made, budget dish in historical center. $

Alcântara
🌐 98

USEFUL ADDRESSES
• **TOWN HALL.** Pça. da Matriz. ☎ 337-1140.
• **POST OFFICE.** R. de Baixo with Pça. da Matriz. ☎ 337-1155.
• **HOSPITAL. Unidade Mista**. R. Direita, Downtown. ☎ 337-1212.
• **SHOPS. Gaivota Artesanato**. ☎ 337-1003. **Terminal dos Passageiros**. ☎ 337-1258.

VISITOR INFORMATION
• **TAXIS AND BOATS.** To cross over to Livramento Island, or to visit other places of interest around Alcantara, contact **Silvia Campos Borba**. ☎ 337-1270. **Paulo Lobato**. ☎ 337-1207. **Maria Eugênia**. ☎ 337-1168. **Marquinho**. ☎ 337-1339.

HOTELS
• **Pousada do Mordomo Régio.** R. Grande, 134, Centro. ☎ 337-1197. Tv, air conditioning, minibar and restaurant. Colonial mansion with agorgeous view over São Marcos Bay and São Luís. $
• **Pousada dos Guarás.** Baronesa Beach. ☎ 337-1339. Bungalows surrounded by tropical gardens. $ $
• **Pousada e Artesanato Planeta Alcântara.** R. das Mercês, 400, Downtown. ☎ 337-1270. Homely, unsophisticated atmosphere. Round the clock snack bar.
• **Pousada e Restaurante da Josefa.** R. Direita, 33, Downtown. ☎ 337-1109. Tv, air conditioning, minibar. Old central building, backpackers' haunt. $

RESTAURANTS
• **Josefa.** R. Direita, 33, Downtown. ☎ 337-1109. Seafood. Tables spread under a massive mango tree. $ $
• **Pousada dos Guarás.** Baronesa Beach. ☎ 337-1339. Seafood and streak. In the hotel's tropical gardens. $ $
• **Restaurante e Lanchonete Palácio dos Nobres.** On corner of R. Direita with R. Grande. Meals and snacks. $
• **Sítio Tipujá**. R. de Baixo. ☎ 9973-1120. Comfortable. Fish. $ $

Carolina
🌐 99

USEFUL ADDRESSES
• **BUS STATION.** R. Lias Barros. ☎ 531-1195.
• **ROAD TRANSPORT. Empresa Transbrasiliana**. ☎ 243-3844.
• **HOSPITAL.** R. Benedito Leite, 57. ☎ 531-1271.
• **BANKS. Do Brasil**. ☎ 531-2200.

VISITOR INFORMATION
• **INFORMAÇÕES TURÍSTICAS.** Av. Getúlio Vargas, 1343. ☎ 531-3421.
• **TOURIST GUIDE. Márcio.** ☎ 531-3833.
• **JEEP (4X4) RENTALS: Valdecí**. ☎ 531-2607. José Flávio. ☎ 531-2965.
• **TOURIST AGENCY. Trilha da Chapada Expedições**. ☎ 531-2097.

HOTELS
• **Balneário da Pedra Caída.** BR-010, km 35. ☎ 531-2318. Bungalows near the waterfalls, surrounded by trees. $ $
• **Hotel Hilton.** Av. Brasília, 741. ☎ 531-2824. Tv, air conditioning, minibar. $
• **Hotel Lírio.** Av. Adalberto Ribeiro, 660. Central. ☎ 531-2317. Tv, air conditioning, minibar. Restaurant. Budget dishes. $ $

• **Imperial Hotel.** Pça. Joaquim Leite, 60, Central. ☎ 531-2151. Air conditioning, tv. Near shopping area. $ $
• **Pousada Cachoeira do Itapecuru.** BR-230 km 30. Bungalows, garage, bathroom, air conditioning, minibar. $ $
• **Pousada dos Candeeiros.** Av. Getúlio Vargas, 1167, Downtown. ☎ 531-2243. Rooms, air conditioning, tv, minibar. $ $
• **Pousadinha.** Av. Getúlio Vargas, 1167, Centro. ☎ 531-2621. Rooms, tv, air conditioning, minibar. $ $
• **Terrinha Palace Hotel.** BR-230, km 39. ☎ 531-3193. Rooms, air conditioning, tv, minibar. $ $

RESTAURANTS

• **Churrascaria do Nonato.** BR-230, km 10. Assorted grilled meats and supplements. $
• **Churrasco Maravilha.** BR-230. Maravilha fuelling station roundabout. Barbecues and supplements (rice, beans, fried potatoes, salad). $
• **Hot Line Pizzarias.** Pça. José Alcides de Carvalho. $
• **Lanches Central.** Pça. Alípio de Carvalho, 66. ☎ 531-2975. Mini barbecues. Tables outside, in the square. $
• **Mocotozim Bar e Restaurante.** R. Cidade de Grajaú, 172. Regional, and home cooking. $
• **Pizzaria Tio Pepe.** R. Diógenes Gonçalves, 437. Log fire pizzas. $
• **Restaurante Lírio.** Av. Adalberto Ribeiro, 660. ☎ 531-2317. Home cooking. $

Cururupu

⊞ 98

USEFUL ADDRESSES

• **TOWN HALL.** Av. Getúlio Vargas, 20, Downtown. ☎ 391-1380.
• **BUS STATION.** ☎ 291-1520.
• **ROAD TRANSPORTATION. Empresa Continental**. ☎ 243-1426.
• **TERMINAL PONTA DA MADEIRA.** ☎ 232-7259.
• **AIRPORT.** The district's landing strip is used by chartered planes. Do Liége. ☎ 391-1497.
• **HOSPITAL. Santa Casa**. Pça. João Vieira, Downtown. ☎ 391-1529. **Flávia Silva**. R. Getúlio Vargas, ☎ 391-1110.
• **BANKS. Do Brasil**. ☎ 391-1331.

HOTELS

• **Hotel Kelma.** R. Cesário Coimbra, Downtown. ☎ 391-1252. 20 rooms, with and without bathrooms. Friendly atmosphere. $
• **Pousada Natalia.** Av. Liberalino Miranda, 53, Jacaré. ☎ 391-2359. 8 rooms, air conditioning, minibar. Homely atmosphere. Excellent breakfast. $
• **Pousada São José.** Pça. João Vieira, 71, Downtown. ☎ 391-2146. 9 rooms with a fan. Communal bathroom. Hospitable. Good breakfast. $

RESTAURANTS

• **Restaurante Kelma.** R. Cesário Coimbra, Downtown. ☎ 391-1252. Seafood and budget dishes. $
• **Restaurante Toc Toc.** R. Raimundo Correia, Downtown. Prepared, budget dishes, with either jerky, chicken or fish. $
• **Samambaia.** R. Dr. José Pires, 10. ☎ 391-1698. Seafood. $ $

Lençóis Maranhenses

⊞ 98

USEFUL ADDRESSES

• **TOWN HALL.** ☎ 479-1343
• **BUS STATION.** ☎ 379-1146
• **HOSPITAL. São Lucas**. ☎ 349-1182
• **BANK. Do Brasil**. ☎ 349-1180
• **CAR RENTAL.** Individual tickets to join an outing can be purchased, or else a jeep can be hired for a self-planned excursion. **Dunas Turismo**. ☎ 349-1614. **Barra tur**. ☎ 349-1779. Excursions starting in Jericoacoara via the Parnaíba Delta, and on to Lençóis via the Jeri Off Road (@ www.jeri.tur.br) can also be arranged. ☎ 669-2022.

VISITOR INFORMATION

• **INFORMAÇÕES TURÍSTICAS.** ☎ 349-1144.

HOTELS

• **Pousada do Buriti e Restaurante.** R. Inácio Lins. ☎ 349-1800. Air conditioning, tv, minibar. Restaurant, swimming pool, motorboats, and jeeps. $ $ $
• **Pousada Filho do Vento.** Povoado de Atins. ☎ 9966-7100. Simple, carnaúba thatched bungalows. Restaurant, motorboat, pony rides. $ $
• **Pousada Porto Buriti.** Praia fluvial de Caburé river beach, on Rio Preguiças. Spacious bungalows with veranda. ☎ 349-1338. $ $ $

• **Pousada Victória.** R. Coronel Godinho. ☎ 349-0016. Ⓢ

TO KNOW MORE

The main sources for the chapters: *Discovering the Northeast, Man in the Northeast* and *Ecological Scenery.*

AB'SÁBER, A. N. **Litoral do Brasil.** Brazilian Coast. São Paulo: Metalivros, 2001.

BUENO, E. **Capitães do Brasil.** A Saga dos Primeiros Colonizadores. Rio de Janeiro: Objetiva, 1999.

BUENO, E. **Náufragos, Traficantes e Degredados.** As Primeiras Expedições Ao Brasil. Rio de Janeiro: Objetiva, 1998.

CALDEIRA, J. **Viagem pela História do Brasil.** São Paulo: Companhia das Letras, 2001.

DIEGUES JR., M. **Regiões culturais do Brasil.** Rio de Janeiro: Centro Brasileiro de Pesquisas Educacionais, 1960.

FERNANDES, C. **Viagem Gastronômica Através do Brasil.** São Paulo: Senac, Estúdio Sonia Robatto, 2001.

FREIRE, G. **Casa-Grande e Senzala** /Nordeste. São Paulo: Livros do Brasil, 1996.

FREIRE, R. **Freire's. Brasil Praias.** São Paulo: Mandarin, 2001.

FREIRE, R. **Viaje na viagem.** Auto Ajuda Para Turistas. São Paulo: Mandarim, 1998.

GARCIA, C. **O que é o Nordeste Brasileiro?.** São Paulo: Brasiliense, 1984.

GARCIA, J. M. **Terra de Vera Cruz.** O Brasil Descoberto Há Quinhentos Anos. Rio de Janeiro: Edinfor, Multinova, 2000.

HUECK, K. **As Florestas da América do Sul.** Ecologia, Composição e Importância Econômica. São Paulo: Ed. da Universidade de Brasília; Polígono, 1972.

JOLY, A. B. **Conheça a Vegetação Brasileira.** São Paulo: Edusp; Polígono, 1970.

MACEDO, M. e PAIVA, F. **Guia de Praias do Ceará.** Fortaleza: Fundação Demócrito Rocha, 2000.

NIMER, E. **Climatologia do Brasil.** Rio de Janeiro: IBGE, 1989.

OLIVIERI, A. C. **Guerras e Revoluções Brasileiras.** O Cangaço. São Paulo: Ática, 1997.

RIBEIRO, D. **O Povo Brasileiro.** A Formação e o sentido do Brasil. São Paulo: Companhia das Letras, 1995.

RIZZINI, C. T. **Tratado de fitogeografia do Brasil.** Aspectos Sociológicos e Florísticos. São Paulo: v. 1-2 HUCITEC, Edusp,1979.

ROSS , J. L. S. **Geografia do Brasil.** São Paulo: Edusp, 2001.

SAMPAIO. T. **O Rio São Francisco e a Chapada Diamantina.** São Paulo: Companhia das Letras, 2002.

SIQUEIRA, R. **Caminhos Pontes e Estradas do Brasil.** Rio de Janeiro: Luminatti, 2001.

TAVARES, L. H. D. **História da Bahia.** São Paulo: Unesp, 2001.

Vários, **Quatro Vezes Fortaleza.** Fortaleza: Fundação Demócrito Rocha, 2000.

Environmental Institutions and Projects

• **IPHAN - Instituto do Patrimônio Histórico Artístico Nacional**
www.iphan.gov.br
SBN Q.02 Ed. Central Brasília 2º andar CEP 70040-904, Brasília - DF Tel.: (61) 414-6101/ Fax (61) 414-6126
An institution linked to the Ministry of Culture with the aims of researching, promoting, inspecting and protecting the Brazilian Cultural Heritage.

• **Projeto Tamar - Ibama**
www.tamar.org.br
Research and protect the life of marine turtles of the Brazilian coast. To develop research programs in partnership with several universities and offer training directed at education in the areas of biology, fishing engineering, veterinary, oceanography and other courses that focus on the environment.
The regional offices in the Northeast are located in Praia do Forte (BA), Pirambu (SE) and in the Marine National Park of Fernando de Noronha (PE).

Updates

We recommend users to always check schedules, prices and other useful information. To keep updated and get further information, visit our site: www.horizontegeografico.com.br. Also send us suggestions, updates and questions through e-mail: redacao@horizontegeografico.com.br, letter or fax.

FAUNA

AMPHIBIAN

Cururu marine toad ►
(Bufo-paracnemis)
The cururu marine toad is 20 cm long and the largest in Brazil. It can be found in Northeast parts of Brazil, down to Argentina. It has mucous glands that also produce a toxic poison which is released only through direct contact with a predator. When mating, the male embraces the female and squeezes her, helping her lay the eggs.

Interesting features:
• Toads inflate themselves when under threat. Some say it's a strategy to appear more menacing.
• The female can lay up to 150,000 eggs in one season.

BIRDS

Black-winged bell-bird ▼
(Procnias averano)

The most visible peculiarity of this bird are the black, beard-like feathers under the beak. It is 27 cm.Its song sounds like an anvil being struck. Bearded bell-birds are also found in other South and North American countries, but in Brazil, only in the North and Northeast regions. It lives in woods and is therefore not easy to observe.

Interesting features:
• The bell-bird, found in Southern regions of Brazil, belongs to the *Procnias nudicollis* specie, which is of the same kind as the black wingedbell-bird.

Eared dove
(Zenaida auriculata)
This dove lives in huge flocks and inhabits camp land, from the Antilles to Tierra del Fuego. It is 21 cm long. It's distinguishable from other species in the family by black markings at the side of the head and on its wings. The peasant population have made this bird part of their meager diets.

Interesting features:
• They are incredibly prodigious breeders. Nests are very rudimentary and, in a little over four weeks, young can survive without their parents.
• It is one of the few terrestrial birds living in Noronha Archipelago.

White-naped jay ►
(Cyanocorax cyanopogon)
The can-can, as it is popularly called, is one of the most typical birds of the semi-arid Northeastern backlands. It lives in flocks, giving sharp warning signals, when there is danger or when food has been found. The local peasants call it 'snake informer'. It's 30 cm long. Because it has the habit of burying food for later use, peasants think can-cans to be maize planters.

Interesting features:
• The white-naped jay can imitate sounds and voices of other birds, animals and even human beings.

◄ Uçá crab: it lives in the swamplands of Brazil

Red-cowled cardinal
(Paroaria dominicana)
The red-cowled cardinal is a typical bird in the Northeast dry lands. It's 17 cm long. It's a solitary bird, but can also join small groups searching for food. It can be found from the South of Maranhão throughout the Bahia backlands.

Interesting features:
• The *galo* in its Brazilian name, is connected to the male's behavior during mating time, when claws and beaks are used to fight competitors.

Chopi blackbird ▼
(Gnorimopsar chopi)
Even the beak of this gregarious

graúna blackbird, which is 25 cm.long, is black. It sings beautifully and strongly, and has many different tunes. It builds its nest inside hollow trees, but also takes advantage of abandoned ovenbird nests and termite mounds. Their habitat is the open camp throughout Brazil.

Interesting features:
• In the Northeast, it is often called 'açum preto'. In the rest of Brazil, it's called 'black-bird'.
• Because it is such a good singer, but also because it gets so very tame, many people have them in cages.

CRUSTACEANS

Uçá crab ▶
(Ucides cordatus)
They are the most celebrated of all the many creatures that live in the swamplands of Brazil. Of the uçá crab, the most valued meat is on the front legs, that end in pincers or claws. The other nine pairs of legs, as well as the body, are usually discarded. When a leg is lost, another grows in its place.

Interesting features:
• At mating time, crabs leave their hiding places and move around slowly, which make them vulnerable.
• Some crabs have an oar-like pair of hind legs. In Brazil, this crab family is called *siri* (Portunidae).

Lobster
(Panulirus argus)
Lobsters live among rocks and reefs. Their shell is hard and their eyes big and protuberant. They have long feelers which can be two thirds the length of their bodies. Lobsters can be found on both sides of the Atlantic Ocean.

Interesting features:
• To conserve the lobster, fishermen dip them alive into boiling water.
• When the female sheds her eggs, she glues them to foot-like attachments on her underside, where she carries them and protects them from predators.

MAMMALS

Humpback whale ▼
(Megaptera novaeangliae)

The humpback whale is very friendly and found in all the oceans.
The female is a little bigger than the male and can reach 19 m and weigh 48 tons. They have immense pectoral flippers, and are known for their acrobatics and for the sounds they produce. Between July and November, they congregate around the Abrolhos Archipelago.

Interesting features:
- When in danger, humpback whales can reach speeds of up to 27 km/h.
- Whale pregnancy lasts 12 months and one baby is born that is suckled for a year.
- The original population has been reduced to 12,000 individuals, according to a 1988 survey.

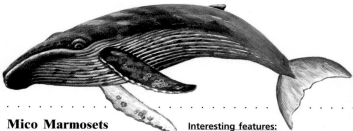

Mico Marmosets
(Callithrix jacchus)

It's one of the most common species in the marmoset group. It has ornamented ears with white tufts, and a white patch on its forehead. Sizes range between 47 and 62 cm. It feeds on insects and tree gum. It lives in the *caatinga* and *cerrado* shrubbery, in the east of Parnaíba River and north of São Francisco. It likes smaller trees, and lives in groups of 7 to 15.

Interesting features:
- The mico is also called the white ear-tuft marmoset.
- Marmosets were introduced into the Tijuca Forest in the Southeast, where they adapted well.

Golden-headed lion tamarin ▶
(Leontopithecus chrysomelas)

The tiny, agile, golden-headed lion tamarin symbolizes the demise of its tropical rainforest home in Southeast Bahia; its only natural habitat. They have long, silky fur, particularly at the shoulders. They are black, but hands, arms and feet, head and shoulders and parts of its tail are an orange colour. They are 50 cm long, and weigh less than a kilo. They move quickly, and family group are of up to 12 individuals.

Interesting features:
- The golden lion tamarin, found only in Southeastern Brazil, was once the most numerous of four species.
- The remaining wild population is now estimated at only 500 individuals, due to incessant clearing of rainforest land for agricultural and ranching purposes, and the illegal pet trade.

Mocó guinea pig ▲
(Kerodon rupestris)
The mocó is a typical rodent in the stony, dry regions of Brazil. It is about 35 cm long. At the first sign of danger, the mocó lets out warning cries to all the others in the group, putting them on guard. They then hide in rocky nooks or among the dry roots for hours, before venturing out again. Mocós are endemic in the arid Northeast and North of Minas Gerais State. It comes out when it's not so hot during the day, and at night.

Interesting features:
* The presence of mocó guinea pigs is believed to be an indication that the environment is being preserved.
* When researching the Chagas disease, it was in a guinea pig burrow that scientists first found the 'barbeiro beetle'.

Tatu bola armadillo ►
(Tolypeutes tricinctus)
The tatu bola armadillo is one of the smallest of its kind in Brazil. It's only 50 cm long (only smaller than the so-called chicken tatu). When in danger, it rolls itself up into a ball, which makes it very difficult for a predator to bite into or otherwise get a hold on. It lives in the Piauí, Minas Gerais and Bahia backlands.

Interesting features:
* Its habits are nocturnal; during the day it seeks shelter in holes of other armadillos or any other cavity suitable for a hiding place.
* Armadillos tuck their legs and tail inside the two-part armor, which is flexible in the middle of the back.

FISH

Blue marlin ▼
(Makaira nigrican)
Marlins are gigantic, high-speed fish. Females are bigger than males and can be up to 5 m long and weigh 700 kg. The blue marlin's upper jaw is elongated into a spear-like structure, in conformity with its streamlined body. They like the warmer waters around cliffs and underwater mountains. In Brazil, they can be found mostly between Fernando de Noronha islands and the São Paulo coastline.

Interesting features:
* When the marlin hunts, it strikes sideways at its prey, because the lateral position of its eyes prevent it from seeing forward.
* Wounds inflicted by a fishing hook heal very quickly and leave no scars.

Spotted jewfish (Mero) ▼

(Epinephelus itajara)

These fish are well known to divers because, although so big, they are trusting and docile, and allows them come into close range. They can be 3 m. long, and weigh 400 kg. Their body is spotted; chiefly on the head and the rear half. They live in coastal and island waters, up to 50 m deep and are often found swimming around shipwrecks.
Jewfish are in all Atlantic and Pacific waters; in Brazil, from the North, down to Santa Catarina.

Interesting features:
- To feed itself, it makes very quick attacks. It also is a sucker fish that draws water and catches crustaceans by suction.
- When specially a large specimen has been caught, instead of putting up a fight, it will hide inside crevices.

Green eel ▼

(Gymnothorax funebris)

This is the biggest eel in the Atlantic. It is 2.5 m long and weighs 15 kg. Like other eels, it's long and looks like a snake. It also looks fearful but is actually quite tame, using its strong jaws and sharp teeth only when threatened. It is not poisonous, but bite wounds will infect because of the micro-organisms in its mouth. It spends most of the time inside holes among the rocks and corals, with only its head sticking out.

Interesting features:
- In Brazil, eels have funny names like caramuru, miroró, mutuca, tororó.
- To breathe, it opens and shuts its mouth, pushing water (and oxygen) into its gills. This constant movement which bares its sharp teeth, gives it its menacing expression.
- Eels have poor eyesight and can mistake human hands for food.

Mullet ▼

(Mugil curema)

It is 60cm long and silvery-grey.
It is common all along the Brazilian coast, but prefers shallow bays and swamp waters. It cruises along the sea floor, around stones and underwater tree trunks, looking for algae, invertebrates or organic matter to eat. Winter is spawning time, when immense shoals are formed that come very close to marshy coasts.

Interesting features:
- The eggs drift with the current and wind into estuaries and marshes, where the fry develop and gradually move to more salty waters.
- It is also is called *parati*, and *curimã* in Northern Brazil.

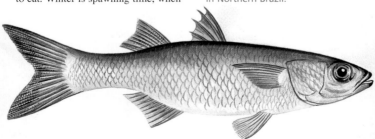

REPTILES

Iguana ►
(Iguana iguana)

These animals can be recognized by a crest of scales that runs along their spine, and by a big round scale under their tympanum. The tail is very long in comparison to the length of the body. Their total length is around 1,1 m of which 80 cm is tail. It lives in trees and uses its strong claws to climb them. It feeds on leaves and fruit.

In caatinga, it has brownish colours.
* Its pouch blows up and its crest stands up, when irritated.
* It is also known as "lazy" because when cornered, it 'freezes' in an attempt to merge with the background it happens to be in.

Interesting features:
* The iguana changes colour according to the environment its in.

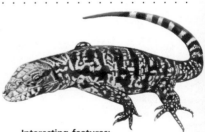

It feeds off algae.The shell is oval and brown, greenish or grey. Even though during the early stages of life they are common along the continental coast, adults prefer the islands of Fernando de Noronha, Atol das Rocas and Trindade also for hatching.

Interesting features:
* Sea turtles have an incredible sense of direction. Every breeding season the female turtle returns to the same beach where it was hatched to lay her eggs.
* Only the female leaves the water, at hatching time. The male stays in the water all its life.
* The sex of the young is determined by the temperature of the sand the eggs have been dug in.

Green Turtle ▲
(Chelonia mydas)

The green turtle, known as *aruanã*, is one of the 5 species found along the Brazilian coast. They are also greatest in number. It measures up to 1.2 m and can weigh as much as 350 kg (though average weight is 250 kg).

Teiú lizzard ►
(Tupinambis teguixim or Tupinambis merianae)

The teiú lizzard is one of the biggest in Brazil, and can be found in most ecosystems in South America. It can reach 1,5 m in length. It is solitary and timid, and when in danger, always tries to flee. Yet when cornered, will bite and use its tail as a whip. It lives in holes burrowed into the ground, which it leaves as the day gets warmer. When it's cold, it stays inside the hole, using up body fat reserves to keep alive. It can often be seen by the roadside, sunning itself. It is omnivorous, with a varied diet of mainly small animals, eggs and fruit.

Interesting features:
* The jaw muscles of the adult teiú are very developed, and form a pouch.
* The teiú can drop its tail when it has been caught by that part, by a predator. A new one will gradually grow.
* Teiús can do a lot of damage in a hen run. It loves eggs, and also chicks.

FLORA

Species in alphabetical
order *320*

Angico ▶

(*Anadenanthera macrocarpa*) Curupay
This is one of the most common trees
of the caatinga. It reaches a height
of from 13 to 20 meters (39 to 60
feet) in the fully-grown state. The
bark has varying aspects: it can be
smooth, wrinkled or cracked in dark
or light colors. The flowers appear in
the form of little white sponges and
the fruit develops in the form of pods.
The tree is found in the Northeast,
Central-west and Southeast of Brazil.
The timber is very heavy and
appropriate for the construction of
houses. The growth of the tree is fast,
and it is often used for reforesting. It
vegetates both in the brush and in the
interior of untouched forest. It prefers
high, well-drained land.

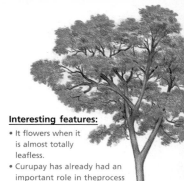

Interesting features:
• It flowers when it
is almost totally
leafless.
• Curupay has already had an
important role in theprocess
of leather tanning asits bark
is rich in a substance called
tannin, whichimpedes
the decomposition
of the hide.

◀ Babaçu

(*Orbignya speciosa*) Babassu
Babassu is a palm-tree, which grows
up to a height of 20 meters (60 feet),
native of northern Brazil. It is very
symbolic of Maranhão where
homogeneous groups are formed.
Of the estimated 18 million hectares
of babassu woods in Brazil, 10
million are in Maranhão. The plant
has many uses. The leaves are used as
thatching for roofs and walls of huts.
A type of milk, flour and oil suitable
for the manufacture of butter, soap
and candles is extracted from the
fruit or kernel, the shell of which is
extremely hard. One palm-tree alone
can produce up to 2,000 fruit per year.

Interesting features:
• The job of cracking
the babassu
coconuts is performed
by women, the
'breakers'.
• Babassu is a vigorous
plant, which invades
open fields and
sometimes is
considered scourge.

Cacau ▶

(*Theobroma cacao*) Cocoa tree
It is a small tree, which can reach
a height of 4 meters (12 feet), native
of the undergrowth of the Amazon
Rainforest or the Central America
forests (there is disagreement among
botanists). It gained importance as an
agricultural crop as the bean, found
inside the fruit, is the basic ingredient
for the production of chocolate. The
white pulp around the seed, although
not as famous, is very tasty.
The cocoa tree adapted well in
southern Bahia, and became the main
agricultural exportation product.
The State has 90% of the Brazilian
cocoa production, establishing the
country as the 5th highest in the world.

Interesting features:
• Cocoa is harvested twice a
year. In Bahia, the principal
harvest occurs from October
to April and a smaller late-
season harvest starts in May.
• The planting uses the system of
'cabruças' (in the shade os native
trees), which preserve the Atlantic Forest.

◀ Brommelia from Chapada Diamantina

Cajá ►

(Spondias mombin)
Yellow Mobin
This is a dense
tree, which grows
up to 30 meters (90 feet) high,
whose trunk is covered by
a thick wrinkled bark.
It produces yellow-colored
fruit in bunches at the end of
branches with a format
similar to that of an egg and
a hard stone inside. In the
Northeast, where humid and sub-
humid zones are common, the fruit
ripen in January to May. The plant is
endemic in tropical forests in several
countries of the American continent.
In the Amazon, Yellow Mobin is
better known as Taperebá.

Interesting features:

• It belongs to the family of anacardiáceas, the
same as the mango (*Mangifera indica*),

cashew (*Anacardium occidentale*), imbu
(*Spondias tuberosa*) and
Jamaica plum (*Spondias purpurea*)

• Old Brazilian Indian tribes treated people
with open wounds and skin ulcers by
burning the stone of the Yellow Mobin and
submitting the patient to the smoke.

• It has been scientifically proved that
substances present in the leaves and the
young branches of the tree have an action
against the herpes virus.

Cajueiro

(Anacardium occidentale) Cashew tree
A short tree reaching a
height of between 5 and
10 meters (15 and 30 feet)
presenting a twisted trunk
common in the Northeastern
fields and restinga forests.
The fruit is an edible nutthat
is highly valued and which
is connected to a fleshy
succulent part, called
the peduncle (stem of the fruit).
The peduncle or pseudofruit,
which people confuse with the
fruit, is yellow or red in color.
It consists of more than
80% water and is well
appreciated eaten pure or
used for sweets and juices.

Interesting features:

• In about 90% of the
Brazilian production of
cashew, only the cashew nut
is used and the pseudofruits
are thrown away.

• Among several medicinal properties
attributed to cashew, the nut has a
reputation as an aphrodisiac.

• Fermentation of the cashew juice to
produce wine has been a habit of the
Indians since, at least, the beginning of
Portuguese colonization.

◄ Cana-de-açúcar

(Saccarum officinarum) Sugarcane
A gramineous semi perennial originally from Asia, it was introduced to Brazil in the 16th century brought from the cultivation zones of the Madeira Island. The species adapted well to the Brazilian climate and soil, principally in Pernambuco and Bahia, and was the main economic drive until the discovery of gold in Minas Gerais. Competition with production from colonies in the West Indies also helped to cause the decline of the crop during the 18th century. At the end of the gold cycle, sugarcane returned to its place of economic importance. Today, Brazil is one of the five top producers in the world. The main production zones are in São Paulo, but the Northeast still maintains large sugar plantations.

Interesting features:

• It was reported in 327 BC, that two generals commanded by Alexander the Great discovered a plant, which they described as "a cane that provides honey without the help of bees". Without a shadow of a doubt this was sugarcane.

Carnaúba ►

(Copernicia prunifera) Carnauba wax palm
This is a typical palm-tree of the flood plains of the semiarid Northeast, where they can be seen in large numbers. Also they are found in Pará and Goiás. They grow up to 10 meters high (30 feet) when adult and can even reach 15 meters (45 feet). The leaves are in the form of a Chinese fan with the petiole (stalk of the leaf) endowed with thorns. The fruit contains oil. When young, the palm-tree conserves the base of the leaves adhered to the trunk. Thus, up to the height of 4 meters (12 feet), the trunk has an aggressive thorny appearance becoming smooth from there upwards. From the young leaves, a wax is extracted which is used in the production of lubricants, candles and varnishes. The dried leaves are used for roofs and walls of huts and for handicrafts such as straw hats, ropes and matting. Sobral, in Ceará, is famous for the production of hats sold throughout Brazil.

Interesting features:

• In the old times, the Indians burned the roots of carnaúba and removed from the ashes a substance, which was used to salt food.

• In the Brazilian wetlands there is a palm-tree very similar to carnaúba, which was even thought to be of the same species. It is called *carandá* *(Copernicia australis)*.

Coqueiro-da-bahia ▶

(Cocos nucifera) Coconut palm-tree
The coconut is the most common
palm-tree of the Brazilian coast,
especially in the region between
Rio Grande do Norte and Bahia.
Extremely well adapted to poor and
well-drained land, it develops well in
the sand on the beach, as it prefers
salty environments. It grows up to
20 meters (60 feet) high and takes
six years from the start to producing.
From the green coconuts, the water is
drunk. When it is ripe, the flesh inside
is consumed as grated coconut and the
fiber is used for the manufacture of
mats, brooms, scrubbing brushes and
as a potting extract for the cultivation
of orchids, as an alternative to xaxim
(Dicksonia sellowiana). The coconut
palm-tree produces fruit all year
round, with the highest production
from July to February.

Interesting features:

• It is not exactly known the region in the
world from where the palm-tree originated.
There are so many places in which it grows
spontaneously that researchers are
undecided between the America and Asia.
But everyone agrees that the fruit can
cross the ocean floating thanks to the
impermeable casing, thick fibrous layer
and the hollow interior of the fruit.

. . . .

Favela ▼

(Cnidoscolus phyllacanthus) Faveleira nut
A small tree which reaches
5 meters (15 feet) high with branches
distributed in an irregular form. The
trunk and the leaves are covered with
thorns and when pricked the wound
burns like the sting of a bee or wasp
provoking painful inflammations,
probably due to the action of the sap.
The white flowers appear in small
bunches. Both the mature leaves and
the bark serve as animal feed. The
seeds are rich in mineral salts and
proteins, and have the potential for
the production of oil and
flour, but currently
without
commercial
value. Faveleira
nut is typical of
the caatinga,
found in
rocky regions
in the strip
between
Piauí and
Bahia.

Interesting features:

• It is said in the *sertão* about the faveleira nut,
that "this here, not even an animal will eat",
because of the thorns on the green leaves
which burn like urtiga (ortiga or nettle tree).

• In the Canudos war, the republican army
attacked from Favela Hill, a neighbor to
the Counsellor's Hamlet. The name was due
to the profusion of plants of the same
name on the hill. After the hostilities, the
war veterans were given houses on a hill in
Rio de Janeiro, which became known as
favela. And this is how favelas (Brazilian
shantytowns) gained
their name.

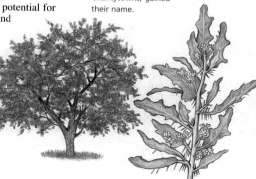

Juazeiro ▶

(Zizyphus joazeiro) Jujube
This small thorny tree does not
grow more than 10 meters (30 feet)
in height. It has a short trunk and
a very dense canopy that almost
touches the ground. It exists on the
border between Piauí and the north
of Minas Gerais, in humid areas.
Even in the dry season, the leaves
remain green as the trees have deep
roots that find water in the subsoil.
Apart from the shade they produce
for the *sertanejos*, the fruit of Jujube
is edible and very much appreciated
by people and animals and has
a high level of vitamin C.

Interesting features:

• Also known as juá and
laranjeira-de-vaqueiro.
• The bark has medicinal properties
and is used in toothpaste.
• Four cities in the Northeast received the
tree's name: Juazeiro, in Bahia; Juazeiro
do Norte, in Ceará; Juazeiro do Piauí,
in Piauí; and Juazeirinho, in Paraíba.

Jueirana-vermelha

(Parkia pendula) Acacia male
This is one of the most
beautiful trees to be found
in the Atlantic Forest of
the Northeast, Espirito
Santo and the Amazon.
Generally it has an almost
flat canopy, supported
above the other trees. It can
attain a height of 40 meters
(121 feet) in the Atlantic Forest
and even higher in the Amazon
rainforest. A peculiar characteristic
of the species is its sprays of flowers
between August and October, which
appear like red baubles that hang
on long peduncles. Acacia male has
a moderately heavy timber.

Interesting features:

• It is also known
as *fava-de-bolota*, visgueiro and
pau-de-arara, among other names.
• It presents aerial roots, roots
which develop on the trunk and
stay above the ground.

are purplish. During the more
prolonged droughts the plant is used,
as a last resort, as animal and human
food. From the base of the widened
and dilated leaves a substance rich in
starch is obtained and used as flour.
From this, a type of bread is made
which is comparable, both the flavor
and consistency, to corn bread.
The flour is also eaten with milk,
meat and similar to pirão (a thick
mixture of manioc flour and water).

Macambira ▲

(Bromelia laciniosa)
This is a large bromeliad native of the
caatinga with leaves of about 1.5 meters
(4.5 feet) long by 20 centimeters
(8 inches) wide when fully grown.
The leaves are lance-shaped with sharp
spikes on the sides. They are pink in the
area above the base and the rest is green,
with rose-colored stripes. The flowers

Interesting features:

• Sertanejos say that if the macambira flour
is eaten with milk or meat it becomes
palatable. But with water and salt it is
intolerable.
• Macambira belongs to the family of
bromelias, which includes the ornamental
bromelias and pineapples.

Interesting features:

- Sertanejos believe that when night-blooming cereus flowers it is because the rains are arriving.
- The thorns of the night-blooming cereus help

◄ **Mandacaru**

(Cereus jamacaru) Night-blooming cereus
Night-blooming cereus is a cactus, the most important symbol of caatinga. It grows on stony sites, almost devoid of soil. It reaches a height of 8 meters (24 feet) and has no leaves and is covered by a thick cuticle, as a strategy for not losing water. The flesh of the plant has a viscous composition, which serves to store the humidity absorbed by its roots. It produces white flowers, which appear in the afternoon and wilt early in the morning. The fruit is edible but the taste is not appreciated.

to protect the plant against animals in the dry periods, as it is one of the few species, which remain green during droughts.

Mangaba ►

(Hancornia speciosa)
When something is excessively easy, it is said that it is mangaba. It is a just reference to the fruit that, when very ripe nearly 'melts' in the mouth, and has a sweet perfumed taste. The mangaba tree, producer of this nectar, attains a height of between 5 and 10 meters (15 and 30 feet) and develops well in poor sandy soils. It bears fruit all year round especially from November to June. When the fruit are completely developed they fall from the tree and complete their ripening on the ground. To gather from the tree, experience is necessary to know the correct time. It is an exclusively Brazilian species, found in the savannahs of the central-west, north of Minas Gerais, a part of Amazon and the northeastern restinga forests.

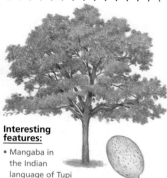

Interesting features:

- Mangaba in the Indian language of Tupi guarani means 'fruit that is good to eat'.
- Sergipe chose the Mangaba tree as its official symbol.
- The latex, which is extracted from the mangaba tree is suitable for the production of rubber, and was exploited in the past.

Moringa ▼

(Moringa oleifera)
This is a short tree, which does not grow higher than 10 meters (30 feet). The flowers are perfumed and white with yellow at the base. It is native of India, however it spread through the tropical regions. In the middle of the 1990's, some organizations divulged a filtration technique for muddy water using the seeds. It is enough to mix the water with macerated seeds and in a few minutes the

mud settles in flakes and it is possible to decant. The leaves are edible and contain the highest concentrations of vitamin A among edible plants.

Interesting features:

- There is a species of Horseradish tree native to northeast Africa, with the scientific name of *Moringa stenopetala* is very similar and has characteristics comparable to Moringa oleifera.
- From the seeds of the Horseradish tree, oil is extracted which in the past was used for the lubrication of delicate instruments.

Palma ▼
(Opuntia fícus-indica) Prickly pear

This cactus is native to the Mexican deserts and was introduced to Brazil in the 19th century. It is formed of structures, which resemble the palm of the hand. The fruits are the round part. Edible, they have a sweet succulent yellow pulp and a slight acid taste and are full of black seeds. The cactus bears fruit all year round, and it is widely cultivated in the Northeast as cattle and goat feed. Besides being perfectly adapted to the semiarid conditions, it is considered to be an excellent high-energy food.

Interesting features:

- It is also known as palmatória
- There is another species known as palm, which is also grown in the Northeast to feed animals. Its scientific identification is *Nopalea cochenillifera - Nopalito, Nopalea.*
- In the Southeast, the palm is named figo-da-India and is planted in fruit orchards.

Pau-brasil ▼
(Caesalpinia echinata) Brazilwood

Brazilwood was intensely exploited at the start of the colonization of Brazil, to the point that the country received its name from it. A substance named brasileina, with a very bright red color, is extracted from its wood, which in the past was used to dye fabric and to manufacture ink. The tree has a thorny trunk and boughs and grows up to 12 meters (36 feet) high, although there have been published reports of specimens of 30 meters (90 feet). The timber is very hard, and has already been used in the construction of ships and until today it is sought after for the fabrication of violin bows. Brazilwood is found in the middle of coastal forests, from Ceará to Rio de Janeiro but is commonest in the south of Bahia. After centuries of exploitation the plant has become rare in all regions.

Interesting features:

- It also is called ibirapitanga, orabutá, pau-rosado and muiapiranga.
- Brazilwood is recommended for landscape gardening because of its size and the beautiful golden-yellow flowers with a pleasant smell. The only problem is the slow growth of the tree.

Piaçava ▶

(Attalea funifera) Piassava palm
Piassava palm is native to the Atlantic Forest in southern Bahia, reaches 15 meters (45 feet) high and exists in the greatest numbers in the stretch between Porto Seguro and Valença. The layer of fiber that is removed from the petiole (the stem of the leaves) is used for the production of brooms, as thatching, for several types of handicrafts and also as thermal insulation. The fibers, which are impermeable and elastic, can grow up to 3.5 meters (10.5 feet) long. Harvesting is achieved mostly by extraction from natural sources, as there are few plantations. Each adult palm-tree, from its seventh year, produces around 10 kilograms (almost 5 pounds) of fibers annually. Besides the fibers, the fruit or nuts are used for food, the production of oil and charcoal.

Interesting features:

• Apart from *Attalea funifera* of Bahia, there is another species of piassava with the scientific name of *Leopoldina piassaba*, commonly known as piaçava-do-pará. It occurs in the Amazon and has a greater commercial value than the palmeira baiana.

• There is another species, *Attalea acaulis*, encountered in the Northeast, but some scholars suspect that it is a common piassava growing in bad soil and water conditions.

· ·

Sisal ▶

(Agave sisalana) Sisal hemp
This is a species of agave native to the Yucatan Peninsula, in Mexico, well acclimatized in the semiarid Northeast. The thorny, fleshy rigid leaves are arranged on the plant in the format of a sort of rosette. The fibers are tough and resistant and are used in ropes, strings, mats and other crafted items. The plant even produces in the prolonged droughts and thus is the salvation of many *sertanejos*. The crop is in decline due to the competition of synthetic fibers and the technological backwardness of the plantations.

Interesting features:

• Sisal flowers only once in its lifetime, dying soon after the formation of the immense spray of flowers.

• Tequila, the traditional Mexican alcoholic drink, is made from one species of agave.

· ·

◀ Umbu

(Spondias tuberosa) Imbu
It is one of the most common fruit trees in the Northeast. It grows up to 7 meters (21 feet) high, it has a short trunk and a diffuse canopy, producing shade for sertanejos and their animals. The roots include organs for storing water and nutrients that guarantee survival of the plant during the dry periods. The imbu tree flowers before the rains and bears fruit, with small regional differences, in January and February.

Interesting features:

• At the start of the dry season, the leaves of the imbu tree start to change color, from green to red until they fall leaving the plant totally bare.

• The tubers of the roots ('cuncas'), are used to manufacture flour in periods of famine.

CREDITS

T: top - C: center - Cl: center-left
Cr: center-right - B: bottom

Legends of the chapter's opening photos

Pages 6-7: Pedro Ribeiro (Tamandaré, PE) – Page 9: Christian Knepper (Praia do Gunga, AL) – Pages 278/279: Tibico Brasil (Rendeira)

Cover: Boat in Canoa Quebrada (CE): Christian Knepper – Peroba Beach (AL): Pedro Ribeiro – Pelourinho (BA): Arlete Soares

Counter-cover: Trekking (BA): Leonardo Pappini - Jijoca Lagoon (CE): Christian Knepper - São Francisco River (BA): Adriano Gambarini - Bumba-meu boi (MA): Christian Knepper - Coco bearer (BA): Ivan Carneiro

Discovering the Northeast

12/13: Pedro Ribeiro – 14: Adriano Gambarini – 15: Christian Knepper – 16: Leonardo Papini – 17T: Leonardo Papini/ 17B: Adriano Gambarini – 18: Christian Knepper – 19: Ivan Carneiro

Ecological Scenery

20/21: Adriano Gambarini – 22: Vitor Andrade – 24: Christian Knepper – 25: David Santos Júnior – 26/27:Christian Knepper – 28: Adriano Gambarini – 29TB: André Pessoa – 29Tr: Adriano Gambarini – 29B: Peter Milko – 30T/B: Adriano Gambarini – 31T/B: Adriano Gambarini

The Man in the Northeast

32/33: Christian Knepper – 34T: André Pessoa/34B: Christian Knepper – 35: Ivan Carneiro – 36T/B: Adriano Gambarini – 37T: Ivan Carneiro/37B: Tibico Brasil – 38T/B: André Pessoa – 39: Adriano Gambarini – 40T: Christian Knepper/40B: Ivan Carneiro – 41: Tibico Brasil – 42/43: Christian Knepper

Bahia

46/47: Fernando Vivas – 50: Roberto Cosulich – 52: Christian Knepper – 53: Pedro Ribeiro – 54: Tibico Brasil – 55: Adriano Gambarini – 56: Adriano Gambarini – 57T: Adriano Gambarini/ 57B: Leonardo Papini – 58T: Leonardo

Papini/58B: Christian Knepper – 59: Agliberto Lima – 60T: Peter Milko/60B: Adriano Gambarini – 61: Adriano Gambarini – 62: Adriano Gambarini – 63: Fabrício Brasiliense – 64: Leonardo Papini – 65: Vitor Andrade – 66/67: Ivan Carneiro – 68T: Adriano Gambarini/68B: Márcio Cabral – 69: Márcio Cabral – 70: Adriano Gambarini – 71: Márcio Cabral – 72: Márcio Cabral – 73: Adriano Gambarini – 74: Ricardo Azoury – 75Cr: Rogério Reis/75B: Peter Milko – 76: Fabrício Brasiliense – 77: Adriano Gambarini – 78: Adriano Gambarini – 79: Ivan Carneiro – 80/81: Adriano Gambarini – 82: Ivan Carneiro – 83: Adriano Gambarini – 84: Adriano Gambarini – 85: André Pessoa – 86: Pedro Ribeiro – 87: Rogério Reis – 88T/ B: Adriano Gambarini – 89: Vitor Andrade – 90/91:Pedro Ribeiro – 92: Vitor Andrade – 93: Adriano Gambarini – 94/95: Adriano Gambarini

Sergipe

96/97: Christian Knepper – 100T: David Santos Júnior – 101T: David Santos Júnior – 102Cl: Roberto Cosulich – 103T: David Santos Júnior – 104B: Álvaro Vilela – 104/105: David Santos Junior – 106T: Adriano Gambarini – 107C: Cangaço Museum reproduction – 108/ 109T: Ivan Carneiro

Alagoas

110/111: Stefan Kolumban – 114: Christian Knepper – 115: Reproduction – 116T: Christian Knepper/116B: Beatriz Santomauro – 117T: Tibico Brasil/117B: Maria Dania Junges – 118: Beatriz Santomauro – 119: Christian Knepper – 120/121: Christian Knepper – 122: Fabio Bonotti – 123T: Christian Knepper/123B: Stefan Kolumban – 124: Adriano Gambarini – 125T: Reproduction/125B: Adriano Gambarini – 126: Roberto Consulich – 127: Christian Knepper

Pernambuco

128/129: Jesus Carlos/HG – 132: Adriano Gambarini – 133: Peter Milko – 134: Peter Milko – 135: Jesus Carlos – 136T: Jesus Carlos/HG/136B: Pedro Ribeiro – 137: Peter Milko – 138: Christian Knepper – 139: Pedro Ribeiro – 140: Beatriz Santomauro – 141A: Illustration J. Borges/141B: Evaldo Parreira – 142: Peter Milko – 143Tl/Tr/B: Cristiano Burmester – 144: Peter Milko – 144/145: Zig Koch – 146/147: Peter Milko – 148: Jesus Carlos/HG – 149T: Peter Milko –

149B: Adriano Gambarini – 150: Jesus Carlos/HG – 151Cr: Jesus Carlos/HG – 151B: Adriano Gambarini – 152: Adriano Gambarini – 153: Adriano Gambarini – 154/155: Christian Knepper – 156: Adriano Gambarini – 157T/B: Adriano Gambarini – 158: Pedro Ribeiro – 159: Peter Milko – 160/161: Pedro Ribeiro

Paraíba

162/163: Augusto Pessoa – 166T: Salomon Cytrynowicz – 166B: Beatriz Santomauro – 168: Beatriz Santomauro – 169T: Beatriz Santomauro/169B: Salomon Cytrynowicz – 170T: Beatriz Santomauro/170B: Ivan Carneiro – 171: Salomon Cytrynowicz – 172: Augusto Pessoa – 173: Beatriz Santomauro – 174/175: Robert Ostrowski – 176: Beatriz Santomauro – 177T: Robert Ostrowski/177B: Ivan Carneiro

Rio Grande do Norte

178/179: Stefan Kolumban – 182: Juca Martins – 183: reproduction Agência Estado – 184T: Juca Martins/184B: Rogério Reis – 185: Vitor Andrade – 186: Memorial Câmara Cascudo reproduction – 187: Juca Martins – 188T: Tibico Brasil/188B: Tibico Brasil – 189: Beatriz Santomauro – 190/191: Vitor Andrade – 192T: Ricardo Azoury/192B: Beatriz Santomauro – 193: Beatriz Santomauro – 194: André Pessoa – 195: André Pessoa – 196: Adriano Gambarini – 197: André Pessoa – 198: Ricardo Azoury – 199: Vitor Andrade –200/201T: Stefan Kolumban – 201B: Beatriz Santomauro

Ceará

202/203: Christian Knepper – 206: Delfim Martins – 207: Vitor Andrade – 208: Adriano Gambarini – 209: Vitor Andrade – 210: Christian Knepper – 211: Ivan Carneiro – 212: Tibico Brasil – 213: Juca Martins – 214: Ivan Carneiro – 215T: Fábio Bonotti/215B: Christian Knepper – 216: Christian Knepper – 217: Ivan Carneiro – 218/219: Ivan Carneiro – 220: Ivan Carneiro – 221: Christian Knepper – 222: Christian Knepper – 223: Peter Milko – 224: Vidal Cavalcante – 225: André Pessoa – 226: Ivan Carneiro – 227: Christian Knepper

Piauí

228/229: Adriano Gambarini – 232: Roberto Cosulich – 234: André Pessoa –

235T: Roberto Cosulich/235B: André Pessoa – 236: André Pessoa – 237: André Pessoa – 238: Adriano Gambarini – 239T/B: Adriano Gambarini – 240/241: Christian Knepper – 242: André Pessoa – 243T/B: Adriano Gambarini – 244T: Adriano Gambarini – 244B: André Pessoa – 245: André Pessoa – 246/247: André Pessoa – 248: André Pessoa – 249: Adriano Gambarini – 250T: Adriano Gambarini/250B: André Pessoa – 251: André Pessoa

Maranhão

252/253: Christian Knepper – 256: Christian Knepper – 257: Adriano Gambarini – 258T/B: Adriano Gambarini – 259: Airton Marinho ilustration – 260T: Vitor Andrade/260B: Peter Milko - 261: Christian Knepper – 262T/B: Christian Knepper – 263T: Christian Knepper/263B: Peter Milko – 264: Vitor Andrade – 265: Christian Knepper – 266/267: Christian Knepper – 266B: Vitor Andrade – 268: Christian Knepper – 269T/B: Christian Knepper – 270/271: Christian Knepper – 272: Christian Knepper – 273T/B: Christian Knepper – 274/275: Christian Knepper – 276: Christian Knepper – 277: Fábio Bonotti

Fauna and Flora

312/313: André Pessoa – 320-321: Márcio Cabral – 330/331: Adriano Gambarini – 335: Jesus Carlos/HG

IMAGE BANKS

Agência Estado
Photographers: Agliberto Lima, Fernando Vivas, Vidal Cavalcante

Fototeca
Photographers: Roberto Cosulich, Pedro Ribeiro

Imagem Latina
Photographers: Jesus Carlos

Pulsar Imagens
Photographers: Delfim Martins, Fábio Bonotti, Juca Martins, Ricardo Azoury, Rogério Reis, Salomon Cytrynowicz, Stefan Kolumban

TBI Imagens
Photographer: Tibico Brasil

Index

CITIES

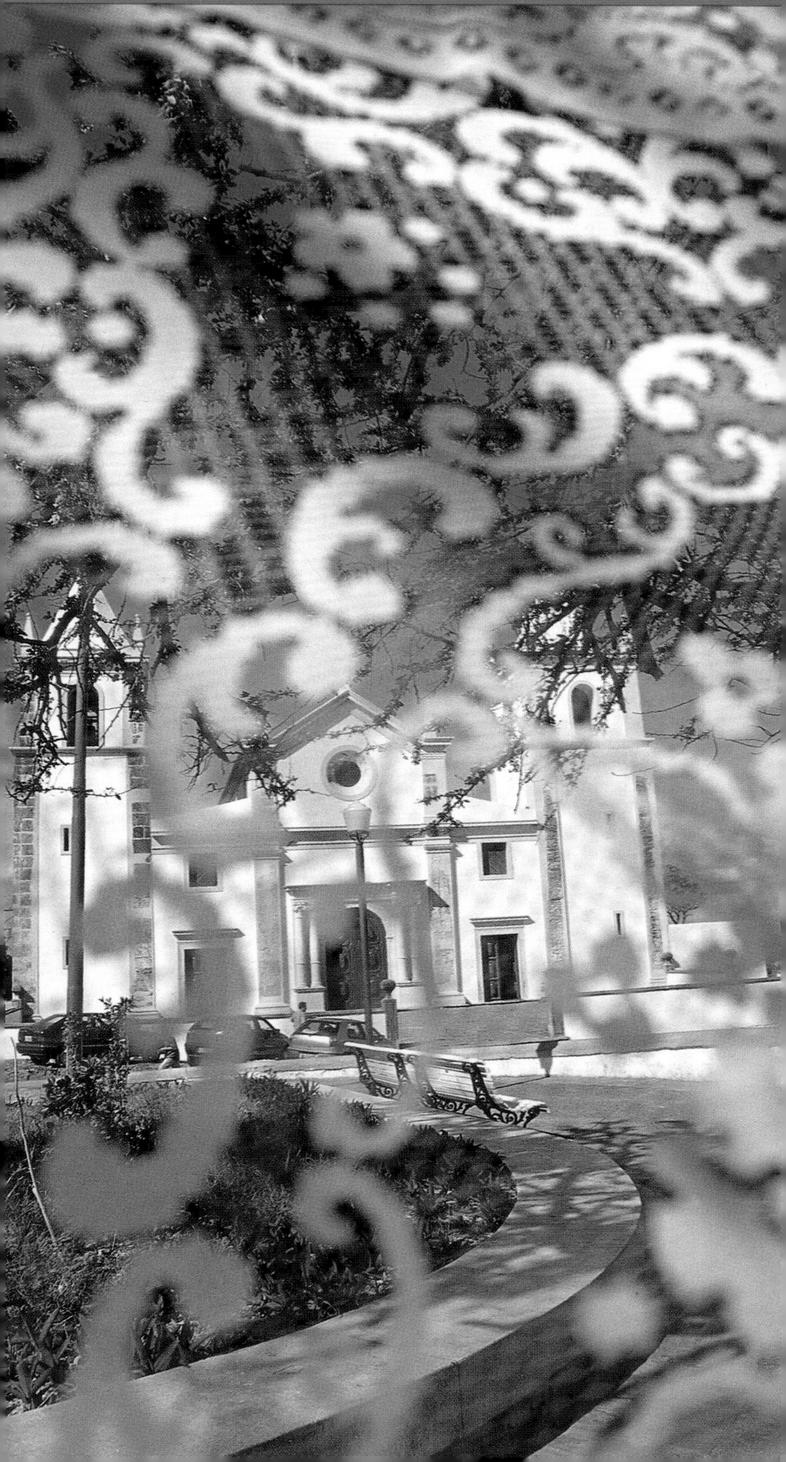

ACKNOWLEDGEMENTS

Adriana Saboya – Tourism Bureau in Ceará
Adriano Gambarini – São Paulo (SP)
André Pessoa – Raízes do Piauí Agency
Andréa and Adriana Tenório – Tourism Bureau in Alagoas
Anthony de Oliveira – Sebrae Touristic Information Bureau, Aracaju (SE)
Augusto Pessoa – Fortaleza (CE)
Aurélio – Restaurant Meio do Mangue, Lucena (PB)
Carlos Cavalcante and Joane – Guest House Costa Branca, Ponta do Mel (CE)
Carmem Vera Lucena – Tourism Bureau in Rio Grande do Norte
Catarina Lucrécia – Tourism Bureau in Pernambuco
Charley Soares e Cláudio – Guest House La Luna
Christine Soares – Tourism Bureau in Sergipe
Cícero Furlani – Guest House HawaiiAqui, Itacaré (BA)
Eduardo Bagnoli - Manary Ecotours, Natal (RN)
Emanuelli Barreto - Tourism Bureau in Natal (RN)
Fernando and Reni – Guest House Erva Doce, Arraial D'Ajuda (BA)
Gilma Buril — Empetur
Hermínia, Dante e Davi – Guest House da Lagoa, Caraíva (BA)
Hugo Veiga and Kilma Fernanda Duarte – Tourism Bureau in São Luís (MA)
Ingrid Clark – Guest House Ilha do Caju (MA)
Joana D'arc — Petrolina City Hall (PE)
João Wharles Portela — Pbtur
Lilian Amarante and Raymundo Mazzei – Bahiatursa
Luiz Phelipe Andrès – São Luís (MA)
Marcos – Restaurant Arca do Bilu, Tambaba (PB)
Maria Auxiliadora - Lajedo de Soledade (RN)
Mariana Lacerda - Peixe-Boi Project, Itamaracá (PE)
Mario Preti – Restaurant Feitiço da Lua, Canoa Quebrada (CE)
Museum of Zoology – USP
Natacha Maranhão – Tourism Bureau in Piauí
Orlando Steylaerts – Piaçabuçu City Hall (AL)
Paulo Rogério – Greentour, João Pessoa (PB)
Pedro Bringel – Tourism Bureau in Carolina (MA)
Publishers: Companhia das Letras, Luminetti, Mandarim, Multinova
Distribuidora, Objetiva, Senac
Reheniglei Rehem – Santa Cruz State University, Ilhéus (BA)
Rodrigo – Guest House Pomar da Pipa (RN)
Rogério Ribeiro – Tourism Guide of Itacaré and Region (BA)
Sérgio Paulo Rodrigues Nascimento – Penedo City Hall (AL)
Sílvia Regina Groto - Pipatour (RN)

**Dados Internacionais para Catalogação na Publicação (CIP)
do Departamento Nacional do Livro**

G943	Philips Guides: Northeast Brazil. – São Paulo: Horizonte, 2002.
	Patrocínio: Projeto Philips Brasilis
ISBN: 85-88031-12-4
	1. Brazil, Northeast – Illustrated books. 2. Tourism – Brazil.
	CDD: 779.991813

Índice para catálogo sistemático:
1. Nordeste : Descrição e viagens